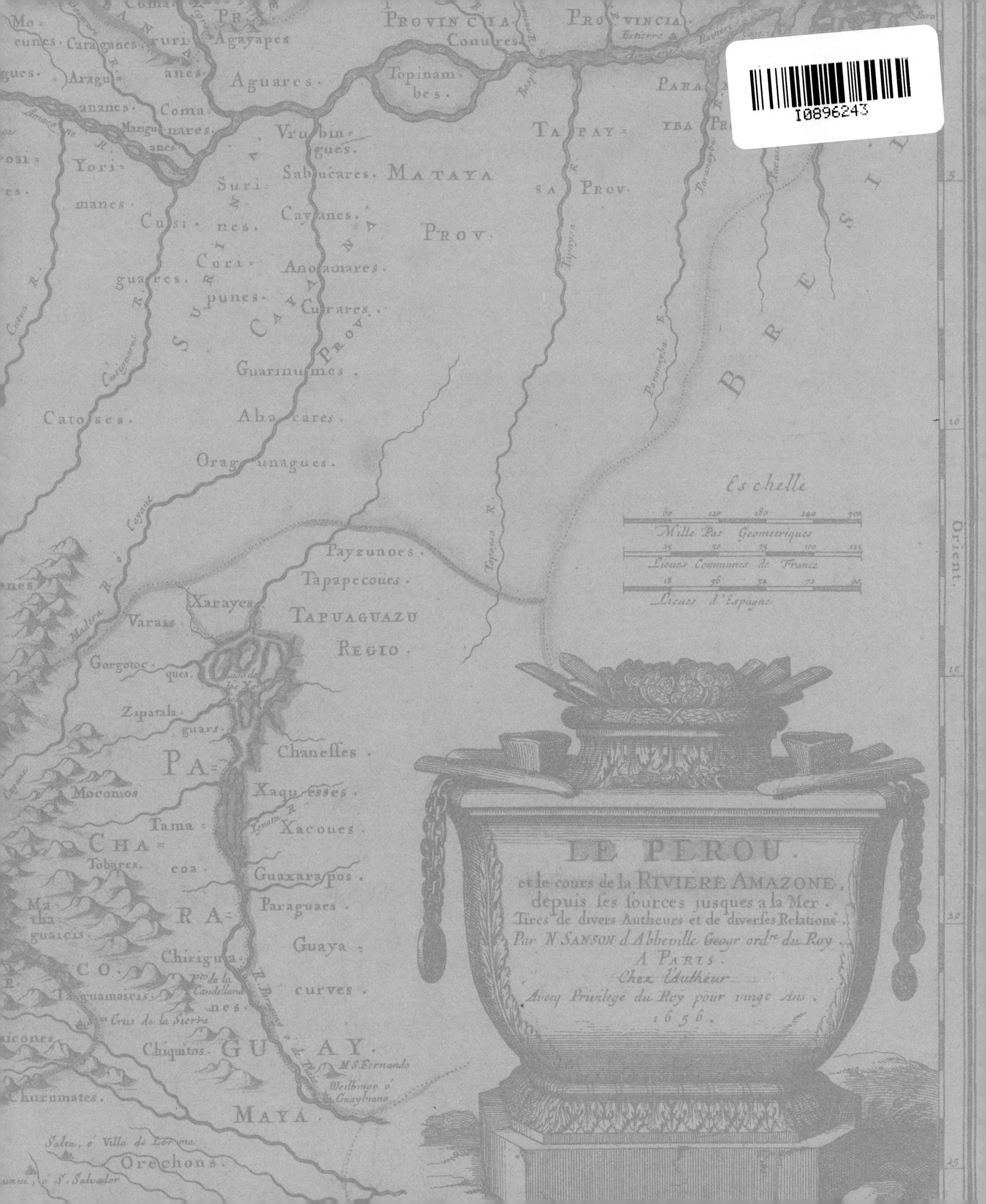
LE PEROU.
et le cours de la RIVIERE AMAZONE,
depuis ses sources jusques a la Mer.
Tirés de divers Autheurs et de diverses Relations.
Par N SANSON d'Abbeville Geogr ordre du Roy.
A PARIS.
Chez l'Autheur
Avecq Privilege du Roy pour vingt Ans.
1656.
Eschelle
Mille Pas Geometriques
Lieues Communes de France
Lieues d'Espagne
Orient.
PROVINCIA
Conures.
Aguares.
Topinambes.
TAPAY
SA PROV.
MATAYA
PROV.
Sabucares.
Cayanes.
Anoamares.
Curares.
Guarinumes.
Abacares.
Oragunagues.
Catosses.
Yorimanes
Cusines.
Coriguares.
punes.
Payzunoes.
Tapapecoues.
Xarayes
TAPUAGUAZU
REGIO.
Varais
Gorgotoques.
Zipatalaguars.
Chanesses.
Mocomos
Xaquesses.
Tama
Xacoues.
Tobares.
Guaxarapos.
Paraguaes.
Guaya
curves.
Chiriguanes
Taguamaicis.
Chiquitos.
GUAY.
Churumates.
MAYA.
Orechons.
M.S.Fernando
Salta, ó Villa de Lerma
BRESIL

# A surviving Legacy in Spanish America

Seventeenth- and Eighteenth- Century Furniture from the Viceroyalty of Peru

GRAPHIC DESIGN **NATALIA ARAKAKI**
EDITION AND PHOTOGRAPHIC ARCHIVES **VERÓNICA IGLESIA**
PROOFREADING IN SPANISH **ARMIDA MARÍA CÓRDOBA - MARINA PÉREZ**
LEGAL ADVISOR **ALFONSO CAMPOS CARLÉS**
PREPRESS **GREGORIO SÁENZ**
PRINTING **BRIZZOLIS**
BOOKBINDING **RAMOS**
TRANSLATION **ESTUDIO MAZZOCCHI**
PROOFREADING IN ENGLISH **DARYL BAINES**

PHOTOGRAPHY CREDITS
**MARÍA CAMPOS CARLÉS DE PEÑA** EXCEPT FOR:
**ARCHIVO HISTÓRICO DE LÍMITES - PERUVIAN MINISTRY OF FOREIGN AFFAIRS:** PAGES XVIII, 1, 4, 6, 12.
**ARCHIVO HISTÓRICO BIBLIOTECA MUNICIPAL DE LIMA:** PAGES 8, 21.
**SPAIN. MINISTRY OF EDUCATION, CULTURE AND SPORTS. ARCHIVO GENERAL DE INDIAS:** PAGE 10.
**MUSEO DE AMÉRICA, MADRID:** PAGE 147.
**BANCO DE CRÉDITO BCP, PALACIO GOYENECHE, LIMA:** PAGE 364.
**DANIEL GIANNONI:** PAGES 26, 42, 49, 53, 60, 69, 77, 87, 96, 97, 104, 109, 113, 141, 151, 169, 177, 179, 181, 201, 219, 222, 227, 233, 234, 239, 289, 299, 300, 329, 340, 383, 386, 390, 391, 393, 394, 395, 396, 410, 415.
**VERÓNICA IGLESIA:** PAGE 427.
**MARÍA JHONG** (MINISTRY OF CULTURE/MUSEO NACIONAL DE ARQUEOLOGÍA, ANTROPOLOGÍA E HISTORIA DEL PERÚ): PAGES 403, 409, 412.
**RAÚL MONTERO QUISPE** (ARCHBISHOPRIC OF CUSCO): PAGES 37, 40, 41, 71, 204, 207, 208, 305, 314, 397.
**ZULLY MERCADO DE GRUPP** (MUSEO DEL MONASTERIO DE SANTA TERESA DE AREQUIPA): PAGE 175.
**JAVIER PRADO HEUDEBERT:** PAGES 21, 82, 142.
**PATRICIO PUEYRREDÓN:** PAGES 5, 7, 428.
**VERA TYULENEVA:** PAGE 209.
**GRAYDON WOOD:** PAGE 261.


ENGLISH VERSION LEGAL DEPOSIT **M-28772-2013**
ENGLISH VERSION ISBN **978-84-940061-8-0**



FIRST EDITION
PRINTED IN SPAIN IN NOVEMBER 2013

DISTRIBUTED BY
**EDICIONES EL VISO**
CASTELLÓ 128, 1° IZDA.
28006 MADRID, ESPAÑA
+34 915 19 65 76
WWW.EDICIONESELVISO.COM/

*BARGUEÑO*
[COVER] Mermaid detail.
Museo de Arte de Lima collection.
Donated by the Prado family.
17TH century.

# A surviving Legacy in Spanish America

## Seventeenth- and Eighteenth- Century Furniture from the Viceroyalty of Peru

MARÍA CAMPOS CARLÉS DE PEÑA

EDICIONES EL VISO

## FOREWORD

Argentine Professor María Campos Carlés de Peña devotes part of her time to teaching at the Universidad del Salvador, the Universidad del Museo Social Argentino and the Museo Nacional de Arte Decorativo de Buenos Aires, and the rest she spends on research into the history of Spanish American and European furniture, among other topics related to Decorative Arts.

The origin of the book we hold in our hands today dates back to 2008, when Professor Campos began her Latin American colonial furniture research and cataloguing project, inspired by valuable material located in Peru. Thus, she undertook the immense task of collating and organising all the information to be found in archival documents about Peruvian colonial furniture, which in turn was based on the material from various cities and regions across the country, such as Lima, Trujillo, Cusco, Arequipa and Puno. With the support of Fundación Carolina, she also embarked on a trip to Spain to carry out research work on the influence of Spanish furniture.

For over four years now, Professor Campos has been conducting a thorough investigation in Peru, carrying out rigorous analysis and preparing a detailed description of the various types of furniture from the viceregal period, both for ecclesiastical and secular use. She has succeeded in presenting a perfectly organised overview of these pieces through the various stylistic periods, and covering a broad span of time, from the 16TH- to the early 19TH-century.

In her book *A surviving Legacy in Spanish America: Seventeenth- and Eighteenth-Century Furniture from the Viceroyalty of Peru* [1], Professor Campos conducts an analytical review of furniture, not only focusing on style, but also the materials used in the production and the function for which such furniture was originally intended; thus reflecting the customs of the that time and that society.

The author of this book explores the world of furniture from the very beginning of the Mannerist transition, with marked Italianising features, all the way to the French

[1] In Lima we were privileged enough to catch a few glimpses of this publication in the form of lectures and seminars which took place between 2011 and 2013.

LIBRARY OF MUSEO DE ARTE RELIGIOSO DEL CONVENTO SAN FRANCISCO Y CATACUMBAS, LIMA.
Partial view.

Neoclassicism of the Enlightenment, going through the full range of Flemish, Spanish and German influences, in the Baroque, mestizo Baroque, French and English Rococo styles, on a tour which shows us the historical evolution of furniture.

This review includes the various materials from which unknown artists fashioned their works: polychromed wood carvings, inlaid with ivory or bone; embossed, polychromed, and studded leather furniture; furniture inlaid with mother-of-pearl, tortoiseshell and mahogany; carved, fretted, polished and gilded wood, and marquetry.

I am certain that this valuable work carried out by Professor Campos will be of great help to researchers and to anyone willing to learn about the significance of furniture production during the viceregal period; furniture which continues to surprise us with its aesthetic and artistic beauty. As the author maintains, this work is intended to encourage further research in the various geographical areas of Spanish America.

*+ Raúl Antonio Chau*

TITULAR BISHOP OF AVEIA
AUXILIARY BISHOP OF LIMA

To my husband Federico, who has always been there with generosity and patience to help me make this dream come true.

## PREFACE

After many years of studying and teaching universal furniture history, I realised that Spanish-American colonial furniture had not yet been explored. Consequently, I faced the inescapable challenge of studying it myself, but without investigating that which had been already researched.

To that end, and with the map of the Americas spread before me, I had to choose suitable places to address the subject. It was not by chance that my work began in Peru; it was an informed decision. Thus, I focused my attention on one of the hubs of the Spanish-American world during the colonial period, based on its public and private cultural heritage. It should be taken into account that this was only a partial view of applied arts and furniture in particular: a true treasure worth making known.

At every stop along my journey, I began the arduous and solitary fieldwork that was essential to create a systematic file of the pieces selected as objects for study.

The curatorial spirit inspiring this book led me to investigate formal aspects that defined the design and manufacture of those pieces of furniture, which became essential points of reference when sorting out a vast artistic structure and discovering its origin and consequences. To this end, it is worth highlighting some key research elements: a vague and uncertain chronology; various scattered production sites; vernacular and Old World artistic styles; influences on a fertile soil and subsequent syncretism; and the wide variety of techniques applied.

It has been very enlightening for me to study and analyse the unending repertoire of Spanish furniture from the 16TH to 18TH centuries in order to understand their essential roots and the analogy with pieces scattered throughout the Peruvian territory. At the same time, I found it essential to establish relationships between art production and weather, tides, earthquakes, vice royalties, royal wars and moods, to find satisfactory answers to the questions which arose as my research progressed.

I also sought refuge in the continuous theoretical support of books containing invaluable help from art historians and researchers specialising in a range of subjects. Authors of the stature of Garcilaso de la Vega (El Inca), Rubén Vargas Ugarte S. J., Raúl Porras Barrenechea, Ricardo Palma, Héctor Schenone, Adolfo Luis Ribera, R. P. Antonio San Cristóbal, Héctor Velarde, Jorge Bernales Ballesteros, Ramón Gutiérrez, Fabio Camacho, Teresa Gisbert, Ramón Mujica Pinilla, Luis Eduardo Wuffarden, Elizabeth Kuon Arce, María Paz Aguiló Alonso, M. Concepción García Saiz, among many others. They helped dispel doubts and allowed me to compare ideas with a valid resource for verifying the information obtained, in order to produce the most rigorous work. Bibliographical references produced unexpected insights into the most significant aspects of the objects of study. Also, the material generously provided by institutional libraries and archives was invaluable and highly significant.

In order to systematize the information gathered, it was essential to conduct a detailed assessment of the Peruvian furniture which I found during my four years of study. The result clearly shows that the makers of these pieces knew how to meet the needs of their customers.

At the theoretical level, I deemed it appropriate to draw a clear distinction between religious and secular pieces, which at that time, were both equally important and essential.

I have established a very special relationship with period furniture, and when my eyes come across any piece, I feel that it always has something to convey. The visual impact which furniture pieces viewed as objects of art has on me is greatly rewarding, and I firmly believe that these pieces may affect any spirit who admires them with the same force; thus becoming elements which mark a difference in art history.

I have put a lot of effort into proving that each language tells a different story: the volumetric, quasi-sculptural feeling of a piece and the materials used, the deep conviction of standing before a witness to its time, and the motivations behind its making are reasons for me to respect and reflect upon them. With each discovery I sensed that the object was waiting to be found, and it comes as no surprise that I felt captivated by a world at whose existence I could only guess.

I have tried to make a careful selection of the pieces which were most representative of each artistic period, to achieve a clear and helpful final result. I intend to contribute to their becoming more widely known, and hope that my work will inspire new projects and eventually promote the restoration of some pieces to their former splendour; fostering their durability.

With this research I fervently hope to encourage scholars to delve deeper into the subject, as there is still room for discussion by those who love period furniture and are interested in the lifestyle of the colonial world.

*A surviving Legacy in Spanish America: Seventeenth- and Eighteenth- Century Furniture from the Viceroyalty of Peru* is just the first stage of a more ambitious project, since I am profoundly convinced that this work must be continued in other South American regions.

*María Campos Carlés de Peña*
BUENOS AIRES, OCTOBER 2013

## ACKNOWLEDGEMENTS

This book would not have been possible without the selfless support, wise advice and extensive collaboration of historians and researchers. Firstly, I want to give particular thanks to Professor Héctor Schenone, who with unparalleled generosity, and a deep love for the topic at hand, trusted and encouraged me to undertake this work; to the Auxiliary Bishop of Lima, Monsignor Raúl Antonio Chau Quispe, who enriched this book by honouring me with his foreword; to Jaime Mariazza Foy, Ramón Mujica Pinilla and Elizabeth Kuon Arce, who gave me invaluable advice and who, with magnanimous and unselfish spirit, opened for me the doors of every institution and private collection in Peru.

I would also like to express my special and sincere recognition to all the institutions which helped me in the difficult task of gathering the information and graphic material necessary for the research work contained in this book:

### IN PERU

**Archivo Histórico de Límites. Peruvian Ministry of Foreign Affairs:** *Edwin Gutiérrez Padrón, Director, and Silvia Patricia Herrera Castañeda.*

**Palacio de Torre Tagle, Peruvian Ministry of Foreign Affairs:** *Daniel Roca, Director; Néstor Miguel Benavides del Solar, Heritage and Cultural Asset Advisor; and Yolanda Gabriela Bisso Drago.*

**Ministry of Culture-Museo Nacional de Arqueología, Antropología e Historia del Perú:** *Carmen Arellano Hoffmann, Director, and Jaime Mariazza Foy.*

**Biblioteca Municipal de Lima:** *Sandro Covarrubias.*

**Instituto Nacional de Cultura-Puno:** *Carlos Miguel Landa Gamio, Regional Culture Director, and Sergio Medina Ticona.*

**Museo del Palacio Arzobispal and Museo del Monasterio de las Nazarenas de Lima:** *Auxiliary Bishop Monsignor Raúl Antonio Chau Quispe and Fernando López Sánchez.*

**Basílica Catedral de Lima and Museo de Arte Religioso:** *Auxiliary Bishop Monsignor Raúl Antonio Chau Quispe and Fernando López Sánchez.*

Arzobispado del Cusco, Basílica Catedral del Cusco, Museo del Arzobispado del Cusco and Parroquia de San Blas del Cusco: *Archbishop Monsignor Juan Antonio Ugarte Pérez.*

Museo Catedralicio de la Basílica Menor de Trujillo: *Monsignor Miguel Cabrejos Vidarte O.F.M., Archbishop of Trujillo.*

Basílica y Convento de Nuestra Señora de la Merced, Lima: *Fray Carlos Nolasco R.P., Prior of Lima, and Father César Medina.*

Compañía de Jesús-Comunidad de San Pedro, Lima: *R.P. José Enrique Rodríguez Rodríguez S.J.*

Convento de Santo Domingo del Cusco and Monasterio de Santa Catalina de Sena del Cusco: *Fray Luis Enrique Ramírez Camacho R.P.*

Convento del Santísimo Rosario de Lima-Basílica and Convento de Santo Domingo: *Fray Luis Enrique Ramírez Camacho and Fray Arturo Eláez.*

Museo de Arte de Lima (MALI): *Natalia Majluf, Director, and Claudia Pereyra Iturry, Chief of Records and Catalogues.*

Museo Pedro de Osma, Lima: *Patricia Pinilla Cisneros, Director.*

Museo de Arte Religioso del Convento San Francisco y Catacumbas de Lima: *Fray Ernesto Chambi Cruz O.F.M., Director.*

Museo de los Descalzos-Convento de los Franciscanos Descalzos, Rímac, Lima: *Alberta Álvarez, Director of the Fundación Descalzos del Rímac.*

Museo de Arte Virreinal del Monasterio de Santa Teresa de Arequipa: *Franz Grupp, Director.*

Monasterio de Santa Catalina de Arequipa: *Lourdes Grupp de Arias and Javier Velarde Talleri.*

Real Monasterio de Clarisas de Santa María de Gracia, Trujillo: *Sister Ginelda Garlequé Pérez O.S.C.*

Iglesia de Santiago Apóstol de Lampa-Puno Diocese: *Oscar Frisancho Deza, Lampa Council.*

Iglesia y Monasterio de El Carmen, Trujillo.

Parroquia San Antonio de Padua, Iglesia San Agustín P.P. Franciscanos, Trujillo: *Fray José Francisco Escurra Mayaute O.F.M.*

Templo de Santo Domingo-Parroquia de San Pedro Mártir, Trujillo: *Fray Jorge Coronado.*

Banco Central de Reserva del Perú, Arequipa Branch-Casa Museo Goyeneche: *Julio Valverde, Chairman of the Board.*

Banco Central de Reserva del Perú, Trujillo Branch-Casa Urquiaga: *Carlos Alatrista Gironzini.*

Banco de Crédito del Perú BCP-Former Casa Goyeneche, Lima: *Álvaro Carulla.*

Banco de Crédito del Perú BCP, Arequipa Branch, La Casa del Moral: *Jhon Guillen.*

Banco Intercontinental del Perú-Interbank-Casa del Mariscal Orbegoso, Trujillo: *Carmen Hoyle.*

Fundación Banco Continental-Trujillo-Casa de la Emancipación: *Carlos Chávez Saldaña.*

Casa de Aliaga, Lima: *Gonzalo de Aliaga and Leticia Niembro de Aliaga.*

La Mansión del Fundador and Parador El Molino Blanco, Arequipa: *Inés García Calderón de Neuenschwander.*

Asociación Civil Museo Enrico Poli, Lima: *Enrico Poli Bianchi.*

### IN ARGENTINA

Museo Nacional de Arte Decorativo, Buenos Aires: *Alberto G. Bellucci, Director, and Hugo Pontoriero, Chief of the Museology Department.*

Museo de Arte Hispanoamericano Isaac Fernández Blanco, Buenos Aires: *Jorge Luis Cometti, Director, Patricio López Méndez, Gustavo Tudisco and Lía Guerrico de Laferrere.*

Fundación Carolina-Argentina: *Guillermo Jaim Etcheverry, President.*

Fundación Fondo para el Patrimonio Argentino: *Carlos María López Ramos, Secretary.*

### IN SPAIN

Archivo General de Indias, Sevilla: *Isabel Simó Rodríguez, Director*

**Fundación Carolina-Spain:** *Mercedes Alcover, Secretary-General.*

**Museo de América, Madrid:** *Concepción García Saiz, Director, and Ana Zabía, Curator.*

**Museo Nacional de Artes Decorativas, Madrid:** *Sofía Rodríguez Bernis, Director.*

**Monasterio de San Lorenzo de El Escorial:** *Almudena Pérez de Tudela, Curator.*

**Monasterio de las Descalzas Reales, Madrid:** *Ana García Sanz, Curator.*

**Monasterio de la Encarnación, Madrid:** *Mari Sol García Fernández, Curator.*

**Museo Lázaro Galdiano, Madrid:** *Amparo López Redondo, Chief Curator.*

**Museo del Traje, Madrid:** *Rodrigo de la Fuente Puebla.*

### IN THE UNITED STATES OF AMERICA

**Hispanic Society of America:** *Margaret Connors McQuade, Assistant Director, and Marcus Burke, Curator.*

I would also like to deeply thank those who contributed to make the publication of this book possible: Ana María Ocampo de Moreyra and Alfredo Pinillos Hoyle.

My special gratitude goes to those who, with great hospitality and generosity, welcomed me and offered their sound advice. Their encouragement was essential so I could gather the material which is reflected in this book:

*María Paz Aguiló Alonso, Armando Andrade, Juan Aurich, Aldo Barbosa Stern and Silvia Stern de Barbosa, María Teresa Belaunde, Mariana Berckemeyer Prado, Alfonso Campos Carlés, Sonia Decker, José and Javier Eguiguren, Miguel Frías, Adrián Gualdoni Basualdo, Ramón Gutiérrez, Rodrigo Gutiérrez Viñuales, María Laura and Henry A. Harman, Roberta and Richard Huber, Rosanna Kuon Arce, José Ignacio Lambarri Orihuela, María Marta Larguía de Arias, Sara de Lavalle, Jaime and Vivian Liébana Evans, Florencia López Romaña, Ricardo Morales Gamarra, Ana María O. de Moreyra, Ramón Mujica Pinilla, Juan Carlos Ocampo, Roxana Olivares de López Romaña, Marita de la Peña Prado, Alfredo Pinillos Hoyle, Marita Prado de Moreyra, Javier Prado Pastor, María del Rosario Prado Rey de Barrios, Magdalena Prado Sosa de Buendía, Paul Rizo-Patrón, Ana and Juan Antonio Saráchaga, Luis A. Sardón Cánepa, Monsignor Ricardo Wiesse Thorndike.*

## CONTENTS

**PERV**
Author: John Ogilvy.
c. 1791.
Courtesy of Archivo Histórico de Límites - Peruvian Ministry of Foreign Affairs (VPE-018).

MAR DEL
ÆQVINOCTIALIS LINEA
ZUR quod et
MARE
PACIFICUM
TROPI CUS
Medius Meridianus est 320 reliqui ad hunc incurvatur ratione sphærica
Cusco metropolis Peru
Leucæ Hispanicæ
Milliaria German
TIERRA DEL FOGO
AMERICA
MERIDIONALIS
Fretum Magellanicu
Rio de la Plata
CHICA
REGIO
Moxos provincia
PARANA
OCCIDENS
Guiana Regnum, auri & omnium animantium feracissimum esse testatur Gualterus Raleg cuius impensis lustrari cœpit anno 1595. In eo multas esse ciuitates asserebat constructas.

# INTRODUCTION:

## KEY HISTORICAL POINTS

## KEY ARTISTIC POINTS

## KEY HISTORICAL POINTS

### AN OVERVIEW OF THE NEWLY CONQUERED NATIONS AND A BRIEF HISTORY OF THE SPANISH CONQUERORS IN THE VICEROYALTY OF PERU

When the Spaniards arrived, the Inca Empire extended over 100,000 square kilometres. Within its borders lived many diverse conquered peoples, ranging from hunting tribes in the Amazon to the Chimú people. The Inca State was rapidly and efficiently organised, controlling every aspect of life from their centre of power. This was achieved through government systems which had already been tried and tested by previous Andean empires.

The Empire's vast domain was controlled by articulating political, military, commercial and religious activities with the utmost efficiency; it included the present-day territories of Peru, parts of Ecuador, western Bolivia, and northern Chile and Argentina. According to the myth, the city of Cusco was founded between the $11^{TH}$- and $12^{TH}$-centuries AD by the first Inca king, Manco Cápac, and his wife, the *coya* or queen Mama Ocllo, although there are no documents to prove that. Cusco was, for four hundred years, the capital city of the *Tahuantinsuyo.*

Cusco, located at 3,355m above sea level in the Southern Andean range, was a *…unique, extraordinary City, in which a profound urbanism was not simply an admirable fusion between geometric possibilities of symmetry and uniformity and an accident of topography, but also a sort of synthetic expression of the political geography of the whole Empire*[1].

***AMERICA MERIDIONALIS***
[OPENING]
Author: Jodocus Hondius (1563-1612).
c. 1597.
Courtesy of Archivo Histórico de Límites – Peruvian Ministry of Foreign Affairs (AMS-029).

**WARDROBE**
[OPPOSITE PAGE] Panel detail.
Vivian and Jaime Liébana's collection, Lima.
$18^{TH}$ century.
Height: 199 cm. Width: 139 cm.
Depth: 84 cm.

[1] Velarde, Héctor. *Arquitectura Peruana.* Colección Tierra Firme. Mexico D.F.: Fondo de Cultura Económica, 1946, pages 37/38.

*CUZCO PROVINCE*
Author: Pablo José Oricain.
1801.
Courtesy of Archivo Histórico de Límites – Peruvian Ministry of Foreign Affairs (VPE-129).

The people were industrious and civilised and their work had made the Inca Empire flourish before the Spaniards arrived. They were skilful in the art of stone carving (stereotomy), and were expert stonemasons. The architectural tradition of the *Tahuantinsuyo* essentially involved the use of stone; a building technique which was suited to the local geography.

Even though there was a wealth of vegetation in the eastern jungle regions, carpentry and cabinetmaking as artistic specialties were brought by the European conquerors. With the arrival of Spanish craftsmen, the natives quickly learned how to work wood in the European sytle, producing furniture, altars, images and other artistic works of marked local flavour, which seemed crude but were of high quality.

The Inca Empire was politically divided and immersed in civil war when, in 1532, the Spanish invasion caught them by surprise. Spearheading the military conquest was Francisco Pizarro (1478-1541), who was appointed governor of Peru by the King of Spain; he performed his duties in this capacity from 1534 to 1541, in the territory which would later become the vast Viceroyalty of Peru.

On November 20, 1542 the King of Spain, Charles V (1516-1556), by virtue of Royal Decree, created the Viceroyalty of Peru, a vast territory —crossed by the Andes from South to North— which at the time ranged from the Magellan Strait to the jungles of Panama, with the exception of present-day Venezuela,

***PORTRAITS OF THE INCA KINGS SUCCESSION AND THE KINGS OF SPAIN***

Illustrated by Didacus Villanova and engraved by Palomino.
In: Juan, Jorge and Ulloa, Antonio de, *Relación Histórica del viage a la America Meridional…*
Madrid: Antonio Marin, 1748.
Courtesy of María Marta Larguía de Arias.

and from the River Plate in the East to the Pacific coast in the West. Cusco on the South Andean Altiplano, Arequipa in a privileged spot between the sea coast and the Altiplano Highlands, together with the coastal cities of Lima and Trujillo, were the places where the most notable and distinguished society of the time was concentrated.

With the consolidation of the conquest, the architecture of Cusco demonstrated Spanish domination translated into great artistic forms, both religious and secular, built on top of the original Inca foundations, streets and walls: in Cusco, […] *the lower part of the buildings is generally Inca, the upper is Spanish.*[2] Thus, the Spanish-American version of a typical Spanish town was born, with its tiled roofs, wooden balconies and Mudejar lattices, displaying attributes resulting from the merger of two cultures, which made it a wonderful and unique city.

Cusco would leave behind its original significance, but because of that […] *it would not lose other well-known attributes. Its very isolation inside the territory would contribute to the survival of many of its qualities.*[3]

Lima, the "City of Kings", was founded in January 1535 and became the capital city of the Viceroyalty of Peru by royal decree. Lima, a walled city, with its main

[2] Velarde, Héctor. Op. cit., p. 62.

[3] Viñuales, Graciela María. *El Espacio Urbano en el Cusco Colonial: uso y organización de las estructuras simbólicas.* Lima: Epígrafe Editores - Cedodal, 2004, p. 13.

***Amérique Méridionale***
Author: Guillaume Sanson.
1669.
Courtesy of Archivo Histórico de Límites – Peruvian Ministry of Foreign Affairs (AMS-023).

***SCENOGRAPHIC LAYOUT OF THE CITY OF KINGS OR LIMA CAPITAL CITY OF THE KINGDOMS OF PERU.***
Engraving.
c. 1740.
In: Juan, Jorge and Ulloa, Antonio de, *Relación Histórica del viage a la America Meridional…*
Madrid: Antonio Marin, 1748.
Courtesy of María Marta Larguía de Arias.

port, El Callao, is located on the banks of the River Rímac, on the Pacific coast [...] *and chained to a series of elevations which are the foothills of the Andes.*[4]

*The city, with its original seventy neighbours and thirty houses, grew little-by-little. On the Plaza Mayor, the beautiful Cathedral, the Palacio del Virrey and the Cabildo were erected; later, many churches, elegant convents, and great mansions of conquerors, noblemen arrived from Spain, and wealthy encomenderos.*[5]

Thus, a cosmopolitan atmosphere was created in Lima... *due to the exquisite cordiality, elegant urbanity and simplicity of its people, one of the most charming cities in the world.*[6]

Soon the city boasted 117 blocks arranged in a quadrangular pattern, known as "Pizarro's draughtboard." Lima and its Plaza Mayor became the centre for celebrating great courtly meetings, ecclesiastical and political ceremonies, such as the arrival of a new viceroy, births of princes in Spain, religious processions honouring patron saints, mournings and festivities in general.

Stately homes were inhabited by the aristocracy of Lima, who adorned their splendid rooms with viceregal furniture characterised by the style of the coastal region, making Lima the most Spanish city in South America.

The city of Trujillo, on the northern coast of the Viceroyalty of Peru, was founded in 1535. It had a booming population, as a result of sugar cane production and its proximity to the ocean shore. In a relaxed and modestly luxurious atmosphere, local rural landowners of ancient lineage settled in the city. Splendid mansions were built in surprisingly good taste and with a rural flavour; they bore coats of arms on the façades, had inner patios and rooms with barred windows in the Spanish style. The quality and soundness of religious architecture, mostly built by natives, is also worth mentioning.

During the colonial period, Arequipa was another important trading centre with its very own characteristics. It was founded in 1540 and its architecture stands out from that found in the rest of the Viceroyalty for its originality and beauty, also as a result of the merger of two cultures. *The urban layout of the early city was adapted to the Renaissance grid and the plots were distributed alongside sixteen streets* [...].[7] The city reveals a European Baroque language in the use of beautiful white ashlar on

---

4 Palma, Ricardo. "Dos tradiciones de Don Ricardo Palma. Un cerro con historia y los azulejos de San Francisco". In: Camacho, Fabio. *Aspectos de Lima.* Lima: Incazteca, Empresa Publicitaria Expresión, 1929, p. XXXVI.

5 Velarde, Héctor. Op. cit., p. 85.

6 Camacho, Fabio. "Lima actval". In: Camacho, Fabio. Op. cit., p. XXXIX.

7 Tord, Luis Enrique. *Arequipa artística y monumental.* Lima: Banco del Sur del Perú, 1987, p. 28.

*PORT OF CALLAO*
[TOP]
Engraving.
18TH century.
Courtesy of Biblioteca Municipal de Lima's Archivo Histórico Municipal.

*EXAMPLE OF COLONIAL ARCHITECTURE – PALACIO DE TORRE TAGLE (LIMA) BUILT BETWEEN 1635 AND 1735*
[CENTRE]
Engraving.
Courtesy of Biblioteca Municipal de Lima's Archivo Histórico Municipal.

*EVOCATION OF LIMA COLONIAL LIFE: IN THE BACKGROUND, THE OLD CABILDO*
[BOTTOM]
Engraving.
Courtesy of Biblioteca Municipal de Lima's Archivo Histórico Municipal.

its facades, which were richly flat-carved with European motifs, for example religious and secular coats of arms, and local symbolism —such as corncob and *kantuta*— in similar and balanced proportions. Due to frequent earthquakes, houses had only one level, with a Spanish layout similar to other Spanish American towns, although roofs were not tiled; windows were small given the intense sunlight.

Villages around the basin of Lake Titicaca, in the Collao region, include Lampa, Juli, Pomata, Chucuito and Zepita. On the road to the Imperial City of Potosí, a region rich in such minerals as silver and mercury —very intensively mined at the time— these isolated villages feature extraordinary churches.

In view of the pressing need to catechise the native population, the Dominican Order and, shortly after, the Society of Jesus were sent to the Viceroyalty. Their buildings were clearly based on European architectural traditions —especially 17TH-century classicism— with elegant flat carved stones spreading over façades with vernacular motifs such as shells, mermaids, parrots, monkeys and pineapples —some of these symbols originating in the Amazon jungle.

Juli, called "the Rome of the Americas" by some historians due to the number of churches erected there, also has markedly indigenous old mansions.[8]

For these reasons, and given such a display of architectural development, it is necessary to bear in mind the critical importance, for over two centuries, of the vast secular and ecclesiastical furniture production intended to meet the demand for equipment. This demand provided a powerful stimulus for manufacturing furniture, which was a very expressive vehicle for symbolism and a highly valuable iconographic source.

## OTHER SOURCES OF WEALTH

Viceroy Francisco de Toledo (1569-1581) laid the groundwork for mining in Peru. He provided native labour for the Potosí mines, where silver was extracted, and the Huancavelica mines, which supplied the mercury needed to purify the silver. The Viceroyalty of Peru became one of the most important silver production centres in the world, and this activity was its greatest source of wealth.

In turn, Spain, which had become the main European power, forged an alliance with Portugal, well-known for its maritime prowess, and decided to explore unknown lands and expand access to markets such as China, India and Japan, which were potential sources of wealth from overseas trade.

---

[8] Velarde, Héctor. Op. cit., p. 141.

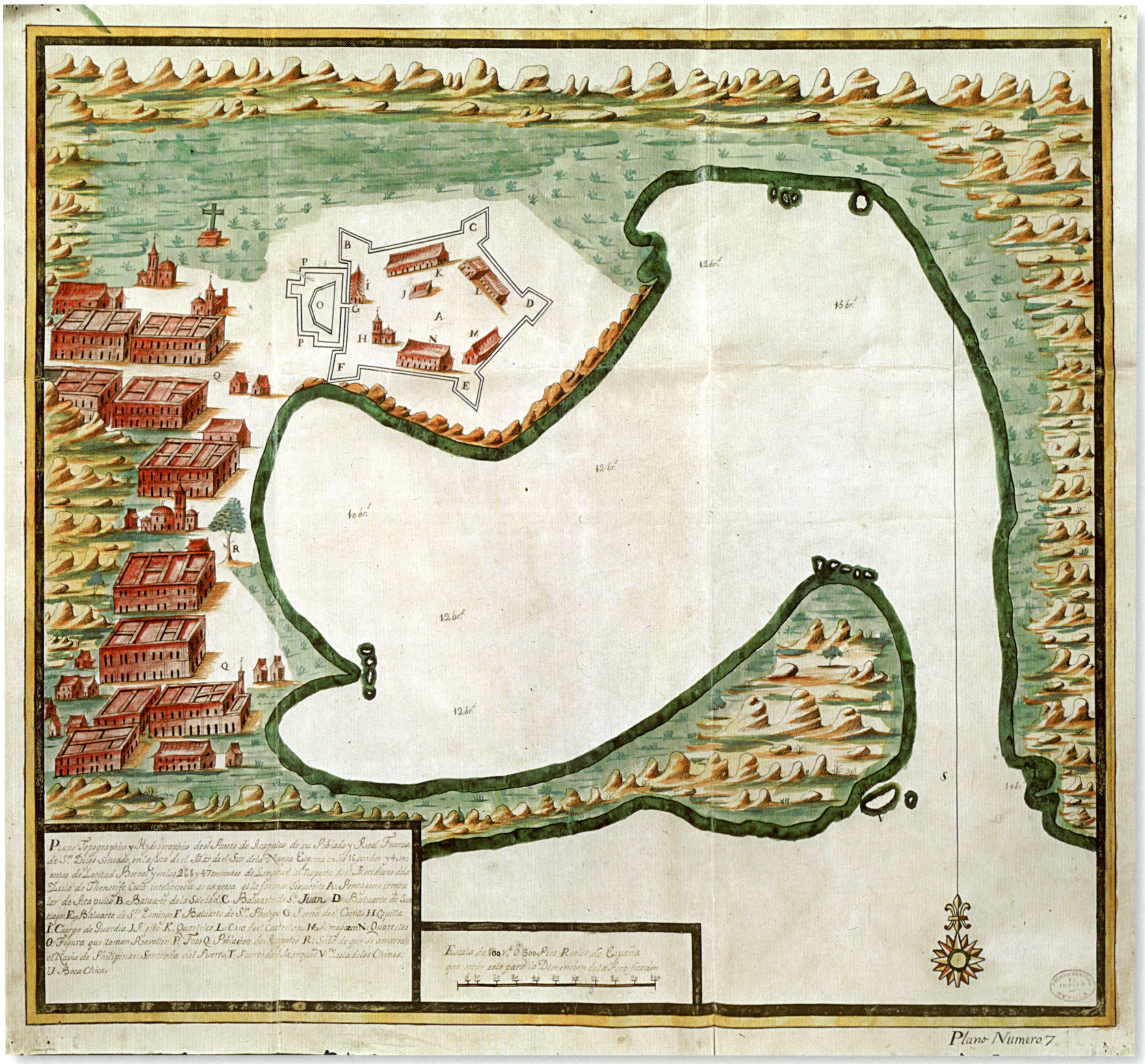
Plano Topographico y Hydrographico deel Puerto de Acapulco de su Poblado y Real Fuerza de Sn. Diego situado en la Costa deel Mar deel Sur dela Nueva España en los 16 grados y 4 minutos de Latitud Boreal y en los 268 y 47 minutos de Longitud al respecto deel Meridiano dela Ysla de Thenerife Cuia inteligencia se expresa en la forma siguiente A: Pentagono irregular de Acapulco B: Baluarte de la Soledad C. Baluarte de Sn. Juan. D: Baluarte de Santiago E: Baluarte de Sto. Domingo F. Baluarte de Sn. Phelipe G: Puerta deel Castillo H: Capilla
I: Cuerpo de Guardia J. Algibe K. Quarteles L: Casa deel Castellano M: Almagazen N: Quarteles
O: Figura que llaman Revellin P: Foso Q: Poblacion de Acapulco R: Seiba de que se amarra el Navio de Philipinas S: entrada deel Puerto T: Puerto deel Marques V: Ysla delos Chinos.
U: Boca Chica.
Escala de 100 vs. ó 300 Pies Reales de España
que sirve solo para la Dimension dela Fortificacion
10 20 30 40 50 60 70 80 90 100
Plano Numero 7

Both empires shared control over maritime routes by signing the Treaty of Tordesillas (1494). Portugal annexed part of the lands of present-day Brazil, the African routes and the Indian Ocean in a South-East direction; Spain, the rest of Spanish-America, and control over the seas in a westerly direction across the Atlantic and Pacific Oceans.

Through these routes, and having colonised the Philippines, the Spanish Crown established a strict control over trade, linking Seville —the "Gateway to the New World"— with Manila, the capital city of the Philippines, through Mexico, until the early 19TH-century. The first Spanish ship to go west set sail in 1565. Thus Spain secured its rule over those remote lands and sealed their fate for the following three centuries.

The "Manila Galleons" or "Nao of China" was the name given to the fleet which carried to Mexico the luxurious objects brought from the East and returned with heavy loads of silver to pay for those trade goods. Upon arrival in Acapulco, on the very beach, a market was set up where some of the cargo from the ships' holds was sold.

*LAYOUT OF THE PORT OF ACAPULCO*
1730.
Spain. Ministry of Education, Culture and Sports. Archivo General de Indias. (AGI, MP-MÉXICO 125).

Part of the cargo was purchased by *encomenderos*, who traded the goods in Peru, since the Viceroyalty was rich in silver and gold mines, and its nobility spent great amounts on luxury goods, regularly buying exotic Asian objects brought by merchants. Another portion stayed in Mexico, while the remainder of the cargo, the most substantial part, was transported by mule to the port of Veracruz before being loaded onto ships and sent to Spain.

Peruvian *encomenderos* were also involved in trade, selling their own products in the main coastal ports of the continent; making stops with their fleets which set off for Mexico.

## KEY SPANISH CONTRIBUTIONS

The Spaniards introduced to the Americas animal species unknown to the indigenous peoples: horses, donkeys, oxen, cows, etc. They also brought with them new techniques for working the land, such as the use of the plough, even though native farmers were reluctant to leave behind their ancestral traditions of using the hoe, or the backstrap loom for weaving. From that time, goods could be transported by mule or on carts driven by skinners from place to place through the vast territories of the Viceroyalty.

The indigenous peoples were skilful metalworkers, an ability which helped them make tools that had been previously unknown in the Americas but commonly used in Europe, such as saws, gouges, chisels, hammers and axes, mostly

*PERVVIAE AVRIFERÆ REGIONIS TYPVS*
Author: Diego Méndez.
c. 1584.
Courtesy of Archivo Histórico de Límites – Peruvian Ministry of Foreign Affairs (VPE-169).

made from iron, another material introduced by Spain to the New World. The local people also learned to appreciate the usefulness of scissors, needles, farming implements and other tools. *Other trades, such as carpentry and silverwork, found trained native craftsmen, who in a brief period are* [sic] *able to achieve the qualified production level of certain areas of Spain.*[9]

## PILLARS OF EDUCATION AND CULTURE

The essential cultural elements for the Viceroyalty's development consisted of books and the printing press: key vehicles for the dissemination of knowledge. The first printing works was established in Lima in 1581 and the first published book was *Doctrina cristiana y catecismo* written in three languages: Spanish, *Quechua* and *Aymara*. Surprisingly, the first Castilian editions of great architects and artists' works, such as the Italian Andrea Palladio… *were frequently found in convent libraries and in the hands of architects and master builders.*[10]

In addition, universities were founded which stood out for their academic achievements: in 1551, the Universidad de San Marcos de Lima, the oldest higher education institution in the Americas; in 1598, the Universidad de San Antonio de Abad, in Cusco; in 1634, the Universidad de Chuquisaca, in Upper Peru (present-day Bolivia); in 1664, the Universidad de Córdoba (present-day Argentina); in 1677, the Universidad de San Cristóbal de Huamanga; in 1719, the Universidad del Gran Padre San Agustín, in Arequipa; and, in 1738, the Universidad de Santiago de Chile.

Church members accounted for ten percent of the Viceroyalty's total population, comprising bishops, regular clergy members, secular clergy members (*doctrineros*), prelates and inquisitor canons. The territory was organised into archdioceses, dioceses and parishes, which developed their evangelising activities in many ways, including the dissemination of knowledge.

The first religious order to arrive in Peruvian lands was the Order of Preachers, or Dominicans, in 1532; the Order of Friars Minor or Franciscans arrived in 1533 and took their task of evangelising to the most remote and inhospitable corners of the Viceroyalty; the Mercedarians, in turn, arrived in 1533; the Order of St. Augustine, in 1551; and finally, in 1568, the Society of Jesus, which was

---

9 Gutiérrez, Ramón (coord). *Pintura, escultura y artes útiles en Iberoamérica, 1500-1825*. Colección Manuales Arte Cátedra. Madrid: Cátedra, 1995, p. 13.

10 Gutiérrez, Ramón. "Transculturación en el arte americano". In: Gutiérrez, Ramón (coord). Op. cit., p. 18.

a new order embracing the Counter-Reformation with great conviction. The difference between convents and monasteries was that convents were located in cities, while monasteries were in areas removed from urban centres, surrounded by large stretches of land, which monks farmed for sustenance.

The indoctrination into the Catholic faith and subsequent baptism of the indigenous people were the primary aims of these religious orders. The Inca society was forced to abandon their ancient beliefs and "pagan practices." A decision was made to destroy their cult objects and put an end to the *huacas* —sacred objects or landforms or old Inca temples for worshipping their ancestors— by erecting, on their foundations, churches suitable for Catholic worship.

In order to carry out the evangelising mission efficiently, there was a need to interact directly with the local population, so fluency in their languages, *Quechua* or *Aymara*, was essential. Jesuits were the first to realise that. To achieve their goals, the various religious orders successfully established relations with the natives, aiming to create an atmosphere which would result in a lasting and fruitful relationship. Thus, familiarising themselves with the local beliefs and learning the languages assisted the task of teaching the basics of Christianity. Religious orders made the teaching of the catechism one of their main virtues. They also taught music, using instruments brought from the Old World, and qualified teachers trained the indigenous people in other minor arts.

The first female orders to settle in the Viceroyalty of Peru were the Incarnation, composed of Augustinian nuns, and the Conception, governed by Franciscan rules. Later, in various regions of the Viceroyalty, congregations of Trinidad, Poor Clares, Saint Catherine, Discalced, Carmelites, Trinitarians, Mercedarians, Capuchinas de Jesús María, Saint Rose of Lima (in 1708), and finally, Nazarenes were founded.

Everyday life in the cloister required suitable equipment, similar to that for secular domestic life. Such needs were met primarily by buying and selling cells, which would be inhabited by nuns from the society of the time. It was a common practice for wealthy families to purchase cells to accommodate their daughters who would take the veil in a particular congregation.

Cells were extremely expensive, and sometimes equipped with the utmost luxury. This was the case with individual cells, which were splendidly furnished and decorated by their owners. In addition, as part of their dowry, novices had to provide the congregation with certain metres of fabric; they could even bring their own servants.

## ARTISTS' GUILDS AND LABOUR ORGANISATION IN *OBRAJES* AND WORKSHOPS

In the late 16TH- and early 17TH-centuries, Spanish painters came to these distant lands to develop their craft and teach their skills to the indigenous population. As teachers, they were entitled to draft ordinances to organise guilds in the Spanish-American world.

Following orders from their superiors, local painters organised themselves into guilds, therefore having to abide by their stringent rules. Guilds were useful, among other things, to dictate styles, and provide protection from unscrupulous traders who would pay a pittance for their work. They were taught the basics of Western art and the value of classical canons. Thus, in Cusco, guilds made up of Spaniards, Creoles, *mestizos* and indigenous people were established with the aim of keeping the relevant art or craft up-to-date.

*During the 17TH-century, constant lawsuits about service procurement* [in Spain] *lead to a comprehensive regulation of the various specialties.*[11] Guilds approved standards for furniture production and a specific division of permitted trades and tasks depending on artisans' training. Presumably, these measures were closely related to those later implemented in Spanish-America.

In Spain, employment and labour standards for Fine Arts (painting, sculpture and architecture) and Decorative Arts (furniture, pottery, silverwork, etc.) were interrelated. Consequently, *obrajes* in cities and towns were especially important in the labour organisation of the Viceroyalty. Numerous workshops concentrated various trades, such as carpentry, cabinetmaking, assembling, gilding, tanning, silverwork; artisans in these trades gathered to work in the large urban centres of the region.

In 1683, conflicts arose between *mestizo* and indigenous painters and their Spanish masters, which resulted in the division of the guild in 1688, an important fact discovered and disseminated by Teresa Gisbert.[12] For this reason, Spanish craftsmen continued to work abiding by the stipulated rules, while indigenous art evolved independently. By doing away with regulations, in many cases these artists worked without licenses, as they did not want to undergo examinations on nudes and basic knowledge of perspective and architecture.

---

11 Aguiló Alonso, María Paz. *El Mueble en España: siglos XVI y XVII.* Madrid: Antiqvaria, 1993, p. 51.

12 Mesa, José de. "La Influencia Flamenca en el Arte Andino". In: Mesa Figueroa, José de *et al. El retorno de los ángeles.* [n.p.]: Unión Latina, [n.d.], p. 133.

Circumstances experienced by artists in the early decades of the 17TH-century in the Viceroyalty allow us to discern and understand the evolution and development of their learning and the production of Decorative Arts works in general and furniture in particular.

There were a large number of artists and master builders working without training, whose skills earned them the title of *"smart in art": religious and military men, or mere officials or neighbours who abundantly express their opinions and produce works on our cultural history* [...].[13]

Many artisans became members of brotherhoods and fraternities, seeking the company of other members of the same trades and performing similar works, as well as ensuring mutual assistance. They shared tastes and beliefs, and were protected by a patron saint.

These artisans had to meet the requirements of their trade, both in terms of quality of work and moral standards, so they tried to avoid, as far as possible, the inclusion of members who were unworthy of practising their trade. *Qualified teachers and workshop owners had the place of honour in that guild structure; journeymen were under contract and supervised trainees.*[14]

Thus, guilds were organised with artisans and builders specialising in various areas, such as geometricians, sculptors, inlay experts, *estofadores* (specialised gilders), wood turners and assemblers. The latter were master carpenters, well-known for their skills —many of whom were part of dynasties in their specialty— who built church altarpieces. Master cabinetmakers also stood out; they were engaged in the production of ecclesiastical equipment, such as pulpits and coffered ceilings in churches and convents.

For the most part, artisanal furniture production was an anonymous work, except in the case of artists, architects and builders of Spanish origin and training —and their most outstanding local disciples— whose authorship was established when they were hired by the Church.

## WAVES OF IMMIGRANTS JOIN THE NATIVE POPULATION

African slaves were forced to settle in the region and worked with the local population to lay the foundations of the Viceroyalty. Slave labourers —used particularly

---

[13] Gutiérrez, Ramón. "Transculturación en el arte americano". In: Gutiérrez, Ramón (coord). Op. cit., p. 18.

[14] Samanez Argumedo, Roberto. "Las portadas retablo en el barroco cusqueño". In: Mujica Pinilla, Ramón *et al. El Barroco Peruano.* Vol. I. Colección Arte y Tesoros del Perú. Lima: Banco de Crédito del Perú, 2002, pages 147/148.

**WARDROBE**
[TOP] Detail of the inner coffered ceiling.
Museo del Arzobispado del Cusco.
Height: 224 cm. Width: 107.5 cm.
Depth: 72 cm.

**TRIBUNE**
[BOTTOM] Lattice detail.
Compañía de Jesús, Comunidad de San Pedro, Lima.
17TH century.
Height: 350 cm. Width: 400 cm.
Depth: 60 cm.

in architectural construction— were given the hardest and most menial jobs. *As early as the 16TH-century, the Spanish and Portuguese colonisation, linked to the Conquest, was combined with the African slave trade and later, with spontaneous migration from Europe and Asia.*[15]

Architects, master carpenters, assemblers, carvers, gilders, *estofadores* and general artisans of Spanish origin, such as Pedro de Noguera, Luis Ortiz de Vargas, Martín de Oviedo, Martín Alonso de Mesa, Gaspar de la Cueva, Juan Martínez de Arrona, Diego Arias de la Cerda and others, who settled in Lima and Cusco, undertook to equip and decorate many churches, convents and other Christian buildings which were in the process of construction. They brought with them —apart from their qualifications— their expertise and the ability to manage workshops for the design and production of pieces of furniture for both ecclesiastical and liturgical purposes. As time went by, carpentry and cabinet-making found in indigenous artisans and builders all skills required for those arts. Their ancestors had mastered stereotomy, i.e. the art of carving stone, but they were able to adapt to the new requirements.

Spanish-Muslim art influenced and inspired Mudejar art, incomparably enriching the Christian artistic world. Among those who worked in this field, it is worth noting some leading artisans of Arab origin who came to the New World drawn by the prospect of much work, and who specialised in metalworking, carpentry, cabinet-making and leatherworking.

---

[15] Ravines, Rogger. "Migración y colonización en el Perú: Preámbulo necesario". *Boletín de Lima.* Lima: El Pino, 1998, Vol. XX, Nº 114, p. 9.

They brought a wealth of ornamental motifs, mostly geometric, and quality and expertise in handling materials —which were remarkably sophisticated and elegant— revealing their solid experience and proven ability. Mudejar influence is evident in most viceregal pieces of furniture, since, as in Spain, cowhide or embossed cordovan were used for upholstering and covering seats and making suitcases and *petacas*. Gilded *guadamecí* was used for more refined decorations, such as parlour carpets and wall linings. *For Christian conquerors, Arab art was, at first, nothing but the expression of the refined lifestyle to which everyone aspired.*[16]

German and Italian artists and artisans settled in these lands in the early 17TH-century, to disseminate their characteristic repertoire of furniture design. Flemish, German and Italian prints inspired detailed and beautiful pieces, which were decorated with pyrographed ivory or bone plaques recreating biblical, classical mythology or European human-centred scenes on tortoiseshell or mahogany backgrounds.

[16] Burckhardt, T. *El mudéjar americano: del Islam al Nuevo Mundo.* Granada: El legado Andalusí, 1995, p. 140.

***HIERBERA***
[TOP]
Museo del Monasterio de Santa Teresa, Arequipa.
Height: 18 cm. Width: 22 cm.
Depth: 25 cm.

***BARGUEÑO***
[OPPOSITE PAGE, TOP]
Museo de Arte Religioso of the Basílica Catedral de Lima.
17TH – 18TH centuries.
Height: 132 cm. Width: 100 cm.
Depth: 36 cm.

***BARGUEÑO***
[OPPOSITE PAGE, BOTTOM LEFT]
Museo de Arte de Lima collection.
18TH century.
Width: 40 cm. Height: 33 cm.
Depth: 30 cm.

***BARGUEÑO***
[OPPOSITE PAGE, BOTTOM RIGHT]
Detail of the side.
Prado Heudebert family collection.
Height: 63 cm. Width: 97 cm.
Depth: 39.5 cm.

Until the late 17TH-century, the above standards were also met by artisans who specialised in manufacturing furniture decorated with inlaid wood to form figurative or abstract patterns clearly influenced by German and Northern Italian styles.

Referring to the furniture production of Upper Peru, Teresa Villegas de Aneiva points out that [...] *it shows fine and delicate inlays of different textures and colours, made from pine, ebony, mahogany, cherry, and other materials* [...].[17]

There is evidence of migration from Japan to the coasts of Peru dating from the 17TH-century, in some cases, via the Philippines. A few people from Japan settled in Lima beginning in 1607.[18] Evidence of the arrival of Japanese people in Spanish-America can be found in the chronicles of Domingo Chimalpahin (1579-1660), a historian whose name, after being baptised, was changed to Domingo Francisco de San Antón Muñón Chimalpahin. In his chronicles he describes the arrival (c. 1610) of the first Japanese diplomatic delegation to the Viceroyalty of New Spain.

The Kano School was a famous dynasty of Japanese craftsmen, who specialised in lacquer treatment. One of them, Kano Domi, moved first to Manila, in 1603, and from there he travelled to Mexico, where he worked with the González dynasty. This was a family of Christianised Japanese artisans who continued to use the traditional technique, to which Tomás González Villaverde and his son, Miguel, added the technique of inlaying mother-of-pearl on wood.

This reveals that, over time, these immigrant waves reached the coasts of Peru, bringing with them refined craftsmanship, which later captivated Peruvian cabinetmakers, who were encouraged to apply the techniques to making the renowned inlaid furniture, among other important contributions.

From the last quarter of the 17TH-century, the Europeanising style of painting and applied arts, including furniture, was almost completely left behind; a fact that paved the way for a creative overlapping of indigenous imaginary elements of great symbolic value, exoticism and local flavour. Thus a renewed kind of art emerged, which adopted

[17] Villegas de Aneiva, Teresa. "El mueble virreinal. Un ejemplo manierista". In: Campos Vera, Norma (ed). *Manierismo y Transición al Barroco: Memoria del III Encuentro Internacional sobre Barroco.* La Paz: Unión Latina - Centro de Estudios Indianos, 2005, p. 142.

[18] Fukumoto, Mary. "Migración japonesa al Perú". *Boletín de Lima.* Op. cit., p. 81.

a *mestizo* aesthetic language, characteristic of the South Andean world, which matured and evolved in all its forms of expression. Its artistic quality persisted throughout the 18TH-century due to local artisans' autonomy in making decisions. This trend extended over a vast area between Arequipa and the Highlands, including Cusco, the banks of Lake Titicaca and the road to Potosí, reaching present-day Bolivia. Its chronology remained independent from the European: it arose from its own reality.

## FOUNDATIONS OF IDENTITY: SECULAR ARCHITECTURE, GERM OF THE IDIOSYNCRASY OF FURNITURE AS AN OBJECT OF STUDY

Secular architecture in Lima between the last quarter of the 17TH- and mid-18TH-centuries, was characterised by the beauty and distinction of palaces and grand houses built in the Andalusian tradition. These Creole mansions, inhabited by wealthy people, displayed coats of arms on their Andalusian Baroque façades, as well as florid bars, projecting balconies with wooden lattices, tiled skirting boards on interior walls, brick or wooden floors, and fountains in inner gardens and on patios. Lima [...] *clearly acquired that aspect, although in a very individual way, because, to the elegance, grace and class of Seville and Lima inhabitants, the latter added a sentimentalism which was as sweet and mild as their climate.*[19]

**ALTAR FRONT**
Mother-of-pearl inlay detail.
Museo de los Descalzos - Convento de los Franciscanos Descalzos, Rímac, Lima.
18TH century.
Height: 102 cm. Width: 292.2 cm.
Depth: 5 cm.

**18TH-CENTURY LADIES AND GENTLEMEN**
[OPPOSITE PAGE, TOP LEFT AND RIGHT]
Engravings.
Courtesy of Biblioteca Municipal de Lima's Archivo Histórico Municipal.

**VIEW OF THE MAIN PATIO AND THE HALLWAY**
[OPPOSITE PAGE, BOTTOM LEFT AND RIGHT]
Casa Prado, Corcovado street, Lima.
In: Prado Heudebert, Javier. *Lima: Arquitectura y Escultura Religiosa Virreynal.* Lima: Talleres Gráficos P. L. Villanueva, 1996. p. 235.
Courtesy of the Prado Heudebert family.

[19] Bernales Ballesteros, Jorge. *Lima, la ciudad y sus monumentos.* Seville: Consejo Superior de Investigaciones Científicas, Escuela de Estudios Hispano-Americanos de Sevilla, 1972, p. 15.

These houses were accessed through a passageway, which led to the entrance hall, on the way to the first patio. After several patios came the drawing room and the study —only for family members and people close to them— next to the main hall, called *cuadra* and intended for important visitors.

The parlour, a room of Arab origin and tradition, which derived from the *harem*, was in the *cuadra*; it was a part of the room and was placed on a platform which could be as wide as the entire *cuadra.* It was especially designed to be used by the ladies of the house and their visitors during gatherings and audiences. The parlour was usually covered by carpets made from wool or gilded and polychromed *guadamecí.* The room was equipped with low chairs, luxurious cushions upholstered with exquisite fabrics, mirrors, work tables, richly decorated jewellery boxes, and other kinds of furniture for female use, as well as braziers for heating, in the Andalusian style.

The decoration was completed with pictures and religious images. According to iconographic sources, during those evenings, Lima ladies drank mate from richly decorated silver containers. Yerba mate or "hierba del Paraguay"[20] —a plant which originally grew in Paraguay and was gradually introduced by the Jesuits throughout South America— was stored in *coqueras* or *hierberas*. Referring to the kettles and stoves where water was heated to make the infusion, Luis Eduardo Wuffarden says: *Since the liquid was kept hot inside, this allowed the preparation of mates and infusions throughout the day. As is known, the favourite drink of that type was hierba-mate* [...] *and its strong roots in the city would result in one of the distinctive social rituals of the 18TH-century Creole elite.*[21]

The dining room was plain and simple, with austerely decorated cabinets, chairs and dining table. Elegance was reserved for the solid-silver tableware, which was more luxurious and less expensive than porcelain, the latter having to be imported from Europe or the East. Given the characteristic religious dedication of the people of Lima, their houses had a "domestic chapel", where a small altar was placed, as well as armchairs and kneelers, religious images and paintings and the essential liturgical utensils.

Bedrooms were private places for rest: domestic spaces which had to be furnished with utilitarian and ornamental pieces, as appropriate. Following the style of the time, they were equipped and adorned with silks, lamps, braziers and carpets.

Containers and supporting furniture —of Spanish tradition and manufacture— arrived on the coasts of Spanish America during the 16TH-century with the conquerors and high dignitaries, whose goal was to begin a new life and settle comfortably in the major urban centres of the Viceroyalty, while trying to preserve the customs of their rank.

Such furniture, which had similar uses as in Spain, adorned the first palaces and mansions. Later that furniture inspired local craftsmen, master carvers and gilders who, after proper training, were able to build such pieces as chests, *bargueños*, wardrobes, and beds with high canopies, among other items. Thus, a furniture production with marked Creole traditions was established. This fertile exchange gave birth to truly Spanish-American furniture styles, which were an

---

[20] Sánchez, Marta. "El mate en la sociedad virreinal". In: Eguiguren Molina, José and Eguiguren Molina, Javier (eds). *El mate en América*. Buenos Aires: Eguiguren y Vega, 2004, pages 39/44.

[21] Wuffarden, Luis Eduardo. "Calentador de agua". In: Bákula Budge, Cecilia *et al. Mestizo. Del renacimiento al barroco andino*. Lima: Impulso Empresa de Servicios, 2008, p. 97.

honest reflection of the syncretism of an important era. Various artistic languages characterised Peruvian colonial furniture, evolving over time according to circumstances influencing their design and construction, including cultural syncretism and the availability of materials.

Items of furniture were made in different shapes, sizes and qualities to suit multiple uses and purposes.

Not only were they essential as elements for everyday life, but also as aesthetic objects which often featured a striking symbolism, becoming vehicles of remarkable expressiveness, clear manifestations of power, devotion or good taste.

A relationship should be established between certain aspects of Spanish-American architecture, both from the coastal and the South Andian regions, and the design and production of colonial furniture —and other applied arts—

WARDROBE
Detail of the upper body (open).
Don Alfredo Pinillos' collection, Trujillo.
Early 17TH century.
Height: 334 cm. Width: 206 cm.
Depth: 111 cm.

which were a true reflection of the former, from the construction as well as the ornamental point of view, particularly in the case of wardrobes and *bargueños*.

## KEY ARTISTIC POINTS

From time immemorial, pieces of furniture were goods designed and made by human hands in order to fulfil certain basic requirements.

## GENERAL CONSIDERATIONS ON ECCLESIASTICAL VICEREGAL FURNITURE

The Viceroyalty was founded on the basis of a profound religious faith, as demonstrated by architectural works which have remained intact until the present day. Cities were organised around a Plaza Mayor, an empty block, so that secular constructions would not overshadow religious architecture. Many churches, convents and monasteries were built over a short period of time; once completed, they had to be furnished with pieces appropriate to their purpose and importance.

These buildings were equipped with furniture, suited to the needs of religious life, whose morphology and symbolic features had a key religious function. This

**GATE**
[LEFT] Detail of a fence and a balustrade on the side.
Iglesia y Monasterio de El Carmen, Trujillo.
Author: Master carpenter Thoribio Ramírez.
1757-1758.

**PULPIT**
[RIGHT] Staircase detail.
Basílica Catedral del Cusco.
Author: Diego Arias de la Cerda, Architect and Master Builder of Catedral del Cusco.
17TH century.

**ALTARPIECE FRAGMENT**
Alcove detail.
Iglesia de Santiago Apóstol de Lampa,
Puno Diocese.
$17^{TH}$ – $18^{TH}$ centuries.

**CONFESSIONAL**
[LEFT]
Iglesia de Santiago Apóstol de Lampa, Puno Diocese.
17th – 18th centuries.
Height: 235 cm. Width: 81.5 cm.
Depth: 100 cm.

**FLOOR LECTERN**
[RIGHT]
Basílica Catedral de Lima.
18th century.
Width: 116 cm. Height: 156 cm.
Depth: 72 cm.

**SACRAMENTARY STAND ON SACRISTY CHEST OF DRAWERS**
Basílica Catedral del Cusco.
17th – 18th centuries.

required a dynamic and vast production to supply an urgent demand. Various types of furniture were designed and built which could be classified as ceremonial or ornamental pieces, particularly columns and altarpieces. It is worth mentioning the pieces for religious use which, attached to the wall, became part of the church architectural structure, including pulpits and counter-pulpits, high and low choir stalls, gates and ambos, tribunes, cathedras and sacristy furniture.

Such pieces stood apart from others which, given their structure and function, could be moved from one place to another, such as confessionals, portable organs, benches, archiepiscopal thrones, portable altars, sacramentary stands, floor and table-top lecterns, kneelers and portable platforms. The latter could be moved easily during ceremonies such as processions, funerals and outdoor masses.

For lighting purposes, especially during religious ceremonies, regular or large

**CANDLESTICKS**
Basílica Catedral de Lima.
Late 18TH century.
Height: 71 cm. Width: 26 cm.

candlesticks, candelabra and hearses were made, as appropriate, from wood, silver or other metals. Sometimes magnificent mirrors hung from church walls, increasing candle light.

## GENERAL CONSIDERATIONS ON VICEREGAL SECULAR FURNITURE

Suited for domestic life in the large towns of the Viceroyalty, the most frequently used types of furniture included chests, coffers, *bargueños*, suitcases, wardrobes, friar's chairs and benches, as well as tables and other supporting pieces.

This does not imply that ornamental furniture was not used in these areas: elegant glass display cabinets and chests of drawers were specifically intended to decorate drawing rooms in the residences of high dignitaries or official buildings. They stood out for the luxury and originality of design, the result of skilled craftsmen's expertise, and the use of rich and exotic materials, all of which made them unique. It is worth noting that mirrors and centre and side tables were also designed for reception areas, such as the *cuadra*.

Chapels in important houses were equipped with pieces of furniture for domestic devotion, such as kneelers, small altars, armchairs, friar's chairs, and glass displays and pedestals for images.

The essential seats were located in different rooms; armchairs or benches were strictly utilitarian pieces, as were beds or bedsteads, cradles, dressers, *bargueños*, coffers, chests, wardrobes, bureau bookcases or writing desks which, as did many others, furnished private rooms hardly frequented by visitors.

Furniture was made mainly from wood, including Nicaraguan or Cusco cedar, mahogany, cocobolo, willow and alder of American origin. Pieces were finished with gold leaf, polychrome, lacquers (of Eastern or local origin: Pasto varnish), tortoiseshell, mother-of-pearl, leather of various qualities, and the most luxurious, with ivory or ebony from India.

Utilitarian containers, such as *bargueños*, chests, coffers and *petacas*, were richly augmented with finely produced locks, latches, corner beads and chiselled silver or iron fastenings.

Household furniture for secular use was similar to and as necessary as those

utilitarian pieces for everyday monastic and convent life, known as "cloister household furniture."

**COFFER**
[LEFT] Detail of silver corner bead and lock.
Private collection.
Formerly, in Don Luis García Lawson's collection.
18TH century.
Height: 25 cm. Width: 32 cm.
Depth: 21 cm.

**COFFER**
[RIGHT] Silver hinge detail.
Museo de Arte Hispanoamericano Isaac Fernández Blanco, Buenos Aires.
Formerly, in Don Martín Noel's collection.
18TH century.
Height: 22 cm. Width: 43.5 cm.
Depth: 33.5 cm.

## ARTISTIC STYLES: RENAISSANCE IN SPAIN. MANNERISM, BAROQUE, ROCOCO AND NEOCLASSICISM IN SPANISH AMERICA

The description and differentiation of artistic styles in the types of furniture listed above should no longer be postponed, as these pieces had characteristic structural and ornamental elements which facilitated their identification on this side of the world.

### SPANISH RENAISSANCE STYLE

The Spanish Renaissance style was born out of three sources which nurtured it and provided the style with a spirit of its very own. These sources were assimilated by Spanish artists, some of whom brought their talent and skills to the Spanish-American colonies.

One source was the appreciation of classical art, which occurred in Italy during the Renaissance. For that reason, in the 16TH-century, many Spanish artists emigrated to receive training in Italy, and to gain a good understanding of the changes based on the use of Greco-Roman patterns.

The salient features of Renaissance style included balanced, eminently classical

***PETACA***

[TOP LEFT] Detail of iron corner bead.
Museo de Arte de Lima collection.
Donated by the Prado family.
18TH century.
Width: 52.5 cm. Height: 21 cm.
Depth: 33 cm.

**CHEST**

[TOP RIGHT] Iron lock detail.
Museo del Arzobispado del Cusco.
Height: 77 cm. Width: 127 cm.
Depth: 53 cm.

**WARDROBE**

[BOTTOM] Iron handle detail.
Palacio de Torre Tagle, Peruvian Ministry of Foreign Affairs, Lima.
18TH century.
Height: 270 cm. Width: 132 cm.
Depth: 64 cm.

proportions, and a wide range of aesthetic values characterised by net volumes, clean lines and spatial symmetry. It was a style which encouraged a display of classical canons in the shape of fluted columns, capitals of every order, pediments, round arches and barrel vaults, and a representation of allegories, grotesques, and stylised anthropomorphic, zoomorphic and phytomorphic figures.

Another source was the intense artistic life of the time in southern Spain, which highlighted the work of many Andalusian artisans, who disseminated Mudejar decorative schemes juxtaposed with the classical spirit. *Horror vacui* was expressed by means of a profuse decoration on wood, leather or metal.

The Spanish Plateresque was combined with the Renaissance style, which became enriched with the abundant decoration used by the silversmiths of the time. *This trend brought together complex and diverse ingredients from Gothic,*

*Mozarabic, Italian Renaissance and Iberian folk art.*[22] This was the third source completing the Spanish Renaissance spirit; it resulted in a style full of identity and unparalleled expressiveness.

Few pieces of Spanish Renaissance furniture came to the Spanish-American world with *adelantados* and conquerors, and even fewer were preserved on Peruvian soil to bear witness to the time. It may be assumed that the few 16TH-century Spanish pieces in the Peruvian artistic heritage arrived later in these lands, purchased by private collectors during the Republican period or in the 20TH-century.

## THE SPANISH MANNERIST STYLE WHICH REACHED THE COASTS OF THE VICEROYALTY OF PERU

*Mannerist trends were fully expressed in Castile by masters who cultivated various arts. In particular two Castilians, Alonso Berruguete and Pedro Machuca, are among the founders of Mannerism in Italy; they continued to cultivate this trend upon their return to Spain,* says Paula Revenga Domínguez.[23]

The above mentioned context of work fostered the strengthening of the Mannerist-Baroque style in Spanish America of the late 16TH-century; it lasted until the first half of the 17TH-century, with highly positive results in the production of a great variety of admirable religious furniture which adorned churches.

Mannerism was a prolific period of artistic production; an arduous journey toward the peak of the Baroque. This style landed in the Spanish-American world in the hands of European artists and craftsmen, approximately between 1575 and 1630. As Elizabeth Kuon Arce points out [...] *it was a subtle but evident phenomenon* [...] *of great relevance for studying the origins of the Cusco school of painting* [...].[24]

Bernardo Bitti (1548-1610), born in Camerino, Italy, was a Jesuit priest who arrived in Peru in 1575 with the goal of "evangelising through art." His great artistic talent made him the most renowned Jesuit painter and sculptor in the Viceroyalty of Peru during the last quarter of the 16TH-century. He worked in the

---

[22] Pignoli, Giorgio; Rosenberg, Lucio; and Altmann, Kenneth. *Diccionario de Estética.* Buenos Aires: Quadrata, 2003, p. 137.

[23] Revenga Domínguez, Paula. "Los lenguajes pictóricos españoles en tránsito". In: Gutiérrez Haces, Juana (coord). *Pintura de los Reinos. Identidades compartidas. Territorios del mundo hispánico, siglos XVI-XVIII.* Vol. II. Mexico D.F.: Fomento Cultural Banamex, 2008, p. 474.

[24] Kuon Arce, Elizabeth. "Del manierismo al barroco en murales cuzqueños: Luis de Riaño". In: Campos Vera, Norma (ed). Op. cit., p. 105.

various houses of the Order: first in Lima, later moving to Cusco and then, in 1585, to Juli —a town near Puno. Bitti even reached Arequipa, Ayacucho and Chuquisaca [...] *where he made plenty of altarpieces and canvasses, some of which are preserved in San Pedro, San Juan de Letrán, and La Asunción churches, along with the altarpiece of the San Pedro Challapampa chapel.*[25]

According to Kuon, Bernardo Bitti: ...*imposed the taste for Roman Mannerism on the major urban centres of the Viceroyalty of Peru, leaving a fundamental work:*

---

[25] Data provided by Instituto Nacional de Cultura - Puno, 2009.

[26] "Bitti, Bernardo". In: Gesualdo, Vicente (ed). *Enciclopedia del Arte en América. Biografías I.* Buenos Aires: Bibliográfica OMEBA, 1968.

*ASSUMPTION OF THE VIRGIN*[26]
Relief.
Author: attributed to Bernardo Bitti (1548-1610).
Museo Nuestra Señora de la Asunción, Juli, Puno.
c. 1584.
Height: 292 cm. Width: 235 cm.

*the basis of Peruvian colonial painting and particularly of Cusco painting.*[27] In turn, Rogelio Ruiz Gomar adds: *His paintings are a part of the Counter-Reformation maniera and atmosphere, "with elongated figures in over-elaborate poses [...]."*[28]

It is also important to acknowledge the relevance of italian artists Mateo Pérez de Alesio (c. 1547-c. 1607), whose works [...] *reflect the changes in style that took place in Italy at the time,* and Angelino Medoro (1557/67-1633). *Italian artists left a lasting mark. The generation which had direct contact with them was dazzled.*[29]

Artistic expressions with Mannerist components were abundant in the decorative arts. They were specifically applied to the construction of liturgical furniture, used for decorating and equipping churches, monasteries and convents which were so urgently erected. All this was reflected in columns, capitals of various orders, balusters, grotesques, arches, cartouches, corbels, but particularly in half-relief anthropomorphic figures carved on bare solid wood, representing saints, martyrs and popes. Carvings adorned backrests of splendid choir stalls, striking sacristy furniture, ambos and lecterns, many of them revealing the strong influence from Montañés. Occasionally, volumes were highlighted with the application to surfaces of gold leaf or polychrome.

Refering to the rood screen in the Convento de San Francisco, Jorge Bernales Ballesteros explains: *They are splendid Baroque stalls which move away from Montañés's influence, evident in the Lima choir stalls of the first half of the 17TH-century.*[30]

**CHOIR STALLS**
[LEFT] Detail of half relief carving on backrest.
Basílica Catedral de Lima.
Authors: Pedro de Noguera in collaboration with Luis Ortiz de Vargas and Martín Alonso de Mesa.
Between 1626 and 1632.

**SACRISTY CHEST OF DRAWERS**
[CENTRE] Column detail.
Museo de Arte Religioso of Convento San Francisco y Catacumbas, Lima.
17TH century.

**LECTERN**
[RIGHT] Shrine detail.
Iglesia y Convento de San Francisco de Lima, Basílica Menor.
Author: Lay brother friar Pérez Gómez.
1678.
Height: 240 cm.
Width of each side: 136 cm.

---

27 Kuon Arce, Elizabeth. Op. cit., p. 105.

28 Ruiz Gomar, Rogelio. "Nueva España: en búsqueda de una identidad pictórica". In: Gutiérrez Haces, Juana (coord). Op. cit., p. 555.

29 Stastny, Francisco. "La pintura en el Perú colonial". In: Gutiérrez, Ramón (coord). *Barroco iberoamericano. De los Andes a las Pampas.* Barcelona: Lunwerg, 1997, pages 111-112.

30 Bernales Ballesteros, Jorge. Op. cit., p. 235.

Juan Martínez Montañés (1568-1649) was a famous Seville-born religious image sculptor and master assembler of altarpieces, who used Renaissance as well as Mannerist and Baroque styles. After an examination before an official jury, he was awarded the degree of master sculptor and assembler, thus authorised to draw architectural and altarpiece designs for works he later carried out. He exerted great influence on the planning and construction of altarpieces in the churches which were built in the City of Kings, becoming a source of inspiration for the first artists and artisans invited to work in these distant lands. It is worth mentioning the magnificent altarpiece dedicated to Saint John the Baptist, which used to be in the church of the Monasterio de la Concepción; this piece is attributed to Juan Martínez Montañés and now adorns the Catedral de Lima.[31]

### THE BAROQUE STYLE ON THIS SIDE OF THE WORLD

The Baroque style originated in Rome in the early 17TH-century. It is related to the second Counter-Reformation, and was an art movement which carried a message of the triumph of the supernatural over the earthly world used by

[31] San Cristóbal Sebastián, Antonio. "La Catedral de Lima en la Arquitectura Virreinal". In: Lohmann Villena, Guillermo *et al. La Basílica Catedral de Lima.* Colección Arte y Tesoros del Perú. Lima: Banco de Crédito del Perú, 2004, p. 106.

**COLUMN**
[TOP]
Museo del Convento de Santo Domingo, Cusco.
Height: 240 cm.

***BARGUEÑO***
[LEFT] Column detail.
Doña Mariana Berckemeyer Prado's collection, Lima.
18TH century.
Height: 51 cm. Width: 86 cm.
Depth: 33 cm.

**PULPIT**
[RIGHT] Detail of double columns.
Iglesia y Convento de Santo Domingo, Cusco.

the Catholic Church to respond to the Reformers and Luther's Reformation. The Baroque was a result of the Counter-Reformation, which was disseminated by the effective *Propaganda Fide.*

Indeed, according to the objectives laid down by the Church, the idea emerged to reinforce its doctrine through the dissemination of artistic expression, which would exalt religion through theatrical messages; light from lanterns creating supernatural effects and causing surprise, appealing to the sensitivity of the population, who was mostly illiterate.

The rhetoric behind this was based on contrast, movement, brightness and volume, features which turned Baroque into an artistic movement rather than a style: elements of previous styles were not replaced by others; rather, they were incorporated and applied in different ways.

The *trompe l'œil* was a common technique for simulating reality by means of perspective; balustrades, cornices and draughtboards were used, among others, to significantly expand spaces. Masks, broken pediments and single, double or triple Solomonic columns attest to the treatment of space and the profuse surrounding ornamentation, and also to the search for highly contrasting effects.

Thus a rich, ostentatious, highly scenographic art sowed the seed which germinated, first in Italy, later spreading to Spain and Portugal, southern Germany and the rest of Europe, to arrive shortly after in the Spanish-American colonies.

**WARDROBE**
[LEFT] Detail of panel with coat of arms.
Museo del Palacio Arzobispal de Lima.
$18^{TH}$ century.
Height: 290 cm. Width: 130 cm.
Depth: 67 cm.

**ARMCHAIR**
[RIGHT] Detail of coat of arms on the reverse of the backrest.
Prado Heudebert family collection, Lima.
$18^{TH}$ century.

***BARGUEÑO***
[LEFT] Detail of squire.
Museo de Arte de Lima collection.
Donated by the Prado family.
17TH century.
Height: 60 cm. Width: 108.5 cm.
Depth: 40 cm.

**WARDROBE**
[TOP RIGHT] Detail of pediment
with a double-headed eagle.
Palacio de Torre Tagle, Peruvian
Ministry of Foreign Affairs, Lima.
18TH century.
Height: 270 cm. Width: 132 cm.
Depth: 64 cm.

**MIRROR**
[BOTTOM RIGHT]
Private collection, Cusco.
Height: 100 cm. Width: 80 cm.

The Baroque movement remained in vogue for two hundred years throughout the Viceroyalty of Peru. Architecture, painting, religious image sculpting, music and applied arts maintained that indelible mark for two centuries; the Baroque became the most prolific of artistic styles, even when it coexisted with others. The archetypal furniture of this style is readily distinguishable according to its purpose: for either secular or ecclesiastical use. Secular furniture includes *bargueños*, chests of drawers, coffers, escritoires, wardrobes, chests, work tables, *hierberas*, suitcases, tables and seats of all kinds; ecclesiastical pieces include magnificent pulpits, choir stalls, sacristy furniture, ambos and lecterns.

This wide variety of Peruvian Baroque furniture, with a European influence, is comparable to that with prevailing *mestizo* or native ornamentation.

Some European motifs applied to secular and ecclesiastical furniture made in the Spanish-American Baroque style are: the double-headed eagle, the imperial symbol par excellence, biblical, mythological, war, hunting or gallant scenes, and the representation of allegories and emblems, squires and conquerors, coats of arms (either ecclesiastical or secular) or sea scenes, often surrounded by vegetation and zoomorphic figures as a background or complement.

Furniture of the time was adorned to a lesser extent with cornucopias, grotesques, single or double columns, pilasters, cartouches, corbels, a wide variety of urns, vases with flowers, rosettes, pearls, as well as classical friezes, ribbons and fruits of the vine completing the decoration.

Occasionally, in prominent areas of certain pieces —made using various supporting structures, materials and techniques— there are oil portraits of Jesus, the

**WALL NICHE**
[TOP LEFT] Detail of Paschal Lamb.
Claustro de los Naranjos, first cell,
Monasterio de Santa Catalina, Arequipa.

**ALTAR**
[TOP RIGHT] Detail of Dominican
Order emblem.
Monasterio de Santa Catalina, Arequipa.
Late 18TH century.
Height: 98 cm. Width: 238 cm.
Depth: 65 cm.

**HEARSE**
[BOTTOM LEFT] Detail of papal
coat of arms.
Iglesia de la Sagrada Familia – Basílica
Catedral del Cusco.
Late 18TH or early 19TH century.

**SACRISTY CHEST OF DRAWERS**
[BOTTOM RIGHT] Detail of central
cartouche with monogram of Jesus
Christ (IHC).
Museo de Arte Religioso of Convento
San Francisco y Catacumbas, Lima.
17TH century.

**PULPIT**
[OPPOSITE PAGE, TOP LEFT]
Detail of sounding board
with pilasters and corbels.
Convento de Santo Domingo, Cusco.
1656.

**WARDROBE**
[OPPOSITE PAGE, TOP RIGHT] Detail
of oil-painted religious image.
Doña Marita de la Peña Prado's
collection, Lima.
18TH century.

**CHEST OF DRAWERS**
[OPPOSITE PAGE, BOTTOM] Detail
of oil-painted religious image.
Prado Heudebert family collection, Lima.
18TH century.
Height: 199 cm. Width: 196 cm.
Depth: 57 cm.

Virgin Mary, patron saints, evangelists, martyrs and popes. There are also centralised religious allegories, such as the Paschal Lamb, the monstrance, the Heart of Christ —symbol of his love— a heart pierced by seven swords, a sacred symbol of the sorrows of Mary ([...] *devotion to the Sorrows, which is easy to recognise because it moved the deep fibres of the faithful's piety*[32]), triumphant angels, and cherubs, to name but a few.

On both the outer and inner sides of colonial pieces, there were monograms

[32] Schenone, Héctor. *Santa María: iconografía del arte colonial.* Pontificia Universidad Católica Argentina "Santa María de los Buenos Aires". Buenos Aires: Educa, 2008, p. 202.

and symbols of the religious orders established in Spanish America, for example, a heart with three nails, the symbol of the Society of Jesus.

Pyrographed ivory or bone plates on drawer and door fronts and wood inlay of contrasting colours distributed over the entire surface of the pieces were alternative methods of decorating Peruvian furniture during this first stage of the Baroque.

## MESTIZO BAROQUE STYLE CREATED IN THE VICEROYALTY OF PERU

The term "mestizo" means combined or mixed. It has different meanings, for example, a person born to an interracial couple; it also applies to the result of the merging of cultures.

Currently, *Mestizo* Baroque means the artistic expression which condenses in its essence European attributes and characteristics and an identity related to its indigenous origins; all these are necessary elements for this style to stand out as such. This syncretism was evident when ornamental motifs of American tradition were applied to European structural forms.

According to Dominique Fernández: *Resulting from a fusion of Spanish influences and indigenous sensibilities, this art has been defined as colonial, but only because it was the custom* [...]. *Let's rather call this Andean art as mestizo art, a culture of encounters.*[33]

Until recently, this from of expression had not been taken into account for its cultural contribution. It was a little explored artistic expression, which was not systematically nor deeply studied, until the International Symposium on Latin American Baroque, held in Rome in 1980; today, many researchers cite this symposium in their papers.

The Andean or *mestizo* Baroque art which originated in the Viceroyalty of Peru in the last quarter of the 17TH-century and was in vogue until the late 18TH-century [...] *identifies the architecture that emerged from the Arequipa region, in southern Peru up to the rich mining centre of Potosí, in Bolivia, including the Collao plateau near Lake Titicaca* [...].[34]

By the end of the 17TH-century, what was later referred to as "*mestizo* Baroque" or "Andean Baroque" began to mature and evolve in the art world of the

[33] Fernández, Dominique. "Donceles y soldados". In: Mesa Figueroa, José de *et al.* Op. cit., p. 42.

[34] Samanez Argumedo, Roberto. "Las Iglesias de Apurimac y Chumbivilcas en el Sur Peruano: Una perspectiva del Barroco Andino". In: Campos Vera, Norma (ed). *Barroco y fuentes de la diversidad cultural: Memoria del II Encuentro Internacional sobre Barroco.* La Paz: Viceministerio de Cultura, Unión Latina y UNESCO, 2004, p. 185.

region, reaching its height during the 18TH-century. In turn, the best results were obtained in furniture production, whose creators remained oblivious to new booming aesthetic trends.[35]

Predominant elements in architecture, as well as in cabinetmaking, its true reflection, were low-relief carvings, as opposed to half-relief carvings, typical of Italian Mannerism. Depending on the case, and with great skill, stone or wood were subtly carved, creating low, bevelled volumes which produced unique lighting effects; more so if carvings were applied to partially or entirely gilded furniture, following the pre-Hispanic tradition, given the high level of symbolism of gold.

The pre-Hispanic indigenous motifs were generous, dazzling and subtle contributions, adequate for decorating both architectural façades and Andean Baroque furniture, which combined universal elements with its own traditions. Therefore, with apparent coarseness, surreptitiousness and caution, a vast iconographic repertoire was added, presenting an example of ancestral sensitivity.

WARDROBE
Panel detail
Private collection, Cusco.
Height: 274.5 cm. Width: 134 cm.
Depth: 80 cm.

Clearly, the invaluable indigenous, *mestizo*, Mudejar, and even African contributions —which had a decisive importance in the artistic development of the Viceroyalty— resulted in a fertile aesthetic combination of unprecedented expressiveness, and proved useful for achieving evangelistic goals.

The frontality, the lack of perspective, the need to fill every space and the unrestrained use of colour were some of the indigenous contributions; thus native idiosyncrasy was expressed on textiles, furniture, metal and ceramic crockery and every other object they made.

The fertile exchange between the Old and New Worlds found its form of expression in the ornamental field, for instance, in applied arts: walls of churches and altarpieces as well as the decoration on the front of a *bargueño* or the embossed cordovan on a friar's chair.

*Mestizo* furniture production became enriched and embellished with details from the indigenous repertoire, combining its highly symbolic iconography and the representation of fruits of the earth with elements from the universal language.

---

35 Villegas de Aneiva, Teresa. "El mueble virreinal. Un ejemplo manierista". In: Campos Vera, Norma (ed). *Manierismo y Transición al Barroco.* Op. cit., p. 141.

Special attention should be paid to certain details, as they are efficient vehicles of expression, for example, indigenous female and male characters dancing; winged, often pregnant, women; child corbels; winged cherubs with indigenous facial features; fantastic figures of green or bearded men, in frontal or profile view, emerging among vegetation; mermaids with large tails of scales or foliage crowned with wreaths of flowers or feathers and strumming a *charango*, guitar or lute.

Those details, of great symbolic value for their creators and their customers, were surreptitiously placed between authorised elements. *However, they failed to prevent instances of religious syncretism or the frequent revelation of artful devices used by natives to hide symbolic practices and elements applied to everyday objects which were related to other iconographies.*[36]

Making reference to the universal mermaid myth, Fontana declares that:

[36] Gutiérrez, Ramón (coord). Op. cit., p. 343.

**CHEST**
[OPPOSITE PAGE, TOP LEFT]
Green man's face detail.
Private collection, Cusco.
Height: 64 cm. Width: 100 cm.
Depth: 59 cm.

**GATE**
[OPPOSITE PAGE, TOP RIGHT]
Angel detail.
Iglesia y Monasterio
de El Carmen, Trujillo.
Author: Master carpenter
Thoribio Ramírez.
1757-1758.

***BARGUEÑO***
[OPPOSITE PAGE, BOTTOM LEFT]
Detail of a triumphant angel
on the reverse.
Don Juan Luis de Aliaga's collection,
Lima.
18TH century.
Height: 45 cm. Width: 98 cm.
Depth: 33 cm.

**PULPIT**
[OPPOSITE PAGE, BOTTOM RIGHT AND THIS PAGE]
Detail of winged cherub and child corbel.
Iglesia Parroquial de San Blas, Cusco.
17TH century.

*Sometimes thought to be hallucinations by sailors starved of female company, mermaids symbolize idealized, elusive feminine beauty, but also vanity and fickleness.*[37]

Indeed, the image of the mermaid in Christian ideology symbolises temptation, but according to the interpretation of Espinosa Medrano, "El Lunarejo", a 17TH-century preacher and theology teacher, it could be associated with celestial music, as Mujica Pinilla explains: *Espinosa Medrano's interpretation of the singing mermaid contextualises the celestial music of the Andean fish-women and explains the fact that they are associated with the heavens and the miracle of the Eucharist because, at least in the Iglesia de Santa Clara, in Cusco, one of them is placed close to the altar; an inconceivable place for a sinful or lascivious mermaid*[38].

Examples: the mermaid carved in stone on the altar front of the Catedral de Puno, where its figure stands out in a festive attitude, and the one on the shaft of a baptismal font in the Museo Religioso de San Pedro —Iglesia de San Pedro Mártir, Catedral de Juli—[39] on Lake Titicaca. This font has a strict liturgical use: to administer the sacrament of Baptism.

Of classical morphology, the piece features *mestizo* ornamentation. On the upper body, it has large leaves carved on the outside of the bowl, while the shaft is decorated with a large-tailed mermaid wearing a crown; from her mouth, a bunch of grapes emerges. The base has winged cherubs with indigenous features. The piece was made from Huamanga stone or *piedra del lago*, a type of alabaster extracted from quarries in the vicinity of Lake Titicaca.

For the Incas, *Inti* was the sun god they worshiped, from whom rulers

**WARDROBE**
[LEFT] Detail of mermaids with guitars.
Vivian and Jaime Liébana's collection, Lima
18TH century.
Height: 199 cm. Width: 139 cm.
Depth: 84 cm.

***BARGUEÑO***
[RIGHT] Mermaid detail.
Museo de Arte de Lima collection.
Donated by the Prado family.
17TH century.
Height: 60 cm. Width: 108.5 cm.
Depth: 40 cm.

[37] Fontana, David. *The secret language of symbols. A visual key to symbols and their meanings.* San Francisco: Chronicle Books, 1994, p. 97.

[38] Mujica Pinilla, Ramón. "El arte y los sermones". In: Mujica Pinilla, Ramón *et al.* Op. cit, p. 306.

[39] Departamento de Registro y Catalogación archives, Instituto Nacional de Cultura, Puno, 2009.

**BAPTISMAL FONT**
Iglesia de San Pedro Mártir - Catedral de Juli, Puno.
Huamanga stone.
18$^{TH}$ century.
Height: 155 cm.
Cup diameter: 97 cm.

descended, and *Mama Killa* or *Quilla*, the moon goddess of fertility. They were siblings as well as husband and wife. This duality was represented through the use of gold —the sweat of the sun— and silver —the tears of the moon. These autochthonous symbols were widely used by indigenous artisans to decorate *mestizo* Baroque furniture.

LARDER
[TOP] Detail of the Sun, the Inca's royal symbol.
Private collection, Cusco.
Height: 185 cm. Width: 138 cm.
Depth: 12 cm.

It is worth noting the repetition of *kantuta* —the sacred flower of the Incas— on various materials as a decorative element in every style. This flower, traditionally dedicated by the Incas to the sun god, was used, with the arrival of the Spaniards, to decorate Christian portable altars or the entrances of houses as a symbol of hospitality.[40]

There are also striking motifs of local fauna, such as the puma, a feline native to the Americas, with open jaws or open jaws and tongue sticking out, as a welcoming symbol; the snake —which alludes to the world of the dead; the *kui*, the viscacha, and the Peruvian hairless dog called *viringo*, the Incas' pet, all of them immersed in the rich decoration of pieces of furniture with western morphology.

Often the hummingbird, considered a winged deity in pre-Hispanic cultures, such as the Nazca, the Moche and the Inca, was depicted on prominent places of the pieces, as it was admired for being an amazing bird which took nectar from flowers and for its ability to fly backwards.

Architectural constructions of different styles were also represented, as well as hunting or local mythological scenes, with male and female figures, children in a playful attitude, groups of musicians playing bass drums, guitars or flutes, cockfights, and monkeys eating grapes. Also turtles were depicted, which were sacred animals to many Amerindian peoples and considered good omens and protectors of human health.

American Baroque furniture was decorated with local fruits of the land, such as corncobs, papayas, pineapples, and also sunflowers, pomegranates and grapes arranged in baskets, or in the form of wreaths or garlands.

[40] Wust, Walter H. *Guía de identificación de especies de la flora y la fauna del Perú.* Lima: Peisa, 2003, p. 4.

The subtle "diamond point" and other small geometric shapes were used not only as background carvings covering the entire piece, but also, occasionally, as distinctive motifs on Cusco furniture. This technique was generally finished with gold leaf, creating an elegant effect.

The vast iconography of great symbolism, a legacy of ancient Peru, is often reflected in viceregal pieces of furniture as remnants of its tangible and intangible cultural heritage.

**CATHEDRA**
[TOP] Backrest detail.
Museo del Palacio Arzobispal de Lima.
18TH century.
Height: 500 cm. Width: 230 cm.
Depth: 70 cm.

**TABLE**
[OPPOSITE PAGE, BOTTOM]
Museo de Arte Religioso
of the Basílica Catedral de Lima.
18TH century.
Height: 75 cm. Width: 78 cm.
Depth: 47 cm.

## ROCOCO STYLE
## THE GROWING EXALTATION OF CURVES IN DECORATIVE ARTS

Rococo style arose in the West around 1730. It was partly inspired by the beautiful and versatile shapes of nature. This artistic expression was not pervaded by religious beliefs, thus artists had a certain freedom of production. The Eastern influence on Europe, from China and Japan —with which Europe traded easily— favoured radical changes in the aesthetic taste of the time, imposing the *chinoiserie*: a valuable trend inspiring stylistic changes, where the use of asymmetrically distributed *rocaille*, scallops and undulating lines naturally adapted to Western taste.

The political relationship between Spain and France and subsequent Bourbon influences were instrumental in shaping artistic tastes. Shortly after this new aesthetic trend became consolidated in Spain it spread to the New World.

Moreover, with the royal consent of Philip V of Spain, House of Bourbon (1683-1746), in the first third of the 18TH-century, England introduced many pieces of Queen Anne —and later Chippendale— furniture to ports of the Viceroyalty of New Spain; these styles were so appealing that they propagated to the rest of the continent, reaching the coasts of Peru. The recently arrived stylistic changes gained prominence, temporarily mitigating the Church's guiding role in every language of artistic production.

The classical orders of the Baroque style, considered rigid and expressionless, were abandoned, as they were not suitable for the intricacies and apparent disorder of the Rococo. Consequently, everything favoured the autonomy of artists and artisans, and customers' tastes became more sophisticated.

*It has been repeated ad nauseam that it is a purely decorative, overelaborate, sickly, effeminate style but rarely have its optical richness and figurative gracefulness been judged non-offensively. During this stylistic transition, ballrooms were decorated, mirror galleries were set up, gold fillets were applied, fine porcelain was produced, and palaces were built. The great artists of this aestheticist movement were the*

**PULPIT**
Detail of custodian angel on the sounding board. Iglesia de San Agustín de los Padres Franciscanos, Trujillo. 18TH century.

**THRONES FOR IMAGE**
[LEFT] Splat detail.
Monasterio de Santa Catalina, Arequipa.
18TH century.

**CORNER CONSOLE**
[CENTRE] Don Armando Andrade's collection, Cusco.
Height: 89 cm. Width: 104 cm.
Depth: 54.5 cm.

**WARDROBE**
[RIGHT] Panel detail.
Museo de Arte de Lima.
18TH century.
Height: 320 cm. Width: 134 cm.
Depth: 64 cm.

*Gauls: François Boucher (1703-1770), Jean-Honoré Fragonard (1732-1806) and Jean Antoine Watteau (1684-1721).*[41] Cabinetmakers as important as Jean-François Oeben (1721-1763) enriched the style in France through a vast production of pieces of furniture filled with Rococo identity.

Among Peruvian secular pieces which bear the characteristics of this style, it is worth mentioning a wide variety of seats, beds and tables, dressers, bureau bookcases, domestic chapels, glass displays and wardrobes for civilian use, as well as magnificent pulpits, sacristy chests of drawers, cathedras, thrones, glass displays, cradles and pedestals for images, lecterns, and catafalques for ecclesiastical use.

Their main morphological features were *cabriole* legs, outwardly curving arms, *bombé* or undulating fronts, crestings on seats and wardrobes, central splats on backrests, and markedly asymmetric panels. All these elements resulted from the application of various techniques to the supporting structures, such as carving, fretting, panelling, marquetry, lacquering —with either clear or coloured lacquers— patination and partial gilding.

These pieces were decorated with gallant and hunting scenes, among others, which were placed within central designs surrounded by undulating and asymmetric curves and frequently adorned with *rocaille*. In the same scene, there

[41] Pignoli, Giorgio, Rosenberg, Lucio, and Altmann, Kenneth. Op. cit., p. 157.

would be characters wearing garments in the European, Creole and indigenous styles. Occasionally, *treillage* could be found in the background, whose diamonds, once again, highlighted an unquestionably exotic Eastern inspiration. Associated with new trends, a tonal palette was selected for applying those motifs; on pieces where bare wood with a clear lacquer finish was not the decoration of choice, pastel colours were commonly used.

## NEOCLASSICAL STYLE. THE ENLIGHTENMENT, A DRIVER OF CHANGE

The neoclassical style began in Europe after the discovery of Herculaneum (1738) and Pompeii (1748) in Italy; these archaeological sites became powerful sources of inspiration for the new neoclassical style which emerged between the last decades of the 18TH- and the early 19TH-centuries. Thus, the classical art of Greece and Rome was appreciated, adding rationality, beauty, harmony and balance.

Also, the consolidation of Enlightenment ideas led to profound changes in the mindset of the time. *Despite the appreciation of subjectivity as a principle, or perhaps precisely because of it, the illustrious individual aspired to order and balance* [...].[42]

During the 18TH-century, known as the "Age of Reason", novel ideas emerged, which altered Western political, economic and spiritual life. Thus, a cultural-philosophical movement called the Enlightenment developed. Its followers believed in the power of Reason, which was useful not only to clarify ideas, but also to rebuild the entire society. *In fact, the Enlightenment could also be seen as a global process of cultural contact, with immense consequences for both the Europeans and indigenous peoples.* [...] *For indigenous peoples, contact with the Europeans often meant the destruction of their societies. In many cases such encounters led Europeans to question the nature of the European society, as well as its supposedly "civilised" character.*[43]

On an artistic level, the appetite for change became evident, given the apparent saturation caused by the excessive presence of the Rococo style in the tastes of the time, which resulted in a gradual abandonment of the ubiquitous curve.

**CONSOLE TABLE**
[TOP]
Museo del Convento de Santa Catalina de Sena, Cusco.
18TH century.
Height: 80 cm. Width: 77.5 cm.
Depth: 64 cm.

**WARDROBE**
[BOTTOM] Detail of flower in panel.
Monasterio de Santa Catalina, Arequipa.
Height: 127 cm. Width: 83.5 cm.
Depth: 57 cm.

---

[42] Barriga Tello, Martha. *Influencia de la Ilustración borbónica en el arte limeño: siglo XVIII*. Lima: Fondo Editorial Universidad Nacional Mayor de San Marcos, 2004, p. 13.

[43] Outram, Dorinda. "Una Ilustración con vocación universal". In: *Panorama de la Ilustración*. Barcelona, Art Blume, 2008, p. 130.

**PULPIT**
Backrest, in detail.
Museo de Arte Religioso of Convento San Francisco y Catacumbas, Lima.
Late 18TH century.

French and English artists and architects were very enthusiastic about organising what was known as the *Grand Tour*: a trip to southern Italy and Greece for studying, researching —and documenting for themselves— the artistic heritage of these countries, which imbued them with the spirit of antiquity. Later, they would recreate and apply these aesthetic values, which were distinctive of the last quarter of the 18TH-century.

In 1777 the Spanish Crown delegated to the Church the supervision of architecture and liturgical applied arts to be developed all over its domains. This evolution of styles took place throughout the history of viceregal art, and even though the above provisions were of a general nature, the lack of integration of the various Viceroyalty regions resulted in a diversity of effects caused by these changes, which had a greater influence and presence in coastal cities, such as Lima and Trujillo.

This supervisory mission was entrusted to the Basque architect and presbyter Matías Maestro, who decided to replace the magnificent and unique works of art in Baroque and Rococo styles which appeared on altar fronts, altarpieces and other religious elements —particularly for liturgical use— with neoclassical style. Despite that, in the secular sphere, master carpenters, cabinetmakers and artisans did not feel the imperative need to adopt this new artistic style; in very few cases did they feel attracted by the classical serenity and take refuge in this new expressive language.

While in the Old World almost everything had been invented, when cabinetmakers, such as Jean-Henri Riesener (1734-1806), had captivated European monarchs with their magnificent creations, the types of furniture which were usually designed and built on this side of the world were perhaps simpler and more austere. Seats and tables of all kinds, corner cupboards, wardrobes and beds are examples of secular furniture; pulpits, counter-pulpits, altar fronts, hearses, floor and table-top lecterns are some of the pieces found in the religious sphere.

Taking neoclassical canons as a point of reference, this type of viceregal furniture had straight lines and right angles, planimetric elements, geometric shapes (particularly ovals), plain or fluted columns with eminently classical bases and capitals, and a marked preference for the Greco-Roman mythological repertoire

**BED**
[LEFT] Detail of an oval on the headboard.
Don Alfredo Pinillos' collection, Trujillo.
Late 18TH century.
Height: 204 cm. Width: 182.5 cm.

**CHOIR STALLS**
[OPPOSITE PAGE] Frieze detail.
Basílica Catedral de Lima.
Authors: Pedro de Noguera in collaboration with Luis Ortiz de Vargas and Martín Alonso de Mesa.
1626-1632.

as main features. The decorative motifs of choice for this style of furniture were cartouches, garlands, acanthus leaves, pineapples, flutings and dentils, pearls and corbels, as well as Greek friezes, eggs, gadroons, and ribbons, which commonly adorned European furniture of that style.

The change in taste, the result of a healthy artistic dynamism, occurs naturally in the evolution of applied arts. Nevertheless, the Spanish-American viceregal neoclassicism should be observed with a critical eye, acknowledging that this was the less representative style of its artistic production. Paradoxically —yet fortunately— it seldom replaced previous styles, which had an immense artistic value.

The Peruvian Baroque furniture of European style, as well as the *mestizo* Baroque which followed it, the surprising Rococo, and the neoclassical from the decline of the Viceroyalty of Peru, create the feeling that, behind every piece and its production, there were builders with remarkable and ancient skills for manual work who also assimilated artistic traditions brought from distant lands; although they were often able to include, with restraint and somewhat surreptitiously, their own iconography and temperament. Thus, they left in their pieces scars and signs which reveal their history; even though those do not represent their signature or "artist's brand", they conceal in their anonymity an implicit message, a heritage.

> *Handmade, the artisanal object stores the fingerprints, either real or metaphorical, of the one who made it. Those fingerprints are not the artist's* signature, *they are not a name, they are not a brand either. They are rather a sign: the almost erased scar commemorating the original fraternity of men.* OCTAVIO PAZ [44]

It is also necessary to take into account the features of every piece and try to appreciate the piece as a witness of its time and the creative spirit of its maker; to accept and imagine for a moment that it ceases to be a seat and becomes a living part of a gathering or a private conversation; that a chest which once stored valuable documents may have witnessed a historic moment; or that from a pulpit eloquent homilies might have been delivered, such as the ones by "El Lunarejo", Juan de Espinosa Medrano (1629-1688)... and that his presence can be still felt.

[44] Paz, Octavio. "El Uso y la Contemplación". In: Alcolea Gil, Santiago *et al. Historia General del Arte: Artes decorativas I.* Madrid: Ediciones del Prado, 1994, p. 9.

# I

## MANNERIST-BAROQUE FURNITURE WITH ITALIAN AND SPANISH INFLUENCES

## CARVED AND GILDED WOOD

Liturgical ecclesiastical, household and secular use

LIMA, CUSCO AND TRUJILLO

# I

It was not by chance that Lima was chosen as the centre of colonial life in South America. It is the ideal city; with all the necessary qualities needed to play that role in such a remote location as the Viceroyalty of Peru.

The Viceroyalty's vast territories stretched from Panama to the Magellan Straits and were bounded by two oceans, the Atlantic and the Pacific.

Spanish dignitaries moved to the Americas to perform duties entrusted to them by the King of Spain; they formed a large delegation consisting of family members and groups of servants and assistants who helped them with their appointed tasks. Skilled craftsmen and builders, who were in charge of organising or building and equipping their homes, came to join them.

Many of these craftsmen, upon completing their assigned tasks, would no longer be under contract, leaving them free to engage in independent handicraft and to organise their own workshops, known as *obradores*.

Spanish America was popular with missionaries from various religious orders including the Mercedarians, the Franciscans, the Augustinians, the Dominicans and the Jesuits, each under the protection of their own patron saint; they engaged in missionary work, using art as a tool. Through their work, the missionaries made a remarkable contribution to the development of colonial artistic life.

Religious congregations tried to meet the demand for labour triggered by the construction of churches, convents and monasteries; inspiring the native community with their pedagogical and evangelising spirit.

At the time there was also an urgent need to meet the demands of the deeply devout society who had emigrated from Spain, by swiftly building churches,

**CHOIR STALLS**
[OPENING] Backrest, in detail.
[OPPOSITE PAGE] Detail.
Basílica Catedral de Lima.
Between 1626 and 1632.
Author: Pedro de Noguera in collaboration with Luis Ortiz de Vargas and Martín Alonso de Mesa.

**CHOIR STALLS**
[LEFT] Backrest detail.
[BOTTOM] Estipite detail.
Basílica Catedral de Lima.
Between 1626 and 1632.
Author: Pedro de Noguera in collaboration with Luis Ortiz de Vargas and Martín Alonso de Mesa.

convents and monasteries, along with private chapels built in homes. All of these were then equipped with the liturgical furniture and fittings needed to perform religious rites.

Italian classical art had an impact on the Spanish Renaissance as many 16TH-century Spanish artists were trained in Italy and influenced by the artistic changes which took place for more than a century.

Andalusian craftsmen with a strong Mudejar background brought an

CATHEDRA
Cresting detail.
Convento del Santísimo Rosario – Basílica y Convento de Santo Domingo, Lima.
c. 18TH century.

ornamental spirit to their decoration. This was revealed in the detailed wood carving with its characteristic *horror vacui.*

The indigenous people were quick to acquire the necessary knowledge and skills with which to produce handicrafts and mechanical pieces. They made them with a level of sensitivity and skill which surprised European professionals and religious leaders, who were often their art teachers.

Examples of the secular furnishings which accompanied the explorers on their journey were Renaissance, Mannerist and Spanish Baroque furniture. These were brought from the Iberian Peninsula during the 16TH and 17TH centuries. They then served as prototypes to be re-created in the Spanish Indies, leading to the first Hispano-Peruvian styles.

Guilds were organised with artists and builders specialising in various fields: geometricians, sculptors, religious image makers, assemblers, painters, carvers, marquetarians, stylists, gilders and *estofadores* (specialised gilders), as well as wood turners. Other prominent artisans were engaged in the manufacture of furniture, altars, pulpits and coffered ceilings for churches.

Creoles and *mestizos* were trained in various crafts; native peoples worked together with Spanish and especially Mudejar artists, who came to the Americas as specialists.

Various types of Spanish-origin religious furniture exhibiting the typical spirit of the period and engraved with great detail were taken as examples to be later replicated in the Americas.

For this reason, the churches, convents and monasteries in Lima were decorated and equipped with liturgical furniture which featured a wide array of Mannerist and Baroque artistic expressions. This is reflected in their columns, capitals, cartouches, corbels and half-relief anthropomorphic figures carved in solid wood.

During the 17TH century, the American Baroque style was influenced by Italian and Iberian art, as reflected in the ecclesiastical equipment. Choir stalls, ambos, lecterns, episcopal and archiepiscopal thrones, cathedras, hearses, sacristy furniture, and tribunes addressing the specific equipment requirements of liturgical celebrations, were crafted, along with utilitarian pieces of furniture such as wardrobes.

The engravers of the time specialised in carving half-relief figures representing saints and martyrs, popes and ecclesiastical dignitaries. They worked the

CATHEDRA
[LEFT] Backrest detail.
Convento del Santísimo Rosario – Basílica y Convento de Santo Domingo, Lima.
c. 18TH century.

CATHEDRA
[RIGHT] Backrest detail.
Convento del Santísimo Rosario – Basílica y Convento de Santo Domingo, Lima.
c. 18TH century.

**CHOIR STALLS**
[TOP] Backrest detail.
[BOTTOM] Seat misericorde.
Basílica Catedral de Lima.
Between 1626 and 1632.
Author: Pedro de Noguera in collaboration with Luis Ortiz de Vargas and Martín Alonso de Mesa.

central panels of the choir stalls' backs using a decorative planimetric carving technique from the classicistic period, and virtuous fretwork, sometimes enhancing it with gold leaf and polychrome.

The usual ornaments include: classical fluted or plain, Solomonic or spirally twisted columns, crowned by all types of capitals, corbels and reversed corbels, religious coats of arms, pinnacles and pilasters, arches, niches and alcoves, balusters, vases, urns and baskets, and all kinds of phytomorphic, anthropomorphic and zoomorphic items, arranged symmetrically, characteristic of that style.

Heroes from Classical antiquity were portrayed in busts, carved on wooden furniture pieces of Spanish origin, such as items for religious use, perhaps representing virtues.[1] Under closer scrutiny, native iconography can be found spread and almost hidden behind European-looking decorative items. Mermaids, corncobs, *kantuta* (a carnation-type plant) and characters with Indigenous features were some of the various elements sneaking into the Western-style decoration, to the surprise of the perceptive eye. Liturgical furnishings include, in order of

[1] Aguiló, María Paz. *El mueble clásico español*. Colección Cuadernos Arte Cátedra. Madrid: Cátedra, 1987, p. 116.

importance, choir stalls, sacristy furniture, pulpits, lecterns, *ceremony dressoir*, cathedras and benches; as merely utilitarian supporting pieces, these items bear true witness to the vast range of furniture produced during this earlier period.

### CHOIR STALLS

Choir stalls are U-shaped multiple supporting structures which usually had two rows of seats, higher and lower, distributed according to rank within the order. These stalls accommodated the religious community which took part in worship and the choir. A great example of these stalls is found in the Basílica Catedral de Lima, currently around the high altar, Gospel side presbytery, central niche and the Epistle side of the space. These stalls were built between 1626 and 1632 by Pedro de Noguera, a master architect and carver of Catalan origin who worked at the Lima school from his arrival in Lima. Luis Ortiz de Vargas, a Seville-born assembler and architect, agreed in 1624 to make the high stalls on the right side and the choir big gate "*following a sketch*"[2], whilst de Noguera himself made the left side and the pulpit.

---

[2] Vargas Ugarte S.J., Rubén. *Ensayo de un diccionario de artífices coloniales de la América Meridional.* [n.p.] Talleres Gráficos A.Baiocco, 1947, p. 223.

**VIEW OF THE NAVE WITH CHOIR STALLS**
Basílica Catedral de Lima.
Courtesy of Monsignor Raúl Chau.

According to Roberto Samanez Argumedo,[3] master carvers and assemblers Martín de Oviedo, Martín Alonso de Mesa and Gaspar de la Cueva, trained in the Seville school and commissioned to build the choir stall in the second decade of the 17TH century, came into serious conflict which in some cases led to them leaving the Viceroyalty.

According to Fabio Camacho,[4] the stalls consist of 75 seats and are divided into sectors: the Gospel and the Epistle sides, which are preceded by a cathedra in the centre, crowned by a canopy and flanked by a pair of ornamental columns which are part of the structure.

Seats can be folded allowing the community to stand up and sing. On the underside of each seat, a misericorde was used for resting during long services and was decorated with feline features. The backs are carved and there are armrests. They were made from solid Nicaraguan cedar, with an incomparable artistic sensitivity.

CHOIR STALLS
Detail of armrest with anthropomorphic figure.
Iglesia y Convento de San Francisco de Lima, Basílica Menor.
17TH century.
Length: 22 m (sides), 12 m (back).

To this liturgical piece, Italian Baroque and Mannerist influences were applied, highlighting motifs where symmetry is of the essence. The piece is decorated with half-relief anthropomorphic figures depicting martyrs, saints, popes and other church dignitaries, separated by fluted columns surmounted by Corinthian capitals. It also includes minor details such as pomegranates, children heads, anthropomorphic figures holding the frieze, shells, masks, garlands, draperies, fountains and birds, and a mythological feline figure which, through repetition, forms the misericorde. All the stalls are crowned by the upper frieze. In the central niche, the Visitation scene can be observed, where the Virgin Mary embraces Saint Elizabeth. This piece is in very good condition even though, according to Guillermo Lohmann Villena,[5] it was redesigned and partly mutilated in the late 19TH century, when it was located in the middle of the nave.

The choir stalls in the Iglesia y Convento de San Francisco de Lima, Basílica Menor, by an unknown maker,[6] is a rectangular supporting structure which could accommodate various members of the order enabling them to sing together in daily religious ceremonies or during special celebrations.

---

3 Samanez Argumedo, Roberto. "Las portadas retablo en el Barroco cusqueño". In: Mujica Pinilla, Ramón *et al.* *El Barroco Peruano.* Vol. II. Colección Arte y Tesoros del Perú. Lima: Banco de Crédito del Perú, 2003, p. 177.

4 Camacho, Fabio. *Aspectos de Lima.* Lima: Editorial Incazteca de F. Camacho, Empresa Publicitaria Expresión, 1929, p. 31.

5 Lohmann Villena, Guillermo *et al. La Basílica Catedral de Lima.* Colección Arte y Tesoros del Perú. Lima: Banco de Crédito del Perú, 2004, p. 132.

6 Camacho, Fabio. Op. cit., p. 141.

The piece currently has 130 stalls on both the upper and lower rows. In order to install the tubular organ built by Inocente Foglia in 1901, three stalls were removed, which are now part of the Hispanic Society of America collection, in New York City.

The central area was occupied by the custodian of the convent, and thus is crowned by the altarpiece which portrays Saint Dominic embracing Saint Francis. This is flanked by Solomonic columns under the protective image of the Immaculate Conception, the patroness of the Franciscan order. The image is located in the upper body of the structure.

The back of the second row has 71 beautiful half-relief Franciscan saints, carved in the characteristic Baroque style of the 17TH century (c. 1678)[7], revealing an Italian influence.

Its decorative elements include a cartouche with religious symbols and cherubs surrounded by scallops. Faces with a variety of expressions are carved on

[7] Harth-Terré, Emilio. "Arquitectura colonial". In: Kirchhoff, Herbert. *Perú Ayer y Hoy.* Buenos Aires: Guillermo Kraft, 1951, p. 36. Bernales Ballesteros, Jorge. *Lima, la ciudad y sus monumentos.* Sevilla: Escuela de estudios Hispano-Americanos de Sevilla, 1972, p. 235.

CHOIR STALLS
[OPPOSITE PAGE, TOP] Detail of the "Embrace of Saint Francis and Saint Dominic" apse.
[OPPOSITE PAGE, BOTTOM] Partial view.
Iglesia y Convento de San Francisco de Lima, Basílica Menor.
17TH century.
Length: 22 cm (sides), 12 m (back).

CHOIR STALLS
Backrest details.
Convento del Santísimo Rosario - Basílica y Convento de Santo Domingo, Lima.
17TH century.
Author: Architect O. P. Fr. Diego de Maroto in collaboration with Pedro de Noguera and his disciples.

the misericorde. In the upper row, serving as armrests, there are female figures with protruding bellies. In the lower row, the seats are divided by corbels representing mythological characters with their tongues hanging out.

This piece was made from carved, solid Panamanian cedar wood and iron and is in very good condition.

The rood screen, located in the upper area of the church and in front of the high altar of the Convento del Santísimo Rosario – Basílica y Convento de Santo Domingo, in Lima, accommodates typical 17TH century choir stalls.

This multiple supporting structure has three sides and 88 seats on two levels (59 upper and 29 lower), distributed according to hierarchy, as students and lay brothers sat in the lower seats.

As with the other examples described above, this ecclesiastical piece of furniture was intended for religious community activities, such as ceremonies and choir singing.

The stall back, made from solid Nicaraguan cedar, was intricately carved with Renaissance/Mannerist ornamentation, representing various saints and martyrs such as Saint Dominic de Guzman and Saint Francis of Assisi. These are located

**CHOIR STALLS**
[LEFT] Backrest detail.
Convento del Santísimo Rosario - Basílica y Convento de Santo Domingo, Lima.
17TH century.
Author: Architect O. P. Fr. Diego de Maroto in collaboration with Pedro de Noguera and his disciples.

**CHOIR STALLS**
[BOTTOM] Polychrome cartouche detail.
[OPPOSITE PAGE, TOP] Detail of the Virgin of Matins in a central niche.
[OPPOSITE PAGE, BOTTOM] Detail of polychrome backrest.
Convento y Basílica de Nuestra Señora de la Merced, Lima.
17TH - 18TH centuries.

in niches crowned by triangular pediments and divided by pinnacles and fluted columns surmounted by Corinthian capitals. Most of its surface is finely carved.

The techniques used were half-relief direct carving and fretwork, and the stalls show cartouches representing an open book from every angle, with a monogram adorned with partial polychrome.

With unquestionable Italian influence, the work was extended by its creator, the architect O. P. Fr. Diego de Maroto (1617-1697). The carving was entrusted to the

architect and carver Pedro de Noguera and several of his students. It is in good condition: the lower row has been partly refurbished and the upper row is original.

In the Convento y Basílica de Nuestra Señora de la Merced there are similar choir stalls. Their construction began in 1628 and was completed in the 18TH century. They were decorated in Italian-inspired strictly Baroque style.[8]

The backrests boast a repetition of peculiar angelic figures dressed as friars in white habits. This decoration also includes Solomonic columns, anthropomorphic columns, coats of arms, curves, acanthus leaves, faces, *rinceaux*, urns, scales and draperies. The top of the central niche has a harquebusier archangel underneath a broken pediment, and the lower row, an image of a sitting Virgin reading, both surrounded by Solomonic columns. *According to a Mercedarian legend* —narrated by Prof. Héctor Schenone— *the monk tending the gates once fell asleep. Upon waking he realised his error, and although Saint Peter Nolasco was already calling the friars to prayer, the community was late for matins. When they reached the choir, they saw that the ceremony had already begun and was now attended by a community of angels led by the Virgin. All the angels were wearing the white habit of the friars they were filling in for. This gave rise to the custom of placing in the main seat of the choir a seated image of the Virgin of Mercy, commonly named the Virgin of Matins, with her prayer book.*

The choir stalls were made by an anonymous artist of the Lima school. The artist who carved the half-relief

[8] Bonet Correa, Antonio. *Monasterios Iberoamericanos*. [n.p.]: Ediciones El Viso, 2001, p. 220.

figures worked closely with architect and sculptor Pedro de Noguera and may have been the skilful carver Friar Luis Montes, originally from Catalonia, who arrived in the Americas when he was very young and took holy orders as a Franciscan in 1632. The materials used were darkened solid wood with partial polychrome figures of angels, etc. It is in delicate condition and the frieze has deteriorated.

## OTHER LITURGICAL PIECES OF FURNITURE: AMBO, LECTERN, SHELF TABLE

The ambo is a liturgical piece of furniture similar to a pulpit; built in pairs, they would be placed on each side of the high altar for reading the Epistle and Gospel during mass. The piece was attached to the core architectural structure and had a small circular rostrum with stairs. The lector stood in front of the congregation. On top of the ambo there was a lectern surrounded by a balustrade.

The ambos in the Basílica Catedral de Lima are two valuable examples of the Lima school with a clear Italian influence and made by an anonymous artist.

They are richly decorated with wood carved flower arrangements at the end of the stairs. In the centre of the rostrum there is a book-shaped lectern held by a kneeling *putto*, carved from wood: a typical example of Baroque style.

While they have classical elements which are characteristic of the last quarter of the 17TH century —the balaustrade, the fluted surface ending in a pineapple—, the pieces were made in the 19TH century during the last reform of the cathedral, when the stalls were placed in the presbytery.

Built on a solid cedar support, these ambos are in very good condition.

The ambo in the Salón de los Diezmos of the Museo Catedralicio at Basílica Menor of Trujillo was one of a pair. Mannerist Baroque ecclesiastical furniture built during the first half of the 17TH century was also outstanding on the northern ocean coast; unfortunately, few examples remain due to devastating earthquakes in the region. This ambo is a liturgical piece of furniture, which, as in other cases, was used for reading the Epistle and Gospel. It was made up of two pieces located on either side of the high altar.

This detached ambo is medium-sized and rests on the floor. Each piece has three flat sides, like a prism, and an inner shelf with a lectern for holy books. Decorative elements were symmetrically placed following the style. It features intertwined curves and counter-curves, ribbons, leaves and pearls on the three framed panels divided by turned columns.

**AMBO**
[LEFT] Lectern detail.
[BOTTOM] Full view.
Basílica Catedral de Lima.
19TH century.
Height: 310 cm. Width: 280 cm.

**AMBO**
[LEFT] Full view.
[RIGHT] Front panel detail.
Museo Catedralicio. Basílica Menor de Trujillo.
17TH century.
Height: 106.5 cm. Width: 93 cm.
Depth: 66 cm.

The ambo has a distinct Italian influence, and is part of the Trujillo anonymous production. It was constructed on a finely carved solid-wood stand, with traces of gold and a clear lacquer finish.

This piece belongs to the Trujillo - La Libertad Metropolitan archbishopric. It is fairly well preserved, except for a few missing elements. The lectern has been refurbished.

A lectern is a choral book holder located in the centre of the liturgical singing area. It is very tall and has a central rotating base. The upper body usually has either two or four flat sides, each with their respective oblique book stand. The lower body which supports the book stand is generally quadrangular or circular, with one or more access doors. It is generally decorated in the style of the furniture and, occasionally, with musical allegories.

The lectern in the rood screen of the Convento y Basílica de Nuestra Señora de la Merced, in Lima, is quadrangular and uneven. It was useful for supporting large scores and psalm books. The piece has a hexagonal socket or base supported on zoomorphic legs.[9]

The lectern is crowned by a tall plinth which contains the image of the Immaculate Conception, attributed to Juan Martínez Montañés (1568-1649), a sculptor born in Seville whose works were of Renaissance and Baroque style.

---

9 Camacho, Fabio. Op. cit., p. 35.

LECTERN
Convento y Basílica de Nuestra Señora de la Merced, Lima.
17TH century.
Stand height: 200 cm.
Shaft height: 120 cm. Base height: 25 cm.
Width of each side: 140 cm.

The piece boasts the clear style of the Lima school, with features of 17TH century ecclesiastical furniture which emphasise Italian influences. Its creator was anonymous and it is in delicate condition. The lectern is decorated with low *rinceaux*, leaves, faces, cherubs, feline figures and claws. Direct carving, polychrome and gold leaf were applied to the darkened solid wood.

The lectern in the rood screen of the Iglesia y Convento de San Francisco de Lima, Basílica Menor, was built in 1678 by lay brother Friar Pérez Gómez[10]. It is similar to the previous example, having a central rotating base and is used for holding choral books. The upper body has four flat sides, each with their respective large oblique bookstands, whilst its lower body is quadrangular with doors divided by eight carved double columns.[11] The lectern is crowned by a shrine whose semi-dome is supported by four columns —a typical feature of the liturgical Baroque style.

The most remarkable decorative elements of the piece have Italian influences and were created by neat, symmetrical carving, using cartouches, grotesques, geometric figures, cherubs and the JHS monogram. The following text can be read on the piece: *"the custodian being the retired lector P.Fr. Pedro Gómez, 1678. Author: Fr. Pedro Gómez, layman."*

Carved from solid wood, the lectern has iron fittings and is in very good condition.

In the Basílica Catedral del Cusco, there are pieces with similar features to those above: choir stalls and the lectern placed next to them. Both pieces were made in the Southern Andean region during the 17TH century.

Their remarkable ornamentation has syncretic features and a clear Spanish influence. Both were made for ecclesiastical use.

The lectern or rotating stand was made around 1650, presumably by the great sculptor

[10] Bonet Correa, Antonio. Op. cit., pages 208-209. Vargas Ugarte S. J., Rubén. Op. cit., p. 178.

[11] Camacho, Fabio. Op. cit., p. 41.

**LECTERN**
[TOP] Basílica Catedral del Cusco.
17TH century.
Height: 226 cm. Width: 184 cm.
Author: Attributed to Master Melchor Huamán Mayta.

**LECTERN**
[OPPOSITE PAGE, TOP] Front panel detail.
[OPPOSITE PAGE, BOTTOM] Full view.
Iglesia y Convento de San Francisco de Lima.
Author: Lay brother friar Pérez Gómez.
1678.
Height: 240 cm.
Width of each side: 136 cm.

and master cabinetmaker, Master Melchor Huamán Mayta. The outstanding quality and beauty of its construction pays homage to the Cusco school tradition, according to Architect Liliana Saldívar Antúnez de Mayolo.[12] It has a large supporting structure for the choir book with four oblique sides and doors on each side. The lectern stands on a platform and rests on double columns. It is topped by a shrine containing an image of the crucified Christ.

The ornamentation of the piece includes planimetrically carved grotesques and classical friezes, as well as double columns, corbels and pomegranates on a supporting structure made of carved solid Cuzco cedar; the piece has iron fittings.

The liturgical shelf table or *dressoir* was intended for displaying liturgical utensils and all the necessary elements for major ceremonies. To this end, it has three

[12] Saldívar Antúnez de Mayolo, Liliana. *Magic and Enthrallment. The Cathedral of Cusco and the Temples of La Sagrada Familia and El Triunfo.* Cusco: Arzobispado del Cusco, 2007.

horizontal divisions. These pieces were usually made as part of a pair, which were occasionally placed on either side of the altar, as described by Professor Héctor Schenone. An example can be found next to the Capilla de Santa Rosa, on the Epistle side of the Basílica Catedral de Lima. An anonymous craftsman made this original, certainly hard-to-find piece. Therefore, it is difficult to say precisely when it was built. It is complete and in good condition, and has not been restored. The piece was ornamented with a pair of pinnacles on each side, a carved front apron and front and rear *cabriole* legs. Classicistic, this table was decorated with acanthus leaves, rosettes, ovals, slightly fluted pinnacles and curved legs with carved goat's feet. It is made of carved, turned and waxed solid cedar wood.

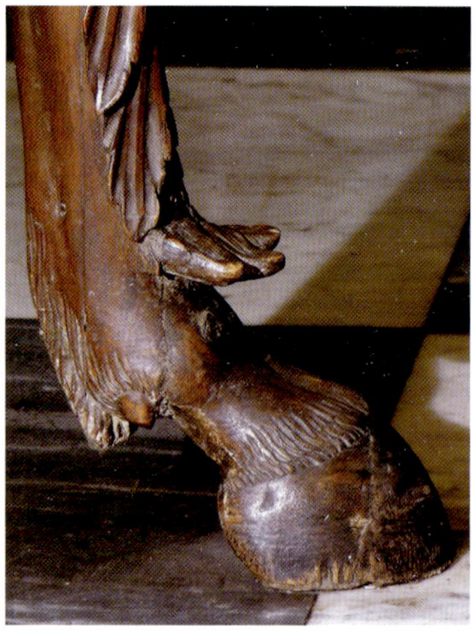

***DRESSOIR***
[TOP] Leg detail.
[LEFT] Full view.
Basílica Catedral de Lima.
17TH - 18TH centuries
Width: 210 cm. Height: 222 cm.
Depth: 145 cm.

**SACRISTY CHEST OF DRAWERS**
[OPPOSITE PAGE] Partial view.
Basílica Catedral de Lima.
Between 1606 and 1618.
Author: Juan Martínez de Arrona.
Length: 18 m. Height: 5.40 cm.

## UTILITARIAN RELIGIOUS FURNITURE: SACRISTY FURNITURE, CATHEDRA, ROSTRUM, WARDROBE

The sacristy furniture consists of ecclesiastical containers placed near altars, with many useful modules for keeping liturgical vestments. It is attached to the wall.

The doors are decorated with quartered and carved panels of various sizes; there are enormous drawers, over one metre deep, to store religious vestments and other liturgical utensils. Juan Martínez de Arrona was the sculptor and master builder at the Catedral de Lima between 1606 and 1635. He built the sacristy chest of drawers in Peruvian Mannerist-Baroque style for the main sacristy.[13] *In his own words: "It followed two styles: the Corinthian and the composite, which are*

[13] "Martínez de Arrona, Juan". In: Gesualdo, Vicente (ed). *Enciclopedia del Arte en América. Biografías II.* Buenos Aires: Bibliográfica OMEBA, 1968.

*the best in terms of beauty, richness and majesty...*"[14] The piece was later restored by Martín Alonso de Mesa and is now in very good condition.

The technique which was used to create this piece involved carving directly onto solid, fine Nicaraguan cedar wood. The piece has iron hinges, small doors on the top cover and larger ones, divided by double columns, below.

At regular intervals, there are fifteen panels carved with images of Christ, the Twelve Apostles, Saint Joseph and Saint John the Baptist; these are flanked by fluted columns, crowned by Corinthian capitals and supported by console tables.

Special attention should be paid to Baroque motifs, such as the door moulding, architecturally arranged in strictly symmetrical panels. The piece is topped by quotations and prayers carved to form circular medallions, branches, ribbons and *rinceaux*, and crowned by other classical friezes such as dentils. This is another example of the Lima school which flourished under the shadow of Italian influence.

A cathedra is the chair where the prior of a religious order sits. It is located in the chapterhouse of a convent or monastery. The chair is a large supporting structure crowned by a canopy and with an ornamented backrest. It was used to preside over meetings, give lessons or defend a dissertation.

The one we are reviewing here is located in the Convento del Santísimo Rosario – Basílica y Convento de Santo Domingo de Lima. It is characterised by the canopy which reveals the status of the person using it, and was made in the Baroque Lima style with Italian influence during the 18TH century.[15]

It has a perfectly symmetrical irregular front, profusely ornamented, with a canopy and six Solomonic two-headed columns dividing its bays. The portrait of Saint Thomas Aquinas is hung in the centre, under the coat of arms of the city of Lima. The chair is decorated with curves, branches, lions, cherub faces, corbels, classical friezes and round arches. It is made of richly carved solid mahogany, decorated with an oil-painted image and a shellac finish. This anonymously made piece is in very good condition.

The lower cathedra in the chapterhouse of the Convento del Santísimo Rosario – Basílica y Convento de Santo Domingo, in Lima is a chair used by ecclesiastical dignitaries of relatively high rank within the order or a guest; for this reason, it has a high backrest.[16]

[14] Vargas Ugarte S. J., Rubén. Op. cit., p. 199.

[15] Bonet Correa, Antonio. Op. cit., p. 232.

[16] Camacho, Fabio. Op. cit., p. 42. Bonet Correa, Antonio. Op. cit., p. 232.

SACRISTY CHEST OF DRAWERS
[TOP] Detail.
Basílica Catedral de Lima.
Between 1606 and 1618.
Author: Juan Martínez de Arrona.

The chair was built in the Baroque style with Italian influence. As a piece of ecclesiastical furniture, it required abundant decoration on the irregular architectural front, which emphasises the bays. The elements are symmetrically arranged. The round arch is placed in the centre, crowned by coats of arms, pinnacles, anthropomorphic and Solomonic columns, cartouches, grotesques, acanthus leaves and rosettes covering its entire surface, which is divided into several bodies split into identical panels. It rests on a pair of feline figures. It is likely that this structure would have originally been attached to the wall as part of the architectural design. The chair was built on a carved solid wood structure covered in lacquer. It is in very good condition.

The chapterhouse of the Basílica Convento del Santísimo Rosario – Basílica y Convento de Santo Domingo de Lima, has a tribune, popularly known as a "Viceroy's balcony".[17] It was built near the top of the room so that dignitaries could attend a chapterhouse meeting or any other ceremony without being seen. It accommodates several people.

The tribune belongs to the ecclesiastical furniture group and probably dates from the 17TH century. Its structure boasts a Baroque style with Italian influence; the abstract ornament arrangement was clearly inspired by the Mudejar style.

This piece of furniture is the result of the positive evolution of the Lima school, in which Andalusian craftsmen or their descendants left their mark on Spanish-American furniture. The characteristic *horror vacui* of Mudejar is revealed through detailed wood carving.

There is abundant decoration on the hardwood stand, which is fretted: this fulfils its specific function of allowing people to see and hear from within. Abstract decoration by the anonymous creator consists of panels divided into

**CATHEDRA**
[OPPOSITE PAGE, BOTTOM]
Convento del Santísimo Rosario – Basílica y Convento de Santo Domingo, Lima.
18TH century.

**CATHEDRA**
[TOP]
Convento del Santísimo Rosario – Basílica y Convento de Santo Domingo, Lima.
18TH century.

[17] Bonet Correa, Antonio. Op. cit., p. 232.

**TRIBUNE OR "VICEROY'S BALCONY"**
[LEFT] Convento del Santísimo Rosario - Basílica y Convento de Santo Domingo, Lima.
c. 17TH century.

**LATTICE BALCONY OR "BALCONY OF PIZARRO"**
[OPPOSITE PAGE, TOP] Museo de Arte Religioso of Convento San Francisco y Catacumbas, Lima.
17TH century.
Height: 350 cm. Width: 800 cm.

**WARDROBE**
[OPPOSITE PAGE, BOTTOM] Cresting detail. Convento del Santísimo Rosario - Basílica y Convento de Santo Domingo, Lima.
Total height: 300 cm. Width: 195 cm.
Depth: 94 cm.

different bodies and a pair of folding lattices in the centre. It was all inspired by the Andalusian way of building balconies, which are commonly found on the streets of Lima. In addition, the piece has a large frieze topped by a triangular pediment fretted with continuous waves. It is in very good condition.

The renowned "Balcony of Pizarro", or lattice balcony, which was once placed in the Viceroy's palace (now the government building), is currently located in the *De Profundis* room of the Museo de Arte Religioso in the Convento San Francisco y Catacumbas, Lima.[18]

The piece consists of a set of eight large panels fretted on the sides and separated by columns, and eight considerably smaller panels on the lower body, as well as a pair of central access doors. Moorish in style, this piece was made in the 17TH century by anonymous artisans from the Lima school. It is a fretted, turned and carved hardwood structure with a clear lacquer finish. The decorative elements which cover almost its entire surface are leaves and branches, pearls, and an upper frieze topped by pinnacles. The piece is in very good condition.

---

[18] *Conjunto monumental "San Francisco de Asís"*. Lima: [n.p.], [n.d.], p. 7.

In the sacristy of the Convento del Santísimo Rosario – Basílica y Convento de Santo Domingo de Lima, there is a wardrobe which falls into the category of utilitarian furniture for both ecclesiastical and secular use. The creator is unknown. It is a two-body containing structure with four front doors. With an Italian inspired design, the piece was made in a refined Renaissance style. Crowned by a triangular broken pediment, it has a central cartouche, flat fluted columns on the side stanchions, Greek friezes, four panels on the front with low-relief ornaments, and another four on the sides. It rests on four bun feet. The piece was made from carved and moulded solid wood, and has a clear lacquer finish. It is in a delicate condition as is riddled with woodworm.

During this period, the use of wardrobes was generalised in Europe; these pieces were aimed to replace traditional chests. This was due not only to the skill level gained by artisans, but also to the evident usefulness of these pieces, since they provided a way to organise contents in an orderly and practical manner.

## CARVED, FRETTED, POLYCHROMED AND GILDED WOOD FURNITURE

### ECCLESIASTICAL, HOUSEHOLD LITURGICAL AND ORNAMENTAL USES IN LIMA, CUSCO AND TRUJILLO

Furniture pieces used to illustrate this section differ from those in the previous part, mainly in their use of gold leaf on wood. This technique enhances the carving and fretwork of certain ecclesiastical pieces of furniture. Using local woods, such as Nicaraguan cedar, the master carver in charge of the work would follow a given sketch and carve and fret specific areas. Finally, the piece would be gilded with gold leaf. This added shine and luxury to the piece —two features typical of a viceroyalty where mining and precious metals abounded, such as Peru. The bare carved wood pieces, as well as the abovementioned gilded ones for ecclesiastical use, are characteristic of the cities of Lima and Cusco.

Types of furniture found in Cusco with a special, almost supernatural, shine of gold on carved wood include the choir stalls in the Cathedral Basilica of Cusco. Their remarkable ornamentation has a strong Spanish influence and a marked

**CHOIR STALLS**
Basílica Catedral del Cusco.
1641 - 1678.
Authors: Architect Diego Arias de la Cerda and master assemblers Melchor Huamán Mayta and Martín de Torres.
Each stall: Height: 102 cm. Width: 109 cm. Depth: 83 cm.

artistic syncretism. Rubén Vargas Ugarte states that they were built by priest and architect Diego Arias de la Cerda, master builder in the cathedral workshop, from 1641, according to the contemporary documents. Not only did he create the magnificent choir, but also the pulpit, ambos and sacristy. Ugarte adds that bishop Mollinedo wrote a letter to the King in 1678 to report the completion of the work.[19] Conversely, Liliana Saldívar Antúnez de Mayolo claims that the piece was produced by master sculptors and assemblers Melchor Huamán Mayta and Martín de Torres.[20]

The features are typical of late Plateresque or Baroque multiple supporting structures from Cusco. They are U-shaped, and placed in the centre of the room, separated by a gate, as was the Spanish tradition. They have 64 stalls, distributed on two levels, and a central episcopal throne for the President of the Ecclesiastical Chapter, topped by the image of the Virgin of the Assumption.

[19] Vargas Ugarte, S.J., Rubén. Op. cit., pages 125-130.
[20] Saldívar Antúnez de Mayolo, Liliana. Op. cit., p. 46.

**CHOIR STALLS**
[LEFT] Detail of image flanked by polychrome and gilded columns.
[CENTRE] Detail of polychrome and gilded column.
[RIGHT] Organ.
Basílica Catedral del Cusco.
1641 - 1678.
Authors: Architect Diego Arias de la Cerda and master assemblers Melchor Huamán Mayta and Martín de Torres.

These stalls were intended for the religious community which took part in worship and choirs. They have balconies on both sides and in front of the organ, and are separated from the nave by a turned wooden gate.

Decorative elements are 83 half-relief sculptures representing, on the upper body, the Virgin Martyrs, and on the lower, Martyr Saints. On both sides of the Virgin of the Assumption, there are Solomonic columns richly ornamented by Corinthian capitals. The sculpture of the Virgin is decorated with a half-relief carving and crowned by a broken pediment; it is escorted by *putti* and cherubs, and the coat of arms of Castile and León.

These choir stalls feature other ornamental details such as niches, fluted columns, balustrades, grotesques, cartouches, classical friezes and round arches, surmounted by pinnacles.

The repetition of a nude and pregnant female on the armrests, supported by a corncob-shaped corbel, should be highlighted as being in contrast to the classical spirit of the rest of the piece, which shows the mixture of elements often found in European ornamentation from this side of the world.

The materials used to build this magnificent piece were solid Cusco cedar wood, with gold leaf and polychrome on certain parts, iron fittings and oil painting on the lower frieze of the organ.

In the chapel's nave at the Real Monasterio de Clarisas de Santa María de Gracia, in the city of Trujillo, there is a magnificent pulpit, made by an anonymous artist, probably of African origin, during the 17TH century. It is Baroque in style, with a distinct Italian influence.[21]

The pulpit is a liturgical supporting structure placed against the wall; used by the officiating priest to deliver his sermon while standing up in front of the faithful. The main structural elements include a tribune divided into four panels, a backrest, a sounding board and some stairs. The abundant decoration of this great piece is arranged symmetrically. The image of the Virgin Mary is enthroned on the backrest, crowned by a broken pediment under a round arch and flanked by Solomonic columns on each side.

There are niches in the tribune with half-relief figures of the four Evangelists resting on a corbel; these are placed inside multi-foil arches and decorated with scallops. On the sides, there are robust Solomonic columns resting on cherub

PULPIT
[OPPOSITE PAGE, RIGHT] Full view.
[OPPOSITE PAGE, TOP] Detail of backrest with an image of the Virgin Mary.
[OPPOSITE PAGE, BOTTOM] Religious image detail.
Real Monasterio de Clarisas de Santa María de Gracia, Trujillo.
17TH century.

[21] González, Elena (ed). *Trazos del pasado: El período colonial en La Libertad*. Lima: Asociación Marsa, 2008. p. 59. Instituto Nacional de Cultura, Trujillo or Dirección Regional de Cultura archives.

bases. Among many elements, there is a child's face covered with stylized leaves.

The top of the sounding board is dome-shaped and covered by carved and fretted volumetric motifs dividing it into segments, where the sculpture of Saint Francis of Assisi, the founder of the order, is enthroned.

The stairs have interesting curved and double-axis Solomonic columns. The image of the Holy Spirit, scallops, corbels, rosettes, pearls, cherubs and child corbels are some of the many ornamental motifs which enhance the piece. These are clear examples of the *horror vacui* which is characteristic of the Andean Baroque. There is a richly carved pendant covered with acanthus leaves which crowns the lower part of the tribune. It is made of carved, fretted and turned wood. The ornamental motifs are partially enhanced with polychrome, gilding and *estofado*, and burgundy patinas decorate the background. The piece is in very good condition, being almost complete. As seen in the next photograph, there is only one column missing, on the left, and some dome segments have been replaced during restoration, despite of this, its beauty remains intact.

## ABOUT THE COLUMNS

The ornamental furniture now simply referred to as 'columns', and considered to be independent and detached, used to decorate churches in the past as part of an altarpiece, tribune or sacristy piece. Lima ancestral homes, such as the one commissioned by the Prado family on Corcovado street in the 18TH century, had several patios. These patios were ornamented with attractive pieces of furniture placed in every corner. In the photograph, there are several pairs of carved and gilded columns hiding among *petacas* and a central fountain on the second patio in the traditional manor[22].

The Museo Pedro de Osma, in Lima, exhibits a pair of columns from Cusco, whose purely ornamental features have an Italian-influenced Baroque style. They were richly decorated with high-relief carving on solid wood, accentuated with gold leaf and the occasional polychrome. These Solomonic columns have decorative carvings depicting a cluster of pomegranates and other fruits, as well as leaves and flowers, surrounded by ribbons. Anonymously

[22] Prado Heudebert, Javier. *Lima: Arquitectura y Escultura Religiosa Virreynal*. Lima: Talleres Gráficos P.L. Villanueva, 1996.

**VIEW OF THE SECOND INNER PATIO WITH COLUMNS**
[OPPOSITE PAGE]
Casa Prado, Corcovado street, Lima.
In: Prado Heudebert, Javier. *Lima: Arquitectura y Escultura Religiosa Virreynal.* Lima: Talleres Gráficos P. L. Villanueva, 1996, p. 235.
Courtesy of the Prado Heudebert family.

**COLUMNS**
[BOTTOM, LEFT AND TOP]
Full column and detail.
Doña Marita de la Peña Prado's collection, Lima.
17TH - 18TH centuries.

**COLUMN**
[BOTTOM, RIGHT]
Museo Pedro de Osma, Lima - Perú.
Height: 193 cm.

made, they are in good condition, except for some missing gold. The pair of carved and gilded columns currently in Doña Marita de la Peña Prado's collection, originally owned by the Prado family, are likely to have been part of an altarpiece. They were made by an anonymous craftsman in a profuse Baroque style; their local wood supporting structure is carved in the shape of a spiral, crowned by Corinthian capitals, and rests on a base. The columns are entirely covered in gold leaf.

## OTHER PIECES WITH A GOLD LEAF FINISH

The tribune is attached to the wall, on both sides of the high altar, with latticework covering almost its entire surface. During religious ceremonies, certain lay or ecclesiastical dignitaries would use it to inconspicuously attend ceremonies.

The pair of tribunes positioned on both sides of the high altar in the Iglesia de la Compañía de Jesús – Comunidad de San Pedro de Lima (built in 1598), and everything around them, is of enormous artistic value, typical of all work

undertaken by Jesuit monks. They were built using carved, fretted wood, gilded with gold leaf. The tribunes are symmetrically ornamented with ribbons and *rinceaux*, crowned by a pediment which boasts a large central cartouche, and flanked by curves and pinnacles. These are supported by corbels and decorative geometric patterns in the centre, which highlight the Mudejar influence.

**TRIBUNE**
Compañía de Jesús - Comunidad de San Pedro, Lima.
17TH century.
Height: 350 cm. Width: 400 cm.
Depth: 60 cm.

The Iglesia y Convento de San Francisco de Lima, which belongs to the religious order known as the "Order of Minor Friars", was commissioned in 1727 by Friar Lucas de Noriega.

Adjacent to the church, in the sacristy, we find the sacristy piece created by Friar Nicolás del Pozo O. M. and builder, Lucas Meléndez. On the façade, which is also Melendez's work, it states that the piece was completed in 1730.

Bonet Correa, however, thinks that the piece was made in the late 17TH century.[23] It is richly ornamented with beautiful carving made in the 18TH century. There are no significant differences from other pieces of that style, except that the wood at the top of the piece is completely gilded, whereas the lower drawers are made of bare wood.

The lower body consists of a set of 13 modules with three large drawers each and two central doors. These modules are decorated with ribbons and plant motifs made from carved cedar wood, and have iron handles on both sides of each drawer. The upper body has panels divided by fluted columns, topped by Corinthian capitals resting on spiral bases. Each central design contains a carved, gilded and polychromed religious image. In the central niche or apse, presiding over the room, there is an image of the Sacred Heart of Jesus enthroned. It is surrounded by cherubs and crowned by a broken pediment bearing a cartouche with the monogram of Jesus on top of the typical feline with open jaws. This remarkable piece of furniture is in very good condition.

[23] Vargas Ugarte S. J., Rubén. Op. cit., pages 253 and 325. *Conjunto monumental "San Francisco de Asís".* Op. cit., p. 8. Camacho, Fabio. Op. cit., p. 40. Bonet Correa, Antonio. Op. cit., p. 204.

SACRISTY CHEST OF DRAWERS
Partial view.
Iglesia y Convento de San Francisco de Lima, Basílica Menor.
1727 - 1730.
Authors: Fray Nicolás del Pozo O. M. and Lucas Meléndez.

AGAMNON
ACH
ILES
NEPTOLEMO
POLYXENA

# II

## BAROQUE STYLE FURNITURE WITH FLEMISH AND ITALIAN INFLUENCES

## IVORY OR BONE, EBONY OR EBONISED WOOD AND TORTOISESHELL AS A BACKGROUND INLAID WOOD

Ornamental secular and utilitarian use

LIMA AND BUENOS AIRES

# II

The lands of Flanders and Naples belonged to the Spanish Empire during part of the reigns of Philip III and Philip IV. In both regions there were workshops producing sophisticated and refined, ornamental *bargueños*, made from luxurious materials, such as ivory, which were sold throughout Europe. The plaques, representing biblical, mythological, gallant or historical scenes, were copied from prints made by renowned artists of the time and pyrographed with a hot burin.

It is worth mentioning furniture pieces made in Naples during the early decades of the 17th century, which were decorated with ivory plaques pyrographed on ebony, such as, among others, that attributed to Jacopo Fiammengo.[1]

Flemish prints containing religious scenes were used to disseminate the Christian faith and came to the Spanish overseas colonies from the Old World in the 17th century. They were printed in Antwerp, Germany, Italy and, to a lesser extent, in Spain. The prints were quickly and efficiently distributed.

It should be noted that two great artists, Maarten de Vos (1532-1603) and Peter Paul Rubens (1577-1640), had an influence on Spanish-American colonial art through graphic arts. *While Maarten de Vos is the most influential Flemish artist in the Americas in the late 16th century, Rubens is the one who dominated the scene during the rest of the century.*[2]

Kelemen highlights: *The immense role played by engravings in the dissemination of the New World's iconographic concepts and pictorial compositions.*[3]

***BARGUEÑO***
[OPENING] Detail.
Museo de Arte de Lima collection.
Donated by the Prado family.
17th century.

***BARGUEÑO***
[OPPOSITE PAGE] Detail with image of the Immaculate Conception.
Museo de Arte de Lima collection.
17th century.

1 Riccardi-Cubitt, Monique. *The Art of Cabinet.* London: Thames and Hudson, 1992, p. 58.

2 Mesa Figueroa, José de, *et al. El Retorno de los Ángeles* [n.p.]: Unión Latina, [n.d.], p. 129. Catalogue from the exhibition of the same name, held in the chapel of the Sorbonne, Paris, 1997.

3 Kelemen, Pál. *Baroque and Rococo in Latin America.* New York: Dover Publications, 1967.

In Spanish America, these prints were a vehicle for cultural transfer, which was later applied to alternative materials; art compositions full of formal Europeanised aspects and content.

Spirituality was renewed as a result of the Catholic Church's pronouncements during the Council of Trent (1545-1563), which was convened in response to the Protestant Reformation in the late 16th century. The Society of Jesus was actively involved in spreading the faith in Spanish America in a rejuvenated and methodical way.

Thus, the printing and subsequent dissemination of engravings and prints in folders and books played a prominent role in South America, where the conquerors were devoted to the task of evangelizing the —mostly illiterate— native population. Any method was valid for spreading the Catholic faith. Art was a particularly useful tool, since visual representations were important and effective.

The conquerors' religious beliefs were expressed in biblical scenes or images depicting the life of the Virgin Mary with gardens and landscapes as backgrounds; acts of beatitudes; visions of the patron saints; all of which were specially designed in copper for easy dissemination.

Classical mythological figures, genre or hunting scenes, combined with plant motifs —later represented on canvas, panels or murals— inspired the early stage of colonial painting paving the way for a later *mestizo* stage.

The contribution made by the Flemish prints to viceregal Peruvian furniture design was key, notably some *bargueños* (Spanish cabinets), escritoires and writing desks. Using inlay technique, materials such as sgraffitoed, pyrographed, carved and fretted bone or ivory were inserted into a structural wood support. These meticulous and elaborate plaques were inlaid using tortoiseshell, mahogany or darkened wood as a background. They were adequate vehicles of expressiveness for American Baroque furniture; Lima and Cusco school pieces were enriched with over elaborate and abstract Mudejar elements.

European artists and artisans, who arrived in the Viceroyalty of Peru with a diverse artistic heritage, such as classic Italian and Spanish schools, as well as Mudejar, Flemish and German trends, together with their *mestizo* and

***BARGUEÑO***
[TOP] Dancing characters, detail.
Museo de Arte de Lima collection.
Donated by the Prado family.
17th century.

***BARGUEÑO***
[BOTTOM] Detail of pyrographed ivory plaques.
Museo de Arte de Lima collection.
Donated by the Prado family.
17th century.

**WRITING DESK**
Detail of hunting scene.
Museo de Arte Hispanoamericano
Isaac Fernández Blanco, Buenos Aires.
Donated by Doña Marietta Ayerza
de González Garaño.
18TH century.

indigenous disciples, formed part of organised unions and guilds, which grouped and protected them until about 1650-1670. Their ornamental skills were exercised not only in Peru but also in Upper Peru, now Bolivia.

Juan Fidel Pérez Espinosa refers to the ivory-inlaid Baroque *bargueños* in the following terms: *...the work is clear proof of trade between three worlds —the East, the Americas and Europe...*[4]

For this reason, these items may have some Asian features, for example, the ivory with which certain Indo-Portuguese furniture pieces were decorated came from Goa, and the same language and techniques were used.

Ornamentation was always positioned on the piece's most visible areas. Fronts, front drawers and folding lids displayed stunning work with interrelated elements.

In some cases, a subtle straight or gentle wavy moulding, made of ebony or ebonized and carved wood, surrounded the plaques containing the compositions mentioned above.

Another moulding technique, of German origin, involved applying marquetry friezes with bi-colour motifs on the perimeter. To this end, local fruit tree woods were used.

The sgraffito technique applied to ivory or bone involved decorating flat pieces of these materials by making small incisions with a burin following a predesigned layout on drawer fronts, alcoves, *bargueño* sides, coffers and escritoires, which gave these plaques a unique aspect similar to Flemish or German engravings. These incisions were often highlighted with black ink. Usually their backgrounds were made of mahogany or tortoiseshell, the latter being a widely used material at the time, both in Europe and America.

---

4 Alfonso Mola, Marina *et al. El Galeón de Manila.* Madrid: Aldeasa, Ministerio de Educación, Cultura y Deporte, 2000. Catalogue of the exhibition of the same name held in the Hospital de los Venerables, Seville, 2000, organised by Fundación Focus-Abengoa.

The most common decorative elements used as aesthetic accessories were architectural: classical and Solomonic columns, open or broken triangular pediments, capitals of different orders, corbels and reversed corbels, niches and alcoves. They surrounded religious representations; secular and ecclesiastical emblems or coats of arms centralised in the piece; figures facing each other; allegories; Spanish conquerors; mythological, courtesan and hunting scenes; as well as natural elements such as flora and fauna, or abstract elements, for example, geometric figures.

The selected furniture is architectural in nature, still associated with the early century Mannerist style. Sometimes the pieces were crowned by combs, pinnacles and pilasters, or a perimeter balustrade made of various materials, as well as vases and urns, baskets, and many other classical ornamental details.

## WITH AN EYE SET ON SOPHISTICATION: SMALL DECORATIVE FURNITURE

***BARGUEÑO***
Detail of the image of Saint Cecilia.
Museo de Arte de Lima collection.
Donated by the Prado family.
17TH century.

*Bargueños*, work tables, coffers, escritoires, chests, desks, wardrobes or pieces with two or more bodies are examples of the type of furniture decorated with sgraffitoed or pyrographed ivory or bone plaques on wood bases, which were framed by a gentle wavy moulding.

The *bargueño* is a Mudejar containing structure, which was specifically intended for storing papers and valuables. It was regular in size, having a flat shape, and in some cases it featured both a front and upper lid. Inside, it had small drawers of various sizes and shapes, and even some secret ones. Usually, it included side handles for transportation. There is an absence of volume due to the particular technique used, which concentrated the creative energy of the artist. These markedly Baroque pieces of furniture demanded a strict use of symmetry.

The materials used for these pieces were fine exotic woods, such as Asian rosewood and ebony, along with American fine woods including mahogany, white cedar, willow and orange. Other materials included pyrographed bone or ivory, which were inlaid in the piece's most prominent places, combined with a balanced proportion of tortoiseshell as a background. Metal fittings were made of silver, iron, copper or bronze. The occasional religious image, centred on the lid or the alcove door, was painted in oils on copper or moulded wood.

Some examples of American *bargueños* are in the Museo Pedro de Osma, in Lima; the Museo de Arte Religioso of the Basílica Catedral de Lima; the Museo de Arte de Lima; or in private collections.

Although utilitarian, the pair of overlapping *bargueños* belonging to the prestigious collection of the Prado Heudebert family[5] of Lima are true works of art and thus, the kind of secular ornamental pieces which used to decorate great mansions during the colonial period. They were likely made around the end of the 17TH century. The anonymous artisans who built them strictly respected the Baroque canons followed for over a century on this side of the world and, as in other cases, these pieces reveal Flemish and Italian inspiration.

Interestingly, this pair of almost identical *bargueños* is presented as a unit, creating a piece of unique magnificence and beauty, yet another example of Lima's furniture production.

**PAIR OF OVERLAPPING *BARGUEÑOS***
[LEFT AND RIGHT] Details.
Prado Heudebert family collection, Lima.
Late 17TH century.

5 Porras Barrenechea, Raúl and Vargas Ugarte, S.J., Rubén. *Historia del Perú desde sus orígenes hasta el presente.* Lima: Sociedad Académica de Estudios Americanos, [n.d.] p. 92.

They have a rectilinear form enriched by some volumetric details enhancing the many (30) drawers and surrounding central alcoves, each crowned by a triangular pediment. This pediment recreates examples of civil architecture of the time, since it simulates rusticated architectural façades.

In both pieces, the decorative items were centralised with hierarchical religious images of the Virgin Mary and St. Joseph, flanked by classical columns crowned by Doric capitals and the Holy Spirit represented on top of each figure. They are surrounded by hunting, military, and musical scenes alternating with various symmetrically arranged zoomorphic and phytomorphic figures. All of them, with a profusion of leaf and flower mouldings, were designed on pyrographed ivory plaques, with a tortoiseshell background on the wood base, and finished with iron fittings.

On the sides there are rhomboids and rectangles, some shapes contained inside others, representing a heart. The grain of the walnut and mahogany of American origin stands out, among phytomorphic figures on small fragments of pyrographed ivory, and is neatly arranged in the four corners and the centre of the rectangle.

These pieces appear to be in very good condition, although if the original design included two legs, one of these is now missing.

A great secular use Baroque *bargueño* dating from the 17TH century was donated by the Prado Heudebert family to the Museo de Arte de Lima collection.[6] This was exhibited at the Philadelphia Museum of Art in the famous exhibition "Revelaciones" in 2006, as noted in its catalogue.[7]

The *bargueño* is a container for storing and carrying valuables. It is rectangular with flat front and sides, many drawers (17) of different sizes and shapes and an alcove-shaped central drawer, larger than the rest. It rests on four bun feet.

There is an architectural concept behind the piece's ornamental structure which distributes the composition in an orderly and symmetrical way. Each drawer was covered with Flemish-style pyrographed ivory plaques, depicting Greek mythological scenes. The central image represents: "Perseus freeing Andromeda." This scene is located in an opening symbolizing a central gate and the upper body is topped by a triangular pediment.

---

[6] Catalogued by José Centurión Padilla on September 7, 1987, according to the museum archives.

[7] Rishel, Joseph J. and Stratton-Pruitt, Susan (eds). *Revelaciones: Las Artes en América Latina 1492-1820.* Colección Arte Universal. Mexico, D.F.: Fondo de Cultura Económica, 2007, p. 491.

**PAIR OF OVERLAPPING *BARGUEÑOS***
Full view.
Prado Heudebert family collection, Lima.
Late 17TH century.
Height: 84.4 cm. Width: 63 cm.
Depth: 41 cm.

This piece is also recorded and described in *El Barroco Peruano*,[8] as an exponent of Baroque furniture which, virtuously, displays the morality tales of Ovid.

The rest of the drawer decoration, with arabesques clearly influenced by Flemish and Neapolitan Art, completes the composition described above.

As was usually the case, it was made and decorated by anonymous artisans. The piece's paneling, inlay and pyrography or sgraffito were made from ebony, ivory and tortoiseshell, and the moulding on the upper frieze, of local darkened wood. It has not been restored and is still in good condition, although some parts are missing.

An interesting *bargueño*, originally from an old Cusco collection, is part of Don Juan Luis de Aliaga's collection, and resides in the library of his ancestral home in Lima. All its sides are clearly Baroque, as can be seen in the various

[8] Mujica Pinilla, Ramón *et al. El Barroco Peruano.* Vol. I. Colección Arte y Tesoro del Perú. Lima: Banco de Crédito del Perú, 2002, p. 40.

techniques used, where the skills of two anonymous artisans are revealed. This piece was probably made in the 18TH century and has obvious Flemish and Italian influences. Made of wood, its front was inlaid and its sides have pyrographed ivory surrounded by tortoiseshell.

On the back, there are polychromes of local origin. It is a flat container with multiple (18) drawers and a central alcove.

This *bargueño* was originally utilitarian and ornamental, designed for secular use. It rests on four bun feet.

Decorated with symmetrically arranged elements, it has three cartouches on the front for inscriptions or coats of arms, with many curves and ribbons on the drawer fronts, which are moulded to simulate spikes.

***BARGUEÑO***
[OPPOSITE PAGE] Museo de Arte de Lima collection.
17TH century.
Height: 50 cm. Width: 86 cm.
Depth: 35.5 cm.

***BARGUEÑO***
[TOP] Front.
[BOTTOM] Back.
Don Juan Luis de Aliaga's collection, Lima.
18TH century.
Height: 45 cm. Width: 98 cm.
Depth: 33 cm.

The sides feature rectangular figures surrounded by suggestive angles forming an architectural pattern. In the centre of the reverse, where the technique used is the polychromy on the front, there is a child's face adorned with plant motifs and flanked by two triumphant angels, as well as flowers, leaves and birds arranged in a grotesque pattern. Importantly, this piece has clearly syncretic features; the Europeanising mark on three of its sides unveils a visually naive language akin to local trends.

This *bargueño* has hidden locks and is in good condition, although the ivory details are in need of restoration.

In this case, the concept of ornamental furniture, so frequent during the 17TH century —and completely alien to everyday activities—, becomes evident in several factors that are closely related to the Baroque style that sets it apart. Particularly relevant is its sumptuous design, enriched with delicate ornaments arranged on the front, where order and symmetry prevail, as key features of the style. In turn, the rich set of materials selected to cover its surface is astonishing due to its extravagance, elegance and beauty, as well as to the skilled treatment they have received.

The specific function of this type of pieces, so richly adorned, was decorative: to provide shine and sumptuousness to drawing rooms in great manors, where their wealthy owners would display them as works of art, as was done in grand palaces of the Old World.

The Museo de Arte de Lima has another *bargueño* donated by the Prado Heudebert family. It is a Baroque-style piece for secular use, made by an unknown artisan, probably during the 17TH century.

It is a flat-sided container for storing and transporting valuables, but it should be noted that due to its outstanding quality and luxury, it has an ornamental, non-utilitarian use. Its salient feature is its Baroque architecture, with many drawers (29) of different shapes and sizes.

The piece has an upper bronze gallery decorated with fretted curves and counter-curves, and crowned by pinnacles around its perimeter. It rests on four claw and ball legs, and has a pair of bronze handles on the sides for transportation.

The central alcove has two religious images, one on top of the other, pyrographed and sgraffitoed on ivory plaques.

The image of God the Father is on the upper body, under a triangular pediment. On the lower body, there is an image representing the Resurrection of Christ, who holds a cross-shaped crosier in his left hand. The composition rests on a sophisticated Mudejar architectural background, under a double triangular pediment, and is flanked by columns.

The side bay drawers are repeatedly decorated by plant motifs and on either side of the piece there are geometric shapes contrasting with the front. Its bronze keyholes display a double-headed eagle.

The piece is in delicate condition, having not been restored and is incomplete.

The *bargueño* donated by the Prado Heudebert family to the Museo de Arte de Lima,[9] is a Baroque-style secular piece with an undeniable European

[9] Catalogued by Amelia Castillo Saavedra in 1987.

*BARGUEÑO*
Museo de Arte de Lima collection.
Donated by the Prado family.
17TH century.
Height: 89.5 cm. Width: 106 cm.
Depth: 36 cm.

impression, which was made in the 17TH century. It was used as a utilitarian container for transporting valuables, but its virtuosity, sophistication and subdued effects are worth mentioning, leading to new insights regarding its uses. The piece seems clearly ornamental, reserved for decorating the living rooms of civil authorities.

The *bargueño* is a rectangular piece with seven drawers on the front.

The side bays have three drawers each and in the centre, there is an important alcove with a triangular pediment resting on an elaborately decorated drawer. The upper balustrade is critical for cataloguing the piece. It rests on four ball or bun legs.

A religious image is engraved on a pyrographed ivory plaque, surrounded by symmetrical branches.

***BARGUEÑO***
Museo de Arte de Lima collection.
Donated by the Prado family.
17th century.
Height: 43 cm. Width: 58 cm.
Depth: 28 cm.

**COFFER - ESCRITOIRE**
Museo Pedro de Osma, Lima - Peru.
17TH century.
Height: 23 cm. Width: 40 cm.
Depth: 40 cm.

The piece was made by an anonymous artisan, from solid wood decorated with inlaid pyrographed and turned ivory and metal knobs. It is in good condition; complete and unrestored.

The coffer or escritoire is a piece of furniture used for carrying writing implements from one place to another. It has a lockable upper lid and inside, many divisions suitable for their various functions.

The coffer or escritoire on a support table, which is in the Museo Pedro de Osma, in Lima, displays ornamentation in inlaid ivory or pyrographed bone recreating Flemish prints. It is a small piece of day-to-day secular furniture commissioned by clients familiar with such luxury objects.

It is an anonymous Baroque piece, with Flemish and Italian influences.

The architectural structure of the piece consists of an upper lid, external drawers and inner compartments. Its fittings include a lock, hinges and a teardrop-shaped handle on the drawer front, all of them made of iron.

The Baroque aesthetics of the piece are revealed by geometric figures such as the two-headed eagle in the centre of the lid, framed by a rhombus and complemented by rustic branching. Fine, gently waved mouldings made of carved, darkened wood frame the perimeter of the lid, base and drawer fronts, and give them a certain volume.

The 18TH century writing desk in the Museo de Arte Hispanoamericano Isaac

Fernández Blanco in the city of Buenos Aires is in the "Dormitorio lusobrasileño" or "Buenos Aires, capital city of the Viceroyalty" hall; a generous donation from Doña Marietta Ayerza de Gonzalez Garaño, which was part of her vast collection.[10] It has the characteristics of a small secular use container: flat front with front and upper folding lids, which hide eleven drawers inside. Its teardrop-shaped fittings and legs are engraved in silver.

The ornamental motifs are Baroque in style: the drawer fronts use geometric language through inlaid shells. Hexagon-shaped friezes surround the perimeter

[10] It is recorded under file No. 107.901/90 in the museum inventory.

**WRITING DESK**
Museo de Arte Hispanoamericano
Isaac Fernández Blanco, Buenos Aires.
Donated by Doña Marietta Ayerza
de González Garaño.
18TH century.
Height: 26.7 cm. Width: 42.6 cm.
Depth: 28.8 cm.

of wide, bare wood spaces. Hunting scenes and floral motifs simulate Flemish prints. The four corners of the lid feature allegorical figures, probably associated with the Inca culture, made in pyrographed ivory. There is a cross on the rounded doorknocker, which is decorated with undulating forms that give prominence to the Baroque decoration of the lock, cast in silver and engraved.

One or more anonymous artisans from the Lima school developed the ivory pyrography and sgraffito techniques and the mother-of-pearl inlay in tropical solid wood. This shows the Flemish, Italian and Oriental influence which inspired the creators of this piece. It is in excellent condition.

**_BARGUEÑO_ WITH SUPPORT TABLE**
Museo Pedro de Osma, Lima - Peru.
18TH century.
Height: 187 cm. Width: 110 cm.
Depth: 52 cm.

Another *bargueño*, made by unknown artisans probably during the 18TH century, belongs to the Museo Pedro de Osma, in Lima. It is a piece for secular use, which rests on an ad hoc support.

The ornamental structure has clear architectural features, and the decoration of its front, made up of eleven drawers and a central alcove with a glass door and three internal shelves, is particularly noteworthy. A pair of columns flank the front at each end. It is crowned by a triangular pediment boasting an orderly ornamentation with leaf and flower motifs on a *treillage* background, which testifies to an oriental influence. Its compositional weight is evenly distributed on a pair of pinnacles on both ends.

The techniques used on the skirt of the support table are comparable to those used for the upper piece. Its legs have been turned in the shape of a rosary and joined by a crosspiece that reinforces the structure; both pieces end in bun feet. Its decorative elements have Baroque features burnt into ivory and bone using pyrographic techniques on all its fronts and on its legs' blocks, which results in a contrasting effect. The repeated geometric patterns decorating this piece reveal the Mudejar aesthetics which emerged from a fertile exchange.

Coffer, portable writing desk or chest of drawers are the different names given to this piece of furni-

ture which belongs to the Museo de Arte de Lima and was donated by the Prado family. It is a small secular-use container which is utilitarian in view of its portability and functionality —although it can be imagined as containing memorabilia, such as letters and lockets, even jewellery— but not because of its materials or the quality of its making.

It is rectangular, resting on bun feet, and has four identically-sized front drawers. Symmetrically arranged and framed *rinceaux* with straight friezes are the ornamental motifs which cover each drawer and allow us to categorise it as a Baroque piece of furniture. As in previous examples, it has Flemish and Neapolitan influences with ornamental details which belong to late 17TH century European furniture.

Solid wood covered in marquetry made from tortoiseshell, or pyrographed ivory or bone, are the materials used by anonymous artisans to create this little marvel, which is in good condition and has not been restored.

In the Sala Schröder or Sala del Tesoro of the Basílica Catedral de Lima, more specifically, in its Museo de Arte Religioso, there is a magnificent *bargueño*. Designed for secular use and markedly ornamental, it was probably made in the late 17TH century and is Baroque in style with Flemish or Neapolitan influences.

The piece is from the collection of brother and sister, Waldemar and Matilde Schröder Mendoza, and is currently owned by the Archdiocese of Lima.[11]

It is a container with a quadrangular front and twenty-one moulded drawers of different shapes and sizes, supported by four Baroque bun feet.

On the piece's central bay, two drawers are alcove-shaped and crowned by a triangular pediment, while the others present a homogeneous decoration based on the contrasting colour of their materials. On the sides, there are geometrical motifs, friezes and branches.

This piece was made with extreme craftsmanship by an anonymous artisan. Made of wood, it features a tortoiseshell or mock tortoiseshell cover. Its creator

[11] Lohmann Villena, Guillermo *et al. La Basílica Catedral de Lima.* Colección Arte y Tesoro del Perú. Lima: Banco de Crédito del Perú, 2004, p. 340.

**WRITING DESK, CHEST OF DRAWERS**
[OPPOSITE PAGE] Museo de Arte de Lima collection.
Donated by the Prado family.
17TH century.
Height: 25 cm. Width: 43 cm.
Depth: 27 cm.
Courtesy of Museo de Arte de Lima.

***BARGUEÑO***
[RIGHT] Museo de Arte Religioso of the Basílica Catedral de Lima.
Donated by Don Waldemar and Doña Matilde Schröder Mendoza.
17TH century.
Height: 83 cm. Width: 75 cm.
Depth: 29 cm.

framed the perimeter of each drawer with pyrographed and fretted ivory in the shape of fine arabesque and scales. The dark wood was fretted in a continuous scallop forming successive friezes.

The sides were covered with wood plaques in different shades, representing finely filleted geometric shapes. Its fittings are made of bronze and may have been replaced.

In the Sala Schröder of the Museo de Arte Religioso, Basílica Catedral de Lima, there is a secular use *bargueño*. It was made using a late 17TH century Baroque style with Flemish and Neapolitan influences; a style once again manifested in these types of pieces.

The piece was donated to Lima's cathedral by brother and sister, Don Waldemar and Doña Matilde Schröder Mendoza from their collection.[12]

[12] Lohmann Villena, Guillermo *et al.* Ibid.

It has the classic features of a very exuberantly ornamented container, the most outstanding being a central alcove surrounded by multiple richly decorated and framed drawers of different shapes and sizes, where a restraint in the use of effects can be noted, stressing their highly aesthetic value.

The various scenes have figures involved in human activities such as conquest, traditions, sailing, and hunting on each drawer with a marked tendency towards a purely figurative ornamental vocabulary which might implicitly carry a historical narrative.

It is also worth mentioning the mirrored alcove, crowned by a broken pediment and surrounded by a mock brick effect, created by contrasting materials. This detail is a glimpse of the architectural sensibility which is sometimes displayed on similar pieces, to great effect.

The upper row of drawers displays a symmetrical decoration repeating the figure of the grotesque in its six spaces. On the sides, there is a decoration based on geometric patterns, which confers a greater prominence to the piece's front, as an intentional stylistic device.

Anonymous craftsmen made this magnificent piece on a wood base with its front fully covered by marquetry, using tortoiseshell, pyrographed ivory, and ebony in different proportions, and also on its sides, with the increased use of various shades of wood. It is in very good condition.

Another interesting Baroque *bargueño* built during the 17TH century was generously donated by the Prado Heudebert family and now belongs to the Museo de Arte de Lima.[13] It is a secular use container for storing and carrying valuables. It is rectangular and has two side bays with three drawers evenly distributed on each, and an alcove with a drawer on top in the central bay. The piece rests on four bun feet.

The piece is adorned with a female mythological figure, framed by an oval, standing on a winged orb. Other motifs were symmetrically placed on the front. The drawers feature stylised ribbons with volumetric and contrasting mouldings. In the background, there are basketwork details and, surrounding the entire front, a

**BARGUEÑO**
[OPPOSITE PAGE] Museo de Arte Religioso of the Basílica Catedral de Lima. Donated by Don Waldemar and Doña Matilde Schröder Mendoza. 17TH century. Height: 68 cm. Width: 105 cm. Depth: 36 cm.

**BARGUEÑO**
[BOTTOM] Detail. Museo de Arte de Lima collection. Donated by the Prado family. 17TH century. Height: 41 cm. Width: 58 cm. Depth: 33 cm.

[13] Recorded in the Asociación Museo de Arte de Lima archives by cataloguer José Centurión Padilla in 1987.

*BARGUEÑO*
Museo de Arte de Lima collection.
Donated by the Prado family.
17TH century.
Height: 41 cm. Width: 58 cm.
Depth: 33 cm.

frieze made of egg or mother-of-pearl semicircles. This demonstrates the influence of the Flemish and Italian schools, as not only did prints arrive here in these Spanish-American lands, but also artisans with striking craftsmanship who trained local artisans in their workshops.

The piece was made of mahogany, decorated on the paneling with ivory and mother-of-pearl inlay, pyrography, turning and moulding techniques, and hand polished with the application of several layers of lacquer. Although some handles are missing, the piece is in good condition.

Another example of a Baroque-style *bargueño*, possibly from the 17TH century, is part of the Museo de Arte de Lima's inventory thanks to donation by the Prado Heudebert family[14]. Including architectural features displayed on a rectangular front, it is made up of ten framed drawers on the side bays, and two large drawers alternating with two smaller ones on the central bay, plus four supporting feet.

[14] It is recorded in the archives of the Asociación Museo de Arte de Lima, catalogued by José Centurión Padilla in 1987.

This secular use piece was made by anonymous artisans, echoing Flemish and Neapolitan aesthetics similar to the previous example.

The decorative elements covering the drawers arranged along the side bays represent various zoomorphic figures in different positions. On the central bay, the upper drawer is decorated with a double-tailed mermaid or caryatid holding a basket and flanked by columns. The lower drawer features a male warrior figure with a bird on his left shoulder. Butterflies and snakes surround both representations.

The syncretism displayed in this piece was achieved through a juxtaposition of elements: a European-style structure, accompanied by local mythological figures, such as the mermaid who lives in Lake Titicaca[15] —wrongly identified as of European origin— and the serpent symbolizing the underworld, i.e., the world of the dead.

Made of wood, the structure is fully marqueted with tortoiseshell in the background and pyrographed ivory. The drawers are framed with carved wood. It is in good condition and has been recently restored.

*BARGUEÑO*
Museo de Arte de Lima collection.
Donated by the Prado family.
17TH century.
Height: 60 cm. Width: 108.5 cm.
Depth: 40 cm.

[15] Gisbert, Teresa. "El elemento indígena en el arte colonial." In: Mesa Figueroa, José de, *et al.* Op. cit., pages 121-122.

*BARGUEÑO*
[LEFT] Museo de Arte de Lima collection.
Donated by the Prado family.
17TH century.
Height: 65 cm. Width: 101 cm.
Depth: 36 cm.

*BARGUEÑO*
[OPPOSITE PAGE, TOP] Gallant scene detail.
[OPPOSITE PAGE, BOTTOM] Full view.
Museo de Arte de Lima collection.
Donated by the Prado family.
17TH century.
Height: 55 cm. Width: 101 cm.
Depth: 35.5 cm.

## OIL PAINTING: AN INSTRUMENT FOR DOMESTIC DEVOTION AND DESCRIPTION OF TRADITIONAL SCENES

A distinguished history precedes another Baroque *bargueño*, being a donation to the Museo de Arte de Lima by the Prado Heudebert family. It was made in the 17TH century, by anonymous craftsmen inspired by the decorative repertoire from the Netherlands and the south of Italy[16]. This secular use piece of furniture has a flat front and a rectangular shape. It has twelve drawers on its identical bays and the base and frieze are of various sizes and shapes.

In the central tabernacle, two religious images are enthroned; one is a highly symbolic representation of Saint Cecilia, the patron saint of music. The other one is unrecognizable, and crowned with a triangular pediment. Both painted in oils, they are flanked by classical paired columns. Once again, religious images are present on Peruvian pieces of furniture —a frequent devotional contribution to domestic furniture throughout the whole colonial period.

On the lateral bays there are scenes showing figures with various characteristics. The piece rests on four bun feet. It is entirely covered in tortoiseshell and ivory marquetry plaques on a wooden structure with carved wood framing. In good condition, this piece of furniture is complete and has not been restored.

Another remarkable *bargueño* was donated by the Prado family to the Museo

[16] Asociación Museo de Arte de Lima archives, catalogued by José Centurión Padilla in 1987.

de Arte de Lima[17]. It is an interesting secular use rectangular container, with a flat front, eight drawers and a central alcove. This piece is decorated following an architectural style. It rests on four bun feet. With clear European influence, the artisans who made it applied the 17TH-century Baroque style, in a way appropriate to the requirements of the time. Ornamental motifs consist of a couple of oil-painted characters dressed in the style of the century and representing a gallant scene in the central alcove, which is crowned by a triangular pediment. On both side bays, there are hunting scenes with anthropomorphic, zoomorphic and mythological (mermaids) figures on moulded drawers, made by inlaying fine materials such as tortoiseshell, ivory or bone on the wood base. It is complete and in good condition, and has not been restored.

This magnificent set of pieces, made in the Viceroyalty of Peru during the early decades of the 17TH century, evidences the close cultural links between Europe and these distant lands, where people enjoyed being surrounded by the same type of luxuries as Europeans did.

[17] Asociación Museo de Arte de Lima archives; piece catalogued by José Centurión Padilla in 1987.

# III

## BAROQUE STYLE FURNITURE COVERED WITH EMBOSSED LEATHER GILDED OR NOT GILDED; POLYCHROMED; STUDDED

Ecclesiastical and secular use

LIMA, CUSCO, AREQUIPA, TRUJILLO, BUENOS AIRES AND MADRID

# III

## LEATHERWORKING TECHNIQUES AND LEATHER USES IN SPAIN AND LATER, IN THE VICEROYALTY OF PERU

Calfskin is a thick and resistant type of leather used for making cordovan. It was one or two millimetres thick and was applied on either plain, unadorned furniture, or furniture decorated using the embossing technique, with a design reflective of contemporary fashion. The cowhide was worked using red-hot metal plates, before dyeing in dark colours. The aim was to highlight the decoration giving it a subtle volume.

From sheepskin, *guadamecil* or *guadamecí* could be obtained, which was a softer and thinner material. It was generally used to cover walls of chapels and domestic altars, as well as on floors, carpets, and cushions in the ladies' parlours of important households. *Guadamecil* was decorated with elaborate Renaissance, Mannerist and Baroque designs using polychrome, embossing, and *estofado* (gilding) with natural motifs.

The original name of this type of leather was *gādāmisī*,[1] from Ghadames, an African village in modern-day Libya, where this technique was applied.

These techniques were developed in the Iberian Peninsula by Andalusian artisans who, during the 15TH, 16TH and 17TH centuries, were noted for their expertise and skill, qualities which should be highlighted since these artisans were the most renowned in Europe at the time.

Many artisans of Arab origin who practiced these skills emigrated to the New

***PETACA***
[OPENING] Detail.
Don Juan Luis de Aliaga's collection.
18TH century.

**BENCH**
[OPPOSITE PAGE] Detail.
Banco Central de Reserva del Perú - Arequipa Branch, former Palacio Goyeneche.
18TH century.

---

1 *Gādāmisī*, word of Arabic origin.

World in search of a promising future, and continued to develop their methods in the colonies. They set up workshops where they trained their students; many of whom were natives. Thus, these techniques were used again and again throughout the history of the Viceroyalty of Peru.

## WHEN LEATHER IS ESSENTIAL TO DEFINE THIS KIND OF PIECE

Leatherworking techniques actively contributed to the production of pieces which were similar to those made in Spain.

Leather was commonly used on specific types of furniture, such as the *frailero* or friar's chair, as it was known in Spanish America; the stool or *faldstool* (folding bishop's stool); and all types of benches. All these kinds of seats were upholstered with cordovan.

The friar's chair, or armchair, was an austere and practical seat which lacked ostentation but had great strength and dignity. Its seat and backrest displayed great ornamentation, mainly on the cordovan.

Only in exceptional cases were fabrics used, for example: velvet embroidered with silk; gold and silver threads; brocades or figured silk.

*Petacas* (leather chests), chests, suitcases and household boxes were generally the ideal utilitarian and portable containers for a changing world, where people

**TRAVEL *PETACA***
[TOP] Studding detail.
Museo del Arzobispado del Cusco.

***PETACA***
[BOTTOM, LEFT AND RIGHT] Fitting detail.
Real Monasterio de Clarisas
de Santa María de Gracia, Trujillo.

moved frequently or merely used them to store their belongings. Metal or thick backstitched-leather handles on both sides of the piece were crucial for carrying on shoulders or on mules. The locks had big latches with keys, corner beads, braces and hinges, all made of metal.

The use of chests and *petacas* was very important at the time. They consisted of rustic wooden structures covered with embossed and dyed leather. For decoration, artisans used decorative studs simply and ornamentally arranged, forming basic shapes such as stars, curves, natural motifs, geometric shapes or in some cases, the owner's monogram.

## FRIAR'S CHAIRS. COMPOSITION AND MORPHOLOGY

The friar's chair was mostly a practical and utilitarian seat for everyday use; it was not devoid, however, of high aesthetic sensitivity and a certain magnificence. The chair was useful during ceremonies or for working at a *bargueño* or writing desk, as well as in drawing rooms around the *cuadra* or dining rooms in private homes, in church sacristies and in convent and monastery walkways.

Very similar to the Spanish armchair, it was known as the *sillón misional* (missionary chair) in the colonies for its close association with monastic life. These chairs were also used by friars and nuns of various religious congregations, as

**FRIAR'S CHAIR**
[TOP] Studding detail.
Banco Interbank - Casa del Mariscal Orbegoso, Trujillo.
18TH century.

**FRIAR'S CHAIR**
[BOTTOM] Studding detail.
Banco Central de Reserva del Perú - Arequipa Branch, former Palacio Goyeneche.

well as by the general population. The key material for backrests and seats was tanned calfskin: a thick, heavy leather which had undergone previous tanning, embossing and dyeing processes. Sometimes it was partially gilded and polychromed as desired.

The seat and backrest structures, of solid quadrangular wood, were covered in cordovan, attached to the frame with widely-spaced, visible metal studs of various qualities and shapes.

Two armchairs owned by Banco Interbank - Casa del Mariscal Orbegoso, in the city of Trujillo, are pieces for secular and everyday use. There is a marked anachronism about these pieces of furniture, with Spanish Renaissance structure and influence.

These pieces have flat backrests and seats, made of embossed leather attached to the frames by Spanish-style engraved studs of considerable size and remarkable making. Their arms and front legs are curved and held together by crossbars and crosspieces.

The backrest and seat are decorated in Rococo style with Bourbon influence, details of which are fully described in Chapter X, page 336. It is worth mentioning that both pieces were anonymously made, possibly by the Trujillo school, which was prone to adopting the stylistic changes that took place during the second half of the 18TH century.

The supporting structure was made of carved local wood. The leather on the seat and backrest is embossed, dyed and attached to the frame with magnificent engraved-iron studs.

The pieces need to be carefully preserved: the leather is in poor condition.

Whenever necessary, the underside of the leather was reinforced with rustic fabrics, or even padded with horsehair for greater comfort.

Friar's armchairs had to be robust and resistant; thus, their structure was

**FRIAR'S CHAIR**
[TOP] Backrest detail.
Banco Central de Reserva del Perú - Arequipa Branch, former Palacio Goyeneche.

**FRIAR'S CHAIR**
[BOTTOM, LEFT] Crossbar detail.
Banco Interbank - Casa del Mariscal Orbegoso, Trujillo.

**FRIAR'S CHAIR**
[BOTTOM, RIGHT] Crossbar detail.
Banco Central de Reserva del Perú - Arequipa Branch, former Palacio Goyeneche.

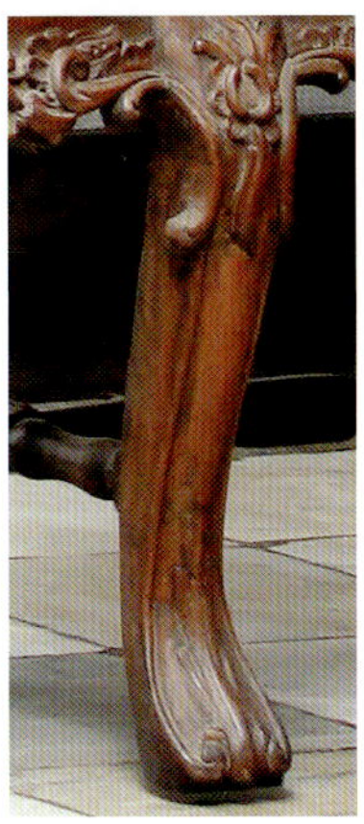

made using local seasoned wood. These chairs were decorated with interesting carvings and, occasionally, fretwork on either straight or curved arms, depending on contemporary styles, which ended in scrolls, rams' heads or lions' paws. A decorative carved or fretted crossbar was placed between the front legs; it was a richly ornate segment and the most noticeable element of the piece. This decoration was not repeated elsewhere, making it a unique piece of furniture.

The anonymously made friar's chair which belongs to Banco Central de Reserva del Perú —Arequipa (former Palacio Goyeneche) branch— has straight legs with a striking carved and moulded crossbar of Spanish influence.

This is a seat for ecclesiastical or secular use, made in the Andean Baroque style. Its crossbar was decorated with a central heart surrounded by undulating and asymmetrical branching representing *kantuta* and acanthus leaves, as well as mouldings with plant motifs. The heart represents love, courage, devotion, pain and joy. When a saint's heart is used, it symbolises love and mercy[2].

The asymmetrical arrangement of elements is a feature of the mid-18TH century, even though a piece may be Renaissance in form. The crossbar in this particular piece is profusely decorated with delicate leaves and flowers.

There is another *frailero* or friar's chair in the collection of Banco Central de Reserva del Perú —Arequipa (former Palacio Goyeneche) branch— which has the characteristic flat oblong backrest of this type of furniture; it is made of embossed leather and dyed in black.

The chair is Baroque in style, with a strong Spanish influence, and is decorated with zoomorphic and phytomorphic figures framed by rectilinear friezes.

Following the Renaissance construction canons and subsequent Baroque and Rococo styles, the earlier seats feature straight legs, later adopting elegant forward curves and later still, *cabriole* legs with the typical and harmonious 18TH century undulations. The rear legs are connected to those at the front via rectangular or H-shaped crosspieces, which are necessary to provide strength to the seat.

**FRIAR'S CHAIR**
[TOP] *Cabriole* leg detail.
Palacio de Torre Tagle, Peruvian Ministry of Foreign Affairs, Lima.
18TH century.

**BENCH**
[CENTRE] *Cabriole* leg detail.
Don Alfredo Pinillos' collection, Trujillo.
18TH century.

**BENCH**
[BOTTOM] *Cabriole* leg detail.
Banco Central de Reserva del Perú - Arequipa Branch, former Palacio Goyeneche.
18TH century.

[2] Ferguson, George. *Signos y Símbolos en el Arte Cristiano.* Buenos Aires: Emecé, 1956, pages 54-55.

## THE EMBOSSED CORDOVAN DECORATION IS WORTHY OF NOTE

Backrests and seats, where upholstered in leather, were usually decorated with the coat of arms of the original owner, or the imperial double-headed eagle. The rest of the decoration consisted of zoomorphic and phytomorphic figures surrounding the central composition. For this, the usual technique was leather embossing; the material generally being dyed in dark colours such as black and brown.

For ecclesiastical pieces, the decoration of choice was the human figure, representing saints, popes, martyrs or conquerors, as well as the mitre, the crosier and other emblems, such as the monograms of religious orders, the chalice, the Paschal Lamb or the monstrance, of highly symbolic content.

The decoration of the seat, although less pretentious, matched that of the backrest. The studs holding the cordovan to backrests and seats of chairs and armchairs were of great beauty, and emphasised the importance of their owners; these decorative elements appeared in a variety of forms, sizes and materials.

The *frailero* or friar's chair in Doña Marita de la Peña Prado's collection is a piece of furniture whose seat and backrest are flat. Classified as a 17TH-century ecclesiastical or secular piece of furniture, it is decorated with Mannerist-Baroque motifs which are surrounded by a leaf frieze. The central oval on its backrest contains a mythological creature flanked by a pair of crowned birds and encircled by abundant vegetation. The backrest upholstery ends in soft waves.

The piece has straight legs joined by crosspieces for greater strength. It features a carved crossbar and its arms are curved and slightly grooved.

The embossed cowhide upholstery is held in place by large bronze studs.

The above description highlights the Spanish influence on this colonial seat, whose unknown creator was likely to have worked at an *obraje* run by a Spanish craftsman of Mudejar origin. The leather on this piece is in poor condition.

The friar's chair exhibited at Casa del Mariscal

**FRIAR'S CHAIR**
Backrest detail and full view. Doña Marita de la Peña Prado's collection, Lima.

Orbegoso[3], in the city of Trujillo, was made in Renaissance style with a strong Spanish influence.

This is a piece for everyday use. Its flat backrest and seat are upholstered with dark embossed leather, attached by large, widely-spaced, engraved studs. It ends in harmonious curves.

This chair has a pair of almost straight arms ending in scrolls, and straight legs connected by crosspieces. A crossbar holds the front parts together. The ornamental motifs are enclosed in the triangles dividing the plane. There is a pomegranate, a pair of felines, a bird and, connecting the angles, a stylized peacock tail. The backrest is bordered with plant motifs and the crossbar is decorated with carved flowers and scales.

The piece was made from local wood, cordovan and iron by an artisan whose identity, as was generally the case, remains unknown.

It is in delicate condition, the leather has deteriorated and some of the original studs may have been replaced.

**FRIAR'S CHAIR**
Full view and backrest detail.
Banco Interbank - Casa del Mariscal Orbegoso, Trujillo.
Height: 109 cm. Width: 61.4 cm.
Depth: 48 cm.

### POLYCHROME CORDOVAN AS AN ALTERNATIVE

In the lobby of Don Alfredo Pinillos' ancestral home, in the city of Trujillo, there is another Baroque friar's chair, built during the 18TH century, both for secular and ecclesiastical use. The skilful craftsman who built it was from the Trujillo school and reveals a strong Spanish influence. The chair's backrest and seat are covered with

---

3 Owned by Banco Internacional del Perú-Interbank.

embossed cordovan dyed in a dark colour, with vivid colours in the ornamental details. The leather is attached to the frame by round and plain metal studs. The chair's front legs are curved forward and held together by a crossbar; the arms are slightly arched.

It is decorated with the Martínez de Pinillos' coat of arms, which is surrounded by plant motifs.

The materials used were carved and polished Nicaraguan solid cedar wood —called cedro de Figueroa in Trujillo— and polychromed embossed leather with traces of gold leaf on the seat and backrest. It is in good condition.

In Casa Chica, at Museo Pedro de Osma in Lima, there is a magnificent Baroque *frailero* made of solid wood. It was built in the 18TH century by anonymous artisans who clearly had a Spanish influence.

It was probably commissioned by the church from a Lima-school workshop, since its coat of arms is crowned by a mitre.

**FRIAR'S CHAIR**
[LEFT] Don Alfredo Pinillos' collection, Trujillo.
18TH century.
Height: 110.3 cm. Width: 61 cm.
Depth: 54 cm.

**FRIAR'S CHAIR**
[RIGHT] Museo Pedro de Osma, Lima - Peru.
18TH century.
Height: 114 cm. Width: 56 cm.
Depth: 41 cm.

**SILLÓN SANTA ROSA – FRIAR'S CHAIR**
[OPPOSITE PAGE] Full view and backrest detail.
Museo de Arte de Lima collection.
18TH century.
Height: 114 cm. Width: 55 cm.
Depth: 41 cm.

The chair is a flat piece of furniture, with an undulating crest rail on the backrest and a rectilinear seat; both seat and backrest are upholstered in polychromed cordovan. It rests on four straight legs, crosspieces, and a crossbar which seems to have been replaced. The straight arms end in subtle scrolls.

Phytomorphic motifs surround a remarkable coat of arms placed in the centre of the backrest. The cordovan was decorated using embossing and polychroming techniques. Seat ornaments match those on the backrest, and deserving of a special mention are the large engraved-silver studs holding the leather in place.

The *frailero* or friar's chair called Sillón Santa Rosa belongs to the Museo de Arte de Lima and was donated by the Prado family. It is a seat for both ecclesiastical and secular use, which was skilfully made in Baroque style during the 18TH century. This piece reveals Spanish influences from earlier centuries.

It is a rectilinear seat with a solid wood structure. As was usual during that period, the backrest and seat were upholstered in embossed cordovan, which was attached to the frame by large, widely-spaced studs.

It has four legs, those at the front ending in scrolls, and a carved frontal crossbar. The legs are connected by crosspieces for greater strength. The side stiles of the backrest stretch out forming upward grooved pendants and curved arms. The central backrest ornamentation represents the image of St. Rose of Lima and the Infant Jesus in a garden, under a round arch representing a cloister; the image is surrounded by local vegetation. It is bordered by a frieze with phytomorphic motifs. The crossbar has a rustic carving forming a central rosette and scales on both sides.

While the museum has catalogued this piece as an exponent of the Cusco School, it is important to note that, according to Professor Héctor Schenone[4], it was likely made by artisans of the Quito School, which usually surrounded religious images with a flower garden, and disregarded perspective.

The piece is made of solid carved wood and upholstered

[4] Interview by the author with Prof. Héctor Schenone in 2010.

in embossed leather, which is decorated with gold and polychrome and attached to the structure by bronze studs. Its creator is unknown. According to data from the museum archives, the piece is complete, but the front leg and backrest are riddled with woodworm and the leather covering the seat is damaged.

### ANACHRONISTIC CURVED LEGS AND ARMS

Special attention should be paid to the morphology of friar's chairs built in the Viceroyalty of Peru during the 18TH century, where the straight lines, characteristic of the strict Renaissance or Baroque periods, were replaced according to the stylistic changes which developed at the time.

Abounding with curvilinear structures, such as outward-bent arms, *cabriole* legs joined by crosspieces, and Rococo features, these anachronistic pieces emerge from a juxtaposition of styles.

At the Museo de Arte de Lima we find, among others, a carved solid wood *frailero*. Its seat and backrest are covered in metal-studded embossed and dyed leather. The curved and robust arms end in scrolls. Its legs have a double curve and an interesting and sinuous crossbar.

This piece was generously donated to the museum by the Prado family. The curved legs and arms are typically Baroque; according to the museum archives, the piece was likely built in the 18TH century.

This chair, made by adept anonymous artisans, was intended for both ecclesiastical and secular use. Its ornaments are sparse and rustic, such as the stylized two-headed eagle surrounded by foliage, on the seat and backrest, and the peculiar undulations on the front apron of the seat, demonstrating Spain's strong influence on the Viceroyalty of Peru. The chair is made from carved solid wood covered with metal-studded, dyed and embossed leather. Some studs are missing and others have been replaced.

In the Sala de los Embajadores at the Palacio de Torre Tagle, next to the portraits of four Marquises of Torre Tagle (the last one painted by the renowned artist Gil de Castro) there is, among other items, a *frailero* or friar's chair of unusual characteristics. It is a Rococo piece with sharp curved arms and cabriole legs connected by an H-shaped crosspiece; it is definitely anachronistic in style, since it has a Renaissance structure with Spanish influence. It is part of the secular-use type of furniture used in drawing rooms of the time. As in many other cases, the creator is unknown. The chair was probably made in the 18TH century, according to the heritage archives of the Peruvian Ministry of Foreign Affairs.

The decorative elements of the piece consist of *rocaille* and stylized leaves highlighting the curved arms and the markedly sinuous goat legs. The chair is made of solid and carved blonde mahogany; metal studs hold the embossed leather to the backrest and seat frames.

It is in very good condition.

The former Palacio Goyeneche, in the city of Arequipa, was built in 1583, and later became the residence of Don José Sebastián de Goyeneche y Barrada, Bishop of Arequipa, appointed Archbishop of Lima in 1856.[5]

There is a *frailero* or friar's chair in one of the rooms; it was part of the Goyeneche family heritage, and its outstanding artistic qualities are worth mentioning.

The creator is unknown. It was probably made in the 18TH century and

[5] It currently houses the Arequipa branch of Banco Central de Reserva del Perú.

**FRIAR'S CHAIR**
[LEFT] Museo de Arte de Lima collection.
Donated by the Prado family.
18TH century.
Height: 119 cm. Width: 61 cm.
Depth: 55 cm.

**FRIAR'S CHAIR**
[RIGHT] Palacio de Torre Tagle, Peruvian Ministry of Foreign Affairs, Lima.
18TH century.
Height: 110 cm. Width: 72 cm.
Depth: 67 cm.

displays Rococo features on a chair of an archaic shape. It maintains the characteristic strictness of the Renaissance; a style which was very popular in Spain.

This utilitarian piece has a flat backrest and seat, both upholstered with embossed leather, which was dyed in dark shades and attached to the frame with brass studs.

The front legs and arms are carved, with pronounced curves and volumes. The H-shaped crossbar connecting the legs is carved to form waves.

The decoration, with marked Spanish and French influences, consists of an exuberant *rocaille*, a central coat of arms crowned by a conqueror's helmet, curves and counter-curves. The *cabriole* legs end in pad feet. There is a detail worth mentioning: the native features of the faces carved on both knees are the fruit of a fertile exchange.

The chair was made from solid local wood, leather and bronze, and the

FRIAR'S CHAIR
[LEFT] Banco Central de Reserva del Perú - Arequipa Branch, former Palacio Goyeneche.
18TH century.

FRIAR'S CHAIR
[RIGHT] Don Alfredo Pinillos' collection, Trujillo.
18TH century.
Height: 107 cm. Width: 62 cm.
Depth: 43 cm.

FRIAR'S CHAIR
[OPPOSITE PAGE] Detail of coat of arms on the backrest and full view.
Prado Heudebert family collection, Lima.
18TH century.

techniques applied were carving, embossing and studding. The leather is deteriorated and the piece is in need of restoration.

The friar's chair in Don Alfredo Pinillos' ancestral home, in the city of Trujillo, may have been intended, like others of its kind, for both ecclesiastical and secular use. It has been classified as belonging to the 18TH century. The piece was made in a Rococo style by anonymous craftsmen of the Trujillo school.

It has curved arms and *cabriole* front legs; a curved and carved crossbar connects the front and back legs. Both seat and backrest are richly upholstered in embossed and studded cordovan, and the backrest ends in a multifoil crest rail.

The Spanish influence is noticeable, again, not only in the morphology of the piece, but also in the decorative details, such as the Martinez de Pinillos' coat of arms, surrounded by plant motifs. The structure is made from carved solid Figueroa cedar wood, covered with embossed and dyed leather; it also has metal elements. It is in good condition, although some elements are missing.

There is another piece from the Prado Heudebert collection in the city of Lima: A *frailero*, friar's chair or armchair featuring embossed leather studded to the seat and backrest. The backrest is crowned with attractive undulations and the seat has a wavy apron. It rests on four legs; the front *cabriole* legs end in pad feet.

This piece combines late Baroque features with Rococo arms and legs, therefore, it would be safe to assume it was made in the 18TH century, since these types of seats were in vogue for over two centuries and this piece has hybrid characteristics.

The Martinez de Pinillos' coat of arms is placed in the centre and surrounded by elaborate phytomorphic motifs. The apron's sole ornament is a central rosette.

The piece was built by anonymous artisans who resorted to Spanish aesthetic patterns.

It is upholstered with embossed leather and attached to a partially carved wooden structure with metal studs. It is in very good condition.

In the Sala Schröder of the Basílica Catedral de Lima, more specifically, in its Museo de Arte Religioso, there is a friar's chair donated by brother and sister, Don Waldemar and Doña Matilde Schröder Mendoza.

It is a utilitarian piece of furniture. Given the type of decoration chosen for its backrest, it seems safe to assume it was built for ecclesiastical use.

The structure emphasises the characteristics of a friar's chair built by anonymous craftsmen. It has a flat backrest and seat, both upholstered with embossed leather; its arms are curved and it is crowned by a multifoil crest rail. The outward curved legs, definitely anachronistic, which are connected by an H-shaped crosspiece, give rise to new speculations.

The Renaissance style of this chair is juxtaposed with a Rococo morphology. For the construction of the piece Spanish structures, materials and techniques were used which were characteristic of earlier centuries. In this piece, the movement of the front *cabriole* legs is worth noting; this feature illustrates the appearance of mid-18$^{TH}$ century late-Baroque or Rococo details. At that time, the Bourbon spirit introduced stylistic changes.

The most remarkable ornament of the piece is a central medallion depicting the Paschal Lamb, which was painted in lively colours on the cowhide and framed in a central circle on the backrest. The piece has a solid wood structure whose seat and backrest are upholstered with embossed and polychromed cordovan; perimeter metal studs hold the leather to the frame.

FRIAR'S CHAIR
Museo de Arte Religioso
of the Basilica Catedral de Lima.
Donated by Don Waldemar
and Doña Matilde Schröder Mendoza.
18$^{TH}$ century.
Height: 120 cm. Width: 67 cm.
Depth: 68 cm.

### BENCH

This bench is another exponent of the Rococo furniture[6] which was part of the Goyeneches of Arequipa collection, and is currently owned by the Arequipa branch of Banco Central de Reserva del Perú.

Its most outstanding features are the straight backrest and seat covered with studded embossed leather in the style of earlier periods. The front legs and grooved arms have very pronounced curves. The backrest and front apron have an interesting decoration, with abundant and asymmetrically

[6] A similar piece, with remarkable crest rail and bearing the Martínez de Pinillos' coat of arms, owned by the Prado Heudebert family, in Taullard, Alfredo. *El Mueble Colonial Sudamericano.* Buenos Aires: Peuser, 1947, figure 121.

distributed carvings. The legs are connected by an H-shaped turned crosspiece.

This is a secular utilitarian piece which reveals two sources of influence: the Spanish, as seen in the Renaissance style of the structure and the embossed cordovan, and the French Rococo style.

Among the decorative elements there is a central coat of arms, crowned by a conqueror's helmet on each segment of the backrest: a reference to its original owner. Also the abundant *rocaille* details, with curves and counter-curves, and framed by straight lines, are worthy of note. It is in good condition, although one crosspiece has been replaced.

Anonymously made in Trujillo, there is a bench from Don Alfredo Pinillos' collection, which is kept in the library of his Trujillo manor.

The piece has abundant Rococo curves: a style which was very much in vogue in the coastal region during the second half of the 18TH century. It has the characteristics of a secular use bench: both seat and backrest are covered with dark embossed leather, attached by metal studs, and feature profuse carved wood mouldings.

Its magnificent fretted and carved wood crest-rail is divided into three

**BENCH**
Banco Central de Reserva del Perú - Arequipa Branch, former Palacio Goyeneche.
18TH century.

**BENCH**
Skirt detail and full view.
Don Alfredo Pinillos' collection, Trujillo.
18TH century.
Height: 145 cm. Width: 150.2 cm.
Depth: 59 cm.

segments and its arms are curved outward. The *cabriole* legs, so fashionable at the time, are joined by a turned crosspiece.

Two kinds of influences are reflected in the piece: the Spanish, in vogue for over three centuries, and the French, which introduced changes in decorative trends to Spanish America during the Bourbon period. The decoration consists of plant motifs surrounding the Martinez de Pinillos' coat of arms, which is replicated on the three segments of the backrest. It also has Rococo elements such as *rocaille* and curves on the carved and fretted wood.

The piece is in good condition, although the leather is timeworn.

There is another bench in one of the halls of Museo del Banco Central de Reserva del Perú, Casa Urquiaga, in Trujillo. It is a secular use piece of furniture made in the mid-18TH century. Its Spanish Renaissance structure is decorated in French-inspired Rococo style.

This bench has an undivided backrest and seat, covered with dark embossed leather, which is attached to the frame by bronze studs. The skilful —although

BENCH
Museo del Banco Central de Reserva del Perú - Trujillo Branch, Casa Urquiaga.
18TH century.
Height: 123 cm. Width: 151 cm.
Depth: 54 cm.

anonymous— work on the solid wood structure translates into abundant and refined carvings on the crest-rail, apron and crossbar. Other elements of this piece's design are the *cabriole* front legs and the outward curving arms.

The striking Rococo decorative elements in its remarkable crest-rail deserve a special mention: the scallop, also called *conchilla en abanico* in the Trujillo region, is profusely surrounded by intertwined *rocaille* and leaf and flower branches arranged on both sides. The embossed cowhide on the backrest has a double-headed eagle with a central heart, a symbol of love and protection.

Since the 16TH century, in the time of Charles V, the double-headed eagle has been a symbol of superiority and integration between the Eastern and Western heritages as successors of the Holy Roman Empire. It is worth mentioning that the wings in this predominant emblem are spread, thus, it is usually called "spread eagle". Being such an important symbol, it was placed on the most prominent part of the bench: the backrest.

The piece is in good condition, although the leather is slightly timeworn.

### USEFUL FOR STORAGE; USEFUL FOR TRANSPORTATION: SUITCASES, *PETACAS*, TRUNKS AND CHESTS

Suitcases, chests, trunks and *petacas* were types of utilitarian containers. Their manufacturing process had several stages: first, carpenters with limited skills built the structure with local wood. Then the outer sides were completely covered in cordovan, which was made using the same technique as used for seats.

The leather —which had been previously tanned— was embossed and dyed. Later, the outer surface was partially gilded and polychromed, following a previously developed design, if so required by the customer.

The owner or religious order's monogram was usually placed prominently in the centre of the lid or front area below the lock.

The external lock and latch (in some cases there were two), the key or occasionally padlock, braces and corner beads, handles and other fittings were made from metal, particularly iron or silver.

These pieces, like any domestic container, were used for storing or transporting personal belongings.

### FUNCTIONAL, SIMPLE AND RUSTIC SUITCASES

The suitcase was a quite rustic quadrangular container whose upper lid was locked or fastened with a belt. It was made from cordovan and the interior was

occasionally lined with fabric: in Spain, during the 17TH century, canvas was used for this purpose.

There was no internal supporting structure except, in rare cases, for wooden strips or metal rods in the corners. The outer sides were decorated with back-stitched leather, or embroidered with leather thongs, using geometric patterns or local motifs. In Spain, suitcases were used to transport belongings on horseback.

Don Armando Andrade's private collection, in Cusco, includes a magnificent local suitcase, made by a very skilled anonymous craftsman of the Cusco school, who was inspired by similar Spanish pieces.

The piece is a utilitarian and portable leather container fastened and decorated with plaited cowhide. It has side handles for easier transportation. There is a frontal projection, typical of the Baroque style. For the greatly refined decoration, the artisan sewed leather thongs in the shape of local zoomorphic figures contained within various central designs.

In the study of a stately home in Barranco, Lima, there is a magnificent large suitcase which, according to its owner, was acquired in Ayacucho. Intended for secular use, it was made by an anonymous craftsman for mule transport, which was very common during the colonial period.

It was used for storing and transporting household equipment, books, weapons, pieces of silverware wrapped in fabrics, and any other element necessary for everyday life.

The suitcase has the characteristic features of a utilitarian container: it has no frame, and its creator used a thick leather support embroidered with leather thongs both for structural and decorative purposes. It is rectilinear, has iron

PETACA
[TOP] Lock detail.
Museo de Arte Hispanoamericano Isaac Fernández Blanco, Buenos Aires.
18TH century.

SUITCASE
[BOTTOM] Don Armando Andrade's collection, Cusco.
Height: 34 cm. Width: 78 cm.
Depth: 45 cm.

**SUITCASE**
[TOP] Private collection, Lima.
Height: 39 cm. Width: 87 cm.
Depth: 51 cm.

**SUITCASE**
[BOTTOM] Detail.
La Mansión del Fundador, Arequipa.

fittings and its upper lid has an iron lock and a pair of side handles for transportation. The symmetrical decoration suggests a Baroque style. The quite rustic geometrical pattern bears a local mark.

This suitcase found in Buenos Aires is a portable container; a classic example of Peruvian manufacture. It has a flat front and an upper lid. It is made of embroidered leather, with an iron lock on the front and leather handles on the sides. This is a utilitarian piece made in Baroque style with predominant rustic elements. The creator, as was usually the case, is unknown and the piece is in very good condition.

The ornamentation consists of a variety of linear and local motifs made from backstitched leather thongs on a supporting structure of cowhide and a very small amount of iron.

The secular use suitcase found in La Mansión del Fundador, in the city of Arequipa, is an incomplete travel container, since its lid is missing. It is a square piece sewn and embroidered with leather thongs. Made in dark and unusually thick leather, it is decorated with consecutive vertical lines. With marked Spanish inspiration, the piece was made in Peru by an anonymous, possibly local, craftsman.

In a novitiate cell at the Monasterio de Santa Catalina, in Arequipa, there is an austere leather suitcase decorated with backstitches and seams. The piece reveals valuable information about life in the cloister, illustrating the needs of a young novice who had to carry her belongings when entering religious life.

It is a cowhide container in the shape of a basket with a lid, and has no supporting structure. It is sewn with red leather strips and decorated with rectangular

**SUITCASE**
[TOP] Casa Saráchaga
(Art auction, November 2010),
Buenos Aires.
Height: 30 cm. Width: 70 cm.
Depth: 45 cm.

**SUITCASE**
[BOTTOM] Monasterio de Santa Catalina,
Arequipa.
Height: 50 cm. Width: 55 cm.
Depth: 38 cm.

shapes. The item is a prototype of a utilitarian piece made in the Spanish tradition by an anonymous local artisan.

## THE *PETACA*: ANOTHER KIND OF PORTABLE CONTAINER

*Petacas* were containers of various sizes, but usually larger than suitcases. Their sizes vary according to customers' needs. The structure is of local wood to provide rigidity and is covered with cordovan or cowhide. The upper lid is secured with hinges and a frontal lock. They are either flat or roof-shaped to avoid the harmful effects of the rain. These pieces rarely have supporting legs.

They are covered in leather treated using various techniques:

1) Embossing: the cordovan[7] was engraved with red-hot metal plates using fashionable designs chosen by the future owner of the piece.

The cordovan acquired a certain volume and was profusely ornamented with simple, repetitive and symmetrically arranged phytomorphic and zoomorphic motifs. Other common decorative elements were the double-headed eagle or the owner's monogram, placed in the centre and framed by simple friezes. The leather surface was dyed in dark colours; gold and polychrome were used to highlight some reliefs.

[7] Rodríguez Bernis, Sofía. *Diccionario de mobiliario.* Madrid: Secretaría General Técnica, 2006, p. 122.

***PETACA***
Detail
Museo de Arte Hispanoamericano
Isaac Fernández Blanco, Buenos Aires.
Formerly, in Don Martín Noel's collection.
18TH century.
Height: 63.5 cm. Width: 92 cm.
Depth: 49.5 cm.

***PETACA***
[TOP] Detail.
Prado Heudebert family collection, Lima.
Height: 49 cm. Width: 92 cm.
Depth: 47 cm.

**BENCH**
[BOTTOM] Detail.
Museo del Banco Central de Reserva del Perú - Trujillo Branch, Casa Urquiaga.
18TH century.

2) Another technique entailed covering a wooden structure with cordovan or cowhide dyed in dark colours. It was decorated with studs forming simple and distinct geometric patterns or natural motifs in the shape of stylized leaves, curves or flowers.

3) These pieces were also decorated with plain cordovan or *guadamecí* leather dyed in vivid colours, which were later polychromed and gilded with designs representing palace, genre, biblical or mythological scenes. Those scenes formed the central design, which was framed by a frieze [8].

These household and utilitarian pieces were essential for keeping personal belongings, silverware, tapestry, weapons, clothes, linen or any other elements which were to be transported or stored by the owner.

Fittings such as hinges, locks, latches, braces and corner beads, were made in metals such as silver, bronze or iron, depending on the use, category and quality of the piece. They were engraved or forged and were useful in providing ductility, strength and safety to these pieces, which contained valuable personal effects.

Like nowhere else in Spanish-America, there is a marked parallel between Spain and the Viceroyalty of Peru in the use of this type of furniture during three centuries.

## FOR STORAGE PURPOSES: THE EMBOSSED-LEATHER *PETACA*

The *petaca* in Don Juan Luis de Aliaga's collection, located in the home of Don Jerónimo de Aliaga, in Lima's historic quarter, is a portable chest-like container whose lid is shaped like a three-sided roof; it has a flat front and sides and handles on both sides. It is intended for both secular and ecclesiastical use. Made by anonymous craftsmen, the piece has a marked Spanish influence, although it is of Peruvian origin. An inscription engraved on the lid reveals the original owner's name: *"Soy DE Dn Jn MANl. MOLLI.NEDO Y ORTEGa" (I belong to Jn MANl. MOLLI.NEDO Y ORTEGa.)*

The piece is a typical container with a local wood supporting structure covered by black embossed leather; it is profusely decorated with leaf and flower branches, zoomorphic figures, a round arch and a circle containing the lock. All these Baroque elements are neatly arranged and framed by friezes. Its lock and side handles are made of iron, and traces of a coloured fabric can be seen under the latch.

[8] See example in Chapter IX, p. 312-3.

An inscription indicating ownership, *"SOI DE Dn FRANo LOPES CALDERON" (I belong to Dn FRANo. LOPES CALDERON)*, is a suggestive detail found on a couple of *petacas* located in the Monasterio de El Carmen cloister, in Trujillo, which belongs to the Discalced Carmelites Order.

This is the same kind of reference found on the previous piece; useful for identifying its original owner whose name is visible on the roof-shaped embossed cordovan lid, revealing, once again, the Spanish influence. These pieces for everyday use were made, as was usually the case, by anonymous artisans. They consist of a solid wood supporting structure completely covered with dark leather. They are finely decorated using the embossing technique, with large plant motifs and dots on the background placed inside Baroque central designs, a style which remained in vogue throughout the 18TH century. As seen in the last two pieces, it was usual to make *petacas* clearly identifiable by engraving on their surfaces the full name of their original owner.

*PETACA*
Don Juan Luis de Aliaga's collection, Lima.
17TH century.

The pieces mentioned illustrate the high value of the monastery's heritage; unfortunately they are not in good condition, since the leather covering them is cracked and dry.

The great *petaca* which belongs to the Real Monasterio de Clarisas de Santa María de Gracia, in the city of Trujillo, is a piece for secular use. It was made in Baroque style with Spanish influence. The Viceroyalty of Peru was the region outside the metropolis where most such pieces were made.

***PETACA***
[TOP] Detail.
Monasterio de El Carmen, Trujillo.

***PETACA***
[BOTTOM] Real Monasterio de Clarisas de Santa María de Gracia, Trujillo.
Height: 65 cm. Width: 105 cm.
Depth: 57.5 cm.

The piece is a rectangular container for household use, where clothes, books, weapons and all sorts of personal effects were kept, both for travelling and for storage purposes. It has a single roof-shaped upper lid and a large lock on the front, with the original key and latch, corner beads, and pair of side handles. From an unknown craftsman, it has a wood supporting structure fully covered with dyed and embossed cordovan; its fittings were made in hammered cast iron. The piece is saturated with a selection of anthropomorphic, zoomorphic, and phytomorphic motifs which are symmetrically arranged, synthesizing the *horror vacui* of the Mudejar tradition.

The face of the green man, a mythological character, occupies a central position under the double-headed eagle on the latch. It is in very good condition.

There is another utilitarian *petaca* at Casa del Mariscal Orbegoso, owned by Banco Internacional del Perú-Interbank, based in Trujillo. It is made in a rustic Spanish-inspired Baroque style using local themes. The date is uncertain and, like all other pieces found in Peru, it was made by anonymous artisans. The piece is a flat-sided container with a roof-shaped lid; as its purpose requires, there are handles on both sides and a large iron lock on the front.

The ornamental structure divides the front into three central designs; the lid is adorned with a star, a profusion of triangles and stylized six-petal flowers. It consists of a local wood structure covered with dyed, embossed, dotted and studded cowhide. Even though the leather is cracked, the piece is in good condition.

## POLYCHROME *PETACAS*

The travelling *petaca* in the Museo de Arte de Lima collection was donated by the Prado family. Suitable for the traditional Creole lifestyle, like the above examples, it has the characteristics of a utilitarian container for carrying personal effects. It has a flat construction and a round top. The structure is made of local wood covered with dyed embossed leather, and it has traces of polychrome. The fretted, shield-shaped lock and the side handles, used for transportation, are made of wrought iron.

Made in 18TH-century Baroque style, this secular piece of furniture bears an

*PETACA*
Banco Interbank - Casa del Mariscal Orbegoso, Trujillo.
Height: 46.5 cm. Width: 102.5 cm. Depth: 51.3 cm.

undeniable resemblance to those built in the metropolis. It is profusely decorated with plant motifs, such as the *kantuta* on the corners of the lid.

Each side is framed by a wide perimeter frieze. The lid decoration is the same on each side.

Another *petaca*, one of the many pieces in the Prado Heudebert's collection, used to be exhibited in the first patio of the renowned Corcovado street mansion, in the historic centre of Lima[9], and now decorates the house of one of the descendants. It is an interesting utilitarian container for secular use, which is in very good condition. It has a roof-shaped lid, flat front and wrought iron fittings, including a pair of handles for transportation.

The piece has a profuse and neat Baroque ornamentation; the artisan selected zoomorphic and phytomorphic elements which were symmetrically arranged. Each side exhibits friezes with flower, fruit and animal motifs; there is a stylized flower on each corner and the imperial double-headed eagle is placed on the lid.

The wood supporting structure is fully covered with polychrome-embossed cordovan, revealing once again the Spanish influence with a Mudejar mark,

9 Prado Heudebert, Javier. *Lima: Arquitectura y Escultura Religiosa Virreynal.* Lima: Talleres Gráficos P.L. Villanueva, 1996. p. 234.

*PETACA*
Museo de Arte de Lima collection.
Donated by the Prado family.
18TH century.
Height: 68 cm. Width: 92 cm.
Depth: 42.5 cm.
Courtesy of Museo de Arte de Lima.

*PETACA*
Full view and detail.
Prado Heudebert family collection, Lima.
Height: 59 cm. Width: 92 cm.
Depth: 47 cm.

*PETACA*
Private collection, Cusco.
Height: 51 cm. Width: 104 cm.
Depth: 56 cm.

which had a positive impact on the production of these kinds of pieces in the Viceroyalty of Peru.

There is a great *petaca*, part of a famous private collection in the north of Cusco, which is a typical regular-size portable container. It has noticeable Spanish features in its *mestizo* Baroque style.

This *petaca* has flat sides, a roof-shaped lid, a pair of side handles and very simple iron fittings. A wood structure, fully covered in polychrome embossed leather with a black and red background and golden traces, makes the piece rigid. It is decorated with phytomorphic and zoomorphic mythological and local-wildlife motifs facing each other; there are feather headdresses on both sides of the lid and each side of the piece is surrounded by perimeter friezes.

In the Museo de Arte Hispanoamericano Isaac Fernández Blanco, in Buenos Aires, Argentina, there is a *petaca* from the private collection of Don Martín Noel[10], which is exhibited in the hall known as "Dormitorio Altoperuano." It was made in the 18TH century by an anonymous Peruvian craftsman in Baroque style with Spanish influences. It is a flat container fully covered in leather, with a round top, a large frontal lock and a pair of side handles.

This everyday use piece of extraordinary artistic quality is decorated with zoomorphic and phytomorphic motifs, double-headed eagles and feather fans on

---

[10] Schenone, Héctor, Ribera, Adolfo Luis y Curt Lange, Francisco. *Historia general del arte en Argentina.* Volume II. Buenos Aires: Academia Nacional de Bellas Artes, 1983, pages 242-3.

**INNER PATIO VIEW**

[OPPOSITE PAGE] Casa Prado, Corcovado street, Lima. In: Prado Heudebert, Javier. *Lima: Arquitectura y Escultura Religiosa Virreynal.* Lima: Talleres Gráficos P. L. Villanueva, 1996, p. 234. Courtesy of the Prado Heudebert family.

**PETACA**

[RIGHT] Museo de Arte Hispanoamericano Isaac Fernández Blanco, Buenos Aires. Formerly, in Don Martín Noel's collection. 18TH century. Height: 63.5 cm. Width: 92 cm. Depth: 49.5 cm.

both sides of the lid, embossed on the cordovan upholstery. There are perimeter friezes on every side.

The piece has a wood structure upholstered with thick embossed and polychromed leather, as well as engraved and wrought iron fittings. It is in very good condition, although the leather is somewhat deteriorated.

A great *petaca* found in the Buenos Aires art market was originally part of Don Gustavo Barreto's collection[11]. It was probably made in the north of Argentina, a region which, in the 18TH century, was part of the Viceroyalty of Peru.

---

[11] Recorded under No. 20 in Pérez Valiente de Moctezuma, Antonio. *Muebles Coloniales: La Colección de Don Gustavo M. Barreto.* Buenos Aires: [n.n.], 1931, p. 22.

***PETACA***
Both sides.
Casa Saráchaga (Art auction, November 2010), Buenos Aires.
Formerly, in Don Gustavo Barreto's collection.
18TH century.
Height: 65 cm. Width: 105 cm. Depth: 58 cm.

As with any other secular travel container, it has flat sides, a large frontal lock, a roof-shaped upper lid, corner beads, and a pair of side handles, which are its key features.

Anonymously made in Andean Baroque style, it was decorated with a subtle embossing on the lid and three sides of the cordovan; the piece has an aromatic wood supporting structure. It is decorated with curves and phytomorphic and zoomorphic motifs surrounded by perimeter friezes. The decoration on the back consists of a polychrome flower arrangement on plain leather.

## SMALLER AND EASIER TO TRANSPORT

It should be noted that, during the colonial period, *petacas* were made in different sizes and shapes, catering to the customer's needs, in order to avoid excessive weight and transportation difficulties.

There is one travel *petaca* in the Palacio del Arzobispado, which houses the Museo del Arzobispado del Cusco. It is a small and portable utilitarian container with an upper lid, a pair of side handles, a simple lock and iron corner beads. It is abundantly adorned with the often present *kantuta* branching arranged in symmetrical central designs, in a *mestizo* Baroque style with Spanish influences. It has a solid wood frame upholstered with embossed leather, gold details and traces of polychrome.

The travel *petaca* in the Museo de Arte de Lima collection, generously donated by the Prado family[12], is a secular use piece anonymously made in Baroque

[12] Asociación Museo de Arte de Lima archives, catalogued by José Centurión Padilla in 1987.

**TRAVEL *PETACA***
Museo del Arzobispado del Cusco.
Height: 21 cm. Width: 55 cm.
Depth: 34 cm.

style with Spanish influence during the 18TH century. This is a rectangular container with a folding lid, and a hammered iron front lock; it is supported by a wood structure covered with partially polychromed and gilded embossed cordovan. The profuse decoration consists of orderly distributed birds facing each other and plant elements on the front.

The sides bear birds spreading their wings framed by an oval surrounded by foliage. The lid perimeter has a sort of apron with subtle curves and figures arranged in a semicircle. It is not in very good condition: there is some leather missing and the damaged lock has not been restored.

In "Espacio Sor Juana" at the Museo de América, city of Madrid, there is an 18TH-century travel *petaca* made by anonymous Peruvian artisans in Baroque style with a strong Spanish influence. The piece is part of the important collection of such items exhibited at the museum[13].

It is a type of utilitarian container which was regularly used all over the Viceroyalty of Peru for long mule-back journeys. It would store the items needed for the journey or the new destination, such as tableware, textiles or books.

Square in shape, it has a top lid and a front lock covered by a remarkable engraved and fretted knocker, and side handles for transportation.

The piece consists of a small cedar wood structure completely covered by thick embossed cordovan which is richly ornamented and held in place by studs.

[13] Information provided by Museo de América, according to data recorded under file No. 06704 in the museum inventory.

*PETACA*
Museo de Arte de Lima collection.
Donated by the Prado family.
18TH century.
Height: 21 cm. Width: 52.5 cm.
Depth: 33 cm.

*PETACA*
Museo de América, Madrid.
18TH century.
Height: 50 cm. Width: 74 cm.
Depth: 45 cm.

Both lid and sides are decorated with compositions contained within perimeter friezes made using the leather tooling technique.

The decoration includes a profuse selection of phytomorphic motifs, such as large leaves, flowers and pomegranates, as well as a double-headed bird with a heart in the centre. There are also lions on both sides of the piece. It is in very good condition.

In the traditional Casa del Moral, in the city of Arequipa[14], there is a quadrangular travel *petaca* with an upper lid, side handles and a wrought-iron lock. It is a household container which was used as travel equipment by *encomenderos* and other Spanish America inhabitants during the colonial period.

The anonymous makers abundantly decorated it with both Spanish and indigenous elements, spreading over its surface figures of birds, pomegranates, leaves and flowers regularly distributed in each central design. The wood structure is covered with embossed and polychrome leather. The piece is not in very good condition, as the leather is cracked.

It is worth highlighting the evident and irrefutable legacy left in the New

---

[14] Currently owned by Banco de Crédito del Perú.

***PETACA***
[LEFT] La Casa del Moral - Banco de Crédito del Perú, Arequipa. Height: 38 cm. Width: 52.5 cm. Depth: 34 cm.

World by Andalusia artisans, who were experts in working the cordovan, and specialists in tanning, engraving, dyening and occasionally, gilding leather. Their expertise was readily assimilated by local artisans, a fact which facilitated the production of a wide variety of containers throughout three centuries.

## WITH STUDDED LEATHER

A travel *petaca* has been found in Museo Arzobispado del Cusco. It is a small capacity, portable, household container. The piece consists of a solid wood structure completely covered with dark leather.

The outer surface was decorated with bronze studs forming *kantuta* branches, which were symmetrically placed on the front.

This is a round top container covered with plain leather. There is a pair of side handles and a rustic lock on the front. It has corner beads to reinforce the structure. All the fittings are made of iron.

The influence of the metropolis is evident in this piece, where scant decoration is reminiscent of Baroque symmetry. It is in delicate condition, as the leather is deteriorated or missing.

In the Sala de Labores of the Monasterio de Santa Catalina, in Arequipa, there is a Baroque household *bargueño*. Its crude manufacture makes it difficult to accurately date the piece.

It has the same morphological features as any *bargueño* and is covered by the

**BARGUEÑO**
[RIGHT] Full view.
[OPPOSITE PAGE, BOTTOM] Detail.
Monasterio de Santa Catalina, Arequipa.
Height: 41.5 cm. Width: 62 cm.
Depth: 31 cm.

**PETACA**
[BOTTOM]
Museo del Arzobispado del Cusco.
Height: 31.5 cm. Width: 92 cm.
Depth: 46 cm.

typical front lid. In order to provide it with additional strength and preserve its contents, the piece was fully covered with dark leather held by studs which have a rustic design. There is a large iron lock on the lid front which reveals a strong Spanish influence. Its maker applied inlaying techniques on the fronts of the inner drawers, using wood panels of two different colours. The leather is deteriorated. Faced with the challenge of settling in these distant lands, travellers —like in Spain— needed to have *petacas*, suitcases and chests that would be useful for the basic needs of a sedentary lifestyle and for carrying their belongings during long overland trips, transported by mule or in carts, as well as during the long sea voyages in which they embarked.

# IV

## BAROQUE STYLE FURNITURE

## WOOD FURNITURE INLAID WITH FIGURATIVE ELEMENTS OR GEOMETRIC PATTERNS

Ecclesiastical and secular use

LIMA, CUSCO, AREQUIPA AND PUNO

# IV

## THE ORIGINS OF INLAY

The inlay technique, which involves setting fragments of wood into a base of the same material, dates back to antiquity. The Egyptians were masters of the art. Carthusian monks in the north of Italy applied it again during the 15TH and 16TH centuries, and it later spread throughout Europe.

The charm of this technique is partly due to the combination of various types of wood in their natural colours, which enhance textures, with the contrasting colours of dyed wood.

Between 1460 and 1510 inlay, or *intarsia*, was put on an equal level with Fine Arts, as it was used to represent images of unparalleled artistic value painted by great masters of the time —such as Botticelli— who made cartoons to later be turned into inlaid pieces.

During the 15TH century, great masters of this art went down in history, who worked in Ferrara, Padua and Urbino. It should be noted that this artistic tradition with a high aesthetic value goes back to the origin of the *certosina (intarsia)* work, used by Carthusian monks during the Renaissance to decorate by means of setting different shades of wood in furniture and wall panels. A wonderful example of this technique is *lo studiolo*, attributed to Baccio Pontelli and Francesco di Giorgio Martini[1], made between 1478 and 1482 for Federico da Montefeltro.

**CHEST**
[OPENING] Detail.
Private collection, Cusco.
18TH century.
Height: 47 cm. Width: 86 cm.
Depth: 43 cm.

**TABLE TOP LECTERN**
[OPPOSITE PAGE] Detail.
Private collection, Lima.
17TH century.

1 Villegas de Aneiva, Teresa. "El mueble virreinal. Un ejemplo manierista." In: Campos Vera, Norma (ed). *Manierismo y Transición al Barroco. Memoria del III Encuentro Internacional sobre Barroco.* La Paz: Unión Latina, 2005, p. 145. Gruber, Alain (ed). *The History of Decorative Arts: The Renaissance and Mannerism in Europe.* New York: Abbeville Press, 1994, p. 444.

Originally placed in the Palazzo Ducale de Urbino, it is currently exhibited in the Metropolitan Museum in New York[2].

Another example worth mentioning is the Santa María Gloriosa choir stalls: a large piece made in 1463 by the Venetian Franciscans, and portraying secular motifs.

The artists began by using geometric shapes, experimenting with different shades of wood, and later became experts in figurative elements, representing vases, grotesques and all sorts of friezes. They finally mastered perspective, creating authentic pictorial compositions in wood[3].

Perspective was applied to the representation of architectural views, cities and ruins, which created imaginary and three-dimensional spaces, as well as to images of saints and prophets, and musical and measuring instruments.

Spanish cabinetmakers made pieces representing prophets, popes and monarchs which were larger than religious, mythological and genre scenes. This art, so deeply rooted in northern Italy, was combined with the Spanish Mudejar inlay technique, which peaked in the late 16TH century. According to Aguiló, it first developed geometric patterns on all sorts of furniture, e.g. coffers and *bargueños.* Later, there was an overlapping of styles, as grotesques and stars were combined with abstract decoration.

This trend became very popular and was also adopted by Central European artisans, particularly those in southern Germany. Magnificent wood inlay works were produced in that region, both for furniture and for architectural accessories, such as doors and *boiserie* covering the walls of palaces.

A superb example *"of the best and most elaborate pieces from Germany, which are well laid out and understood"*[4] is the set of four German doors leading to the King's hall at the Royal Monastery of El Escorial. It is not certain if those doors were originally placed there.[5] They were a gift from Emperor Maximilian II to the King of Spain, Philip II.

## THE VICEROYALTY OF PERU; THAT ISOLATED PART OF THE WORLD

Inlay was the technique of choice for Cusco furniture, which demonstrated a link to the European trends mentioned above. Skilful craftsmen and master carpenters

---

2 Raggio, Olga. "The Gubbio Studiolo". In: Peck, Amelia *et al. Period Rooms in the Metropolitan Museum of Art.* New York: Metropolitan Museum of Art, 1996, pages 41-47.

3 Aguiló, María Paz. *El mueble clásico español.* Colección Cuadernos Arte Cátedra. Madrid: Cátedra, 1987, pages 139-150.

4 Sancho, José Luis. *Real Monasterio de San Lorenzo de El Escorial.* Madrid: Reales Sitios de España, 2002, p. 142.

5 Aguiló Alonso, María Paz. *Orden y decoro: Felipe II y el amueblamiento del Monasterio de El Escorial.* Madrid: Coleccionarte, 2001, pages 82-85.

disembarked in the Americas and implemented this technique as a useful vehicle to express themselves.

Furniture manufacture in the South Andean region gave rise to a new style. The inlay of natural or dyed local wood was its leitmotif. European themes were combined with local zoomorphic and phytomorphic motifs, which pervaded the inner and outer surfaces.

As a result of this fertile exchange, Spanish-American art produced a vast repertoire of containers; a clear, though not the only, example of the American Baroque style. Those pieces were both utilitarian and ornamental. Indigenous artisans put a great deal of care, expressiveness and attention to detail into their work.

In the 18TH century, *bargueños* and chests with *mestizo* characteristics, decorated using the above technique, flourished in Jesuit and Franciscan missions in tropical areas near the Amazon basin, at the foot of the Andes.

As already mentioned, this kind of decoration was achieved by inlaying wood fragments of various sizes and shapes onto a wood base, which was either flat or slightly curved, neatly arranged and generally moulded, following a predetermined layout.

Especially noteworthy are pieces for secular use, including *bargueños*, chests and escritoires, where symmetry played a predominant role.

## A *BARGUEÑO* WITH A DIFFERENT PALETTE

The *bargueño* or desk is a container of Andalusian origin. It was made and used across Spain; a typically Spanish type of furniture. There are three well-known types of *bargueño*, according to the kind of furniture supporting them: *taquillón* (placed on a chest of drawers), *mesa de fiadores* (on a money lender's table) and *pie de puente* (on a small trestle table).

As a general characteristic of Andalusian architecture, the outside of these pieces is almost undecorated: its beauty lies within.

The *bargueño*, useful for storing valuables and documents, is an essential portable piece of furniture for keeping male household items. It is rectangular in shape, with a large folding lid covering the entire front, and contains many drawers of various sizes and shapes. It may also have secret drawers.

Its engraved iron fittings are of outstanding decorative value. The latch and corner beads reveal the skilful metalworking of the Spanish-Arab culture, which maintained its quality upon arrival in the Americas. It has handles on both sides for transportation purposes.

The *bargueño* spread throughout Europe in the 16TH and 17TH centuries under different names: *cabinet* in France and England, and *stippo* in Italy. In the Spanish American colonies, this kind of furniture was very popular and production continued until the late 18TH century.

## FIGURATIVE REPRESENTATIONS

The concept of figurative art involves representing in a brief sketch, objects, characters, symbols and scenes drawn from reality, mythology or imagination.

The scenes on the piece are readily identifiable: they are produced on a predetermined layout, whose representation is easy to understand. This representation serves a dual purpose: it is deeply symbolic and also simply descriptive and iconographic, without disregarding the mandatory ornamental aspect.

All the elements in these containers, including drawers, doors, alcoves and lids, as well as every front, were covered with exuberant decorative motifs in local wood of contrasting colours.

The subject matter consisted of American mythological figures drawn from local legends and beliefs, such as "the god of the walking stick", or local animals and plants, and native characters dressed in the European style of the time, or

**TABLE TOP LECTERN**
[TOP] Detail.
Private collection, Lima.
17TH century.
Height: 29.5 cm. Width: 36 cm.
Depth: 25 cm.

**GLORY BOX**
[LEFT] Inside the lid, in detail.
Museo de Arte de Lima collection.
18TH century.
Width: 131 cm. Height: 68 cm.
Depth: 68.5 cm.

vice versa; this syncretism helps to understand the Spanish-American mindset.

Paucartambo is a province located nearly 100 kilometres from Cusco, in the Paucartambo river valley, 2,900 metres above sea level and north of the Andean mountains. In that province, there is an old town, Paucartambo, which has paved streets, white houses and balconies painted with a characteristic blue colour. It was an important trading centre during the colonial period, and is renowned for its chests and *bargueños* inlaid with fruit-tree wood.

Among inlaid furniture with figurative decoration, there are also some elements of formal Baroque style, for example, Solomonic columns, triangular broken pediments, niches and alcoves, as well as anthropomorphic figures facing each other.

Native or European characters, local flora and fauna, architectural constructions and liturgical elements string together, with unusual expressiveness, a figurative discourse representing hunting, genre and gallant scenes on all sides of the pieces.

There is the ubiquitous fruit of the vine, as well as local elements such as corncobs and pineapples. Anthropomorphic figures with indigenous features and native mythological characters are also recurrent.

In the Asociación Civil Museo Enrico Poli, in the city of Lima, there is a secular use *bargueño* or chest. This was anonymously built by an artisan who chose

***BARGUEÑO***
Asociación Civil Museo Enrico Poli, Lima.
18TH century.

a Baroque figurative design. It would not be wise to accurately date the piece, but it was likely made in the 18TH century.

**BARGUEÑO**
Drawer detail.
Asociación Civil Museo Enrico Poli, Lima.
18TH century.

This *bargueño* is a utilitarian container made by Cusco artisans. for storing valuables and important documents. It has flat shapes and a classical morphology; the front is made up of nine drawers of various shapes and sizes and a central alcove. There is no folding lid; a common feature of this kind of piece.

Using the traditional inlay technique, its maker decorated the central alcove with a monstrance: a classic element of domestic devotion, necessary for the religious practices of the society of the time. The entire front of the drawers surrounding the alcove is adorned with male and female *mestizo* characters representing sequential rural and symbolic scenes from Andean tradition, which are framed by an inlaid frieze.

Stylized floral and animal motifs, and a central vase, are repeated along the

**CHEST**
Private collection, Cusco.
18TH century.
Height: 47 cm. Width: 86 cm.
Depth: 43 cm.

sides of the piece. There is a wood support inlaid with Cusco cedar wood and other contrasting or dyed fruit-tree woods. It is in very good condition.

This chest belongs to a private collection located not far from Cusco. It was made in Paucartambo, a town northeast of Cusco on the banks of the river which bears its name; a tributary of the Urubamba River.

The piece is an everyday use container for storing personal belongings; it has flat sides and a roof-shaped lid divided into three bays. It was probably built in the 18TH century.

This chest is decorated using the inlay technique and has mouldings along its perimeter. In addition to the local style used, it has southern German and Lombard influences. The artisan worked with local wood of contrasting colours on an orange-tree wood base.

Andean Baroque decorative elements make up the central composition on the front and sides of the piece: there are real and fantastic anthropomorphic and zoomorphic figures, hunting scenes and rustic constructions, all of them placed within a central design framed by flowers and fruits, and accompanied by jungle animals. The metal latch on the front displays a double-headed eagle.

Revealing normal wear and tear, the piece is in good condition, although some mouldings are missing.

This table top lectern which is part of a private collection in Lima has the characteristics of a desktop book holder. It is usually placed on altars to hold liturgical books during mass.

This piece, with a surprising classical serenity, was anonymously made in the Baroque style, probably in the 17TH century, when schools and colonial *obrajes* were occasionally run by craftsmen from the Old World. It was built in Peru, and has strong Italian or German influences. There are religious symbols on its remarkable front, distributed within straight lines.

Its upper body is decorated with a central monstrance resting on papal emblems. At both ends, triumphant characters hold wind instruments. On the lower body, there is a central urn bearing a heart with seven swords which represent the Seven Sorrows of the Virgin, who is escorted by guardian angels.

*The devotion to and iconography of the Virgin of the seven swords were born in Flanders in the late 15TH century. It was Juan de Coudenberghe who organised the first confraternity of Our Lady of the Seven Sorrows, and it was Margaret of Austria, ruler of the Netherlands, who founded, also in Bruges, the first convent dedicated to Our Lady of the Seven Sorrows, and offered the church of Brou-en-Bresse a votive*

TABLE TOP LECTERN
Detail
Private collection, Lima.
17TH century.
Height: 29.5 cm. Width: 36 cm.
Depth: 25 cm.

**TABLE TOP LECTERN**
Private collection, Lima.
17TH century.
Height: 29.5 cm. Width: 36 cm.
Depth: 25 cm.

*painting with the Virgin's image. Finally, it is in an engraving dedicated to Charles V, published in Antwerp in 1509, where the seven swords, arranged in a fan pattern, appear for the first time.*[6]

The abovementioned decoration, an eloquent testimony to Christian devotion displayed on a piece of furniture, is encircled by curves, leaf and flower branching, and framed with volumetric mouldings. The lower body reveals two round arches placed in the centre of the apron that supports the piece. The surrounding decoration consists of details which suit the style of the piece.

This Baroque *bargueño*, possibly made for household use during the 18TH century, is part of the Museo de Arte de Lima collection and was donated by the Prado family.[7]

---

6 "La virgen de las siete espadas." Historiarte.net [online] [last access on February 29, 2012, 4.30 pm] <at www.historiarte.net/iconografia/sieteespadas.html>. Source: Réau, Louis. *Iconografía del arte cristiano.*

7 Asociación Amigos del Museo archives, catalogued by Amalia Castillo Saavedra in 1987.

The piece stands out as a quadrangular container with flat sides; the front lid is moulded with profuse wood carvings. It rests on four bun feet and has seven drawers with turned-wood knobs.

There are stylized floral motifs on the lid, surrounding a flaming heart placed in a circle. Inside the piece, there is a central alcove with the monogram of Christ under a round arch, and a heart resting on plant motifs, which also appears on the rest of the drawers. A vase containing fruits of the land adorns the top drawer. It was decorated using the inlay technique, of evident German influence, on wood of various colours. The front lid is moulded with a remarkable frieze featuring floral carvings.

The artisan's identity, as is generally the case, remains unknown. The piece is in good condition, except for a missing knob.

This Andean Baroque *bargueño* was designed for everyday use. It currently belongs to a private collection in the city of Lima. It is conceivable that during the first half of the 17TH century, the European artisans who arrived from the Old World and set up assembly and cabinetmaker's workshops trained natives in these skills; finding in them a fertile soil.

The *bargueño* is a quadrangular container. Its front folding lid has a large latch; metal handles are placed on the sides. Inside are 19 drawers of various sizes and shapes. The central drawer has an alcove flanked by columns which are repeated on the side drawers.

***BARGUEÑO***
Museo de Arte de Lima collection.
18TH century.
Width: 40 cm. Height: 33 cm.
Depth: 30 cm.

*BARGUEÑO*
Private collection, Lima.
Formerly, in Don José Antonio de Lavalle's collection.
17TH century.
Height: 54.5 cm. Width: 66 cm.
Depth: 41 cm.

The drawers are decorated with plant motifs surrounding mythological creatures and fantastic animals, such as a unicorn and a snake which, according to local traditional beliefs, symbolises the world of the dead. The drawers have flat and symmetrically arranged mouldings. Geometric patterns on the sides give the piece a harmonious aspect.

This piece was made from a wood base to which various techniques were applied: inlay using various local woods, and woodturning for the columns. Its movable fittings are made of metal; it should be noted, though, that they do not chronologically match the piece.

This is one of those pieces which would have remained outdoors in Lima for long periods of time, with the sole protection of gallery roofs, a fact which could have been detrimental to its upkeep.

The 17TH-century glory box in the Museo de Arte de Lima collection was donated by the Prado family.[8]

This piece is a secular utilitarian container for storing and transporting trousseaux. It has a flat structure with a roof-shaped upper lid and an interesting

---

[8] Catalogued by José Centurión Padilla in 1987, according to Asociación Amigos del Museo de Arte de Lima archives.

**GLORY BOX**
Inside the lid in detail and full view.
Museo de Arte de Lima collection.
18TH century.
Width: 131 cm. Height: 68 cm.
Depth: 68,5 cm.

lock whose engraved-iron latch rests on the front. The Baroque decoration is noticeable in the coat of arms placed in the centre of the piece, as well as in the geometric, irregular, and quartered shapes containing natural motifs in the central designs.

These ornaments were the result of inlaying light-coloured wood in a solid wood structure. The piece is a classic example of the Cusco school.

This glory box is complete and in good condition; it has never been restored.

*BARGUEÑO*, WRITING DESK
Don Armando Andrade's collection, Cusco.
Height: 24 cm. Width: 42 cm.
Depth: 22 cm.

At Don Armando Andrade's residence, in the city of Cusco, there is a strictly utilitarian *bargueño* or writing desk for secular use. It has simple features, typical of a small rural piece of furniture. With a flat front, it has seven drawers: the central of which is vertical and simulates an alcove.

Undulating friezes mould the central designs decorated with inlaid flowers, fruits and leaves, which are arranged on the front of each small drawer. The central alcove has a religious decoration inserted under the arches and flanked by turned columns.

Following Spanish patterns, unknown artisans of the Cusco region managed to build this rustic container which has a solid cedar base and details in lighter-coloured wood. The piece is in good condition, although some parts are missing.

## INLAY WITH ABSTRACT PATTERNS

Decorative geometric and abstract patterns of Mudejar origin reveal the presence of Andalusian artisans in the Viceroyalty. Skilled in the inlay technique since the Spanish Renaissance, these artisans brought with them a wealth of knowledge to the Americas for which they stand out in these forms of expression.

It is a well-known fact that Muslim beliefs prohibit the representation of nature, which is why Muslims tended to decorate with geometric shapes. This kind of ornamental work was applied to utilitarian pieces intended for transporting documents and valuables, where drawers, doors or alcoves were needed.

Alcoves were placed in the centre, the most prominent place of the piece, and were surrounded by drawers of various shapes and sizes. This central location was chosen not only due to the architectonic forms of the alcoves but also to the selected decorative motifs which, in some cases, were of symbolic representation. These depictions were generally of religious images, such as crosses, sword-pierced hearts, monograms of religious orders, patron saints, etc. The viceregal population's evident Christian devotion was transferred to the domestic sphere through these displays.

The techniques and materials used were flat wood bases inlaid with wood of contrasting colours, as well as mouldings with little volume. The most frequently used materials were Cusco cedar wood, orange tree and other types of local wood in various natural or dyed colours. Fittings were made of silver and iron.

In the Doña Marita de la Peña Prado collection, in the city of Lima, there is another *bargueño* which is similar to the above pieces. Possibly made in the South Andean region during the 17TH century, it evokes the Baroque style with techniques similar to those used in northern Italy and southern Germany.

*BARGUEÑO*
Doña Marita de la Peña Prado's collection, Lima.
17TH century.
Height: 42 cm. Width: 70 cm.
Depth: 36.5 cm.

**BARGUEÑO**
Monasterio de Santa Catalina, Arequipa.
Height: 41.5 cm. Width: 62 cm.
Depth: 31 cm.

This rectilinear utilitarian container has twelve drawers of various sizes and shapes which are decorated with symmetrically arranged ribbons. The alcove in the central drawer is inlaid with a Christian Cross flanked by columns. It was built and decorated using various types of very aromatic local wood, and its fittings were made of metal. The piece is in very good condition.

It should be borne in mind that young women of noble birth who entered the novitiate of any religious order carried with them rich and luxurious belongings, which enabled them to lead a comfortable life in the cloister. These belongings included containers, such as chests and *bargueños*, which are currently exhibited, as in a museum, in the Monasterio de Santa Catalina.

The utilitarian *bargueño* in the Sala de Labores of the Monasterio de Santa Catalina, in Arequipa, was made in Baroque style; two shades of wood were used. The piece has iron fittings and is covered by leather held in place and decorated using studs, with a clear Spanish influence. (See Chapter III, page 149)

Its anonymous maker resorted to the inlay technique to decorate the inside of the container, which is covered by a folding lid and has an iron lock on the front.

The piece has twelve irregular drawers, the central one being alcove-shaped.

These drawers were decorated, with a certain tendency to abstraction, using ribbons and stylized leaves symmetrically arranged in moulded central designs.

It is in delicate condition, the leather having deteriorated and some handles are missing.

The novitiate of the Monasterio de Santa Catalina, in Arequipa, exhibits a regular-sized *bargueño* with a front lid. The piece contains ten drawers of various sizes, the central of which is quadrangular.

It is a Baroque secular use piece decorated with geometric shapes forming flat panels and angles in all four corners, divided by Greek friezes. These central designs contain curves, circles and scrolls.

The piece, whose maker is unknown, was likely produced by the Arequipa school, which drew on Spanish influences. It was made on a local wood base and inlaid with wood of two different colours.

It is in delicate condition and some parts are missing.

In the above examples, it is noteworthy that both pieces at the Monasterio de Santa Catalina, in Arequipa, are everyday-use items, which reveals that, in their convent life, cloistered nuns used containers to keep valuables.

Despite that, it is worth noting that *bargueños* were especially made for men, who at the time were the most educated (literate) population group.

*BARGUEÑO*
Monasterio de Santa Catalina, Arequipa.
Height: 42 cm. Width: 83 cm.
Depth: 40 cm.

# V

## BAROQUE STYLE
## FURNITURE
## PORTABLE NATIVITY SCENES

## CARVED WOOD AND OTHER MATERIALS; POLYCHROME AND GILDED PIECES

Ecclesiastical use

LIMA, CUSCO AND AREQUIPA

Gloria in Excelsi Deo

# V

## ECCLESIASTICAL USE WITH A MISSIONARY PURPOSE

The first religious orders to arrive in the Viceroyalty of Peru were the Franciscans and Dominicans, followed by the Mercedarians, Augustinians and later, the Jesuits. Members of these religious orders travelled continuously from Spain to the colonies, until the decline of the colonial period.

Their presence revealed the evangelizing vocation not only of their own congregations, but also of the Spanish Crown, which encouraged them.

Creoles, Spaniards and Europeans in general could be ordained as priests. Natives and blacks were ordained as lay brothers. There were plenty of friars and nuns establishing their congregation's main houses in Spanish-American cities. They also took their ministry to outlying and isolated areas where there was often no colonial presence.

The indoctrination and conversion of natives was successful for many reasons. Churches and monasteries were built, schools were founded for children, and craft workshops were established for adults in out-of-the-way populations, providing the areas with schools of arts and crafts which bore the fruit of high quality *mestizo* handicraft. This was partly due to the astonishing speed with which natives learned to apply their skills.

Priests and monks involved in this task studied indigenous languages, not only to be able to communicate fluently, but also to write in *Quechua*, the Catechism, poetry and plays representing and illustrating Biblical History.

In order to achieve a fluid understanding, they also became interested in local traditions, beliefs and history, with a commendable teaching spirit. They

**PORTABLE NATIVITY SCENE**
[OPENING] Museo Pedro de Osma, Lima - Peru.
18TH century.
Height: 46 cm. Width: 108 cm.
Depth: 44 cm.

**PORTABLE NATIVITY SCENE**
[OPPOSITE PAGE] Manger detail.
Museo del Monasterio de Santa Teresa, Arequipa.
Height: 115 cm. Width. Closed: 205 cm, open: over 3 metres.
Depth: 86 cm.

established a calendar of religious holidays, which were celebrated according to rites the natives were strongly attracted to, as a way to achieve their mission's religious goals.

With identical aspirations, Nativity scenes or Nativity chests —as these portable mangers were called— were devised. These are very popular Spanish American pieces of furniture which were made throughout the Viceroyalty in the 17TH and 18TH centuries, particularly in the cities of Cusco and Quito. They were considered an essential tool for conveying the basic teachings of the Catechism.

According to oral traditions, the origin of the Nativity manger dates back to 13TH-century Italy. Some authors attribute the narrative of the life of Jesus as an object of devotion and piety to St. Francis of Assisi. The Society of Jesus recovered this valuable tradition in the 16TH century.

According to Ramón Mujica Pinilla: *The Nativity or Christmas manger dates from 1223 and was created by St. Francis of Assisi (d. 1226) himself, who turned the historical Jesus' life into a paraliturgical object of pious meditation*[1].

Derived from the *retablo de cajón* (a portable altarpiece), the portable Nativity scene is a rectangular container with an upper lid and either a folding front lid or front doors. Inside, it is divided into several bodies, which contain many characters representing the life of Jesus and various stories from Biblical History, including episodes from both the *Old* and *New Testaments.*

Depending on the scene, different images were placed inside, representing different moments in the life of Jesus. The Virgin Mary, St. Joseph, the Magi, angels and shepherds, as well as the Doctors of the Temple, surrounded him in adoration.

Among vegetation and other elements, there were also conquerors; secondary characters, often with native features; local flora and fauna; and surrounding elements, *…resulting in syncretic versions of the indigenous and rural worlds*[2].

These small sculptures were made in various sizes and materials, such as wood or moulded paste, in order to represent relatively simple but authentic scenes, and surrounded by mountains, skies, trees, fruits, flowers, altars and fountains. Thus, an essentially descriptive stage effect was achieved which could replace the written word.

---

1 Mujica Pinilla, Ramón. "La devoción al Niño Jesús." In: *Orígenes y devociones virreinales de la imaginería popular.* Lima: Universidad Ricardo Palma; Instituto Cultural Peruano Norteamericano-ICPNA, 2008, p. 75.

2 Gutiérrez, Ramón (coord). *Pintura, escultura y artes útiles en Iberoamérica, 1500-1825.* Colección Manuales Arte Cátedra. Madrid: Cátedra, 1995, p. 356.

Carrying the piece on their shoulders, priests and monks of all orders went on missions visiting many indigenous communities and recounting Biblical History in the simplest terms.

The Baroque format was sometimes anachronistic. Despite the arrangement of the various elements and figures, depth was difficult to achieve when compared with the rigor of European works. The characters' hierarchical perspective was generally altered, and so were the proportions of surrounding flora and fauna. It is worth noting that, when the piece was closed, each character would fit perfectly between the others, maintaining its original position: the piece was then ready for a new exhibition.

Various materials were used: characters were made from carved wood which was polychromed with a vibrant palette, or built from maguey (agave stems) covered with gummed cloth. Various fabrics were used to dress the figures, and gold leaf, to enhance certain light effects.

Characters were dressed in the style of Spanish and American religious images. Glass, crystal, Huamanga stone, and porcelain details were some of the resources which also contributed to an impressive and substantially didactic stage effect.

The exterior of the boxes is of no particular interest: they are simple and sparsely painted local wood bases with a rustic finish. They always have a pair of

PORTABLE NATIVITY SCENE
Museo Pedro de Osma, Lima - Peru.
18TH century.
Height: 46 cm. Width: 108 cm.
Depth: 44 cm.

handles on the sides for transport, and a metal front lock. Several pieces with similar characteristics have been found. One of them is the Nativity scene or Nativity chest of Cusco origin, owned by the Museo Pedro de Osma, in the city of Lima. This container has a flat front, an upper lid and a folding cover. Inside there is a portable manger with a myriad of images which fit perfectly. ... *the themes of Paradise, the Annunciation, Joseph's Dream, the Nativity, the Presentation at the Temple, the Circumcision, the Arrival of the Magi, the Flight into Egypt, the Massacre of the Innocents, Jesus among the Doctors and, finally, the story of the Baptism of Christ* can be seen there.[3]

The chest has the characteristic scenographic design of the 18TH-century Baroque style applied to rural Peruvian architecture. Aimed at teaching episodes from the life of Jesus, it contains a variety of images representing scenes from his birth and childhood, surrounded by biblical characters and conquerors, dressed

[3] Fundación Pedro y Angélica de Osma Gildemeister. *Museo Pedro de Osma.* Lima: [n.n.], 2004, pages 144-145.

PORTABLE NATIVITY SCENE
Detail.
Museo Pedro de Osma, Lima - Peru.
18TH century.
Height: 46 cm. Width: 108 cm.
Depth: 44 cm.

**PORTABLE NATIVITY SCENE**
Museo del Monasterio de Santa Teresa, Arequipa.
Height: 115 cm. Width. Closed: 205 cm, open: over 3 metres.
Depth: 86 cm.
Courtesy of Franz Grupp.

in the Spanish-American fashions of the time. On the inner side of the upper lid there is a painting of a heavenly image. Solomonic columns, balustrades, round arches in galleries and fountains repeatedly appear all over the piece.

It was built by anonymous artisans using local wood which was carved, turned, gilded and painted. Characters were constructed from wires and a paste made with fabric that was glued and polychromed with golden glass ornamental details; the hinges were made from iron.

It is in very good condition.

The manger or Nativity chest located in the Sala de la Natividad or Sala de la Sagrada Familia, in the Museo del Monasterio de Santa Teresa, which belongs to the Carmelites of Arequipa[4], was donated by Don Pedro de Arbe, who was the priest of Puquina at the time.

It is probably *...the piece of highest artistic quality; the largest and best preserved portable manger in the country;* it seems to be a mixed production, since ... *According to the* Crónica de Santa Teresa, *the manger was "transported by mule from Quito, Ecuador"*[5] and decorated with colours which are more luxurious than those pieces of unquestionable Peruvian origin.

In turn, its Quito origin is revealed in the quality of the piece and the special characteristics of its images, even though, in Franz Grupp and Zully Mercado de

---

4 Carty, Charles L. *Arequipa, Ciudad inolvidable.* Arequipa: [n.n.], 2008, p. 70.

5 Grupp, Franz and Mercado de Grupp, Zully. *El Monasterio de Santa Teresa de Arequipa.* (Unpublished).

Grupp's view, the structure may have been finished in Arequipa. They also claim that the background ornamentation has evident Cusco school features, as seen in the European bucolic landscapes typical of that school.[6]

It should be noted that this manger is an ecclesiastical piece, made in Baroque style in the early 18TH century. It has the shape of a *bargueño*, with an upper lid, a pair of front doors, and side handles for easy transportation. The decoration consists of Solomonic columns, round arches, cartouches, pendants and natural motifs, such as pomegranates. All these elements form part of a rich tableau, where multiple characters of unusually large size are represented by colourful carved wood sculptures.

This piece displays eleven panoramas with over a hundred characters. Such scenes include the Holy Family, the Adoration of the Magi and the Shepherds, the Baptism of Jesus, the Garden of Eden, the Massacre of the Innocents, Jesus among the Doctors and the Flight into Egypt.

The chest was built by unknown artisans from carved wood, which was covered with fabrics and partially decorated with gold leaf. It is very well preserved.

In the Sala de Labores of the Museo del Monasterio de Santa Catalina de

6 Grupp, Franz and Mercado de Grupp, Zully. Op. cit.

PORTABLE NATIVITY SCENE
Details.
Museo del Monasterio
de Santa Catalina de Sena, Cusco.
Height: 125 cm. Width: 148 cm.
Depth: 140 cm.

**PORTABLE NATIVITY SCENE**
Museo de Arte Religioso
of the Basílica Catedral de Lima.
Donated by Auxiliary Bishop
Monsignor Alberto Brazzini Díaz Ufano.
Height: 40 cm. Width: 50 cm.
Depth: 40 cm.
Courtesy of Monsignor Raúl Chau.

Sena, in the city of Cusco, there is another manger or portable Nativity scene: a container used by monks of various congregations for teaching purposes.

When the top and side lids are opened, many characters can be seen representing scenes from the birth and life of Jesus, as well as other episodes from Biblical History.

On the lid there is a representation of the Holy Trinity in heaven surrounded by an orchestra of angels. The chest itself is decorated with a Baroque balustrade and arches, and a blown-glass fountain which may have been added later.

Solid wood, carved, fretted and covered with fabric; gold leaf; coloured patinas; and *lattimo* or blown glass with gold threads were the materials of choice for this piece, which is in good condition.

In the Sala Brazzini of the Basílica Catedral de Lima's Museo de Arte Religioso, there is another portable Nativity scene which was donated to the museum by Auxiliary Bishop Monsignor Alberto Brazzini Díaz Ufano.

This container was probably made in the 18TH century. Its flat sides have a pair of front doors; it also has a backward-sloping roof, which gives the piece a certain architectural dimension.

The *mestizo* Baroque style is noticeable inside, where a Nativity scene takes place in a cave under the sky and the watchful eye of God the Father. Multiple popular characters surround the Infant Jesus, the Virgin Mary and St. Joseph, who are topped by a frieze and protected on only one side by a balustrade.

This devotional and utilitarian piece is yet another example of local inspiration and the Italian style which, under express instructions from monks of various orders, were applied to the piece by unknown local artists. It has a solid wood structure, which has been carved, polychromed and partially gilded. The various characters, scenographically arranged within the piece, were made from various materials, such as maguey, gummed cloth and carved Huamanga stone, and finished with remnants of wool. On the apron which crowns the scene, there is a golden mirror, a highly valued object in those times.

It is in very good condition and, as was generally the case, some characters and animals were added later.

The Nativity chest which was part of the magnificent collection of Auxiliary Bishop Monsignor Alberto Brazzini Díaz Ufano, located in one of the Brazzini halls of the Basílica Catedral de Lima's Museo de Arte Religioso, was made in a popular Baroque style, probably in the 18TH century.[7]

It is a rectangular Creole portable container, with a flat folding upper lid and front doors. The inner part is covered with a mirror from which the images of God the Father and the Holy Spirit hang among the angels of heaven; these details were probably added later.

Inside the chest, amidst profuse vegetation, there are Solomonic columns, balustrades, anthropomorphic and zoomorphic figures and a round arch; these elements create the appropriate atmosphere for the birth of Jesus in the manger of Bethlehem. It is an ecclesiastical utilitarian piece used for evangelisation; it was commissioned to anonymous artisans by a religious congregation.

Made from a carved and turned, solid, local wood base, it was decorated with mirrors and beads, and covered with paint and gold leaf, of which only traces remain. Metals were used for the indispensable fittings.

The piece is in good condition.

---

7 Lohmann Villena, Guillermo, *et al. La Basílica Catedral de Lima.* Colección Arte y Tesoros del Perú. Lima: Banco de Crédito del Perú, 2004, p. 342.

**PORTABLE NATIVITY SCENE**
[BOTTOM] Details.
[OPPOSITE PAGE] Full view.
Museo de Arte Religioso of the Basílica Catedral de Lima.
Donated by Auxiliary Bishop Monsignor Alberto Brazzini Díaz Ufano.
18TH century.
Height. Closed: 44 cm, open: 79 cm.
Width: 84 cm.
Depth. Open: 76 cm.
Courtesy of Monsignor Raúl Chau.

# VI

## BAROQUE STYLE FURNITURE

## FLAT CARVED, BARE, GILDED AND POLYCHROMED WOOD

Secular and religious, utilitarian and ornamental use

LIMA, CUSCO, AREQUIPA, PUNO AND TRUJILLO

# VI

Direct carving onto wood on 16TH and 17TH century furniture cannot be attributed to any particular region of Spain, but this kind of furniture was certainly among the personal effects brought to the Americas by the conquerors to furnish their homes.

The design and production of colonial furniture and other applied arts were a true reflection of certain aspects of Spanish American architecture. The architectural inspiration for some pieces becomes especially evident in certain types of containers, including wardrobes, chests, and *bargueños*.

Their decoration had little volume and was similar to that found on church façades. This was achieved by profuse decoration, and applying flat carvings to all their faces, following an aesthetic pattern of balanced proportions.

According to Bailey: ... *an excellent example of* mestizo *style is the profusely embellished façade of the Jesuit church of Santiago in Arequipa (1698)*. He also maintains that this type of carving *is not unique to Mexico or Peru. In fact, planimetricism occurs all over the Iberian empires.*[1]

Referring to a silver tabletop lectern, an example of applied arts which can be linked to the furniture production of the Peruvian Highlands, Luis Eduardo Wuffarden says: *...it evokes the decorative repertoire of the South Andean frontispieces during the second third of the 18TH century, which coincides with a boom in the planiform or "mestizo" architectural style.*[2]

Flattened or three-dimensional carvings were referred to as *planimetric*

**WARDROBE**
[OPENING] Detail.
Vivian and Jaime Liébana's collection, Lima.
18TH century.
Height: 199 cm. Width: 139 cm.
Depth: 84 cm.

**LOW WARDROBE**
[OPPOSITE PAGE] Front panel detail.
Don Alfredo Pinillos' collection, Trujillo.
17TH century.
Height: 133 cm. Width: 145.5 cm.
Depth: 65.2 cm.

[1] Bailey, Gauvin Alexander. *Art of Colonial Latin America*. New York: Phaidon, 2005, pages 79/87-88.

[2] Bákula Budge, Cecilia *et al. Mestizo. Del renacimiento al barroco andino*. Lima: Impulso Empresa de Servicios, 2008, p. 60.

*carvings.* It is worth noting the aesthetic differences between pieces decorated with *mestizo*-style flat carvings and those with half-relief carvings described in Chapter I. The latter, in a typically European Mannerist style, were ornamented with direct carvings on wood, figures in high-relief, columns, capitals and corbels, among other items. For example, the choir stalls built in the Americas during the 17TH century were true reflections of classical Italian architecture and furniture.

*It is very common for the sensual and fleshy Baroque forms to lose their original sensuality and acquire a marked chasteness under persistent smoothing and spreading, reminiscent of a typical system of pre-Hispanic goldsmithing.*[3]

Local artisans used artistic patterns taken from European engraving and drawing books. This valuable data allowed them to decorate the pieces with Europeanised morphology by juxtaposing local elements.

In the Viceroyalty of Peru, the Spanish Baroque style experienced changes as a result of the influence of the typically Andean ornamental fantasy, which was hungry for creativity. The merger of Hispanic symbols and indigenous theogonies, a very specific iconography, gave rise to a *mestizo* style. It is worth noting the syncretism which this merger represents.

Thus, different and profusely arranged motifs coexisted, forcing keen observers to discover the persistent presence of figurative and very symbolic *mestizo* elements and, in some cases, a Spanish-Arab influence.

The use of ornaments from such different cultures on the same piece suggests an apparent crudeness of the wood carvings, but also reveals the artists' creative impulse.

This is how a new aesthetic trend was born which nourished designs of both secular and ecclesiastical American Baroque furniture, and which was in vogue from 1650 to about 1800; a trend that was both a classic example of, and heir to, Cusco's art world.

The three-dimensional volume was achieved by bevelling noble and ductile woods, turning them into flat, archaic forms which covered almost the entire surface of the pieces.

Sometimes, carved wood was wholly or partially gold leafed, and patinas and polychrome were also applied, giving the piece unprecedented expressiveness. Decoration was completed by turning and fretting the wood.

This way of covering the surface reveals the *horror vacui* which was characteristic

[3] According to Francisco Gil Tovar's, renowned Spanish Art critic and Director of the Museo de Arte Colonial in Bogotá, in 1975.

of this kind of furniture. A distinctive Baroque feature was the use of symmetry with a suitable distribution of compositional weight, which gave the piece a certain harmony.

The outer sides of doors, drawers, lids and lateral faces of these containers were usually carved. Generally, motifs were repeated on each face, and a rich decoration was hidden inside, painted on a flat base. With singular art, this decoration represented a story on the bottom and inner sides of doors. The pieces were ornamented with a traditional iconographic repertoire or genre scenes on a background landscape: human-centred, gallant, hunting or religious scenes, often framed by slightly volumetric mouldings.

Pieces were made from solid Nicaraguan and Cusco cedar, as well as alder, mahogany, cocobolo and willow woods. Locks and other fittings were made from engraved silver or wrought iron.

Predominant motifs consisted of a profusion of natural elements, such as flora and fauna, as well as local motifs including *kantutas*, corncobs, fruits of the

CHEST
Detail
Museo Pedro de Osma, Lima - Peru.
Height: 63 cm. Width: 114 cm.
Depth: 61 cm.

vine and hummingbirds. Anthropomorphic figures with indigenous features were some other elements used for decoration, along with the rich local iconography representing flora and fauna of different regions: monkeys, tropical fish and lizards of the Amazon jungle, local fruits, and also typical images of the Altiplano, such as child corbels and winged cherubs.

Baroque architectural motifs surrounded and completed the composition with a profusion of crowns, triangular pediments, cornices, friezes, niches and alcoves, arches, detached or engaged columns, classical or Solomonic half-columns with capitals of every order, corbels, reversed corbels, pinnacles, pilasters and balustrades, as well as vases, urns and baskets.

Depending on their characteristics and purpose, both secular and ecclesiastical pieces were decorated with liturgical ornaments, human or animal figures facing each other, musical instruments, cartouches, monograms and coats of arms.

The types of furniture onto which the flat carving technique was most frequently applied were wardrobes —famous from Cusco for their quality and excellent carvings— chests, coffers, escritoires, benches, sacristy furniture, pulpits, coca goblets or gourds and *coqueras* or *hierberas.*

## FLAT CARVED, SOLID WOOD FURNITURE FOR SECULAR USE

In the Museo Pedro de Osma collection, in the city of Lima, there is a chest which was produced by unknown artists from the Cusco school. It has an upper roof-shaped lid, straight lines in its lower body and a wrought iron lock.

This Baroque container of notable Spanish influence is a secular piece of furniture for household use. It was intended for storing linen or trousseaux. When closed, it could be used as a seat.

Other more rustic and simpler pieces, almost without decoration, *were designed for grain or household equipment storage*[4].

This chest has a solid wood supporting structure entirely decorated with direct carving, a central urn on the front surrounded by branches and *rinceaux*, and an abundance of *kantuta* leaves hanging from the branches. All these elements, encircled by friezes, are symmetrically arranged.

In Don Alfredo Pinillos' ancestral home, in Trujillo, there is a regular-sized utilitarian chest. Its most remarkable structural feature is a slightly curved upper lid with flat lines on all four sides. It has a great iron latch on the front which rests in a carved socket.

---

4 Aguiló Alonso, María Paz. *El Mueble de España: siglos XVI y XVII.* Madrid: Antiqvaria, 1993, p. 85.

**CHEST**
Museo Pedro de Osma, Lima - Peru.
Height: 63 cm. Width: 114 cm.
Depth: 61 cm.

The chest was made in Baroque style during the 17TH or 18TH century. It is a well-known fact that these pieces were manufactured until the late 18TH century: the date when this piece was probably produced.

The Spanish influence becomes evident in its structure and the Cusco school influence through the wonderful flat carvings that are repeated throughout the piece and which are a typical artistic expression in the South Andean region. The piece, however, can be considered a Trujillo production, not only because it was found in that city, but also because it is made from Figueroa cedar wood, a material widely used in the coastal area of northern Peru.

Decorative motifs were symmetrically arranged around a central latch in the shape of a coat of arms, as well as on the lid and all its faces, which were overwhelmed with decoration. There is an interesting selection of plant motifs and grapes on either side. Mouldings consist of classic friezes of little volume carved on the lid perimeter, the faces and the socket.

The chest is in excellent condition.

This chest, which belongs to a private Cusco collection, demonstrates the *mestizo* Baroque spirit applied to a utilitarian piece of furniture. It was produced by the Cusco school; as in most cases, its creator is unknown.

It is a container with an upper lid and flat front and sides, resting on four legs ending in corbels. The chest was decorated with direct carvings on solid alder wood; it has engraved iron fittings.

Ornamental exuberance was marked by the representations of natural elements: local flora and fauna, surrounded by friezes on each side, were symmetrically arranged.

A remarkable expressiveness was achieved by including a feline face on the front with leaves coming out of its mouth; this image is greatly symbolic. With evident crudeness, angles are supported by carvings representing large leaves and strings of pearls. Two large rosettes are placed on the sides.

The piece is in very good condition, although some elements are missing.

In the Brazzini Halls of the Basílica Catedral de Lima's Museo de Arte Religioso, there is an 18TH century Baroque coffer/escritoire made by Cusco artisans.[5]

It is a container for storing and transporting documents. This portable escritoire has flat front and sides, a pair of drawers in the lower frontal body, and an upper lid. There are small compartments inside.

The sculptor of its abundant decoration, consisting of symmetrically

**CHEST**
[OPPOSITE PAGE, TOP]
Don Alfredo Pinillos' collection, Trujillo.
18TH century.
Height: 72 cm. Width: 120.5 cm.
Depth: 62.5 cm.

**CHEST**
[OPPOSITE PAGE, BOTTOM]
Private collection, Cusco.
Height: 64 cm. Width: 100 cm.
Depth: 59 cm.

**COFFER - ESCRITOIRE**
[BOTTOM] Museo de Arte Religioso of the Basílica Catedral de Lima.
Height: 42 cm. Width: 64 cm.
Depth: 38 cm.

---

5 Data from the museum archive, provided to the institution by the INC (Instituto Nacional de Cultura).

**COFFER - ESCRITOIRE**
Open.
Museo de Arte Religioso
of the Basílica Catedral de Lima.
Height: 42 cm. Width: 64 cm.
Depth: 38 cm.

arranged local flora and fauna motifs, remains unknown. A central rosette, moulded friezes, and robust stile have strong Cusco and Italian influences. The piece is made from solid cedar wood and has a wrought iron central latch. It is in critical condition and has not been restored.

In the sacristy of the Basílica Catedral del Cusco, there is a magnificent seat supported by a chest. In the 17TH and 18TH centuries, Italians used to refer to this type of piece as a *cassapanca*. It is a seat with a backrest, while the lower body is a container.

It could be linked to the sumptuous Spanish piece made from oak by Adrián Lombart in 1553, which was inspired by Italian typologies of the time, and belongs to the Dukes of Medinaceli's collection.[6]

This piece has straight backrest and sides; the arms are slightly curved toward the sides. There is a container in the lower body, and the upper lid is divided into

---

6 Aguiló Alonso, María Paz. Op. cit., p. 358. Feduchi, Luis. *Historia del Mueble*. Barcelona: Blume, 1986, p. 53.

two parts, each with an iron lock. The piece boasts profuse Baroque decoration and its compositional weight is well balanced.

There is a pair of carved vases on both the backrest and the lower body, surrounded by symmetrically arranged branches with leaves and fruits of the vine, and moulded with successive pearl and dentil classical friezes, with rosettes on the sides. The stiles are crowned with corbels. Thus, it contains classical ornamentation with a hint of indigenous elements.

It is made from solid and darkened Cusco cedar wood and has iron fittings.

The piece is in reasonably good condition, although the base of the lower body has somewhat deteriorated.

In one of the halls in Casa Chica, an annex to the Museo Pedro de Osma, in the city of Lima, there is a Baroque console table made by anonymous artisans from the Cusco school. Probably constructed in the 17TH or 18TH century, it is a Spanish table for salting bacon.

This secular table was decorated by applying direct carvings to solid cedar wood. Its skirt, under a flat projecting lid, has a large drawer which rests on four turned legs held together by crosspieces and dados.

The decoration consists of a central heart on the front and cartouches on the sides, surrounded by very symmetrical ribbons and acanthus leaves. The perimeter of each side is moulded with rosettes and scales. The straight legs of the piece are turned forming a rosary and connected by two dados.

BENCH WITH CHEST
Basílica Catedral del Cusco.
Arzobispado del Cusco.

The table is in fairly good condition, although some wood pieces are missing.

The wardrobe which used to be part of an old Cusco family collection, now owned by Museo Pedro de Osma in Lima and exhibited in the Casa Chica annex, makes a great visual impact.[7]

It is a secular-use container whose Baroque style can be observed in its suggestive ornaments; the piece is a true exponent of the 18TH century Cusco school in the Viceroyalty of Peru.

Unknown yet possibly local artisans managed to combine the front and side ornaments with planimetric carvings on the outer face of the upper body and on the four lower drawers. Under a projecting cornice, a great frieze crowns the doors, where a central mascaron stands out representing a feline face.

Compositional weight was skilfully distributed in order to arrange the decorative motifs making good use of a fertile aesthetic exchange. Classical round arches, vases and urns were distributed on the front and the sides, as well as a profusion of indigenous birds facing each other amidst local vegetation to make up the central axis.

---

7 Fundación Pedro y Angélica de Osma Gildemeister. *Museo Pedro de Osma.* Lima: [n.n.], 2004, pages 180-181.

**CONSOLE TABLE**
Museo Pedro de Osma, Lima - Peru.
Height: 83 cm. Width: 165 cm.
Depth: 78 cm.

**WARDROBE**
[OPPOSITE PAGE]
Museo Pedro de Osma, Lima - Peru.
18TH century.
Height: 187 cm. Width: 119 cm.
Depth: 76 cm.

**WARDROBE**
[LEFT] Inside the door, in detail.
[RIGHT] Closed. Detail.
Museo Pedro de Osma, Lima - Peru.
18TH century.
Height: 187 cm. Width: 119 cm.
Depth: 76 cm.

**WARDROBE**
[OPPOSITE PAGE]
Museo Pedro de Osma, Lima - Peru.
18TH century.
Height: 215 cm. Width: 123 cm.
Depth: 67 cm.

Inside the upper body, painted on a flat wood base, the warm and rich polychrome decoration dazzles the eye. Gallant scenes filled by characters in typical costumes and local fruit baskets with proportions altered, are unique examples of cultural syncretism. Each frame is carved and gilded forming scales.

Insistently describing the known world, and emphasising the surrounding elements, Mesa says that: *the Cusco painter replaced this landscape with a flower garden, including birds that were not in the model. He added a parrot and replaced the naughty dog with a lamb*[8].

This wardrobe is a clear example of a piece of furniture where the indigenous, Spanish and Creole legacies coexist.

Apparently built and carved from Cusco cedar wood, this piece has wrought iron handles and hinges, as was usual in the region.

The piece is in very good condition.

There is another magnificent wardrobe of considerable size, which has been recently acquired by Museo Pedro de Osma. It is a household piece of furniture, probably made in the 18TH century by anonymous Cusco school builders. The Italian Baroque and Renaissance influences can be seen not only in the variety of techniques applied, but also in the morphology of the piece.

---

8 Mesa Figueroa, José de *et al.* *El retorno de los ángeles.* [n.p.]: Unión Latina, [n.d.], p. 134.

With flat front and sides, the wardrobe is divided into two bodies, upper and lower; each body has two doors and three drawers in the skirt. It is topped with a "cardinal's hat" and rests on a typical Renaissance base.

The architectural features are profusely, orderly and symmetrically decorated, combining ornamental techniques to enrich the piece. Direct carvings on most of the surface, with gold leaf traces and mouldings on each panel, coexist with friezes reminiscent of the southern German style, which were inlaid with light wood forming geometric patterns. The composition on the inner side of the doors is similar to that of the exterior.

The decoration evokes a clearly European repertoire through a moderate use of grotesques, *rinceaux*, pearls and scales.

The construction is from solid Cusco or Nicaraguan cedar wood with wrought iron fittings.

The piece is in very good condition.

The vast wardrobe (over three metres high and two metres wide) anonymously built in the first third of the 17TH century, which belongs to the famous collection of Don Alfredo Pinillos, is one of the items in the library of his ancestral home in the city of Trujillo.

It is a two-bodied container with flat front and sides. There are four front doors and drawers in the skirt. It is worth noting that the piece bears three unique carved and fretted crest rails resting on an impressive projection.

The Baroque decorative elements have a classical influence and are symmetrically arranged. Stylised and refined Italianising urns rest on corbels surrounded by leaves and flowers. The composition was achieved by bevelling the wood, creating a subtle volume, an

**WARDROBE**

[LEFT] Full view.

[OPPOSITE PAGE] Detail of *il bamboccio* figure.

Don Alfredo Pinillos' collection, Trujillo.

Early 17TH century.

Height: 334 cm. Width: 206 cm.

Depth: 111 cm.

effect inspired by Cusco wood treating techniques. Drawers were adorned with curves carved with plant motifs. There are three suggestive cherubs on the upper frieze, recreating the *il bamboccio* figure.

As an exponent of Trujillo production, this piece was made from solid Figueroa cedar wood; iron hinges and handles are its only metallic elements.

This piece is in very good condition.

In the late 16TH and early 17TH centuries, particular importance was given to this type of furniture —wardrobes— because, being more practical than chests, lead to people gradually leaving behind said pieces, mainly in their sedentary life.

The low wardrobe in Don Alfredo Pinillos collection, exhibited in his Trujillo house, is a splendid example of local furniture; its morphology is very different from the Cusco double-bodied pieces.

Its structure has flat front and sides, with a pair of front doors, and three drawers in the skirt, a typical feature of Trujillo production. It is only one metre and thirty-three centimetres high.

The piece was decorated following the Baroque canons of the 17TH century, when it appears to have been made. With the flat carving technique, stylized and refined urns were produced and placed on corbels, leaves and flowers; curves with floral motifs decorate doors and drawers. All these elements are symmetrically arranged.

Anonymous craftsmen built the piece using solid Nicaraguan cedar wood

LOW WARDROBE
Don Alfredo Pinillos' collection, Trujillo.
17TH century.
Height: 133 cm. Width: 145.5 cm.
Depth: 65.2 cm.

—known in Trujillo, for unknown reasons, as *cedro de Figueroa*— and completed with iron hinges.

The piece is in excellent condition.

In the workroom of the Real Monasterio de Clarisas de Santa María de Gracia, in the city of Trujillo, there is another utilitarian low wardrobe. It is a container with two doors, three drawers in the skirt, inner drawers and a lid bordered by a frieze.

It has Baroque decorative elements which place an emphasis on symmetry. On panels, delicate guards enclose a composition including grape bunches, urns and birds facing each other, all produced with the flat carving technique, revealing an unmistakable Cusco influence on the Trujillo production of the time.

The piece's maker selected Figueroa cedar wood for the supporting structure, and iron for fittings and hinges. It is in very good condition.

It is important to mention one of the wardrobes located in the refectory of the Museo del Monasterio de Santa Catalina de Sena, in Cusco, which illustrates domestic aspects of monastic life.

Its morphology, with Italian Renaissance influence, is characteristic of colonial wardrobes consisting of four doors and two drawers in the skirt. The piece is topped by a hip roof, a typical stylistic feature of Andean viceregal art, which gives the piece an architectural style.

Made by anonymous Highlanders, the piece was richly ornamented with subtle carvings on the flat faces and inner shelves, which were designed for storing and displaying crockery. Reliefs were highlighted with partial gilding, and turned spheres crown a magnificent frieze.

**LOW WARDROBE**
Real Monasterio de Clarisas
de Santa María de Gracia, Trujillo.

Vases of various shapes, as well as leaves and flowers, adorn the quartered

panels, all moulded with successive friezes representing pearls, scales, leaves and rosettes.

The piece was made from solid Cusco cedar wood; wrought iron was used for the fittings.

It is in delicate condition, since some elements are missing.

On grand display in the Museo del Monasterio de Santa Teresa, in Arequipa, is a beautiful coca goblet or mate gourd, a domestic piece made in *mestizo* Baroque style. It was used as a container for drinking mate, a beverage which is sipped through a silver straw.

This goblet is a spherical utensil made in one piece, whose support and circular base are turned. It was decorated with direct carvings on local hardwood, possibly cocobolo: a tree native to the Peruvian Amazon.

The object was made by an anonymous craftsman, profusely decorated on the outside with jungle zoomorphic figures, such as felines, pigs and monkeys, and surrounded by vegetation in a symmetrical and well proportioned manner.

WARDROBE
Museo del Monasterio de Santa Catalina de Sena, Cusco.
Height: 210 cm. Width: 121 cm.
Depth: 62 cm.

COCA / MATE GOURD
[OPPOSITE PAGE, TOP] Museo del Monasterio de Santa Teresa, Arequipa.
Height: 23 cm. Diameter: 18 cm.

*COQUERA*
[OPPOSITE PAGE, BOTTOM] Museo de Arte de Lima.
Misiones Jesuíticas de Moxos.
Donated by the Prado family.
18TH century.
Height: 21 cm. Width: 31 cm.
Depth: 26.5 cm.
Courtesy of Museo de Arte de Lima.

The *yerba mate* is a local infusion made from a plant which initially grew in Paraguay and was gradually introduced by the Jesuits throughout South America. According to iconographic sources, mate was the favourite beverage of viceregal society, and was enjoyed by women during their parlour gatherings[9].

This *coquera* or *hierbera* from the Jesuit Missions of Moxos or Chiquitos was probably made in the 18TH century (c. 1780).[10] It was donated by the Prado family and is now part of the Museo de Arte de Lima collection, enriching the collection's artistic heritage.

When *yerba mate* or *yerba del Paraguay* arrived in Peru, introduced to the colonial society by the Jesuits, there was a need to build containers for storing dried leaves. This container was a household item used to store and transport *yerba* or coca leaves. *There are many testimonials on the subject left by European*

[9] Sánchez, Marta. "El mate en la sociedad virreinal". In: Eguiguren Molina, José and Eguiguren Molina, Javier (eds). *El mate en América.* Buenos Aires: Eguiguren & Vega, 2004, pages 39-41. Illustrative engraving in: Tord, Luis Enrique and Gjurinovic Canevaro, Pedro. *El Palacio de Torre Tagle y las Casonas de Lima.* Lima: Asociación de Funcionarios del Servicio Diplomático del Perú, 2001, p. 157.

[10] As a background, it is worth noting that this piece was described in Eguiguren Molina, José y Eguiguren Molina, Javier (eds). Ibid. p. 194.

*chroniclers and draughtsmen on their way to Lima and other urban centres of the South Andean region. That may have been the place where the term coquera originated: a fact which reveals the persistence of a ritual and the lavish use of coca leaves among certain Andean elites.*[11]

This piece is a small, solid, cocobolo, hardwood container, with an upper lid, an engraved cartouche-shaped latch, a silver bolt and a lock with a key.

Unknown artisans carved it profusely with plant motifs and four legs which represent the Atlanteans. The lid is shaped like a trefoil scallop, with curves and counter-curves, as well as natural elements and *putti* alternating with gadroons and pearls. This ornament is surrounded by feathered and serrated friezes, both on the lid and the container. It is lined with red tufted and buttoned silk.

A similar piece is thoroughly described: *Designed for the most refined society, because of the deep-rooted custom of drinking mate, boxes were made by silversmiths of these lands to store leaves and the necessary lime; some of them had scalloped tops*

[11] Wuffarden, Luis Eduardo. In: Bákula Budge, Cecilia *et al.* Op. cit., pages 133-134.

*and others, a circular egg-and-dart outline and a lid [...] these coqueras always have locks.*[12] This is a description of a silver *coquera*, while the previous one is made from hardwood.

## FLAT CARVING ON ECCLESIASTICAL FURNITURE

At the entrance to the tower of the Iglesia y Convento de Santo Domingo del Cusco, hidden from inquisitive eyes, there is a piece of sacristy furniture: a particularly original example of Cusco production. The South Andean Baroque style is once again revealed in this two-bodied piece for ecclesiastical use, which has four doors and five drawers.

It is worth mentioning the combination of techniques used to produce the piece, which are proportionally subordinated to the architectural language. The upper body has a roof-shaped top and side balconies supported by columns. The lower body has a pair of drawers in the skirt and a projecting lid. It rests on four carved legs.

On the outside of the piece, panels are moulded by other decorative carved elements, such as continuous friezes adorned with beads, scales and rosettes. On the inner side of the doors and at the back, there are brightly coloured oil paintings: figures of the time with a gallant aspect, framed by a floral frieze, an element which casts doubt upon the use given to the piece. Other elements, in disproportionate arrangements, include fuchsia (*ñucchu* in *Quechua*) leaves, and vases containing fruits such as pomegranates, pears and bunches of grapes.

Unknown makers built the piece using Cusco cedar wood. It has silver or tin fittings and there are traces of gold leaf on the carved surface. It is in good condition, although part of the paint on the lower doors is missing.

In the Iglesia Parroquial de San Blas del Cusco, on the left side of the nave, there is a famous pulpit made during the last quarter of the 17TH century, during the time of Bishop Manuel Mollinedo, the governor of the region and a generous patron.

With some reservations, this work has been attributed to indigenous architect, carver, assembler, sculptor and gilder Juan Tomás Tuyru Túpac, a native of Cusco, who is said to have been related to the Inca nobility. According to the legend, he suffered from leprosy and it took him four years to finish the piece; moreover, he did not charge anything for his work.

---

[12] Gutiérrez, Ramón (coord). *Pintura, Escultura y Artes Útiles en Iberoamérica, 1500-1825*. Colección Manuales Arte Cátedra. Madrid: Cátedra, 1995, p. 396.

**SACRISTY FURNITURE**

Open and closed. Detail.
Iglesia y Convento de Santo Domingo, Cusco.
Upper body: Height: 130 cm.
Width: 126 cm. Depth: 58 cm.

Ruben Vargas Ugarte states: *There are very few arguments to attribute the authorship of the famous pulpit of San Blas to him.* And he adds: ... *the work itself does not belong to him but to the rather famous Cusco assembler, Martín de Torres*[13]. A view shared by Harold Wethey, as ... *for him, Tuyru Túpac's authorship does not make any sense.*[14]

This mention of the controversial authorship of the San Blas pulpit may be of interest since it implies that clarification is required.

It's a magnificent piece of ecclesiastical furniture, a container designed and built in Baroque style. The piece is, however, a worthy exponent of Cusco ecclesiastical furniture for its exceptional aesthetic values, simultaneously evoking the European decorative repertoire and the creative Andean ornamentation.

As is generally the case, the piece is attached to the wall and consists of a canopy or sounding board crowned by the image of St. Thomas, with a skull placed at his feet. It is surrounded by the images of nine doctors of the Church:

---

[13] Vargas Ugarte S.J., Rubén. *Ensayo de Diccionario de Artífices Coloniales de la América Colonial.* [n.p.]: Talleres Gráficos Baiocco, 1947, pages 272-273.

[14] Viñuales, Graciela María. *El Espacio Urbano en el Cusco Colonial: uso y organización de las estructuras simbólicas.* Lima: Epígrafe Editores - Cedodal, 2004, p. 144.

**PULPIT**
[OPPOSITE PAGE] Detail of sounding board with the image of St. Thomas.
[RIGHT] Tribune support detail.
Iglesia Parroquial de San Blas, Cusco.
Arzobispado del Cusco.
17TH century.

St. Bernard, St. Basil, St. Jerome, St. John Chrysostom, St. Leo, St. Augustine, St. Gregory the Great, St. Thomas Aquinas, and St. Bonaventure.[15]

The rostrum is circular and contains representations of Our Lady of Good Success and the Four Evangelists. On the backrest, between the sounding board and the rostrum, there is a half-relief carving of San Blas.

Supporting the rostrum, there are eight semi-nude heresiarchs, their backs bent with guilt, which … *seem to represent Martin Luther, John Calvin, Henry VIII, Elizabeth I, Arius, Photios and Katharina von Bora*[16]*;* all of them are surrounded by a decorative extravagance which was used to add drama to the sermon. Around these images, there are seven chimeras with bunches of grapes in their mouths as additional stylistic features.

Other decorative elements include: niches containing images, separated by richly turned triple Solomonic columns, child corbels, "green man" mascarons with tropical fruits coming out of their mouths, cartouches, grapes and leaves of various sizes and shapes. The piece ends in a pendant with fretted acanthus leaves. It also has a side balcony which leads to the access stands.

It was skilfully crafted by direct carving and fretting of solid Cusco cedar wood, which makes this great piece from the Peruvian Highlands unique.

PULPIT
Iglesia Parroquial de San Blas, Cusco.
Arzobispado del Cusco.
17TH century.

The pulpit with Italian Baroque influences in the nave of the Basílica Catedral del Cusco was made after the 1650 earthquake by Martín de Torres[17], a master assembler and carver, and a disciple of Juan Toledano.

Its authorship has also been attributed to the priest and architect Diego Arias de la Cerda, who was appointed Master Builder of the Catedral del Cusco in 1641 by Bishop Ocón … *as it will be seen, this great building was almost entirely constructed by this renowned architect, including its magnificent choir, pulpit, ambos, sacristy, the famous "María Angola" bell and the Triumphal tabernacle.*[18]

This liturgical piece is a hanging structure, which is attached to the wall and has three parts: rostrum, canopy and staircase with access door.

On the rostrum backrest, there is an image of St. Peter which is profusely carved in high relief, framed by a round arch and flanked by Solomonic columns.

---

[15] Rivero L., Víctor T. *Cuzco Incaico y Colonial.* Madrid: Ediciones Serrano, 1966, pages 94-95.

[16] Mujica Pinilla, Ramón *et al. El Barroco Peruano.* Vol. I. Colección Arte y Tesoros del Perú. Lima: Banco de Crédito del Perú, 2002, p. 243.

[17] Saldívar Antúnez de Mayolo, Liliana. *Magic and Enthrallment. The Cathedral of Cusco and the Temples of La Sagrada Familia and El Triunfo.* Cusco: Arzobispado del Cusco, 2007, p. 60.

[18] Vargas Ugarte S.J., Rubén. Op. cit., p. 126.

**PULPIT**

[LEFT] Basílica Catedral del Cusco. Arzobispado del Cusco. Authors: Architect Diego Arias de la Cerda, Martín de Torres and Melchor Huamán Mayta. 17TH century.

**HEARSE**

[OPPOSITE PAGE] Iglesia y Convento de Santo Domingo, Cusco. Courtesy of Convento de Santo Domingo, Cusco.

On the rostrum, paired Solomonic columns divide compositions, which are decorated with symmetrical corbels, pinnacles, classical friezes, curves and scales.

A side staircase designed in the artistic style of the late 18TH century, before Neoclassicism, gives access to the pulpit.

The piece was entirely built of solid Cusco cedar wood, which was carved, turned and fretted. It has wrought iron fittings.

The piece is in very good condition; it has been restored and some parts have been replaced.

There is a hearse at the entrance to the tower of the Iglesia y Convento de Santo Domingo, in the city of Cusco. It is an impressively large triangular candelabrum for liturgical use, which used to be lit during Tenebrae of Good Friday. Its fifteen candles would be gradually extinguished until there was complete darkness.

Made in Baroque style by anonymous Cusco craftsmen, possibly commissioned by the Order, the piece cannot be accurately dated.

It consists of metal candle sockets, placed on a triangular moulding, supported by a single large central shaft shaped like a Solomonic column and divided by a *kantuta*.

Other ornamental motifs include continuous and voluminous guards representing pearls and scales around the upper triangle.

This piece, made from carved Cusco cedar wood, has traces of paint. It is in good condition.

## CARVED, FRETTED AND POLYCHROMED WOOD
## LIMA, CUSCO, PUNO AND LAMPA

### UTILITARIAN FURNITURE FOR ECCLESIASTICAL AND SECULAR USE

There are pieces of furniture built and decorated in the 17TH and 18TH centuries which have similar morphologies and techniques to those described in the previous section, but which have wholly or partially polychromed carvings. Their metal fittings are engraved.

It is worth mentioning some pieces found in Lima and produced in the South Andean region, such as wardrobes and tables, confessionals, organs, rood screen gates and other richly decorated fragments, which might currently be serving other purposes.

A splendid wardrobe of Cusco origin which used to belong to the Brignardello family was acquired by collectors Vivian and Jaime Liébana, from Lima. It was specifically designed for storing personal items, especially clothing or trousseaux.

It is important to mention that the piece was part of "The Arts in Latin America, 1492-1820" exhibition held in Philadelphia, in 2006.[19]

In this piece, whose structure was made with obvious Italian Baroque influences, the artistic mark of 18TH century Cusco furniture stands out in the use of local elements producing a *mestizo* Baroque style which is full of surprises.

This rectilinear piece with four front doors divided by two drawers in the skirt is topped with a projecting cornice and rests on a base.

Unknown artists designed this large wardrobe with ornamental exuberance,

---

[19] Rishel, Joseph J. and Stratton-Pruitt, Suzanne (eds). *Revelaciones: Las artes en América Latina, 1492-1820.* México D.F.: Fondo de Cultura Económica, 2007, p. 502.

**WARDROBE**
[RIGHT] Full view.
[OPPOSITE PAGE, TOP] Frieze detail.
[OPPOSITE PAGE, BOTTOM] Drawer detail.
Vivian and Jaime Liébana's collection, Lima
$18^{TH}$ century.
Height: 199 cm. Width: 139 cm.
Depth: 84 cm.

unprecedented expressiveness and a harmonious distribution of compositional weight. With remarkable aesthetic sense, they focused on arranging every decorative element in strict symmetry.

A double-headed eagle can be seen in the centre of each drawer surrounded by grotesques on both sides. Guitar-playing mermaids and fantastic animal faces surrounded by local flora and moulded with perimeter friezes were carved on the upper door panels.

On the side stiles, curious observers may find a very expressive female face with its eyes closed. On each bottom door, there is a centralized vase, ornamented with a sunflower surrounded by acanthus leaves, grapes, cacao fruits, pomegranates and other natural motifs framed by repeated guards.

The piece is topped by a frieze with a head of a notably symbolic "green man", an image of remarkable syncretism. The sides have quartered decorations with a profusion of pearl friezes.

**TABLE**
Real Monasterio de Clarisas de Santa María de Gracia, Trujillo. Height: 77 cm. Width: 75 cm. Depth: 50 cm.

**ORGAN BOX**
[OPPOSITE PAGE] Iglesia de Santiago Apóstol de Lampa, Puno. 17TH – 18TH centuries.

The entire surface is bevelled on a solid Cusco cedar base. Details of the various compositions are polychromed with a vivid and varied palette.

In the Real Monasterio de Clarisas de Santa María de Gracia, in the city of Trujillo, there is a pair of Baroque utilitarian tables which cannot be accurately dated. These are small side tables with rectangular tops decorated with a carved apron. Each rests on four oblique legs connected by crosspieces.

They are ornamented with carved and turned scales, waves and beads. The tables were built using a local wood base, with dark patinas and gold leaf applied in prominent places. They are in very good condition.

In the choir of the Church of Santiago Apóstol, in Lampa, we find the box of an organ (a wind instrument originally from the Netherlands) made between 1675 and 1775 by local artisans in *mestizo* Baroque style.

The profuse decoration consists of paired Solomonic columns on both sides, with a great carved and fretted comb forming an arch; winged cherubs and plants

are distributed across its entire surface. These elements have a certain volume and are full of ornamental fantasy. Details were highlighted with paint and gilding.

This ecclesiastical piece was made from solid cedar wood, carved by anonymous craftsmen influenced by European trends. It belongs to the remarkable Puno Diocese heritage and is in good condition.

In the vast La Libertad region, in the church of Monasterio de El Carmen, in Trujillo, which belongs to the Discalced Carmelites, there is a Baroque rood screen gate made by master carpenter Thoribio Ramírez, who … *reveals his authorship of the fences and rood screen railings in the church of El Carmen in Trujillo in a statement of his will (July 11, 1757): "his clothes and tools are in Monasterio de El Carmen".*[20]

The structure is supported by four large columns topped by an upper frieze and alternated with a grid covering the entire rood screen front, becoming a part of the church architecture.

**ROOD SCREEN GATE**
[OPPOSITE PAGE, TOP] Frieze detail.
[OPPOSITE PAGE, BOTTOM] Partial view.
[BOTTOM] Column detail.
Monasterio de El Carmen, Trujillo.
Author: Thoribio Ramírez.
c. 1757-1758.

Its selected decorative elements belong to the 18TH century late Baroque style. These are clear and strikingly naive examples of the Trujillo school with a Moorish influence, including smiling faces, stylized leaves and dentils; all these elements are highlighted with a vibrant palette of reds and greens.

Built from solid wood, it is alternately covered with gold leaf and polychromes, producing an effect in which beautiful carvings are combined with the subtle fretting that characterises the piece.

The piece is in excellent condition.

In the Church of Santiago Apóstol, in Lampa, against the wall of the nave, there is a confessional which is part of the Puno Diocese heritage. It was made by anonymous artisans, in Andean Baroque style, between 1675 and 1775.

It is a liturgical piece of furniture, consisting of an inner seat for officiating priests, side walls, and a canopy. It has lattices on the sides for the priest to confess women without seeing them; men, on the other hand, would kneel in front of the priest.

This piece has a strong Italian influence in its morphology and decoration, but it also has local elements.

The confessional consists of a solid wood base which was partially decorated using flat carving, turning and fretting. Quartered

---

[20] Data provided by Professor Ricardo Morales Gamarra; records in Archivo Regional Histórico de La Libertad, Trujillo. Notarial / Deed. López Collado, Gregorio. File. 370 fol. 120 (1757-1758).

spaces framed by volumetric friezes contain a plethora of decorative motifs, including symmetrically arranged rosettes, flowers and scales. Carvings are highlighted by patinas of various colours. The piece has wrought iron fittings.

In the Church of San Pedro Mártir, Juli Cathedral, there are two interesting fragments, which are attached to the benches located on either side of the high altar. They may have once been part of an altarpiece or a frieze decorating a religious setting. They belong to the Prelature of Juli, Museo Religioso de San Pedro, in the Department of Puno, Province of Chucuito[21].

These pieces were probably made in the late 16TH or early 17TH century —according to Professor Héctor Schenone— in Andean Baroque style with a strong Italian influence.

They are decorated with religious symbols, the "Instruments of Crucifixion or Passion", immersed in overlapping cartouches, surrounded by symmetrically arranged fruits of the vine, interlaced motifs and acanthus leaves.

*The Instruments of Passion. Weapons of Christ, the instruments used in the torture of the Lord; on this subject, plastic arts have represented no less than thirty different objects, especially the cross, the spear, the whips, the sponge, the crown of thorns and the nails; also the ladder, the hammer, the ropes, the Veil of Veronica, etc.*[22]

This reveals, once again, that the ornaments selected by anonymous artisans for those pieces were useful to illustrate a highly significant moment from Biblical History.

**CONFESSIONAL**
[OPPOSITE PAGE] Iglesia de Santiago Apóstol de Lampa, Puno.
18TH century.
Height: 170 cm. Width: 84 cm.
Depth: 100 cm.

**FRAGMENTS**
Iglesia de San Pedro Mártir - Catedral de Juli, Puno.
Late 16TH – early 17TH century.
Height: 226 cm. Width: 50 cm.
Height: 230 cm. Width: 50 cm.

[21] Instituto Nacional de Cultura-Puno. Archivo del Departamento de Registro y Catalogación.

[22] Becker, Udo. *Enciclopedia de los símbolos.* Barcelona: Swing-extra, 2008, p. 226. Ferguson, George. *Signos y símbolos en el arte cristiano.* Buenos Aires: Emecé, 1956, pages 254-267.

To that end local solid wood was carved in low relief, enhanced with gold leaf applied on the background and finished with partial polychrome.

Despite some cracks, they are in good condition.

It is a positive thing that fragments like the ones described were restored after the destruction of altars and altarpieces by several earthquakes in the area or after changes in the liturgy in the mid-20TH century.

## CARVED, FRETTED, GILDED AND POLYCHROME WOOD. LIMA, CUSCO, AREQUIPA AND PUNO

### A GILDED AND POLYCHROME FLAT CARVING VARIANT ON UTILITARIAN FURNITURE FOR ECCLESIASTICAL AND SECULAR USE

Console tables, larders and two-door dressers are a few types of secular furniture decorated using the flat carving technique and occasionally enriched with a total or partial application of gold leaf.

Ecclesiastical furniture decorated with this technique includes sacristy furniture, pulpits, sacristy chests of drawers, wardrobes, cupboards, columns, lecterns, altars with or without altarpieces, portable platforms, mirrors, candlesticks and candelabras.

The types of wood used to make these pieces include Cusco cedar, alder and willow. Carvings were highlighted by applying gold leaf and polychrome; fittings were made from metal.

### A SELECTION OF FLAT-CARVED SECULAR PIECES WITH A GOLD LEAF FINISH

In a famous private collection from Cusco, there is a splendid console table which is part of the household furniture. A console table is a piece of furniture intended to be placed against walls, and so is elaborately decorated on only three sides. A typical piece of household furniture of the time, its origins can be traced back to well-known European consoles.

It is a utilitarian and ornamental table for secular use which has flat sides, a projecting top and one large drawer taking up the entire front of the skirt, ending in wooden knobs. The piece rests on four profusely carved straight legs which are connected by a crossbar.

This table was made in Andean Baroque style by anonymous local artisans with a predominance of planimetric carvings. Decoration includes a repetition of ornamental motifs, such as concave grooves on the drawer front, which emphasise an appreciation of classical art. Scales and rosettes frame the drawer, thus compositional weight is evenly distributed.

Remarkable skill is displayed in the use of the flat carving technique, warm and vivid patinas, and partial gildings on the solid wood, resulting in a superb piece of South Andean furniture.

Thanks to the generous donation by Doña Clorinda Málaga de Prado, Museo de Arte de Lima owns a secular use two-door dresser or low cabinet made in Cusco. This piece has been recently restored.

Despite its lavish ornamentation, it is a utilitarian container. It has three drawers of two different sizes in the skirt and two front doors with four moulded panels on each. Two corbels support the projecting lid and the dresser rests on a base which may have been restored.

It is decorated with Baroque motifs: a profusion of flat carved vases surrounded by foliage, quartered on each panel and framed by friezes. All these

CONSOLE TABLE
Private collection, Cusco.
Height: 92 cm. Width: 139.5 cm.
Depth: 68.5 cm.

elements are distributed across a blackened solid wood structure, which was partially covered with gold leaf. The piece has metal locks.

There is a splendid and famous cupboard[23] in the sacristy of the Basílica Catedral del Cusco, which is part of its artistic heritage. This piece was built in the *mestizo* Baroque style of the Highlands by unknown craftsmen from Cusco in 18TH century; it was intended for both ecclesiastical and secular use.

DRESSER OR LOW WARDROBE
Museo de Arte de Lima.
Donated by Doña Clorinda Málaga de Prado.
Height: 122 cm. Width: 140 cm.
Depth: 78 cm.
Courtesy of Museo de Arte de Lima.

[23] Aguiló Alonso, María Paz. *El Mueble Clásico Español.* Colección Cuadernos Arte Cátedra. Madrid: Cátedra, 1987, p. 222. Porras Barrenechea, Raúl and Vargas Ugarte S.J., Rubén *et al. Historia General de los Peruanos.* Lima: Peisa,1986, p. 576.

Its morphology has Plateresque features inspired by Spanish art. The piece, however, has a notably local flavour in its monumental scale; typical of furniture production in the prosperous viceroyalty.

This two-door container, exuberantly ornamented, boasts a front upper cresting and two symmetrical lateral ones resting on a large projection. The doors have several turned columns for ventilation, which suggests that this cupboard was used for storing food. It rests on four claw and ball feet.

The distinctive decorative features on the front and flat sides of the piece consist of a central cartouche resting on a triangular pediment which holds a religious order's monogram: on the cresting, there are also multiple pinnacles that have been replaced. The ornamental moulding surrounding the vases, arranged in various patterns on quartered divisions, completes a design akin to Spanish-Arab motifs.

The piece is built from solid wood, probably Cusco cedar, decorated with direct carvings, and partially covered with gold leaf, which enhances the volume of the wood. It has iron locks.

Some elements have been replaced and the piece has been obviously adjusted.

In the collection of the Museo de Arte de Lima, there is a dazzling and majestic secular wardrobe, which was also donated by Doña Clorinda Málaga de Prado[24]. This piece was built in the last quarter of the 17TH century by unknown Cusco artisans who had an Italian influence.

One of the most remarkable features of this large container is its classical morphology. It has four doors, two drawers in the skirt, and it rests on four legs decorated with phytomorphic designs. Following local traditions, its upper panel has an architectural profile, hidden by a large comb-shaped top on the front and sides which is abundantly decorated and fretted, and rests on an important carved cornice.

Inside the upper body, there is a pair of shallow shelves, protected by a turned-wood balustrade, and a third hexagonal shelf, supported in the centre by a rotating terminal and placed under a canopy which is decorated with floral motifs.

The profuse and symmetrical Andean Baroque decoration on each door and side panel consists of classical vases surrounded by vegetation with birds facing each other and moulded friezes. The sides are decorated with volutes. All these

---

[24] Catalogued in the Museo archives by José Centurión Padilla in 1987.

elements were distributed over a solid wood supporting structure and enhanced with partial gold leaf, thus creating interesting volumetric effects.

The magnificent piece has a wrought–iron central lock, and the ring–shaped handles of the characteristic drawers, placed on the skirt dividing the piece, are made from the same material. The piece was restored in 1991 and thus is in very good condition.

**WARDROBE**
Basílica Catedral del Cusco.
Arzobispado del Cusco.
18TH century.

**WARDROBE**
Museo de Arte de Lima.
Donated by Doña Clorinda Málaga de Prado.
17TH century.
Height: 285 cm. Width: 137 cm.
Depth: 93 cm.
Courtesy of Museo de Arte de Lima.

## SELECTION OF FLAT CARVED AND GOLD-LEAF FINISHED ECCLESIASTICAL FURNITURE

A pair of columns decorated with Italian influence and intense local flavour, which were made in the 17TH century, are part of the Museo Pedro de Osma collection, in the city of Lima. They are round pieces intended for ornamental purposes. It is reasonable to think that they used to be part of an altar or some other piece for ecclesiastical use.

The columns are regular-sized; they have mixed decoration in Baroque style, consisting of rhomboidal volumetric carvings on the lower body. Their upper body is gilded and polychromed with vibrant colours. Bodies are separated by a subtle pearl frieze.

Unknown artisans made them from a wood structure, and decorated them with grotesques representing cherubs with a royal crown, as well as *rinceaux*, leaves and floral motifs on the upper body.

COLUMN
[LEFT] Museo Pedro de Osma, Lima - Peru.
17TH century.
Height: 136 cm.
Maximum diameter: 60 cm.

COLUMN
[RIGHT] Private collection, Cusco.
16TH – 17TH centuries
Height: 240 cm.

There is a Mannerist-Baroque pair of columns of singular beauty in a remarkable private collection in the city of Cusco. They are currently decorative pieces of furniture which in the past must have formed part of an altarpiece.

Made by anonymous artisans between the late 16TH and the early 17TH centuries [25], their style reveals strong Italian influences and a marked local flavour. The decorative elements were distributed with moderation, resulting from a fertile aesthetic exchange.

The upper body has a grooved shaft topped by Corinthian capitals; the lower has low-relief figurative carvings representing winged cherubs and cartouches containing anthropomorphic figures. Their ornamentation consists of light and dark green patinas, polychromes and gilding on a solid local wood.

There are some elements missing from these pieces.

In the art gallery of the Iglesia y Convento de Santo Domingo in the city of Cusco, there is a pair of Solomonic half-columns, which were sculpted by unknown artisans with an obvious Italian Baroque influence and South Andean inspiration. Such notable pieces may have been part of an altarpiece which was eventually dismantled.

[25] Interview of the author with Prof. Héctor Schenone in 2009.

Made from solid wood, they were profusely carved, forming anthropomorphic figures which were covered with gold leaf and polychrome. An acanthus leaf frieze divides the shaft into two bodies, a detail repeated on a base which is turned to form smooth circles. Figures and faces of children with headdresses and crowns, as well as local plant motifs, are distributed all over the surface. These columns are in very good condition, since they have been restored recently.

In a private Cusco collection, there is a magnificent *mestizo* Baroque tabernacle, monstrance or prayer niche possibly built during the 17TH century by a master carver, and gold leafed by a gilder; both artisans were probably indigenous.

This is a liturgical container which was used for storing the ciborium and consecrated hosts; it was generally placed on the centre of altars.

The piece has a pair of front doors flanked by half-columns; the doors and sides are divided into two panels, which are separately decorated. The tabernacle is topped by a diminished arch placed on a projecting frieze and rests on an interesting socket. It has a barrel vault inside. Another decorative motif consists of a fine pearl frieze framing the perimeter of each central design, which contains European Baroque elements.

Made from local wood, the piece is gilded, carved and polychromed. Its hinges are made from iron.

There is some gilding and polychrome missing, some of which has obviously been replaced.

There is a throne for a religious image or icon exhibited in one of the Salas Brazzini of the Basílica Catedral de Lima's Museo de Arte Religioso. It is an ecclesiastical piece of furniture made in the late Baroque style which was in vogue in the Viceroyalty of Peru well into the 18TH century. It is small, but of adequate size to enthrone a richly dressed image of the Infant Jesus.

Much can be said about its features. Its backrest boasts a superb oval crest rail, and the moulding consists of several friezes inlaid with glass paste. In the centre, a child's face is surrounded by ornaments.

The curved arms end in carved cherubs; the four legs have a marked inward curve and are connected by an H-shaped crossbar with complimenting waves which curve upward from the centre, matching the decoration on the

arms. All these details are a true display of luxury and exquisite taste. Maintaining the characteristic symmetry of this style, the creator of the piece arranged the decorative motifs across the entire surface. These motifs include mascarons, cherubs, doves on acanthus leaves carved on the arms of the piece, stars in the sky, hunting scenes, birds, horns of plenty and plant elements.

The materials and techniques used consisted of: a flat-carved wood structure largely covered with gold leaf, and an eglomise (glass painted on the reverse) mirror, which creates the feeling of standing in front of a piece with Venetian inspiration; a fact which, once again, highlights the strong influence of Italian art in these distant lands.

The wood has also been polychromed, turned and fretted. Both seat and backrest are upholstered in red velvet, which has probably been replaced. The piece is in very good condition, which reveals that it has been treated carefully.

The glass cabinet hanging in parlour Nº 1 of the Real Monasterio de Clarisas de Santa María de Gracia, in Trujillo, was made by anonymous Trujillo artisans in *mestizo* Baroque style with Italian influences.

The piece is a rectangular utilitarian container for ecclesiastical or secular use in which symmetry predominates; it is useful for displaying religious images or ornaments.

The great cresting is decorated using subtle curves with straight terminals on both sides; there are two glass doors on the front, and it ends in a carved and fretted apron.

This gilded and polychromed wood piece is ornamented with corbels, leaves,

**FRONT HALF COLUMN**
[OPPOSITE PAGE, TOP] Museo de la Iglesia y Convento de Santo Domingo, Cusco.
Height: 240 cm.

**TABERNACLE, MONSTRANCE**
[OPPOSITE PAGE, BOTTOM] Private collection, Cusco.
Height: 100 cm. Width: 80 cm.

**THRONE FOR IMAGE**
[RIGHT] Full view.
[TOP] Arm detail.
Museo de Arte Religioso of the Basílica Catedral de Lima.
18TH century.
Height: 71.5 cm. Width: 36 cm.
Depth: 45 cm.

flowers, cherubs and perimeter friezes on each panel. It is in very good condition.

In the aisle leading towards the sacristy of the Basílica Catedral de Lima, there is a pair of beautiful candlesticks which belong to the Archdiocese of Lima and are part of the liturgical utensils necessary for religious services. These candlesticks were made by unknown craftsmen in Andean Baroque style, probably in the 18TH century.

They consist of metal sockets for one candle, supported by a central rectilinear shaft which rests on three eagle-headed figures placed on a pedestal that, in turn, is held by three legs in the shape of claws.

The candlesticks are typical examples of local production, made from carved and turned solid wood, on which vermilion patinas alternate with the contrasting glitter of gold and quicksilver. They are in very good condition.

In the chapel of the Salas Brazzini, in the Basílica Catedral de Lima's Museo de Arte Religioso, there is a great candlestick for liturgical use. It used to belong to the important collection of the Auxiliary Bishop, Monsignor Alberto Brazzini Díaz Ufano[26].

This candlestick cannot be accurately dated: it should be emphasised that these types of pieces were made and decorated in a similar manner until the late 18TH century. This particular piece was made by anonymous school artisans, probably from Cusco, with distinctive Andean Baroque features which also reveal an Italian influence.

It is a torch holder, useful for special celebrations, such as the Mass on Easter Sunday. It consists of a central bulb-shaped shaft with soft, harmonious curves, which rests on a socket split into four, ending in bun feet.

Made from local wood, its structure was covered with red patinas; carvings were enhanced with gold leaf and the background was gilded. Its decoration consists of subtle carvings with little volume representing plant motifs, such as leaves and canes, as well as neat and symmetrical curves. There are fine pearls around its neck and on the base, dividing the composition.

[26] Lohmann Villena, Guillermo *et al. La Basílica Catedral de Lima.* Colección Arte y Tesoros del Perú. Lima: Banco de Crédito del Perú, 2004, p. 342.

**GLASS DISPLAY**
[OPPOSITE PAGE, TOP]
Real Monasterio de Clarisas
de Santa María de Gracia, Trujillo.
Height: 110 cm. Width: 125 cm.
Depth: 16.5 cm.

**CANDLESTICK**
[OPPOSITE PAGE, BOTTOM]
Basílica Catedral de Lima.
Height: 75 cm. Width: 30 cm.

**LARGE CANDLESTICK**
[LEFT] Museo de Arte Religioso
of the Basílica Catedral de Lima.
Donated by Auxiliary Bishop Monsignor
Alberto Brazzini Díaz Ufano.
Height: 149 cm. Base width: 46 cm.

**FLOOR LECTERN**
[RIGHT]
Monasterio de El Carmen, Trujillo.
Height: 137 cm. Width: 71 cm.
Depth: 62 cm.

On the high altar of the Monasterio de El Carmen Chapel, in the city of Trujillo, there is an interesting floor lectern which is part of the liturgical furniture of the Discalced Carmelites Order.

It was made in Trujillo in a Spanish-American late Baroque style with a Cusco influence. Its central shaft, in the shape of a Solomonic column, holds the oblique book rest, which is used to support the missal. It rests on a socket decorated with four fretted and carved panels and four bun feet.

This lectern was anonymously decorated with grape bunches, leaves, curves, and a strange zoomorphic head on its feet.

On the wood structure, other materials were used, including gold leaf and red (oxblood) patina as a background; carvings and fretting add a special flavour to the piece. It is in very good condition and seems to have been recently restored. It should be noted, however, that a shelf was added which was not in the original piece.

This pair of mirrors is located in Sala Nº 11, or Sala de los Espejos, at the Museo Arzobispal del Cusco. They form two magnificent and exuberantly decorated pieces, made in the characteristic Baroque style of the South Andean region which incorporates various craft specialities from Cusco.

They are square pieces with a silver mirror in the centre; the mirrors are small, as was usually the case in the 17TH century, and with remarkable carved moulding and several surrounding friezes.

Each frieze has rosettes contained within diamonds forming a striking central geometric frieze; the external frieze has acanthus leaves divided by elegant pearls.

The selected materials adapt themselves to the local hardwood structure, which is entirely covered in gold leaf and polychrome. A subtle volume was achieved by carving the wood or by means of *pastiglia*, an Italian technique for moulding and for gilding plaster.

The piece is in good condition, although some wood and gold leaf are missing from both pieces.

**MIRROR**
[LEFT]
Museo Arzobispal del Cusco.
Arzobispado del Cusco.
Height: 76 cm. Width: 71 cm.

**MIRROR**
[RIGHT]
Iglesia de la Sagrada Familia – Basílica Catedral del Cusco.
Arzobispado del Cusco.
Height: 100 cm. Width: 120 cm.

There is a set of mirrors in the nave of the Iglesia de la Sagrada Familia, which is adjacent to the Basílica Catedral del Cusco. These mirrors are extremely fine and have high aesthetic value. Designed for ecclesiastical use, their fundamental purpose was to multiply light, even though mirrors themselves were important ornamental objects of the time given their exceptional brilliance and elegance; this suggests that they were intentionally placed there.

A Baroque style is clearly revealed in their Italian morphology which, coupled with a local aesthetic expressiveness, defines the pieces, made with great skill by Cusco craftsmen, as a *mestizo* production.

The mirrors are rectangular and their elegant decoration was achieved by flat carving and fretting a solid wood base, which was subsequently gold leafed and partially polychromed.

They are decorated with multiple mouldings covered with symmetrically distributed plant motifs. The set is crowned by a central cartouche containing a religious monogram, with a scallop at the top.

Adorning the nave walls of the Iglesia de la Sagrada Familia, in the Basílica Catedral del Cusco, is a set of Spanish-American Baroque mirrors, the fruit of an unnamed creative impulse which drew on the Italian Baroque style for reference.

Cusco craftsmen took to their task in their usual way, applying their expertise to the smallest of details. These are ornamental pieces for both ecclesiastical and secular use, designed to increase lighting in any room. The small, oblong mirrors are framed by several mouldings.

MIRROR
Iglesia de la Sagrada Familia – Basílica Catedral del Cusco. Arzobispado del Cusco.

Their solid carved and fretted wood was treated with the *pastiglia* technique, creating a false stone-like effect. A gold leaf finish produces a tangible impression of elegance, common in these regions.

Curves and counter curves were used for decoration, as well as symmetrically arranged plant motifs; the pieces are topped by cartouches.

In the Iglesia de la Sagrada Familia, which is adjacent to the Basílica Catedral del Cusco, there is another set of mirrors, made in South Andean Baroque style and placed on the nave perimeter, alternating with the previously mentioned ones.

These decorative pieces are clear evidence of the luxury and pomp which prevailed in the Viceroyalty, both in the ecclesiastical and the secular world. They evidence the need to illuminate liturgical ceremonies and private drawing rooms.

Each piece consists of two bodies: an oblong mirror moulded with multiple friezes, both straight and curved, and another body crowned by motifs akin to those of the outer frieze, with a cartouche at the top and a mirror in the centre.

Their solid wood structure, covered with gold leaf, was carved and fretted to produce attractive ornamentation.

The small altar located in the Salas Brazzini of the Basílica Catedral de Lima's Museo de Arte Religioso was used for private services which took place in oratories or domestic chapels of ancestral homes during the colonial period. It was probably made in the late 17TH or early 18TH centuries.

**MIRROR**

[TOP] Iglesia de la Sagrada Familia – Basílica Catedral del Cusco.
Arzobispado del Cusco.

The altar belongs to the great collection of the Auxiliary Bishop, Monsignor Alberto Brazzini Díaz Ufano[27]. The front and sides of this piece are small and flat; its ornamentation is divided into three bays, those on the sides having six panels.

The piece has Italian Baroque decorative elements with local influences. A central coat of arms, rosettes, urns, *rinceaux*, curves and geometric shapes are contained within moulded central designs.

The materials and techniques used to build the altar were a carved local wood base with inlaid mirrors, covered with gold leaf. The piece is in excellent condition.

The high altar or predella in the altarpiece of Nuestra Señora del Rosario, in the Templo de Santo Domingo, Parroquia de San Pedro Mártir, city of Trujillo,

[27] Lohmann Villena, Guillermo *et al.* Op. cit., p. 342.

was built between the 17TH and 18TH centuries[28] (no accurate dating available) in Spanish American Baroque style.

The flat local wood front, distinctly ornamental, is covered with gold leaf and mirrors. This piece dazzles the observer as a magnificent example of Trujillo production with a marked Cusco influence.

The piece is decorated with abstract motifs and geometric shapes of various sizes distributed over the entire front. It is very well preserved.

The San Francisco Solano portable platform is permanently stored in the Sala de Andas of the Museo de Arte Religioso, Convento San Francisco y Catacumbas, in Lima. It is exhibited every July 16 in the central nave of the Church and

[28] González, Elena (ed). *Trazos del pasado: El período colonial en La Libertad.* Lima: Asociación Marsa, 2008, p. 53.

**DOMESTIC ALTAR**
Museo de Arte Religioso of the Basílica Catedral de Lima.
Donated by Auxiliary Bishop Monsignor Alberto Brazzini Díaz Ufano.
Height: 102 cm. Width: 160 cm. Depth: 67 cm.

Convent of San Francisco de Lima, Minor Basilica, in order to honour the patron saint[29]. It is a functional piece for ecclesiastical use, intended for supporting and transporting the religious image during the procession. It is made up of three bodies, one on top of the other, and some rods (new) for transport. The upper body is rounded and the lower ones, quadrangular. The saint's image rests on a polychrome half-sphere representing the sky, which is placed on acanthus leaves. It also has four flower vases at the corners.

The piece was built by anonymous craftsmen, possibly from Lima, in a Classicistic-Baroque style with an undeniable Italian mark. It was made in the 18TH century (c. 1732) for the solemn canonisation festivities of Saint Francis Solanum.

The platform is adorned by cartouches with polychrome reliefs illustrating different scenes from the life of the saint, and making up a narrative. These are surrounded by corbels, classical friezes, leaves, rosettes, spheres and garlands.

The solid wood structure, partially covered with gold leaf and polychrome,

**ALTAR FRONT**
[TOP] Templo de Santo Domingo, Parroquia de San Pedro Mártir, Trujillo. Height: 105 cm. Width: 290 cm.

**SAN FRANCISCO SOLANO PORTABLE PLATFORM**
[OPPOSITE PAGE] Sala de Andas in Museo de Arte Religioso of Convento San Francisco y Catacumbas, Lima. c. 1732.
Height: 130 cm. Width: 178 cm.
Front: 192 cm.

29 *"San Francisco de Asís" historical monuments.* Lima: [n.n.] [n.d.]

was ornamented using carving, half-relief carving, fretting, polychrome and gilding techniques. It is in very good condition.

In the Iglesia de San Pedro Mártir, Catedral de Juli, on the shore of Lake Titicaca in the middle of the Peruvian Altiplano, there is a portable processional platform which was likely made by artisans from Puno.

This piece is used for transporting devotional objects during processions. The pedestal is transported on the shoulders of four men, who keep it high in the air so it can be seen from a distance. These Christian rituals are some of the traditions the conquerors brought with them to these lands.

Made by anonymous craftsmen with Italian-inspired Baroque morphology, possibly during the 18TH century, it is a typical piece of Andean colonial art. It is a quadrangular platform divided into two bodies: the upper body is smaller than the lower one and they are supported by four rods.

The piece is made from gilded and carved solid wood where traces of polychrome are still noticeable. It has iron fittings.

The decorative elements, including rosettes, cartouches and plant motifs, are symmetrically arranged within geometric figures.

The piece currently belongs to the Prelature of Juli, Museo Religioso de San Pedro, in the Department of Puno, Province of Chucuito[30].

In the Chapterhouse of the Monasterio de Santa Teresa de Arequipa, there is an altar with an altarpiece of outstanding features which dominates the room[31].

[30] Data from the Departamento de Registro y Catalogación archives, INC Puno. Department of Puno-Peru.

[31] Carty, Charles L. *Arequipa, ciudad inolvidable.* Arequipa: [n.n.], 2008, p. 73.

**SAN FRANCISCO SOLANO PORTABLE PLATFORM**

[TOP] Detail.
Sala de Andas in Museo de Arte Religioso of Convento San Francisco y Catacumbas, Lima.
c. 1732.
Height: 130 cm. Width: 178 cm.
Front: 192 cm.

**PORTABLE PLATFORM**

[BOTTOM] Iglesia de San Pedro Mártir - Catedral de Juli, Puno.
Height: 206 cm. Width: 83 cm.
Depth: 82 cm.

The front of the altar is simple, square and made from flat bare wood, with a carved and gilded perimeter frame. In the centre, there is a coat of arms with the monogram of the Order.

The altarpiece, built in the 17TH century in Andean Baroque style, has a remarkable moulding around the image of Our Lady of Mount Carmel. This frame illustrates the creative impulse of the anonymous artists. Topping the piece, a projecting multifoil fretted comb stands out, teeming with beauty, like the sides, which were adorned in a similar manner with double friezes that imitate filigrees.

The piece is supported by a wide carved frieze or by *pastiglia* work of little

**ALTARPIECE**
Museo del Monasterio de Santa Teresa, Arequipa.
17TH century.
Height: 450 cm. Width: 450 cm.

volume. Each of its four panels is moulded in relief and ornamented with vases and plant motifs on the sides. Above the panels, there are corbels and sockets for the candles that illuminate the Virgin's image, which is exuberantly decorated, with the plants, pearls and eggs surrounding it.

Its carved, fretted and gilded wood has a unique shine. Clearly, the splendour of this magnificent piece aims to honour the Virgin.

It would not be wise to include altarpieces as elements of decorative or applied arts. It is the first and only time, however, an altarpiece is mentioned in this book, as the piece had such a profound impact on the author that she felt the need to include it as an example of skill and expressiveness.

The pulpit located in the nave of the Convento de Santo Domingo, in the city of Cusco, was built in 1656[32] in Spanish-American Baroque style by unknown artists. It is a piece of liturgical furniture which leans against the church wall. The piece has a hexagonal rostrum for the officiating priest to deliver the sermon and is located high on the side of the nave. There is a staircase for access. The rostrum is decorated with alcoves crowned by broken pediments and flanked by Solomonic columns —key elements of the Counter-Reformation discourse— alternating with little angels painted on mirrors. It is topped by a carved pineapple.

The sounding board glorifies the polychrome and moulded image of Saint Vincent Ferrer surrounded by a cluster of pinnacles and corbels. The image of Saint Augustine is represented on the backrest, crowned by a round arch and flanked by columns. Large rosettes adorn the staircase.

There are other elements which highlight the Italian inspiration of the piece, such as classical friezes, panels, plant motifs and symmetrical curves.

The upper image is highly volumetric; there are half-relief carvings on the backrest and some planimetric carvings in the surrounding decoration, all of which was designed on a Cusco cedar base. This highly artistic pulpit was further decorated with gold leaf, oil paintings and polychrome mirrors, resulting in a piece which inspired many sermons and is consistent with the evangelising vocation of the colonial period.

It is also worth mentioning that the shine of gold should be linked not only to Christian symbolism, but also to local beliefs.

It has been recently restored and is in very good condition.

**PULPIT**
Sounding board detail and full view.
Iglesia y Convento de Santo Domingo, Cusco.
1656.

[32] Bonet Correa, Antonio. *Monasterios Iberoamericanos.* [n.p.]: Ediciones El Viso, 2001, p. 138.

# VII

## BAROQUE STYLE FURNITURE

## INLAID WITH MOTHER-OF-PEARL AND TORTOISESHELL

Ecclesiastical and secular, ornamental and utilitarian use

LIMA, AREQUIPA, BUENOS AIRES AND NEW YORK

# VII

## HISTORY OF TRADE BETWEEN THE EAST AND THE AMERICAS

**BUREAU CABINET**
[OPENING] Cresting detail.
Palacio de Torre Tagle, Peruvian Ministry of Foreign Affairs, Lima.
c. 1740.
Donated by Doña Teresa Blondet de Cisneros.
Height: 245 cm. Width: 119 cm.
Depth: 54.5 cm.

**ALTAR FRONT**
[OPPOSITE PAGE] Panel detail.
Capilla de la Virgen del Carmen.
Museo de los Descalzos - Convento de los Franciscanos Descalzos, Rímac, Lima.
18TH century.
Height: 102 cm. Width: 292.2 cm.
Depth: 5 cm.

After the Spanish colonisation in 1571, the archipelago of the Philippines became a dependency of the Viceroyalty of New Spain: present day Mexico. Heavy maritime traffic then began to flow between Europe and the Far East through the Spanish-American colonies.

Manila, the capital of the archipelago, founded by the Spanish conqueror Miguel López de Legazpi, was essential for trade between Spain and the East. Thanks to its outstanding port, the city became a strategic hub for communication between the distant lands of India, China, Japan and the New World.

The city grew into an important port for trade, enabling regular and uninterrupted trips between Manila and Acapulco for two and a half centuries (1571-1815). Chinese junks and Japanese ships would easily arrive in the harbour, all of them loaded with precious goods.

These coveted trade items, scarce or nonexistent in other parts of the world, drew much attention to the Metropolis. For this reason, Chinese and Japanese merchants accumulated great quantities of goods over the years in huge warehouses, known to the Spaniards as the Sanglay market and Japanese market. These were two independent and unconnected markets, from which precious goods were shipped twice a year in Spanish-flagged vessels; an event that involved the entire city of Manila.

The "Manila Galleons" or "Nao de China" were Spanish vessels which sailed from Manila to Acapulco, taking three to six months to complete the trip.

This journey was referred to as "the Route to Asia" or "the Pacific of the

Iberians", and crossed the "Spanish Lake", as the Pacific Ocean was then known. The network of Spanish-American ports suitable for trade on the Atlantic Ocean included Havana, Veracruz, Nombre de Dios (later Portobelo) and Cartagena de Indias, while on the Pacific lay Acapulco, Panama and El Callao.

From Acapulco, precious goods were transported by mule to the port of Veracruz to be shipped to Seville. These Spanish ships carried in their holds all kinds of goods which had a decisive influence on Western taste.

A strategic alliance forged in the 16TH century between Spain and Portugal facilitated the defence of their commercial fleets from Dutch and English pirate attacks within their region of influence. Under the Treaty of Tordesillas, Portugal monopolised the passage around southern Africa, forcing Spain to use alternative maritime routes.

The Manila Galleons transported silver bullion or coins with the portrait of the King of Spain to the East in order to pay for the luxury goods produced and offered in those distant locations. On their journey (*tornaviaje*) the ships carried many luxury Asian products that would be traded in the metropolis via the Viceroyalty of New Spain, for example, spices, pearls, silk, ivory, ceramics, East India Company porcelain, screens and furniture lacquered with *Namban* lacquer, from China and Japan; all of them surrounded by an aura of exoticism and secrecy.

Priests and monks of various religious orders also moved to these far-away destinations, as representatives of the Spanish Crown, to carry out their important evangelising mission; thereby justifying their presence.

There is evidence of migration from Japan to the coasts of Peru in the 17TH century. A few people from Japan settled in Lima from 1607. *The 1613 census, carried out in Lima to register Indians, and Asians were considered as such, revealed a total of twenty Japanese, who were called "japonex" ... (Del Busto 1989).*

*The Japanese who arrived in Peru during this period came from the Philippine Islands. At that time Japan had close ties with Manila [...]. Some of them had been enslaved by the Portuguese [...] in Lima they became free. Some had been born in Japan, but others, in Goa (India) of Japanese parents or grandparents*[1].

Most likely, over time, some of them would become craftsmen and carpenters trained in the decorative technique of *Namban* lacquer, developed in Japan. Later, they would pass their skills to Creole and native craftsmen.

---

[1] Fukumoto, Mary. "Migración japonesa al Perú". *Boletín de Lima.* 1998, year 20, vol. XX, N° 114, p. 81.

**CHEST**
[LEFT AND RIGHT] Detail of the front and the decoration inside the lid.
Museo Nacional de Arte Decorativo, Buenos Aires.
Origin: Japan.
Late 16TH or early 17TH century.
Height: 78 cm. Width: 159 cm.
Depth: 60.4 cm.

## HISTORY OF THE LACQUER ARRIVING FROM THE EAST: *NAMBAN* LACQUER, A JAPANESE TECHNIQUE WHICH INSPIRED AMERICAN INLAID FURNITURE

While the lacquer technique used to decorate everyday and ornamental pieces originated in China, it arrived in Japan as early as the 7TH century AD. It attained a high degree of technical and artistic development during the Momoyama period (1573-1615).

In the 16TH century, trade between East and West resulted, among other things, in the birth of a hybrid Japanese artistic movement called "*Namban* Art" (*Namban* meaning "Southern Barbarians", i.e. foreign), which appeared on pieces of furniture of European, mainly Spanish, morphology and style, made using Eastern materials and techniques.

This artistic style, which peaked between 1580 and 1624, was not reserved to the West: it also became popular in peripheral regions of the Far East. *This open and direct contact between Japan and Europe peaked for a short time until the government of Japan, jealous of and worried about the growing power and possessions of the Catholic Church, closed its borders to foreigners in 1639.*[2]

As these pieces of furniture were intended exclusively for the export market, their design differed from Eastern traditions.

The *Namban* style was characterised by the profuse decoration of a wood base with abundant mother-of-pearl inlay, as well as inlaid metals and exquisite woods, which were covered in clear lacquer.

Their use, secular and, occasionally, ecclesiastical, was unknown to the

---

[2] Kawamura Kawamura, Yayoi. "Obras de laca del arte *namban* de los Monasterios de la Encarnación y de las Trinitarias de Madrid". *Reales Sitios*, year XXXVIII, Nº 147, p. 3.

CHEST
Details of the decoration outside the lid and on the reverse.
Museo Nacional de Arte Decorativo, Buenos Aires.
Origin: Japan.
Late 16TH or early 17TH century.
Height: 78 cm. Width: 159 cm.
Depth: 60.4 cm.

Japanese craftsmen who made them to order for their new customers. Chests with roof-shaped or round-top lids, coffers, writing desks, *bargueños*, support tables, religious images, lecterns, frames and portable tabernacles were just some of the many pieces decorated with *Namban* lacquer.

This technique consisted of applying several layers of lacquer with monochrome pigments, especially black *urushi*, onto a very dry local wood base. Lacquer was dried in a warm and humid chamber called *furō*.

To achieve the desired shine, the surface was polished between layers with powdered charcoal, bone dust or fine sandpaper mixed with abundant water.

To the last *urushi* layer, while fresh, designs were applied which consisted of plant and mythological motifs, Eastern animals and geometric shapes; all of them contained within central designs of various shapes unknown to Eastern artistic traditions. For this purpose liquid gold and silver were mixed with sap, black lacquer was applied on the background and gold or silver paints were put on with a brush: a technique known as *maki-é*.

The ornamentation was completed with *raden*: pieces of inlaid mother-of-pearl cut into various shapes, forming friezes which framed the composition. With a Baroque distribution of elements, alien to Japanese aesthetics and sensitivity, fragments of mother-of-pearl were also applied forming leaves or other figurative motifs, and endowing the pieces with a dazzling splendour.

In order to create a colourful and contrasting palette, pieces were also inlaid with light or dyed woods. Occasionally metals were also applied, such as silver,

**CHEST**
Latch and side handle details.
Museo Nacional de Arte Decorativo, Buenos Aires.
Origin: Japan.
Late 16TH or early 17TH century.
Height: 78 cm. Width: 159 cm.
Depth: 60.4 cm.

tin, copper or bronze, creating an iridescent effect. A clear lacquer covering, or several layers of an oily and refined sap finish, completed the pieces; producing a hand polished effect on the surface.

It was usual for fittings, such as hinges, side handles and corner beads, to be made from engraved metal (bronze).

The technique and the external decoration could be repeated inside, where the same elements were chosen but not so profusely distributed.

This attempt to achieve just a visually rich ornamentation, without focusing on quality, in view of the limited time available for carrying out the work, resulted in *Namban* pieces made for the Americas often having fewer layers of lacquer than those produced for the Japanese market. This lack was made up for with the use of the oily sap mentioned above.

Ships from the British and Dutch East India companies also sailed the area, engaging in close and direct trade relations with Japan. This is the reason why pieces decorated with this technique are also found in England and the Netherlands.

Importantly, these types of pieces can currently be found in prestigious museums around the world, bearing witness to this short period when *Namban* furniture was produced.

There are examples of *Namban* furniture in the Museo de Artes Decorativas in Las Descalzas Reales; the Monasterio de la Encarnación in Madrid; the Museo Diocesano de Arte Sacro in Vitoria-Gasteiz; the Musée National des Arts

Asiatiques Guimet in Paris; the Kunsthistorisches Museum in Vienna; the Convento de Monjas Capuchinas, Castellón de la Plana, in Mexico City; and in the Toshiba Collection of the Victoria and Albert Museum in London.

In 1624, trade with Spain (Japan-Philippines) was banned by the Tokugawa Shogunate and for this reason the production of such precious furniture was discontinued.

CHEST
Full view and detail of the side.
Museo Nacional de Arte Decorativo, Buenos Aires.
Origin: Japan.
Late 16TH or early 17TH century.
Height: 78 cm. Width: 159 cm.
Depth: 60.4 cm.

## NAMBAN LACQUER PIECE LOCATED IN BUENOS AIRES

The chest in the Salón Renacimiento of the Museo Nacional de Arte Decorativo, Buenos Aires, under inventory Nº 1804, is a good example of a piece with the above morphological, stylistic and technical features.

It is an ornamental secular and utilitarian piece, made in the late 16TH or early 17TH century by anonymous Japanese craftsmen for the Western market.

It is a portable container with a roof-shaped or round-top lid, whose surfaces are all flat. It features a pair of side handles, four hinges, two European cases protecting the locks, and engraved-bronze corner beads.

The outer surface and the inside of the lid were decorated with *Namban* lacquer; motifs were applied to a flat base resting on an architectural and quartered composition in Baroque style. Inside the lid, the mother-of-pearl ornaments are not as abundant as on the outside.

The materials used for building and decorating the piece were a thin wood

base, fruit-tree woods for the ornamental details, black *urushi* lacquer, black lacquer with gold (*maki-e*) and mother-of-pearl on black lacquer (*raden*); all these elements are necessary for making a *Namban* piece.

The black-lacquer background is divided into panels by straight lines with geometric patterns. On the front are three symmetrically arranged multifoil central designs of identical size. The one in the centre contains a pair of birds, possibly cranes, which are messengers of good and luck in the East; these images are surrounded by profuse foliage. In the designs on the sides, fantastic lion-shaped animals are also surrounded by a background of plant motifs.

*BARGUEÑO*
Detail of the side.
Prado Heudebert family collection, Lima.
18TH century.

The outer side of the lid has a rhomboid in the centre, made from chained curves and straight lines. Five circles with stylised flowers lie in the centre and on the angles. A subtle floral background covers the outside of the rhomboid, surrounded by a perimeter frieze.

The profuse decoration of the piece reveals the *horror vacui* which was characteristic of these kinds of pieces. Although it has not been restored and some pieces are missing, it is in good condition.

### ORIENTAL SKILLS RELOCATED TO COASTAL PERU: INLAID FURNITURE

A combination of the traditions which travelled with the large migration flows from different places and arrived in the Viceroyalty of Peru, gave origin to wonderful pieces of furniture in local cabinetmaker's, carpenter's and assembly workshops… *Even if we include in the list the many "art intellectuals": religious and military men, or mere officials or neighbours who abundantly express their opinions and produce works in our cultural history, it is true that those people and most Creole artists were trained by the master…*[3] and can be considered skilful artisans.

The Eastern influence on coastal Peruvian and Mexican furniture began in the mid-17TH century with the arrival of Japanese craftsmen, either Christianised or not, who specialised in *Namban* lacquer. They brought with them their expertise in the use of lacquer in combination with mother-of-pearl and other materials. They provided training in these skills to European craftsmen from various backgrounds. Converted Muslims and natives, all of whom already had experience in the arts, quickly learned the technique and were thus able to plan, design

3 Gutiérrez, Ramón (coord). *Pintura, escultura y artes útiles en Iberoamérica, 1500-1825*. Colección Manuales Arte Cátedra. Madrid: Cátedra, 1995, p. 18.

and build luxurious pieces of furniture. These were called "inlaid" and replaced the *Namban* furniture of Japanese origin. Covered in mother-of-pearl and tortoiseshell —the latter replacing lacquer as a background— the pieces were made following different European typologies. Their construction and artistic quality were excellent, and they were later exported to the Viceroyalty of New Granada, now Ecuador, and the Pacific coast.

Comparing the Peruvian inlaid furniture with other pieces of furniture produced in the region, Peter Gjurinovic Canevaro states … *they are dramatically different from those made in Peru. Thus, it can be shown that, due to an Eastern influence, these inlaid pieces were developed with characteristics of their own in their respective countries*[4].

For these pieces, a strictly Baroque ornamentation was selected, in order to convey a strong feeling of opulence; the pieces also featured a distribution of elements that were alien to the Japanese style, which was slowly left behind.

The profuse decoration reveals the *horror vacui* that was characteristic of these kinds of pieces.

A preliminary sketch was drawn by craftsmen trained in the *Namban* lacquer technique, which they combined with their own artistic background of both Mudejar and indigenous roots, thus resulting in truly Peruvian pieces of furniture rich in cultural symbiosis.

It is worth noting the natural inclination of the Arab craftsmen living in the Viceroyalty of Peru to abstract motifs, which were key to their style and distinctive of their way of viewing art. Those motifs are also seen in the geometric transformation of ornaments, friezes and ribbons, which appear repeatedly, reflecting a Spanish influence, typical of Spanish-Mudejar furniture.

The predesigned sketch was transferred to the flat sides of the wood structure, which were inlaid with tortoiseshell as a background, small polished fragments of mother-of-pearl and, occasionally, artistically arranged ivory or bone details. The highly contrasting colours of these materials were combined creating a refined and appealing effect, as each detail was fully highlighted.

The work was completed with turned solid wood forming balusters or half-round mouldings which divided the pieces into bodies and bays or crowned them producing suggestive architectural effects.

**CHEST OF DRAWERS**
[OPPOSITE PAGE, TOP LEFT]
Detail of religious image on the front.
Museo Pedro de Osma, Lima - Peru.
18TH century.
Height: 219 cm. Width: 175 cm.
Depth: 61 cm.

**WARDROBE**
[OPPOSITE PAGE, TOP RIGHT]
Cresting detail.
Doña Marita de la Peña Prado's collection, Lima.
18TH century.

**CHEST OF DRAWERS**
[OPPOSITE PAGE, BOTTOM LEFT]
Religious image detail.
Prado Heudebert family collection, Lima.
18TH century.
Height: 199 cm. Width: 196 cm.
Depth: 57 cm.

**TABLE TOP LECTERN**
[OPPOSITE PAGE, BOTTOM RIGHT]
Detail of religious monogram.
Museo Pedro de Osma, Lima - Peru.
Height: 29 cm. Width: 32 cm.
Depth: 23 cm.

**THRONE FOR IMAGE**
[BOTTOM] Detail of religious monogram.
Private collection, Lima.
Height: 31 cm. Width: 26.8 cm.
Depth: 16.5 cm.

4 Tord, Luis Enrique and Gjurinovic, Pedro. *El Palacio de Torre Tagle y las casonas de Lima.* Lima: Asociación de Funcionarios del Servicio Diplomático del Perú, 2010, p. 205.

Quite often, a small religious image, which was oil-painted on a copper or wood base, was placed on the front. Since this detail was an object for domestic devotion, it was placed on the main bay of the piece, in an alcove topped by a pediment and surrounded by elements imitating architectural fronts with columns, arches, balusters, etc.

The different types of furniture were designed on the basis of the Spanish tradition, with the aim of meeting the local market demands. In institutions and private collections, there is a great variety of inlaid furniture for domestic use, such as chests of drawers, with their matching bases or several bodies, one on top of the other, as well as wardrobes, coffers, *bargueños*, chests with roof-shaped lids, work tables, general tables and frames for artworks.

With regard to the small number of ecclesiastical pieces found, it is worth mentioning altar fronts, table top lecterns, thrones for holding religious images or icons, and small chests or chrismatories: liturgical elements for exhibiting religious symbols.

The inlay technique was enthusiastically adopted in Peru, as a result of a trend which began in the late 17TH century and lasted until the late 18TH century; this technique was emblematic of the luxury furniture of the time and very expensive indeed. The technique was strictly intended for decorating parlours of the most important houses in Lima. It consisted of the use of various shades of mother-of-pearl (also called nacre) alternating with tortoiseshell, on a solid wood base, usually mahogany —a high-quality American wood with a close grain and a shine of its own— which was often partially exposed. The work was completed by applying thin layers of clear lacquer.

Tortoiseshell replaced the dark lacquer traditionally used as a background in Japanese pieces. The thin mother-of-pearl was cut into oval, circular or square fragments, which were selected in order to execute a predetermined design and to cover the gaps in the piece, creating iridescent effects. Thus, the decorated surface turned out to be perfectly smooth and flat. This led to repeated and continuous patterns representing nature through stylised phytomorphic motifs, which were framed by successive friezes.

Nacre and tortoiseshell were at hand due to the abundance of large turtles from the Peruvian Amazon, such as the Charapa turtle, *Podocnemis expansa*, among the largest in South America, whose shell can measure up to 70 cm, or the

**CENTRE TABLE**
[TOP] Detail of the top.
Palacio de Torre Tagle, Peruvian Ministry of Foreign Affairs, Lima.
18TH century.
Height: 77 cm. Diameter: 64 cm.

**COFFER**
[BOTTOM, LEFT AND RIGHT] Details of silver lock and reverse with silver hinges.
Museo de Arte Hispanoamericano Isaac Fernández Blanco, Buenos Aires.
Formerly, in Don Martín Noel's collection.
18TH century.
Height: 22 cm. Width: 43.5 cm.
Depth: 33.5 cm.

**COFFER**
[TOP LEFT] Detail of silver leg.
Museo de Arte Hispanoamericano Isaac Fernández Blanco, Buenos Aires.
Formerly, in Don Martín Noel's collection.
18TH century.
Height: 30.5 cm. Width: 55.5 cm.
Depth: 29 cm.

**COFFER**
[TOP RIGHT] Silver latch detail.
Prado Heudebert family collection, Lima.
17TH - 18TH centuries
Height: 24 cm. Width: 92 cm.
Depth: 49 cm.

**BUREAU CABINET**
[BOTTOM] Silver hinge detail.
Palacio de Torre Tagle, Peruvian Ministry of Foreign Affairs, Lima.
Donated by Doña Teresa Blondet de Cisneros.
c. 1740.
Height: 245 cm. Width: 119 cm.
Depth: 54.5 cm.

Brazilian giant tortoise, *Geochelone denticulata*, with a shell up to 82 cm.[5] Therefore, these species were likely used as key materials for decorating inlaid furniture. The Pacific coast and the fresh water of certain rivers provided the mother-of-pearl used to complete the decoration.

Depending on the period, and in order to improve the whole piece, the hinges, locks, latches, cases, keyholes, corner beads and legs of the most luxurious pieces were made from engraved silver, with Baroque or Rococo ornamentation in prominent places.

There were great differences between the inner and outer decoration. In many cases differing materials and techniques were chosen, creating a contrasting effect which was noticeable on opening a lid or door. Sometimes, the inside would display geometric marquetry, created with various fruit tree or dyed woods, or would be covered with Chinese or Japanese lacquers, like the magnificent piece found in Museo de Arte Hispanoamericano Isaac Fernández Blanco, in Buenos Aires, Argentina.

## INLAID ECCLESIASTICAL FURNITURE

It is worth mentioning some pieces found in Lima which were used as liturgical furnishings, such as small inlaid table-top lecterns or thrones for holding

5 Vogt, Richard C. *Tortugas amazónicas.* Lima: Gráfica Biblos, 2008, pages 8 and 90.
Wust, Walter. *Guía de identificación de especies de la flora y la fauna del Perú.* Lima: Peisa, 2003.

religious images or icons. These pieces were made in the Lima Baroque style. The lecterns have front and side aprons and rest on four bun or bracket feet which add a touch of luxury to the piece.

In addition to the usual Baroque decoration, those pieces would display in the centre the monogram of Jesus or the Virgin Mary, an ecclesiastical coat of arms or a double-headed eagle, the imperial symbol.

In the Museo de los Descalzos, Convento de los Franciscanos Descalzos, Rímac, in the city of Lima, there is an exceptional inlaid altar front with an obvious Eastern influence.[6] Made in the 18TH century, it has the magnificence of a unique piece.

The altar front has a refined Lima Baroque style; it is flat, with three front panels divided by perimeter friezes and mouldings. Stylised flowers and leaves decorate each panel, and are placed into central designs surrounded by friezes; urns and geometric figures complete the composition.

Anonymous artisans produced it on a wood base, where a background of tortoiseshell was inlaid with mother-of-pearl.

The piece is in delicate condition, since some elements are missing.

The table top lectern exhibited at the Museo Pedro de Osma, in the city of Lima, is a good example of a liturgical book holder. It has an oblique supporting

[6] Bernales Ballesteros, Jorge. *Lima, la ciudad y sus monumentos.* Seville: Consejo Superior de Investigaciones Científicas, Escuela de Estudios Hispano-Americanos de Sevilla, 1972, p. 212.

**TABLE TOP LECTERN**
[OPPOSITE PAGE, TOP LEFT]
Museo Pedro de Osma, Lima - Peru.
18TH century.
Height: 29 cm. Width: 32 cm.
Depth: 23 cm.

**TABLE TOP LECTERN**
[OPPOSITE PAGE, TOP RIGHT]
Museo de Arte Religioso of the Basílica Catedral de Lima.
18TH century.
Height: 37 cm. Width: 35 cm.
Depth: 23 cm.

**TABLE TOP LECTERN**
[OPPOSITE PAGE, BOTTOM]
Museo de Arte Religioso of the Basílica Catedral de Lima.
18TH century.
Height: 30 cm. Width: 33 cm.
Depth: 23 cm.

**ALTAR FRONT**
[BOTTOM] Capilla de la Virgen del Carmen.
Museo de los Descalzos - Convento de los Franciscanos Descalzos, Rímac, Lima.
18TH century.
Height: 102 cm. Width: 292.2 cm.
Depth: 5 cm.

structure and an apron with a decorative cartouche. The piece rests on four Baroque bun feet.

In the centre, there is a cartouche within a circle which contains the monogram of the Society of Jesus. The surrounding decoration consists of scales and other stylised elements.

The mother-of-pearl and tortoiseshell covering all the faces are obvious evidence of Japanese influence.

Another pair of table top lecterns, magnificent pieces designed to hold liturgical books, is located in the Museo de Arte Religioso of the Basílica Catedral de Lima[7].

One of them is crowned with a fretted pediment, which is decorated on both sides with winding volutes and rests on four legs. The piece is decorated with a double-headed eagle on the central cartouche, a profusion of surrounding foliage and a frieze framing and containing them. Its key features include symmetry as a predominant Baroque element, and soberly arranged undulating curves.

The Japanese inspiration is revealed in the wood base inlaid with mother-of-pearl and, to a lesser extent, tortoiseshell.

---

[7] Lohmann Villena, Guillermo *et al. La Basílica Catedral de Lima*. Colección Arte y Tesoros del Perú. Lima: Banco de Crédito del Perú, 2004, p. 340.

This inlaid table-top lectern, part of a private collection in Lima, was made by unknown craftsmen, probably in the 18TH century. It has the morphology of a table-top holder for liturgical books, having an oblique supporting structure, a top crown and undulating sides.

For its Baroque ornamentation, the symbol of Our Lady of the Seven Sorrows was selected: a heart pierced by seven swords, surrounded by stylised flowers and leaves. It was made from wood and its decoration was finished with mother-of-pearl and tortoiseshell details. Some parts are missing and the piece is in need of restoration.

There is a suggestive throne for holding a religious image or icon which belongs to the same Lima private collection. It is an ecclesiastical piece; a small holder used to enthrone the image of the Infant Jesus.

Possibly made in Lima, it is decorated with Baroque motifs. The monogram of Jesus is placed in the centre of the backrest, surrounded by flowers and other elements. It also has straight quadrangular arms and legs, the latter ending in spheres.

**TABLE TOP LECTERN**
[LEFT] Private collection, Lima.
18TH century.
Height: 40 cm. Width: 40 cm.
Depth: 24 cm.

**THRONE FOR IMAGE**
[RIGHT] Private collection, Lima.
Height: 31 cm. Width: 26.8 cm.
Depth: 16.5 cm.

This piece was inlaid with tortoiseshell on a wood base and has very fine mother-of-pearl details. It is in good condition.

## INLAID FURNITURE FOR SECULAR USE: ORNAMENTAL, UTILITARIAN AND FOR DOMESTIC DEVOTION

The wide variety of furniture for secular use —both ornamental and utilitarian— which was decorated with the inlay technique includes coffers, chests, *bargueños*, side and coffeecentre tables, work tables, jewellery boxes, foot rests, large wardrobes, dressers with several bodies, glass cabinets and bureau-cabinets.

The materials used were the same as those for ecclesiastical furniture, i.e., onto a wood base, a mother-of-pearl layer was applied and combined with fragments of tortoiseshell, ebony or ebonised wood (darkened wood imitating ebony). Ivory was occasionally used on decorative details. The supporting structure was made from local woods, such as mahogany, walnut or Nicaraguan cedar, and the pieces would have silver fittings.

On the front of certain pieces, in the most prominent places, or inside the lid, there were one or several religious images oil-painted on a wood or copper base. These are deeply symbolic details which emphasise the religious devotion of the original owners of the pieces. The number of images would vary according to the piece size and number of bodies.

An exceptional chest of drawers decorated with the inlay technique was made in the 18TH century in Baroque style. It used to be a household item in Don Felipe Pardo y Aliaga's [8] old manor; nowadays, it is part of the artistic heritage of the Museo Pedro de Osma in Lima.

This large container has three detachable bodies, the upper two resting on the lower. The arches on the supporting structure have six legs in the shape of paired Solomonic columns which rest on crosspieces and end in bun feet.

The irregular front is divided into five panels by Solomonic columns; it has multiple drawers, six on each side, and a central alcove on each body. All these elements obviously reveal a Mudejar influence on this stunning piece. Each alcove contains an oil-painted religious image.

Both upper bodies are crowned by a fretted perimeter gallery and an upper

---

[8] Tord, Luis Enrique and Gjurinovic, Pedro. Op. cit., pages 204-205.
Fundación Pedro y Angélica de Osma Gildemeister. *Museo Pedro de Osma.* Lima: [n.n.], 2004, pages 176-177.
Rishel, Joseph J. and Stratton-Pruitt, Suzanne (eds). *Revelaciones: Las artes en América Latina 1492-1820.* Mexico D.F.: Fondo de Cultura Económica, 2007, p. 498.

cornice decorated with scrolls and divided by pinnacles. *Rinceaux*, curves, arabesques, *kantutas* (the national flower) and other natural elements, contained within curves interlaced with straight lines, as well as floral friezes, appear repeatedly on the front mouldings of drawers.

This is a reinterpretation of the use of *Namban*, an example of syncretism in a piece of inlaid furniture made in the Americas by local artisans using Japanese techniques. Thanks to the unprecedented expressiveness achieved by the careful use of mother-of-pearl, tortoiseshell, oil painting and imperceptible iron fittings, it became an ornamental inlaid piece designed to stand out as a work of art in important Lima parlours.

This magnificent Lima Baroque chest of drawers is a secular container; its two bodies match the table on which they rest. It was anonymously made in the 18TH century and belongs to the Prado Heudebert family collection, in the city of Lima. Its general appearance reveals a marked Eastern influence; its structure and ornamentation, however, show an Europeanising Baroque spirit.

CHEST OF DRAWERS
Museo Pedro de Osma, Lima - Peru.
18TH century.
Height: 219 cm. Width: 175 cm.
Depth: 61 cm.

The stacked bodies are divided into three sections, one central and two oblique ones at the sides, divided by columns. The upper body is crowned by alternating pinnacles and fretted pediments. The table, designed ad hoc to complete the work, rests on four legs turned in the shape of a rosary and connected by crosspieces.

The upper body has four drawers on the front, while the lower, between a set of drawers, has a central alcove with an oil-painted image of Jesus framed by a round arch and flanked by columns: evidence of the religious fervour of Lima society of the time.

Stylised plants, including *kantuta*, are some of the motifs selected for the decoration of this chest, as well as octagonal shapes with a distinct volume arranged on the sides. All the elements of the piece are distributed symmetrically.

The materials for building this unparalleled luxury piece and decorating it with the inlay technique include a mahogany base, blackened wood, large amounts of mother-of-pearl, tortoiseshell for the background, and iron for the hinges. The piece is in very good condition.

There is a superb three-bodied piece in the remarkable Don Juan Luis de Aliaga's private collection, located in the house which used to be Don Jerónimo de Aliaga's ancestral home, in the historic centre of Lima.[9] The richness, quality

9 Arrarte, Eduardo R. *et al. Casa Solariega de Aliaga.* Lima: Stimulus, 2004, p. 44.

and functionality define the piece as a strictly ornamental container.

It has an architectural structure, with three sides divided by columns. There is a spacious glass display on the lower body, which is larger than the others. In the upper bodies, there are many drawers, some of them hidden, and a central alcove where a religious image is exhibited.

The cresting is profusely decorated with fretwork, a decorative detail which suffices to link this piece to Mudejar art. The upper cornice is inlaid and fretted, as is the rest of the piece, and divided by fluted columns and turned wood pilasters.

The piece is supported by a socket which rests on four bun feet.

Although it was made in the early 18TH century, the arrangement of elements is Baroque. Its most significant motifs are phytomorphic and Mudejar geometric shapes; these motifs are flat and symmetrically arranged.

The piece is mostly adorned with the inlay technique, which gives it a superb appearance. A volumetric moulding with small undulations, as well as columns and capitals, divide the sides.

CHEST OF DRAWERS
Full view and detail of the side.
Prado Heudebert family collection, Lima.
18TH century.
Height: 199 cm. Width: 196 cm.
Depth: 57 cm.

The Virgin's image in the central alcove was painted in oils on a flat base. This detail demonstrates once again the religious fervour in the City of Kings during the colonial period.

The artisans who made the piece remain unknown. They used solid wood and decorated it with ebony or blackened wood, which was inlaid with mother-of-pearl and ivory. The piece also has bronze details. The glass display on the lower body has three moulded-glass sides to showcase ornaments.

After 1929, Ayres Maia Montero purchased in London this magnificent and luxurious four-drawer cabinet, built in Lima for secular use. The piece was inherited by his son, Roberto Maia Montero, born in Petrópolis, Rio de Janeiro. In 2004, its current owners, Roberta and Richard Huber, acquired it from Notus Art LLC, an antique shop in New York City, to increase and enrich their magnificent private collection.[10] This ornamental piece, whose magnificence and impressive features used to adorn some Lima drawing room, is now part of the remarkable Huber collection in the United States, which is specialised in

[10] Stratton-Pruitt, Suzanne and Castro Mark A. (eds). *Journeys to New Worlds. Spanish and Portuguese Colonial Art in the Roberta and Richard Huber Collection.* Philadelphia Museum of Art, 2013, pages 190-191.

THREE-BODIED PIECE / GLASS DISPLAY
Don Juan Luis de Aliaga's collection, Lima.
18TH century.

CABINET
[OPPOSITE PAGE] Roberta and Richard Huber's collection, New York.
Mid-18TH century.
Width: 100 cm. Height: 53 cm.
Depth: 33 cm.

Iberoamerican art (Spain, Portugal and their colonies). It is showcased in the Journeys to New Worlds exhibition in an annex to the Philadelphia Museum of Art: the Perelman Building.

Its date is uncertain and the subject of discussions within the academic world, but the piece was likely made in the mid-18TH century, as many others, since the mother-of-pearl inlay trend was in vogue throughout that century in the City of Kings, where skilful local artisans mastered the technique.

It is a rectilinear container divided into three sections, one central and two oblique ones on the sides, which rest on four bun feet. On the front, four drawers of various shapes and sizes, with keyholes, are flanked by two detached columns supported by dadoes.

An emphatic Baroque language can be observed in its architectural structure, a characteristic of the style, in its orderly and symmetrical ornamentation —with every element arranged as dictated by the style—, and in the materials and techniques used, revealing European and Eastern influences in similar proportions.

All the above elements highlight, once again, that this artistic style remained in vogue in coastal furniture.

**CABINET**
Drawer detail.
Roberta and Richard Huber's collection, New York.
Mid-18TH century.
Width: 100 cm. Height: 53 cm.
Depth: 33 cm.

The four drawers, surrounded by mouldings, display repeated patterns of phytomorphic motifs and subtle geometrical friezes. The shaft of both columns is ornamented with swirling leaves; the supporting dadoes reveal delicate rosettes. The drawer in the lower body has central flower and leaf branches extending towards the sides. Decorations on the sides are Mudejar in style, i.e., abstract motifs were applied.

There is nothing as subtle and refined as the mother-of-pearl inlay technique for creating the desired iridescent effects. To that end, thin fragments of nacre were inlaid in a tortoiseshell background creating an extremely beautiful contrast, highlighted with elegant silver dots on the traditional *kantuta* calyx. This luxurious set rests on a fine carved frieze with tenuous undulations made from solid bare wood.

It is in excellent condition. According to the owners of the piece, this chest only required minor restorations for the exhibition.

A wardrobe built with the characteristic Baroque splendour of the 18TH century, at the height of the inlaid furniture trend, is part of Doña Marita de la Peña Prado's important Peruvian collection.

The hexagonal shape of the piece, the two front doors, together with the remarkable fretted cresting, all of them resting on an essential socket, are the most noteworthy structural features.

The piece is a container decorated with a double-headed eagle, centred on the outstanding upper pediment where an oil painting depicts the Sacred Heart surrounded by fretted ribbons.

It has a symmetrical and profuse ornamentation on three faces, where geometric shapes frame leaf and flower motifs, a syncretic merger of Eastern, Mudejar and Spanish influences, and a valuable example of Lima's anonymous production.

The piece consists of a base made from exquisite woods, including mahogany, which were inlaid with mother-of-pearl, tortoiseshell and ivory. It is in excellent condition.

In the Sala de los Tratados of Palacio de Torre Tagle, in the city of Lima, there is an example of Lima inlaid furniture known as bureau-cabinet, whose quality is remarkable. It was a generous donation made in 1978 by Doña Teresa Blondet

**WARDROBE**
Doña Marita de la Peña Prado's collection, Lima.
18$^{TH}$ century.

de Cisneros in memory of her husband, Don Manuel Cisneros Sánchez, who had acquired it.[11]

Its structure has English influences which are characteristic of the period we are dealing with: the mid-18TH century. The piece alludes to the Rococo style enthusiastically adopted in Lima under Bourbon influence (see chapters IX and X).

The piece consists of two bodies: the upper has two front doors, drawers and small shelves —*cartonnier*— inside, while the lower is a container desk (a bureau) with three large bottom drawers and an oblique lid resting on them. The piece is supported by flat bracket front legs and straight rear legs.

The outside of the piece is completely inlaid with an almost white covering of scale-shaped mother-of-pearl, filleted with light coloured wood. It has fine engraved silver fittings.

The inside of the upper part is fully covered with marquetry panels and decorated with diamond shapes made from different shades of fine woods and forming a geometric pattern.

It is crowned by a remarkable fretted cresting, with a double-headed eagle at the centre, flanked by fretted *rinceaux* on the front and on the side combs. The piece has been recently restored and is in very good condition.

In the Sala Buenos Aires capital del Virreinato, at the Museo de Arte Hispanoamericano Isaac Fernández Blanco, city of Buenos Aires, there is a coffer which was part of the collection of architect Martín Noel, a great collector of American colonial art who spent long periods in Lima throughout the 20TH century building what would later become the Argentine Embassy in Peru.

The technical features of this ornamental piece of furniture are similar to those of the abovementioned piece in Palacio de Torre Tagle, in Lima. Both pieces were made in Lima, in the mid-18TH century, by unknown craftsmen. It could be inferred that they are connected and were made in the same workshop.[12]

This particular coffer is a small container, with an upper lid and a front lock, and has a side drawer. It rests on four claw-shaped legs made from engraved silver.

The external decoration, with a distinct Japanese influence, was the result of applying the inlay technique using tones which were almost white. The piece has flat surfaces covered with a profusion of scales made from nacre fragments filleted with light coloured wood.

---

[11] Tord, Luis Enrique and Gjurinovic, Pedro. Op. cit., p. 91.

[12] Interview of the author with Prof. Héctor Schenone in 2009.

**BUREAU CABINET**
Closed and open.
Palacio de Torre Tagle, Peruvian Ministry of Foreign Affairs, Lima.
c. 1740.
Donated by Doña Teresa Blondet de Cisneros.
Height: 245 cm. Width: 119 cm.
Depth: 54.5 cm.

Its stylised phytomorphic Baroque elements are symmetrically arranged and placed within central designs surrounded by several friezes on all sides of the piece. The lion-paw legs, braces and rosette-shaped front lock were made from engraved silver.

Inside, it was decorated with geometric marquetry work in the shape of diamonds which cover all the sides.

The coffeecentre table in the Sala de los Tratados at Palacio de Torre Tagle, in Lima, is a quality piece from the institution's artistic heritage. Made in the 18TH century, it can be said to be a Baroque ornamental piece.

It is an inlaid piece of exquisite taste made in Lima, which probably adorned a luxurious parlour, in keeping with the lavish customs of the City of Kings' high society during the Bourbon period.

This table has a circular top decorated with a

**COFFER**
Open and closed.
Museo de Arte Hispanoamericano
Isaac Fernández Blanco, Buenos Aires.
Formerly, in Don Martín Noel's collection.
18TH century.
Height: 30.5 cm. Width: 55.5 cm.
Depth: 29 cm.

CENTRE TABLE
Palacio de Torre Tagle, Peruvian Ministry of Foreign Affairs, Lima.
18TH century.
Height: 77 cm. Diameter: 64 cm.

scalloped apron and supported by a central prism-shaped shaft with an octagonal base. It is adorned with undulating lines and stylised foliage.

The piece consists of a local wood base, completely covered in mother-of-pearl creating an almost white palette, interspersed with light-coloured wood filigrees. The inlay technique, as in other cases, reveals once again the Japanese influence on coastal Peruvian furniture. This piece needs to be adequately restored. There are some elements missing.

Within the various styles nurturing inlaid furniture production it is necessary to emphasize this one, consisting in the almost exclusive use of mother-of-pearl —which has a white palette with iridescent hues— and the application of stylized decorative schemes within a fine wood or tortoiseshell fillet. This type of finishing should be associated with the one seen in Gujarati production —from Gujarat, western India— which, during the 16TH and 17TH centuries created magnificent decorative art pieces with Western morphology and a similar kind of work. It could be assumed that this source of inspiration somehow reached the west coast of the Americas.

The unique coffeecentre table which belongs to the Prado Heudebert family collection, located in the city of Lima, is a piece for secular use made in Lima in the 18TH century.

Its structure is made up of a circular top with a polygonal central shaft, whose base is divided into segments and ends in an octagon. It rests on double bun feet. The piece was made from mahogany, which was covered in mother-of-pearl and tortoiseshell.

This is an inlaid piece decorated with undulating and abstract motifs in a Baroque style of Eastern inspiration. The contrasting tortoiseshell and nacre colours create remarkable aesthetic effects. The piece is in very good condition.

In the Sala Bartolomé María de las Heras, at the Museo del Palacio Arzobispal, in the city of Lima, there is an 18TH-century coffee or auxiliary table made in late Baroque style for secular or ecclesiastical use. Its base, which enhances its height, is reminiscent of those pieces placed beside altars during religious services.

It is a small piece, with an octagonal top and base and a polygonal central shaft. Made in Lima, it is decorated with curves and stylised flowers; the composition is framed by two symmetrical friezes.

The wood structure was covered in mother-of-pearl and tortoiseshell by anonymous artisans who applied the Eastern-inspired inlay technique. In turn, the base and part of the skirt are decorated with carved exposed wood. This piece is in very good condition.

There is another interesting coffeecentre table at Museo Pedro de Osma, in Lima. It is a piece with striking lines and remarkable syncretic features due to its impressive Baroque ornaments. Those features consist of the Japanese-inspired inlay technique based on *Namban* art, the Mudejar spirit reflected in the use of a predominantly abstract language —as seen in the elements inside the geometric

**CENTRE TABLE**
[OPPOSITE PAGE] Prado Heudebert family collection, Lima.
18TH century.
Height: 63.5 cm. Diameter: 62.5 cm.

**CENTRE TABLE**
[LEFT]
Museo del Palacio Arzobispal de Lima.
18TH century.
Height: 47.5 cm. Diameter: 48 cm.

**CENTRE TABLE**
[RIGHT] Museo Pedro de Osma, Lima - Peru.
Height: 74 cm. Diameter: 58 cm.

**CENTRE TABLE**
Detail of the top.
Museo Pedro de Osma, Lima - Peru.
Height: 74 cm. Diameter: 58 cm.

figure placed in the centre of the top— and the local flavour added by floral motifs, such as *kantuta.*

This table has an octagonal top and an undulating skirt. A central shaft serves as a base; the top rests on a socket and turned bun feet.

The materials used to make the piece include a base, probably local wood, as well as mother-of-pearl, tortoiseshell, and ebony or ebonised wood as a background: all the elements required for the application of the local inlay technique.

There is yet another coffeecentre table in the Museo Pedro de Osma collection, city of Lima. As with previous examples, it has Japanese influences and was made by anonymous artisans.

It is similar to the piece described above. The table is circular, its octagonal central shaft is placed on a hexagonal base, which rests on bun feet that supposedly have been replaced or added.

Baroque motifs are symmetrically arranged within geometric central designs; there is an interesting rosette on the top, and phytomorphic patterns, e.g. *kantuta*, framed by several friezes.

There is also wood —possibly dyed— mother-of-pearl, blonde tortoiseshell and ivory on the supporting structure, typical elements used by the inlay technique.

**CENTRE TABLE**
[LEFT]
Museo Pedro de Osma, Lima - Peru.
18TH century.

**CENTRE TABLE**
[RIGHT] Doña Marita de la Peña Prado's collection, Lima.
18TH century.

On the top perimeter, there is a gently undulating moulding revealing harmonious and beautiful triangles and curves.

In the private collection of Doña Marita de la Peña Prado of Lima, there is another coffeecentre table or gueridon. Like many other similar pieces, it was produced in the 18TH century by artisans in Lima workshops.

It has decorative and morphological features typical of the Baroque style, with an obvious Japanese influence. This is a magnificent ornamental piece for secular use.

The circular top is supported by a central shaft resting on a polygonal base which is placed on an octagonal socket.

Its whole surface is decorated with stylised mother-of-pearl floral elements, framed by several concentric circles. A central rosette and triangular shapes on the perimeter complete the top ornaments. The socket is decorated with scales. The profusion of elements clearly points to the typical *horror vacui* of the Baroque style.

Anonymous craftsmen covered the wood structure of the piece with mother-of-pearl, tortoiseshell and ivory. It most definitely is in a delicate condition.

A magnificent coffer was found in the Sala En contacto con Oriente at the

**COFFER**
Open and closed.
Museo de Arte Hispanoamericano
Isaac Fernández Blanco, Buenos Aires.
Formerly, in Don Martín Noel's collection.
18$^{TH}$ century.
Height: 22 cm. Width: 43.5 cm.
Depth: 33.5 cm.

Museo de Arte Hispanoamericano Isaac Fernández Blanco, city of Buenos Aires. It once belonged to Don Martín Noel's collection.[13] It is a small Baroque container with Eastern influences made in the 18TH century for secular use.

This luxurious inlaid piece, with flat sides, has an upper lid faceted in two levels. It has small inner drawers of various shapes and sizes covered with vermilion and gold lacquer. Phytomorphic motifs were engraved on its front lock, hinges and legs by a clearly talented master silversmith.

Unknown craftsmen designed decorative motifs which were applied as follows: on the outside there are several stylised designs forming friezes framed by delicate dark fillets. Plain friezes divide the spaces with a contrasting palette; two of them are wider than the rest and have stylised flowers.

Inside there are several landscapes with Chinese motifs. Those details highlight once again the aesthetic link between the East and the Americas through a sophisticated combination of the inlay technique on the outside and an artistic and chromatic display inside.

The materials used for the structure and decoration are wood, mother-of-pearl, Eastern lacquers or chinoiserie and silver. It is in excellent condition.

This inlaid chest, made in the Peruvian coastal tradition, is part of the Prado Heudeberts' important Lima collection. Probably made in the 18TH century, with Baroque characteristics and Japanese inspiration, it is a secular ornamental container.

Its small structure, suitable for use as a jewellery box or small coffer for storing correspondence or important documents, has a suggestive front lock. It has straight lines on every side, a polygonal upper lid, and rests on four turned bun feet.

The maker covered much of its wood surface in mother-of-pearl, using tortoiseshell only for fillets, which provide the piece with an intense brightness.

Decorative elements, such as stylised flowers, are scattered across the surface in a balanced and symmetrical manner. It is in good condition, like the rest of the pieces in this collection.

This remarkable coffer, another high-quality example of Lima furniture, also belongs to the Prado Heudebert collection. It was made in Baroque style with marked oriental influence in the 17TH or 18TH century.

Given its singular form, this container is strictly for ornamental and secular

---

[13] Schenone, Héctor, Ribera, Adolfo Luis and Curt Lange, Francisco. *Historia General del Arte en Argentina.* Vol. II. Buenos Aires: Academia Nacional de Bellas Artes, 1983, p. 180.

use. Due to its large width, contrasting with its reduced height, it cannot possibly have been for household use.

It has flat surfaces and a roof-shaped lid divided into three sections.

It rests on four bun feet and is further ornamented with engraved-silver hinges and a front lock.

As for the rest of the decoration, the supporting wood structure is entirely covered in mother-of-pearl forming plant motifs, curves, *rinceaux* and stylised scales. It is in very good condition.

In the Prado Heudebert family collection there is also a pair of *bargueños* which were probably made in the 18TH century. These magnificent pieces are some

**COFFER**
[LEFT] Prado Heudebert family collection, Lima.
18TH century.
Height: 20.5 cm. Width: 44 cm.
Depth: 35 cm.

**COFFER**
[BOTTOM] Prado Heudebert family collection, Lima.
18TH century.
Height: 24 cm. Width: 92 cm.
Depth: 49 cm.

of the secular ornamental pieces which used to decorate major Lima parlours. Both the decorative elements and the structure of these *bargueños* display the elegance of their Baroque architecture. Also, a strong artistic Eastern influence can be seen in their inlaid details, a syncretism which gives the pieces a special character.

They are small containers with irregular fronts. There are four drawers in the upper body and one in the lower; all of them are flanked by turned Solomonic columns entirely covered in leaves. Both pieces rest on four bun feet. Their friezes have baluster-shaped crestings on the front and sides.

The pieces were made by anonymous artisans from local wood and their entire surface is covered with striking tortoiseshell plaques, mother-of-pearl fragments, pyrographed ivory and metal in balanced proportions. Stylised plant motifs frame the drawers and geometric shapes adorn the sides. They are in good condition.

The sofa table in the above collection is useful for supporting one of the aforementioned *bargueños.*

This piece has a flat top, drop leaves on both sides, rounded corners and two drawers in the skirt, one on top of the other. It rests on straight legs connected by a turned crosspiece, obviously revealing the English influence which, at the time, inspired not only Lima artisans but also others from various Spanish American regions.

It is a piece for secular use, like the matching *bargueños*, produced around the 18TH century and decorated with an aesthetic language which straddles the Baroque and Rococo styles.

*BARGUEÑOS*
Side detail and full view.
Prado Heudebert family collection, Lima.
18TH century.

The ornamentation selected by its anonymous makers consists of diamonds and other geometric shapes inlaid in the top, and carved plant elements on the drawer fronts, which have simple wooden *tirettes*; the legs end in carved lions' paws.

This table was made from a wood supporting structure, covered with mahogany or some other hardwood and inlaid with ivory or pyrographed bone.

It has bronze friezes embedded both in the drawer perimeter and the clear lacquer cover. Fortunately, it is in good condition.

**SOFA TABLE**
[TOP] Prado Heudebert family collection, Lima.
18TH century.

***BARGUEÑO***
[OPPOSITE PAGE] Detail of oil-painted image in central alcove and full piece.
Doña Mariana Berckemeyer Prado's collection, Lima.
18TH century.
Height: 51 cm. Width: 86 cm.
Depth: 33 cm.

It is worth noting that the sofa table is a piece of English furniture which was originally designed during the Queen Anne period, in the early 18TH century and remained in vogue until the Edwardian period, in the early 20TH century. Strictly utilitarian, the table would be placed against the back of the sofa that gives the piece its name and temporarily moved to the front when it was time to lay the table for tea. Its shape is based in distinct lines. It has a flat top, drop leaves on both sides and rests on a skirt, which consists of one or two drawers. Two legs connected by a crosspiece hold the structure together.

In Doña Mariana Berckemeyer Prado's collection, originally from the Berckemeyer Pérez Hidalgo family collection, there is a striking Baroque ornamental *bargueño* for secular use, a true example of the 18TH-century coastal furniture.

It is a flat sided container whose upper body is flanked by Solomonic columns; there is a central alcove crowned by a pediment and surrounded by seven drawers. The lower body has a pair of drawers framed by subtle waves, which reappear on the socket perimeter.

It should be noted that the niche decorative motifs consist of a pair of *putti* (plump children) painted in oil on wood or copper in the central compartment, pointing out the domestic devotion of the time. Plant motifs adorn drawers and other parts of the piece.

Built by unknown craftsmen on a mahogany architectural structure of classical inspiration, the piece reveals a certain Eastern influence in the use of the inlay technique, achieved through the insertion of fine fragments of mother-of-pearl in a tortoiseshell background and the addition of pyrographed ivory details.

The sides, covered in fine woods, show skilful marquetry work representing repeated geometric patterns, which highlight the front decoration and the difference between the sides and the front. It is in good condition.

In the Prado Heudebert family collection, there is a coffer on a support table. It comprises two pieces with similar structural, decorative and technical features, both with mother-of-pearl inlay and made approximately in the same period by anonymous artisans with similar artistic skills.

They are secular pieces inspired in the late Baroque. They were likely made in the 18TH century, as the Baroque remained in vogue throughout the century, coexisting with other, more innovative, aesthetic trends.

The coffer is a small portable container with flat sides. Its lid top has a slight curve and remarkable fretted metal locks on the front and the bottom drawer; this piece has useful side handles for easy transportation. In its lower body, a

drawer runs from side to side. The piece rests on four bun feet. The decoration on each segment generates a grid of different sizes and shapes which form central designs containing symmetrically arranged plant motifs, following predetermined layouts.

The lid and socket are framed by slight waves carved around their entire perimeter in European style.

The support table on which the coffer rests consists of a top with similar decoration and four slightly oblique legs turned in the shape of a rosary and connected by straight crosspieces for extra strength. They were both made from wood, probably of local origin, which was covered with tortoiseshell as a background and

COFFER WITH SUPPORT TABLE
Prado Heudebert family collection, Lima. 18TH century.

mother-of-pearl decorative motifs. The fillets framing the central designs are made of ivory or bone and the fittings, of finely fretted and engraved iron.

A refined secular coffer is part of the Prado Heudebert family collection. It was built in the 18TH century in Lima, where Baroque lines were maintained through repeated decorative patterns and techniques inspired by the Eastern traditions which gave rise to the inlay technique.

This container, anonymously built as was usually the case, has a wood supporting structure, flat faces, a lid on the top and a front drawer at the bottom. Inside, there are drawers for storing small items.

The decorative motifs are presented between rectangular shapes surrounded by several stylised floral friezes. In the centre of the piece, geometrical and phytomorphic figures are placed around a star. This decoration was achieved by inlaying the background tortoiseshell with small fragments of mother-of-pearl, and adding some marquetry details to produce contrasting effects. It is in very good condition since it has evidently been restored.

COFFER
Detail of flower design and open piece.
Prado Heudebert family collection, Lima.
18TH century.
Height: 37 cm. Width: 61 cm.
Depth: 32 cm.

COFFER

Reverse.

Prado Heudebert family collection, Lima.

18TH century.

Height: 37 cm. Width: 61 cm.

Depth: 32 cm.

COFFER

Don Juan Luis de Aliaga's collection, Lima.

18TH century.

The coffer or container in Don Juan Luis de Aliaga's collection was occasionally used for storing valuables, although it was a luxury piece intended for decorating important Lima parlours.

This secular piece could be classified as coastal Baroque due to the inlay technique, of marked Eastern influence, which was applied in the region until the mid-18TH century.

It is a small coffer with flat sides, a slightly curved top lid, a hidden drawer in the lower front and four bun feet.

Phytomorphic decorative patterns stand out, with repeated *kantutas* and curves on both sides and sunflowers on both ends of the lid. All these elements are contained within geometric central designs; a perimeter frieze forming semicircles surrounds the bottom of the piece.

The piece was built from a solid wood base inlaid with tortoiseshell and ivory fillets, which frame spaces decorated with mother-of-pearl following a predetermined pattern. Its lock and side handles are made of engraved and fretted bronze.

In the Sala Buenos Aires capital del Virreinato, in the Museo de Arte Hispanoamericano Isaac Fernández Blanco, city of Buenos Aires, there is another coffer. It used to be part of the collection of architect Martín Noel. The piece is strikingly similar to those above and a true example of the 18TH-century Lima Baroque style, with obvious Japanese influences.

It is an anonymously made functional container for secular use with a slightly curved or roof-shaped upper lid, a drawer in the lower front, a central lock, and a pair of side handles for transportation.

The piece has plant motifs on the outside, contained within quartered central designs of various kinds, which are symmetrically arranged as dictated by the style.

Made from wood, probably of local origin, it is covered in mother-of-pearl fragments with tortoiseshell in the background and has a lacquer finish.

On the lid and base perimeters, subtle undulations are carved in wood. The front lock is ornamented with a coat of arms.

The inside has rhomboidal shapes made using marquetry technique with various shades of fine woods. In the centre, an unknown character is painted in oil.

The coffer located at the Asociación Civil Museo Enrico Poli, in Lima, is an exquisite piece which stands out among the secular pieces made by coastal artisans in the 18TH century. Due to its refinement and beauty, it is a faithful witness to the characteristic splendour of the City of Kings.

In this case, its unique decoration consists of a geometric pattern forming a draughtsboard, a typical ornament of the Spanish-Arab world which can be associated with Gujarati art —an obvious relationship established at that time due to overseas trade. These patterns are connected by symmetrically arranged branches and framed by abstract friezes and fillets which contain the elements within a given area.

It is a rectilinear container in which right angles prevail. The piece has five drawers of differing sizes and shapes and flat bracket feet.

The piece consists of a local wood structure inlaid with mother-of-pearl and tortoiseshell. Its small fittings in the shape of drops or tears were made from iron.

This 18TH-century work table, one of Doña Ignacia García de Rivero's household items, now in the private collection of her great-great-granddaughter, was adorned with the inlay technique.

COFFER
Museo de Arte Hispanoamericano Isaac Fernández Blanco, Buenos Aires. Formerly, in Don Martín Noel's collection. 18TH century. Height: 33 cm. Width: 63 cm. Depth: 34 cm.

**CHEST / COFFER**
[TOP] Side detail and full view.
Asociación Civil Museo Enrico Poli, Lima.
18TH century.

**WORK TABLE**
[BOTTOM]
Private collection, Arequipa.
Formerly, in Doña Ignacia García de Rivero's collection.
18TH century.
Height: 15 cm. Width: 37 cm.
Depth: 36 cm.

It is a small, anonymously made container, used for needlework. In all likelihood, it was originally intended for the family parlour, a room usually found in important houses.

The square structure features a top lid and a front lock. It rests on four turned bun feet. The piece's supporting structure is made from solid wood decorated with mother-of-pearl fragments on a tortoiseshell background. Its lid and lower

**PORTABLE ESCRITOIRE**
Open and closed.
Prado Heudebert family collection, Lima.
18TH century.

body perimeters have darkened and carved wood mouldings with some volume. It has metal fittings.

The piece is decorated with stylised Baroque plant motifs, which are symmetrically arranged within double mouldings.

The lock and corresponding key are missing.

COFFER
Front and side view.
Casa Naón —Art auction, August 2010— Lot Nº 672, Buenos Aires.
Formerly, in Don Luis García Lawson's collection.
18TH century.
Height: 25 cm. Width: 32 cm.
Depth: 21 cm.

The travel escritoire in the Prado Heudebert family collection is a small secular or ecclesiastical writing desk designed for transporting writing implements. It has an upper lid with a lock. Inside the lid, there is an oil-painted image of the Sacred Heart.

Although it is a small 18TH-century piece, there are symmetrically arranged plant elements, such as *kantutas*, revealing once again the inclination of some artisans towards the Baroque style.

Structurally, it is a European piece of furniture, although its decoration has Eastern influences. It consists of a wooden supporting structure made by unknown craftsmen of the coastal region. The outer sides are covered with small fragments of mother-of-pearl and bone or ivory. Small undulations were carved on the perimeter moulding, which was coated with lacquer. On the front, there is a lock without a key.

This 18TH-century Baroque coffer used to be part of the famous Argentine colonial art collection of Don Luis García Lawson. Its last owner, before the auction which broke up the collection, was Don Fernando García Balcarce.

It is a piece for secular use and was likely used as a ladies' jewellery box.

This coffer is small, has flat sides and an upper lid with a marked roof shape. It has a front lock, fretted and engraved silver fittings and four bun feet. Plant motifs are profusely distributed in a balanced way. On the socket, the entire decorative composition rests on an abstract frieze.

The piece's surface is entirely covered with tortoiseshell and mother-of-pearl inlaid in a wood base. The refined silver details were carved and fretted.

In the Sala En contacto con

Oriente, in the Museo de Arte Hispanoamericano Isaac Fernández Blanco, city of Buenos Aires, there is a secular coffer which was made and decorated in the coastal Baroque style of the Viceroyalty of Peru.

Originally from the famous private collection of Doña Celina González Garaño, it was showcased at the Los tesoros de la muy noble Iberoamérica exhibition in the above museum. It currently belongs to the museum collection.[14]

This piece is a small container with a roof-shaped lid, a front lock, and four spherical legs. The simple decorative elements represent undulating zoomorphic and phytomorphic figures of various colours and contrasting materials. These elements were inlaid and profusely arranged on the sides, which are framed by filleted friezes.

The wood has inlaid mother-of-pearl details, which are combined with

[14] Recorded under file Nº 343 in the museum inventory of 1982.

**COFFER**
Full view and detail of zoomorphic figure.
Museo de Arte Hispanoamericano
Isaac Fernández Blanco, Buenos Aires.
Formerly, in Doña Celina González
Garaño's collection.
Height: 17.5 cm. Width: 30.5 cm.
Depth: 18 cm.

**FOOTREST / FOOTSTOOL**
Prado Heudebert family collection, Lima.
18TH century.
Height: 8.3 cm. Width: 39.5 cm.
Depth: 25.2 cm.

lighter shades of wood. The front latch was made from engraved silver. The piece is slightly deteriorated and the original key is missing.

The footstool or footrest is a small utilitarian piece of furniture for resting one's feet while sitting. This particular piece may have adorned some corner of an important Lima house. However, analogous examples can be found in religious iconography, where the Virgin Mary is portrayed with her feet resting on pieces with a similar morphology. This shows once again that European stylistic guidelines were transferred to the Viceroyalty of Peru.

This footstool, which used to be part of the Prado Heudebert family collection, was built in the 18TH century with Baroque ornamentation and Japanese inspiration.

It is small, rectangular, flat, and rests on bun feet. The techniques and decoration applied to the piece are comparable to those described in the two previous pieces. Given its refined construction, it was probably used with a small cushion which helped to preserve it.

The piece was built by anonymous artisans and consists of a wood structure inlaid with mother-of-pearl and tortoiseshell. It is in very good condition.

Pieces decorated with the above technique have the common characteristic of being an ornament in themselves; regardless of their specific function.

This is due to the fact that they were made with an amazing beauty and unusual refinement, the result of the subtle combination of rich and exquisite materials and the skills of the carpenters who designed and built them.

# VIII

## BAROQUE STYLE FURNITURE

## TURNED, CARVED AND GILDED WOOD

Secular and ecclesiastical use

LIMA, CUSCO, AREQUIPA, PUNO AND TRUJILLO

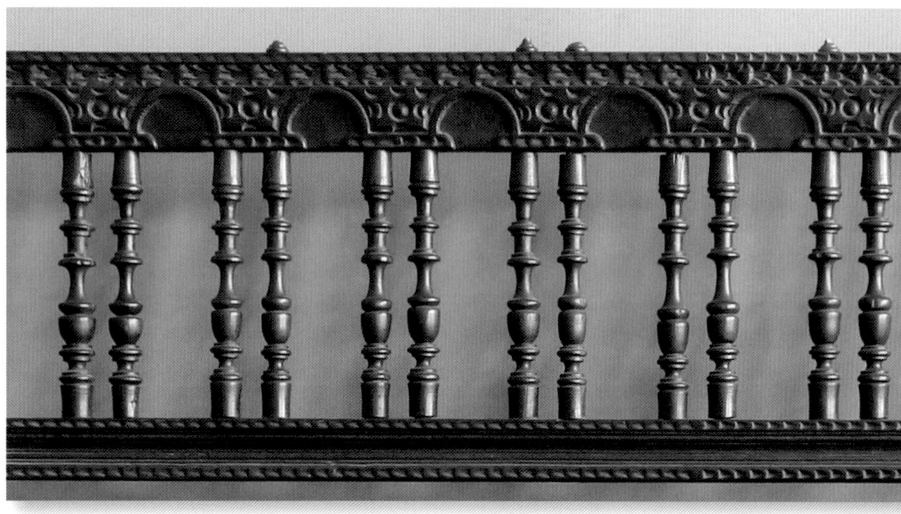

# VIII

## SIMPLE BENCH IN THE SPANISH TRADITION

The bench is a type of seat of Muslim origin. *It evolved from the* sarir, *the enlarged throne of the* Umayyad *and* Abbasid *caliphates, which was first used in aristocratic circles and then spread to other social groups*[1]. Referring to the Andalusian bench design, Aguiló Alonso states: ...*since the mid-$17^{TH}$-century it has had a low backrest with balusters, and has been used especially in brotherhoods and fraternities*[2]. This type of seat emerged as a variant of traditional Spanish benches and spread throughout the Viceroyalty in the $17^{TH}$- and $18^{TH}$-centuries, also reaching rural areas in Spanish America. It was also known as a "reception bench".

Of debatable functionality, because its seat is narrow, rigid and very straight, the bench is only a place to pause for a rest.

Benches were useful in public spaces such as church atriums, convent and monastery entrances and as ecclesiastical seats; although benches could also be found in private house entrance halls and lobbies for visitors to wait more comfortably. Benches would be placed against walls and, when made in pairs, the two pieces would face each other.

The bench was the typical Baroque seat; it was made in solid rustic wood and adorned with simple carvings and rudimentary turnings.

Benches could be up to three metres long and were equipped with flat, elongated, unpadded seats; the backrest was rigid and straight; there were arms

**BENCH**
[OPENING] Backrest, in detail.
Prado Heudebert family collection, Lima.
$17^{TH}$ - $18^{TH}$ centuries
Height: 172.3 cm. Width: 202 cm.
Depth: 64 cm.

**BENCH**
[OPPOSITE PAGE] Backrest detail.
Museo de Arte de Lima.
$18^{TH}$ century.

---

1 Rodríguez Bernis, Sofía. *Diccionario de mobiliario.* Madrid: Secretaría General Técnica, 2006, p. 159.

2 Aguiló Alonso, María Paz. *El Mueble en España: Siglos XVI y XVII.* Madrid: Antiqvaria, 1993, p. 143.

on both sides and straight legs resting on crosspieces or bases to strengthen the structure.

The backrest was usually ornamented using various techniques, such as carving and turning; the latter would produce a series of columns in the shape of balustrades on one or two bodies. The stiles could be topped by pinnacles or other simple ornaments at both ends. Occasionally, the fretting technique was applied to highlight selected decoration.

In some cases, the seat was connected to the front legs by a crossbar, which was merely a copy of the balustrade on the backrest.

If the piece (although made from local wood) was designed for an important house, it could be fully or partially covered with gold leaf. If it was intended for meeting basic needs in more modest environments, the wood was simply preserved with waxes or oils.

BENCH
Backrest detail.
Iglesia de San Pedro Mártir - Catedral de Juli, Department of Puno.
Height: 109 cm. Width: 237 cm.
Depth: 43.5 cm.

### BENCHES IN THE VICEROYALTY OF PERU

A Baroque bench with an obvious Spanish influence, donated by the Prado family to the Museo de Arte de Lima, is exhibited in the hall of this museum. It was made by anonymous artisans during the 18TH-century[3].

The bench was presumably intended for secular use. It has a flat backrest and seat and slightly curved arms and front legs ending in scrolls. It also has a double balustrade on the back and under the seat.

Built from solid carved and turned wood without any sort of finishing, this bench has arches on the backrest and on the longitudinal segment under the seat. The decoration consists of simple friezes and undulating arms ending in corbels.

The piece is probably originally from Lima; its condition is delicate and it has not been restored.

The bench in the main hall of the Parador del Molino Blanco, in the city of Arequipa, is a utilitarian Baroque piece which cannot be accurately dated. This type of furniture has been regularly produced for centuries. It was likely made by an anonymous Arequipa craftsman with Spanish influence.

There is a large seat with straight arms at both ends. The skirt is connected to the crossbar by a turned colonnade. The piece is supported by four quadrangular legs resting on bases. Its side stiles end in carved corbels.

---

3 Archives of the Asociación Museo de Arte de Lima. Catalogued by José Centurión Padilla on September 8, 1987.

**BENCH**
[TOP] Museo de Arte de Lima.
18TH century.
Width: 160 cm. Height: 107 cm.
Depth: 54 cm.

**BENCH**
[BOTTOM] Parador del Molino Blanco, Arequipa.
Height: 110 cm. Width: 243 cm.
Depth: 63 cm.

The decoration is simple and the rustic result consists of straight lines formed by a series of columns, placed on the backrest and the front, which hold the crossbar. The backrest is crowned by high, turned pinnacles. The piece was made from local solid wood, presumably willow.

At Casa del Moral[4], in the city of Arequipa, there is a rustic Baroque bench, probably for secular use, which was inspired by Spanish pieces.

This is a seat whose backrest is made up of turned columns which give the appearance of a fretted backrest. The stiles on both sides of the backrest are crowned by simple corbels. The bench has straight arms and four quadrangular legs resting on bases and connected by a narrow crosspiece.

Repeated rustic Baroque motifs were carved from local solid wood by anonymous craftsmen. The robustness of the bench structure is due to the use of entirely visible hardwood pegs and mortise and tenon joints.

The piece is in good condition.

**BENCH**
[TOP] Side detail.
La Casa del Moral, Arequipa.
Height: 103 cm. Width: 225 cm.
Depth: 67 cm.

**BENCH**
[OPPOSITE PAGE] Real Monasterio de Clarisas de Santa María de Gracia, Trujillo.
Height: 112 cm. Width: 253 cm.
Depth: 60 cm.

In the entrance of the Real Monasterio de Clarisas de Santa María de Gracia, in Trujillo, there is another simple bench. It is very well situated, since it stands in a walkway, where people wait to be received. It was made in Baroque style by unknown artisans, probably from Trujillo, and intended for secular or ecclesiastical use. It is not possible to accurately date the piece.

It is a piece with a Spanish influence, made from solid wood which has not been upholstered; the backrest and seat are flat. The bench has a pair of quadrangular armrests on each side and four straight legs ending in bases. Regular-sized, as was usually the case, the bench features a single turned-wood decorative motif: a simple continuous baluster repeated on the backrest, under the seat, between the skirt and the crossbar, and on the sides. The piece is in good condition due to meticulous care.

This pair of benches is to be found on each side of the high altar in Iglesia de San Pedro Mártir - Catedral de Juli, in the Collao Region. The pieces currently

4 It currently belongs to Banco de Crédito del Perú.

belong to the Prelature of Juli, Museo Religioso de San Pedro, in the Department of Puno, Province of Chucuito. They are pieces of ecclesiastical furniture, made by anonymous craftsmen probably from Juli.[5]

[5] Departamento de Registro y Catalogación archives of the Instituto Nacional de Cultura de Puno. December 2010.

This is a pair of flat seats. Their backrests have round arches supported by double turned columns. In the lower bodies, containers with lids function as seats and replace the legs. The arms at both ends of the seats are straight.

The decoration is completed with very simple carved rosettes and diamonds arranged across different areas.

The stylistic characteristics of the benches straddle the Renaissance and Baroque with an evident Spanish influence. Their decorative elements include arches, turned columns forming balustrades and rosettes within diamonds.

The benches were built from turned and carved solid cedar wood and have iron hinges.

They are in good condition, although some elements are missing.

BENCH
[TOP] San Pedro Mártir - Catedral de Juli, Department of Puno.
Height: 109 cm. Width: 237 cm.
Depth: 43.5 cm.

BENCH
[OPPOSITE PAGE] Prado Heudebert family collection, Lima.
17TH - 18TH centuries.
Height: 172.3 cm. Width: 202 cm.
Depth: 64 cm.

## LUXURIOUS BENCHES IN PARLOURS OF IMPORTANT HOUSES

In important Lima and Cusco houses, benches would have various shapes and sizes, but their great elegance was mostly due to their fine carving and gold leaf finish. They were significantly smaller than those previously described, and owed their imposing presence to their robustness and strength.

This solitary bench from the Prado Heudebert family collection was made in Cusco, as revealed by its wood treatment.

It has a clearly Baroque style with marked Spanish influence and may be one piece of a pair. As background information, it is worth mentioning that an identical piece is or was part of the La Torre-Lastres family collection, in Lima.[6]

This secular ornamental bench was designed to adorn the parlours of the most important Cusco and Lima mansions of the time —from the late 17TH-century and through the 18TH-century. It was made by highly skilful anonymous carvers and gilders. The bench has a broad, over two-metre wide backrest and is

6 Taullard, A. *El Mueble Colonial Sudamericano.* Buenos Aires: Peuser, 1947, figure 148.

crowned by a dazzling cresting which increases its height. It has a flat backrest and seat; the quadrangular arms and sturdy front legs are straight. Along the seat there is a diamond-point skirt, alternating with decorative corbels.

Diamond point predominates in the chosen overlapping ornamentation. A carved and fretted comb with a central blank cartouche stands out, adorned with leaves and curves projecting beyond the backrest.

A double balustrade alternating with pendants decorates the backrest and the crowning frieze, and under the seat there are also subtle friezes. The arms are topped by pinnacles.

The piece was made from solid wood, presumably Nicaragua cedar, given its strength and outstanding quality. The entire surface is covered in gold leaf. It is in excellent condition.

At Museo de Arte de Lima, there is a remarkable bench which was donated by Doña Clorinda Málaga de Prado. It was anonymously made in Baroque style, with an obvious Spanish influence, during the 18TH-century.[7]

For secular use, the piece is characterised by the usual flat backrest and seat, slightly curving arms ending in scrolls, and straight legs resting on a base on each side. The main decoration consists of wood turnings on the backrest and under the seat.

The decorative motif is a balustrade on both bodies of the backrest, a detail which is also seen under the seat. Two richly carved crosspieces with scale and rosette motifs connect the legs. The refined relief on the upper frieze, which is topped by short pinnacles adorning the backrest, is carved with plant and zoomorphic motifs and has a chalice at the centre.

The distinctive features of this type of seats are the choice and saturation of the decorative elements applied to each face of the piece. It is worth mentioning, among other elements, the turned wood balausters, either bare or gilded, as specific and exclusive ornaments decorating backrests and crossbars from side to side.

The piece is made from solid wood covered by traces of gold leaf; a fact which suggests it is of Cusco production.

The technical record provided by the institution reveals that the piece has deteriorated, although it is complete and has not been restored.

BENCH
[TOP] Column, cartouche and backrest details.
Prado Heudebert family collection, Lima.
17TH - 18TH centuries
Height: 172.3 cm. Width: 202 cm.
Depth: 64 cm.

BENCH
[OPPOSITE PAGE]
Backrest detail and full view.
Museo de Arte de Lima.
Donated by Memoria Prado.
18TH century.
Width: 249 cm. Height: 133 cm.
Depth: 46.5 cm.

---

7 As recorded in the archives of Asociación Museo de Arte de Lima under file v-2.3-00130, catalogued by Ana María Tolentino on December 17, 1987.

## BEDS AND IMAGE CRADLES

In the Museo de Arte de Lima collection, there is a bed[8] which was part of Doña Rosa Prado Garland's collection; it is a type of furniture known in French as *meuble d'apparat.* It would be used for special occasions, such as the birth or wake of a family member.

This piece of secular furniture was made in the late 17TH-century using a local Baroque repertoire of abundant decoration. It can be safely attributed to Cusco artisans. The form reveals both Italian and Spanish influences.

With architectonical morphology, and headboard and footboard of almost the same height, it is completely ornamented with eight elaborately turned balusters of various sizes. It also has a blanket and curtains which cover and embellish

---

[8] Catalogued by José Centurión Padilla in 1987. Recorded in Rishel, Joseph J. and Stratton-Pruitt, Suzanne (eds). *Revelaciones: las artes en América Latina 1492-1820.* Mexico D.F.: Fondo de Cultura Económica, 2007, p. 490.

BED
Museo de Arte de Lima.
Donated by Doña Rosa Prado Garland.
Late 17TH century.
Headboard height: 216 cm.
Footboard height: 186 cm.
Width: 169 cm. Total length: 244 cm.
Courtesy of Museo de Arte de Lima.

it. The canopy and curtains are stored in the museum warehouse. This bed is decorated with *rinceaux*, leaves, pineapples, pomegranates, feathers, scales, and pearl and dentil friezes distributed over its entire surface. There are four turned columns adorned with leaves, and scrolls at the corners for support. Superb combs resting on a series of turned spheres top the headboard and footboard.

Above the headboard, there is also a central scallop flanked by leaves and *rinceaux.* A pair of pinnacles and lions hold a central coat of arms, which has three *fleurs-de-lis* and is topped by a crown. There are rampant lions at the ends of the footboard.

The structure is made from local solid wood and entirely covered with gold leaf. It has wrought iron fittings. The piece was restored in April 1992 and is in very good condition.

Image cradles would sometimes be significant elements for novices and cloistered nuns going about their everyday activities, since, following the liturgical calendar, they would adorn both cradle and sacred image for whatever particular occasion.

In the Museo del Monasterio de Santa Teresa de Arequipa, of the Carmelite Order, there is a strictly religious piece of furniture: an image cradle for the Infant Jesus, located in the Sala de la Natividad or Sagrada Familia.

The piece was likely designed and made during the 18TH-century in Spanish American Baroque style, with an obvious Spanish influence. There are some similar examples in the Monasterio de las Descalzas Reales, in Madrid.

The piece has the same structural features as a child's cradle. The difference lies in its size, since it is intended for the glorification of a carving of a reclining Infant Jesus.

There are four columns supporting a canopy with a remarkable apron around the perimeter. The headboard and footboard are of equal height and rest on four legs. The entire piece was made from turned and carved solid wood, which was covered with gold leaf and a mirror.

It is symmetrically ornamented with plant motifs on the canopy perimeter; pinnacles and flat spheres adorn the columns.

The image cradle exhibited in the Salas Brazzini of the Museo de Arte Religioso de la Basílica Catedral de Lima is a small rectilinear piece for holding and displaying an image of the Infant Jesus for worship. The headboard and footboard are of identical height.

Skilfully made by unknown craftsmen, it is decorated in a Baroque style with

**IMAGE CRADLE**
Museo del Monasterio de Santa Teresa, Arequipa.
Height: 60 cm. Width: 30 cm. Length: 47 cm.

**IMAGE CRADLE**
Museo de Arte Religioso of the Basílica Catedral de Lima.
Height: 28 cm. Width: 22 cm. Length: 50 cm.

European influences. There are bright-red rosettes on the backrest and a balustrade on each end. It is made from flat-carved, turned and gilded wood.

This piece is in very good condition.

There is another image cradle, a smaller one, in the same halls of the Museo de Arte Religioso de la Basílica Catedral de Lima. It was intended to support for worship the image of the Infant Jesus. It has strong influences from Italian and Spanish Baroque art; similar to those found in pieces from the Highlands.

This is an anonymously made rectilinear supporting structure for religious use, possibly domestic, whose headboard is higher than the footboard.

The piece is ornamented with balustrades, pinnacles and bun feet; all these elements were flat-carved from wood, and then turned and completely gilded. This gold leaf cover is closely associated with the sacred aura reflected by the image.

Although some parts have been replaced, the piece is in very good condition.

IMAGE CRADLE
Museo de Arte Religioso of the Basílica Catedral de Lima.
Height: 51 cm. Width: 28 cm. Length: 51 cm.

# IX

## TRANSITIONAL BAROQUE-TO-ROCOCO FURNITURE

## POLYCHROME AND GILDING ON FLAT SURFACES

Secular and ecclesiastical use

LIMA, CUSCO, AREQUIPA AND PUNO

# IX

## EARLY ROCOCO FEATURES OF HOUSEHOLD ECCLESIASTICAL AND SECULAR PIECES DECORATED WITH EMBLEMS AND ALLEGORIES

In the Viceroyalty of Peru during mid-18TH-century, renewed aesthetic values developed in furniture design: the Baroque style would coexist with an incipient Rococo language. Pieces of furniture were ornamented with polychrome on broad flat surfaces, almost entirely covered in decorative elements, within one or more central designs on pastel or vibrantly coloured backgrounds.

Rococo is an artistic style which emerged in Europe during the late Baroque, when aesthetic fashions arriving from distant China changed both Old and New World tastes. A characteristic feature of this new style is the artists' marked interest in including bold and asymmetrical curves in a constant representation of nature, especially the underwater world; for example the rocaille, which gave this style its name. Rococo is also notable for frequently disregarding the characteristic order and rigidity of the classical language —which remained in vogue throughout the Baroque— in order to adopt, for a brief period of time, lightness, grace and exoticism.

Thus, religious, allegorical, historical or mythological motifs or simple landscapes were applied to the fronts of chests, *petacas*, screens, positive organs, *bargueños*, fitted larders and cabinet doors.

The increasing secularisation of decorative themes in these pieces reveals a shift in artists and artisans' mindset, as well as in the sensibilities of society at the time. Interesting examples of pictorial compositions were executed with a true artistic sense and unquestionable freedom of expression on the fronts and insides of lids and doors.

***BARGUEÑO***
[OPENING] Inside of the lid in detail.
Museo del Arzobispado del Cusco.
18TH century.

***PETACA***
[OPPOSITE PAGE] Front detail.
Asociación Civil Museo Enrico Poli, Lima.
18TH century.

**CONFESSIONAL**
[LEFT] Monogram of the Society of Jesus in detail.
Iglesia de San Pedro Mártir - Catedral de Juli, Department of Puno.

***BARGUEÑO***
[OPPOSITE PAGE] Detail of treillage and *kantuta*.
Museo del Arzobispado del Cusco.
18TH century.

***PETACA***
[OPPOSITE PAGE] Detail of Creole nobility portrait.
Asociación Civil Museo Enrico Poli, Lima.
18TH century.

***BARGUEÑO***
[OPPOSITE PAGE] Gallant scene detail.
Private collection, Arequipa.
18TH century.

Other decorative elements include religious or secular symbols, such as images of the Virgin Mary, the Sacred Heart or a patron saint, and civil or ecclesiastical coats of arms within cartouches surrounded by foliage or scallops placed in prominent places on the piece.

In some cases, those elements adorned rustic furniture which was not intended for decorating great mansion parlours, but rather private areas in more modest houses, convents or monasteries; while in others, the pursuit of virtuosity and quality shows that the public was eager for a change. To this end, various techniques and materials were applied to local wood or leather, which were decorated with gilded details and wrought and engraved iron fittings.

Background paint was used to decorate the surface or highlight the decoration covering it and to provide a durable coating for the supporting structure, making it imperishable.

Importantly, a precise iconography was used to ornament and illustrate: genre, hunting or biblical scenes, or allegories, with a common theme, adorned the pieces and were repeated on the sides. These scenes were circumscribed and enriched by friezes or asymmetric central designs which were inspired in the rocaille and had 18TH-century characteristics; their decoration consisted of local zoomorphic and phytomorphic motifs.

***BARGUEÑO***
[BOTTOM] Inside the front lid in detail.
Museo Pedro de Osma, Lima - Peru.
18TH century.

The traditional Chinese treillage, widely used for porcelain decoration, was another technique of background decoration. It consists of a fully interlaced diamond pattern, of relative aesthetic importance, always placed in the background and used to cover the space around the composition. Treillage is found in multiple pieces of European furniture, since this decorative detail set a trend during the Bourbon period (1730-1760).

In both gallant and hunting scenes, the Creole nobility was often portrayed with European features and dressed in typical costumes of the Andean upper classes; this reveals a marked syncretism in the decorative repertoire produced in Spanish America.

Also important is the inclusion of local flora and fauna elements, such as *kantutas*, pineapples and corncobs, as well as hummingbirds, cougars, monkeys, guinea pigs and fighting cocks, which coexisted harmoniously within the abovementioned compositions.

These pieces were entirely covered with a painted finish, which preserved them from damp and other potentially damaging factors. Local wood was generally used in their construction, since they did not require the same wood quality as pieces of furniture or altarpieces which would remain bare.

At the Museo Pedro de Osma, in Lima, there is a portable *bargueño* or writing desk suitable for storing documents and valuables; as suggested by its traditional Spanish-Arab morphology. Flat in shape, it has top and front lids, and contains twelve drawers of various sizes: these elements prove once again that the Baroque style was still in vogue in the 18TH-century.

Its drawers are moulded and topped by a series of relief-gilded arches, an expression of ornamental richness.

The paintings inside the upper and bottom lids evoke scenes from a book on political emblems entitled *Emblemata Centum Regio Politica*, and published in 1657 by an important intellectual of the time, Juan de Solórzano Pereira (Madrid, 1575-1655)[1].

The scenes demonstrate the European decorative repertoire of the period, which was based on allegories inspired by works of great artists[2]. They can be linked to the themes selected for 17TH-century tapestry cartoons.

1 Fundación Pedro y Angélica de Osma Gildermeister. *Museo Pedro de Osma.* Lima: [n.n.], 2004, p. 182.

2 Mujica Pinilla, Ramón *et al. El Barroco Peruano.* Vol. I. Colección Arte y Tesoros del Perú. Lima: Banco de Crédito del Perú, 2002, pages 40-41.

On the top lid, there is a representation of "Emblem V" which shows the goddess Fortuna, a winged female figure holding a rudder-shaped wheel and standing on a pair of spheres. The goddess is surrounded by birds which are immersed in the landscape; it is moulded by a broad frieze of flowers and leaves.

The bottom lid is decorated with "Emblem LXIXV" *(sic)*,[3] which represents a blindfolded Lady Justice holding scales and a sword in her hands. On a background of trees, there is a large bird and the Justice figure rides a feline. The composition is framed by plant elements.

This unique secular piece was made by anonymous Cusco artisans. It was decorated by covering a wood base with fine leather (*guadamecí*), which was gilded (*estofado*) and polychromed; the wood has a gold leaf finish. This *bargueño* has an iron lock.

The leather on both sides has deteriorated; the unique quality of the piece, however, is still apparent.

In a private Arequipa collection, there is a fragment of a piece which was made with European influences somewhere in the vast South Andean region. The fragment's shape reveals that it may have been a small *bargueño* lid, as it bears the marks of bolts.

Rectangular in shape, it features a strictly Baroque oil panel-painting. It was likely made in the late 17TH- or early 18TH-century. There are traces of inlay on the back of this piece.

***BARGUEÑO***
[OPPOSITE PAGE]
Museo Pedro de Osma, Lima - Peru.
18TH century.
Height; closed: 47 cm, open: 82.5 cm.
Width: 77.5 cm. Depth: 39 cm.

***BARGUEÑO***
Detail of the lid.
Private collection, Arequipa.
17TH - 18TH centuries.
Height: 26 cm. Width: 48 cm.

---

3 Fundación Pedro y Angélica de Osma Gildemeister. Op. cit., p. 182.

It is safe to assume that this fragment was part of a secular utilitarian piece. Unknown craftsmen applied various techniques to it: inlay, which unfortunately disappeared over time, and oil panel-painting, depicting the Old Testament story of Samson killing a lion (Judges, 14:5-20)[4].

This magnificent and unique stretched-leather *petaca*, which was gilded and polychromed, belongs to the collection of the Asociación Civil Museo Enrico Poli, in the city of Lima. This portable container, made in mestizo Baroque style with exceptional quality and artistic sensibility, is in excellent condition.

With four flat sides, it has a roof-shaped lid divided into three and an iron

---

[4] *La Biblia de Estudio. Dios habla hoy con Deuterocanónicos.* Brazil: Sociedades Bíblicas Unidas, 2004, pages 243-244.

***PETACA***
Lid detail and full view.
Asociación Civil Museo Enrico Poli, Lima.
18TH century.

lock on the front placed on top of a gilded double-headed eagle. It was decorated by applying polychrome and gold-leaf (*estofado*) to the cordovan or *guadamecí* covering the entire solid wood structure of the piece. On the front, there are two parallel palace scenes which can be easily related to each other. On the one hand, there is a landscape and a group of knights riding horses; on the other, a palace scene where a queen is sitting on a throne, sheltered by a large canopy and surrounded by the ladies of the court, who are all dressed in Spanish-American style. The type of clothing can be compared with the 18TH-century fashions in Spanish America, as ladies dressed up with "Creole" court luxury; this information is useful for dating the piece.

As in many other Baroque pieces, a distinctly European hunting scene is portrayed on the lid. There is a character, accompanied by a typical horse and dressed in Bourbon style, which is surrounded by a landscape typical of the time.

Although intended for a specific use, its morphology, profuse ornamentation and the ostentation of the themes described cast doubt on its purpose, which was generally that of storing and carrying personal belongings.

The compositions were created using a vibrant palette which gives the *petaca* an unprecedented expressiveness. Each composition is framed by a floral gilded frieze on a red background. The creators of the piece, which is in good very condition, remain unknown.

In Sala de los Espejos at the Museo del Arzobispado del Cusco, there is a *bargueño* for secular use, made in late Baroque style with local and Bourbon influences, following the mid-18TH-century fashion. It was produced by anonymous artisans, possibly in a workshop in the Chinchero region, near Cusco.

This *bargueño* is a container who's top and front lids, as well as its sides, are flat. It has thirteen moulded drawers inside.

Every side is adorned with polychrome on saffron-coloured backgrounds. There is a pair of ovals surrounded by rocaille on the upper lid; inside these ovals, Creole characters with European garments of the time are represented in a gallant scene within the landscape. A treillage surrounds and completes the compositions, together with local zoomorphic figures, fruit and flowers, such as *kantutas*.

The combination of ornaments makes up a compendium of information which is useful for dating the piece accurately; also, this harmonious decoration inspires admiration.

It has no exterior decoration. Inside, towards the front, there is a turned and gilded colonnade which functions as a baluster. It also has moulded drawers

that are decorated with repeated symmetrical motifs. The structure was made from local solid wood and embellished with polychrome and gold leaf. The piece has iron fittings.

It is in delicate condition: three drawers and some columns and mouldings are missing.

The pedestal in the Casa Chica wing of the Museo Pedro de Osma, in Lima, is divided into two bodies forming orderly curves and has a projecting lid.

The piece has several undulations created by direct carving. To that end, local wood was likely used, which was decorated with gold leaf and covered with polychrome. Various floral motifs complete the decoration: on the front, there is a cockerel, representing resurrection, pride and courage. On the central body there is a cartouche with a pair of lions facing each other and holding a coat of arms. While on the base there is a crowned double-headed eagle: an imperial symbol. All these elements demonstrate the value of ostentation in colonial society.[5]

The piece is in good condition, although some elements are timeworn.

In the Capilla de la Virgen María, at the Palacio Arzobispal del Cusco, there

---

5 Bruce-Mitford, Miranda. *El libro ilustrado de signos y símbolos. Miles de signos y símbolos de todo el mundo.* Buenos Aires: El Ateneo, 1997, p. 64.
Fontana, David. *The secret language of symbols. A visual key to symbols and their meanings.* San Francisco: Chronicle Books, 1994, p. 83.

**BARGUEÑO**
[OPPOSITE PAGE]
Museo del Arzobispado del Cusco.
18TH century.
Height; closed: 46 cm, open: 84 cm.
Width: 88.5 cm. Depth: 41 cm.

**PEDESTAL**
[RIGHT] Front detail.
Museo Pedro de Osma, Lima - Peru.
18TH century.
Height: 94 cm. Width: 78 cm.
Depth: 50 cm.

**PEDESTAL**
Museo Pedro de Osma, Lima - Peru.
18TH century.
Height: 94 cm. Width: 78 cm.
Depth: 50 cm.

is a small portable and manually activated organ, usually referred to as a "positive organ".[6] The instrument was most likely made in Europe in the 16TH-century and the organ case, in the 18TH-century. It is believed to have been the first of its kind to arrive in the Americas. The makers of both pieces are apparently unknown.

On the outside of the case, there are Rococo gold paintings, vehicles of expression at the time, while the wind instrument inside is Renaissance in style.

Flat lines abound on each side of the organ case, which has two front doors,

[6] Gutiérrez, Ramón (coord). *Pintura, Escultura y Artes Útiles en Iberoamérica, 1500-1825*. Colección Manuales Arte Cátedra. Madrid: Cátedra, 1995, p. 361.

**PORTABLE OR POSITIVE ORGAN**
Side detail, open and closed.
Capilla de la Virgen María del Palacio Arzobispal del Cusco.
Musical instrument: 16TH century.
Organ case: 18TH century.
Height: 83 cm. Width: 104 cm.
Depth: 59 cm.

some handles and side drawers. The upper lid is decorated with carved feline figures which activate the bellows; this function is evident to the naked eye.

The ornamentation outside and inside the piece differs. On the outside, there are urban landscapes, such as a view of the Basílica de San Pedro and a Venetian *veduta*, surrounded by floral friezes. These images contain characters dressed in 18TH-century European fashions.

Inside each door, there is an altarpiece surrounded by friezes. Around the keyboard, there is an architectural structure exhibiting a marked Italian Renaissance influence. A series of niches decorated with little faces, caryatids, angels and grotesques adorn the piece, as well as columns and arches with great classical serenity,[7] all of them applied to a wood base. The musical instrument was decorated with golden bronze; keys are made from ebony and ivory and the case is upholstered in dyed and gilded leather.

The piece is in delicate condition: there are some missing elements, particularly from the instrument.

This *bargueño*, belonging to a private Arequipa collection, is renowned for having been a household item of Doña Ignacia García de Rivero. It was made by anonymous craftsmen in the South Andean region of the Viceroyalty of Peru during the second half of the 18TH-century. With a Rococo decoration, the piece has Bourbon influences which are expressed using a local rustic language.

It is a small and flat container. The front lid has an iron lock. There are drawers and a central alcove, in keeping with its morphology. The piece rests on bun

[7] As Professor Héctor Schenone told the author in 2009.

***BARGUEÑO***
[BOTH PAGES]
Private collection, Arequipa.
18TH century.
Height: 40 cm. Width: 65 cm.
Depth: 33 cm.

feet which have been replaced. The solid wood base is richly yet simply decorated with polychrome against a vermilion background; gold brushstrokes give the piece its finishing touches.

It has decorative motifs on all sides, placed within central designs. These rocaille-shaped motifs are surrounded by vegetation. There are depictions of male characters dressed in European clothing and women in Creole garments, as was the fashion of the time, all displaying a gallant attitude.

These scenes may be associated with the "*casta* paintings", portraits of interracial couples, produced in the Viceroyalty of New Spain. *…accepting the extensive miscegenation that took place in Spanish America, they were moved to capture on canvas* [in this case, on panels] *the various racial mixtures produced over two centuries of colonial domination. Therefore, casta paintings aimed to show the world the racial diversity in the Spanish overseas territories, and thus highlight its status as a great empire.* [8]

The piece is in delicate condition, as the paint has deteriorated.

The *imagen de vestir* (dressed image) of Our Lady of the Rosary holding the Infant Jesus in her arms is placed on a monstrance at the side of the nave in the

---

[8] O'Phelan Godoy, Scarlett. "El vestido como identidad étnica e indicador social de una cultura material". In: Mujica Pinilla, Ramón *et al. El Barroco Peruano.* Volume II. Colección Arte y Tesoros del Perú. Lima: Banco de crédito del Perú, 2003, p. 112.
*Artes de México. La pintura de castas.* Mexico: Artes de México y del Mundo, Nº 8, summer, 1990.

Iglesia de Santiago Apóstol de Pomata, in the Collao region. Its main appeal lies in the inner decoration of its doors, highlighting iconographic details which are worth analysing, since it is a prototype of Andean Baroque ecclesiastical furniture[9].

This piece, made in Puno by unknown artisans, is a religious image container. Inside, there are overlapping and interrelated scenes depicting some miracles performed by the Virgin, which are painted with bright colours on a panel and framed by flowers and large leaves.

The image was made from local carved, painted and partially gilded wood, as well as iron, silks and various fabrics, among other materials.

There are no features to allow the dating of this piece, which is in delicate condition, since there are some cracks and missing elements.

In a farm house near the city of Cusco, there is a pair of peculiar pieces of furniture which belong to a private collection: two polychromed solid-wood larder doors. These are boards supported by a frame built into the wall. It is difficult to accurately date these pieces, which bear the "*Mdina*" signature on the top right.

These utilitarian pieces for secular use, so typical of rural areas, were made by craftsmen from the Cusco school; in these areas there was a markedly syncretic decorative style, as was generally the case, including European Baroque elements and important local features. The advantage of this type of design was that with few resources —wood and polychromes— a container was made which was suitable for storing household equipment.

This syncretism can be appreciated in the selected ornamentation: a central coat of arms crowned by three feathers in vibrant colours which contains the Eucharistic Heart of Jesus pierced by swords —the religious symbol of Sacred Love— flanked by *Inti* and *Mama Quilla or Killa* (the Sun and the Moon). There

9 The piece belongs to the Prelature of Juli, Administration of the Municipal District of Pomata.

**MONSTRANCE**
[OPPOSITE PAGE] Inside of doors in detail.
Iglesia de Santiago Apóstol de Pomata,
Department of Puno.
Height: 155 cm.

**LARDER DOORS**
[RIGHT]
Private collection, Cusco.
Author: Mdina (top right).
Height: 185 cm. Width: 138 cm.
Depth: 12 cm.

is a red bow above an inscription which reads "*DOMUS DEI & PORTACQLI*", and a perimeter moulding made up of two friezes of different colours: one undulating and one straight.

These doors were made from a wood base and have iron hinges and nails. Both paint and wood have deteriorated.

## RUSTIC FURNITURE FOR RELIGIOUS OR SECULAR USE ADORNED WITH COLOUR AND OUT OF PROPORTION DETAILS

During the 17TH- and 18TH-centuries, in the South Andean region of the Viceroyalty of Peru, there emerged a type of rural rustic furniture intended for both ecclesiastical and secular household use.

Pieces were decorated by local peoples with naive paintings representing the surrounding nature, as well as zoomorphic and phytomorphic iconography with altered proportions and a vibrant palette; further decorative elements included mouldings.

In places of worship, monasteries and convents of the Arequipa and Collao regions, both furniture and walls were adorned with birds and other indigenous animals along with plants, flowers and tropical fruit placed in baskets, interpreted with simple local colours.

Various types of pieces are worth mentioning, such as confessionals, pulpits, organ cases and cabinets, ornamented on flat wood fronts or other surfaces with no relief or volume.

## RELIGIOUS FURNITURE WITH COLOUR EFFECTS

Located on one side of the nave of the Iglesia de Santiago Apóstol, in Pomata[10] —a jewel of *mestizo* Baroque architecture— there is a pulpit designed for liturgical use which was made by unknown craftsmen in Andean Baroque style.

It has a hexagonal projecting tribune crowned by a canopy, placed on top of a remarkable turned shaft which rests on a base. The access stairs are balustrade-shaped and entirely covered with polychrome.

The pulpit is ornamented by various polychromed and gold leafed carvings: the characteristic image of the patron saint of the Dominican Order flanked by Solomonic columns; the usual presence of the Holy Spirit on the canopy; the Virgin Mary on the backrest. In contrast, there are fantastic figures with indigenous iconography reclining on the canopy dome, and pearls and rosettes on the surrounding friezes.

Of particular interest for this chapter are the frescoed wall supporting the piece and supplementing its ornamentation, and the stairs decorated with vegetable elements of undeniable local flavour. They are wood and mortar structures

[10] Capital of the Pomata District, considered the "Philosophical Balcony of the Altiplano", in the Province of Chucuito, Department of Puno, on Lake Titicaca.

covered with paintings, carved and turned to create a volumetric effect. The fresco work can be linked to the words of Antonio Bonet Correa [11], who describes the murals in the cell of friar Francisco de Salamanca (1660-1737) at the Iglesia de Nuestra Señora de la Merced, city of Cusco, and makes a special mention of the characteristic use, in the Andean region of the Viceroyalty of Peru, of this clearly rustic type of mural decoration with altered proportions.

The piece is not in very good condition and there are some images missing from the tribune niches.

[11] Bonet Correa, Antonio. *Monasterios Iberoamericanos.* [n.p.]: Ediciones El Viso, 2001, p. 239.

**PULPIT**
Base, shaft and staircase in detail, and full view.
Iglesia de Santiago Apóstol de Pomata, Department of Puno.

In the rood screen of the same church there is a magnificent architectural organ case[12] which houses the wind instrument. It is a piece for ecclesiastical use that was made by unknown Puno school artisans in Andean Baroque style.

As with the previous piece, large and brightly coloured flowers and leaves were selected as decoration. Under a gabled roof, there is a top gallery with a remarkable cornice adorned by arches placed on turned columns.

The lower body is a flat container made from carved and turned wood which was ornamented with polychrome. Due to the inaccessibility of the piece, it was not possible to assess its condition.

The confessional in the nave of Iglesia de San Pedro Mártir - Catedral de Juli[13] is a Baroque liturgical piece of furniture. Made by anonymous Puno artisans;

[12] It currently belongs to the Prelature of Juli, Administration of the Municipal District of Pomata.

[13] It currently belongs to the Prelature of Juli, Museo Religioso de San Pedro, in the Department of Puno, Province of Chucuito. Data from the Departamento de Registro y Catalogación archives, INC Puno.

**ORGAN BOX**
Iglesia de Santiago Apóstol de Pomata, Department of Puno.

it has Spanish influences and an evident local flavour. The piece contains a seat with arms where the priest sits to administer the sacrament of confession. It has walls on the sides, an external kneeler for female penitents and a front door for the men. It is topped by a canopy.

The piece has carved wood lattices on the sides so ladies of the time could confess without being seen.

There is a polychromed central cartouche on the backrest which bears the monogram of the Society of Jesus surrounded by clouds, a frieze on the cornice and plant elements ending in a bunch of grapes.

This rustic piece was made from solid wood, polychrome, gold leaf and iron. It was constructed and decorated using carving, gilding and painting techniques.

Despite having been restored, the piece is deteriorated: it is cracked and some elements are missing.

In M. Dolores Llamosas's cell, at the Monasterio de Santa Catalina in the

CONFESSIONAL
Detail of the side.
Iglesia de San Pedro Mártir - Catedral de Juli, Department of Puno.
Height: 206 cm. Width: 83 cm.
Depth: 82 cm.

city of Arequipa, there is a wardrobe for secular use. This piece of furniture is small, and its rustic and naive features are extremely attractive. It cannot be accurately dated. This flat-fronted container has two doors; the ornaments on each side are distributed within quartered designs. It is crowned by a frieze and its lock is hidden.

**WARDROBE**
Monasterio de Santa Catalina, Arequipa.
Height: 127 cm. Width: 83.5 cm.
Depth: 57 cm.

**LARDER DOOR**
Museo del Monasterio de Santa Teresa, Arequipa.
Height: 145 cm. Width: 93 cm.

The stylised, vibrantly coloured zoomorphic and phytomorphic figures on each panel were made in Andean Baroque style, in which the proportions of the elements were altered, as was the case in many Spanish-American regions. Unknown artisans used solid local wood to build this piece, which was then decorated with polychrome, mouldings and iron.

It is not in very good condition, since both wood and paint are missing.

### WITH DISTINCTIVE CHINESE DECORATION

Covarrubias's definition of "larder" is *...a hole in the wall, with doors and shelves, used as a cupboard;*[14] this type of furniture was part of the Iberian Peninsula home fittings for everyday use from the 16TH-century. It is safe to assume that furniture such as this arrived shortly after in Spanish America and was also used for household purposes.

This particular piece is a larder door decorated in Chinese style which was probably made in the 18TH-century. It can be found in the chapterhouse of the Monasterio de Santa Teresa de Arequipa.[15]

This built-in larder has only one front door, which is right-handed. Made from local wood (probably willow), it is completely covered with polychrome in vibrant colours on a gold leaf background. Its quartered decoration has large phytomorphic elements forming diamonds by way of a treillage. The piece has iron hinges and lock.

The piece may have contained shelves for storing liturgical implements or been used as a cupboard, a simple way to solve everyday storage needs.

[14] Quoted by Aguiló Alonso, María Paz. *El Mueble en España: siglos XVI y XVII.* Madrid: Antiqvaria, 1993, p. 122.
[15] Tord, Luis Enrique. *Arequipa Artística y Monumental.* Lima: Banco del Sur del Perú, 1987, p. 125.

Venditio Iosephi. 1. B. Mose 37. C. v. 24. 28.

# X

## ROCOCO STYLE FURNITURE

## CARVED, FRETTED, POLISHED, POLYCHROMED AND GILDED WOOD

Secular and ecclesiastical, utilitarian and ornamental use

LIMA, CUSCO, AREQUIPA, PUNO AND TRUJILLO

# X

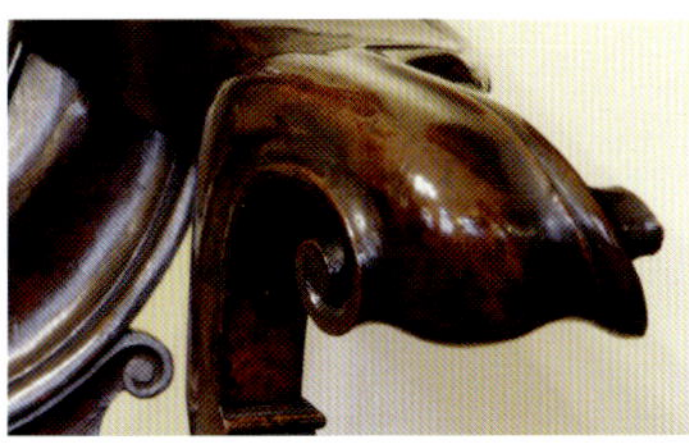

*The 18TH century is characterised by remarkable complexity: throughout a hundred-year period, a series of far-reaching transformations take place in every area of life and thought […]. In the Arts, not only opposing, but contradictory trends coexist: the last Baroque developments; the Rococo style …*[1]

The Rococo style began in The West during the first half of the 18TH century, partly due to the persistent Eastern artistic influence from China and Japan, which established an easy trade with Europe. In addition, Encyclopaedism and the Enlightenment, which pervaded the thinking of the time, gave the artists a certain freedom to create their works.

These factors resulted in a style of furniture and applied arts whose design can be linked to the aesthetic trends which arrived in Spain under the influence of the Bourbons. They were introduced by King Philip V of Spain, House of Bourbon, Duke of Anjou —the grandson of Louis XIV and Maria Theresa of Austria. Born in Versailles in 1683, he ruled Spain from 1700 to 1746. He had a great taste for things French: his education in France provided him with a cosmopolitan spirit and a mind that was open to the aesthetic changes which took place in England.

Both the French and the English Rococo stood out for an abundance of *rocaille*. The main characteristics of these styles included elegant and asymmetrical sinuosity, curves, plant motifs and above all, underwater landscapes, typical

**SACRISTY CHEST OF DRAWERS**
[OPENING] Panel detail.
Convento y Basílica de Nuestra Señora de la Merced, Lima.
18TH century (before 1773).
Chest of drawers height: 122 cm.
Depth: 124 cm.

**WARDROBE**
[OPPOSITE PAGE] Cresting detail.
Origin: Cajamarca.
Prado Heudebert family collection, Lima.
18TH century.
Height: 270 cm. Width: 180 cm.
Depth: 68 cm.

**ARMCHAIR**
[TOP] Arm detail.
Museo del Palacio Arzobispal de Lima.
18TH century.
Height: 163 cm. Width: 76 cm.
Depth: 60 cm.

[1] Checa Cremades, F., García Felguera, M.S. and Moran Turina, M. *Guía para el estudio de la Historia del Arte.* Cuadernos Arte Cátedra. Madrid: Cátedra, 1987, pages 127-128.

of *chinoiserie*, among other decorative elements which gave this style its own identity. Throughout the 18TH century, England maintained a brisk trade with Spain; thus, these artistic developments and changes in taste disseminated throughout Spain and, later, the Spanish-American colonies.

In short, there were two ways in which Eastern influence reached the viceroyalties of the Americas. The direct route was that of the Manila Galleons which, via the Philippines, transported manufactured products such as porcelain, furniture and fans from China and Japan to Spanish-American shores. The indirect route went through England and France, and introduced changes to the American continent which had been processed by European taste.

In addition, it is worth noting that English merchants flooded the Mexican market with a wide range of English furniture when trade between England and Mexico was opened in 1700, through the port of Veracruz. Sometime later, the Viceroyalty of Peru also started to trade with England.

Regarding mid-18TH-century Mexican furniture, whose aesthetic features were English-inspired and spread to and imposed on the rest of the Spanish-American world, Marita Martínez del Río de Redo stated that …*The influence of English furniture, especially evident in dressers, chairs and bureaus, begins after Queen Anne's reign (1702-1714) thanks to the direct delivery of pieces from England*

**MIRROR**
[LEFT] *Rocaille* detail.
Convento del Santísimo Rosario - Basílica y Convento de Santo Domingo, Lima.
18TH century.
Height: 230 cm. Width: 150 cm.

**CENTRE TABLE**
[RIGHT, TOP] *Rocaille* detail.
Don Alfredo Pinillos' collection, Trujillo.
18TH century.
Height: 84 cm. Width: 149 cm.
Depth: 95 cm.

**WARDROBE**
[RIGHT, BOTTOM] Detail of *treillage* on cresting.
Museo de Arte de Lima.
18TH century.
Height: 320 cm. Width: 134 cm.
Depth: 64 cm.

*to Spain [...]. English furniture is reproduced with such perfection that it is sometimes difficult to tell its origin.*[2]

The Queen Anne and, later, Chippendale styles were either inspired by the Chinese spirit, both in the lacquered, polychrome and gilded finish and in the carved bare wood, which was fretted and covered with clear lacquer, or attempted to mimic structural elements characterising the Chinese furniture that was in vogue in China during the Ming period (1368-1644), such as the *treillage* applied to any part of the pieces or the central splat on the backrest of most types of seats.

[2] Martínez del Río de Redo, Marita. "Mueble Civil". In: Carmen Aguilera *et al. El mueble mexicano. Historia, evolución e influencias.* México, Fomento Cultural Banamex, 1985. pages 64-65.

**BENCH**
[LEFT, TOP] Splat detail.
Museo del Monasterio de Santa Catalina de Sena, Cusco.
18TH century.
Height: 104 cm. Width: 206 cm.
Depth: 48.5 cm.

**CENTRE TABLE**
[LEFT, BOTTOM] *Rocaille* detail.
Don Alfredo Pinillos' collection, Trujillo.
18TH century.
Height: 84 cm. Width: 149 cm.
Depth: 95 cm.

**ARMCHAIR**
[RIGHT, TOP] Skirt detail.
Museo del Palacio Arzobispal de Lima.
18TH century.
Height: 163 cm. Width: 76 cm.
Depth: 60 cm.

**CHAIR**
[RIGHT, BOTTOM] Splat, oblong detail.
La Mansión del Fundador, Arequipa.
18TH century.
Height: 130 cm. Width: 56 cm.
Depth: 48 cm.

In $18^{TH}$-century Lima parlours, there were low seats with Queen Anne backrests, since ladies rarely used traditional Arab cushions in those rooms.

On the coast of Peru, especially in the "City of Kings" and Trujillo, furniture was built and decorated with local and incorruptible hardwoods which were resistant to damp and insects. Those included mahogany, brought from the Peruvian Amazon or Santo Domingo, cocobolo from the Amazon and to a lesser extent Nicaraguan cedar, known in Trujillo as "Figueroa" cedar. Wood was covered in clear lacquer, a technique arriving from The East in the early $17^{TH}$-century which was useful to preserve the wood and make it more attractive by providing a moderate shine.

In October 1746 there was an earthquake that devastated the city of Lima and its port, El Callao, which was flooded by a raging tsunami. After a period of mourning, the people of Lima diligently undertook the reconstruction of the city under the supervision of Viceroy Don Antonio Manso de Velasco, Count of Superunda, who consequently was considered its second founder.

Those years of feverish city rebuilding, in the third quarter of the $18^{TH}$-century, saw enormous changes which followed French aesthetic canons. These were soberly reflected in façades, altarpieces, furniture and silverwork, adapted to new stylistic trends which left behind the traditional Lima Baroque and revealed an increasing secularisation.

The techniques used to build furniture were those in which artisans were naturally skilled: carpentry, assembly, carving and fretting. Occasionally, they resorted to pastel coloured patinas and gold trimmings that gave the pieces a singular appearance and evoked the European decorative repertoire, which was similar to Venetian Rococo.

Mirrors, wardrobes topped with large combs, chairs, armchairs, benches, tables of various shapes and for different purposes, were some of the elements providing a high level of comfort to secular life.

There is, among others, a magnificent sacristy piece in the Basílica y Convento de Nuestra Señora de la Merced, in Lima; a remarkable example of Rococo ecclesiastical furniture, whose creator was determined to make the change in taste quite evident following the spanish influences which arrived in the Viceroyalty of New Spain and the Viceroyalty of Peru.

Viceroy Manuel Amat y Junyent Planella Aymerich y Santa Pau, of Catalan origin, served from 1761 to 1776. He took singer-actress and comedienne Micaela Villegas, *La Perricholi*, as a lover. Of renowned beauty, she was said to have had a

**IMAGE GLASS DISPLAY**
[TOP] *Cabriole* leg detail.
Monasterio de las Nazarenas, Lima.
$18^{TH}$ century.

**BED HEADBOARD**
[BOTTOM] Polychrome detail.
Don Alfredo Pinillos' collection, Trujillo.
$18^{TH}$ century.
Height: 141 cm. Width: 131 cm.
Depth: 7.3 cm.

certain influence over matters of State: ... *full owner of the Viceroy's sexagenarian heart, La Perricholi completely dominated his spirit.* [3]

Her celebrity was such that Jacques Offenbach wrote an operetta in three acts entitled *La Périchole.* Henri Meilhac and Ludovic Halévy's libretto in French, inspired by the life of the artist, was based on Prosper Mérimée's novel *Le Carrosse du Saint-Sacrement.*

The lady in question was extremely fond of fashion arriving from Spain. She became immediately attracted to the Rococo style, which she declared to be of the upmost desirability. Her house reflected a rustic Rococo style.

At that time, Lima adopted a refined and worldly lifestyle, and dressed its parlours in gold. Luxurious interior decoration was accompanied by the appropriate kind of furniture.

Types of furniture in this outstanding style had no other purpose than to furnish homes. They include four-poster beds, dressers, wardrobes, chairs and armchairs, sedan chairs or litters, parlour or image seats, benches, as well as side tables and centre tables, consoles, glass displays, mirrors and bureau cabinets.

Those pieces were built using various techniques and materials: direct carving, fretting, hand polishing, polychrome and full or partial gilding. Gold leaf was applied to local woods such as mahogany, cocobolo and Nicaraguan or Figueroa cedar.

[3] Lavalle y Arias de Saavedra, José Antonio de. "La Perricholi". In: Camacho, Fabio. *Aspectos de Lima.* Lima: Editorial Incazteca de F. Camacho, Empresa Publicitaria Expresión, 1929, pages XXIV-XXVIII.

MANSION OF "LA PERRICHOLI"
"Voyage de la Bonite", reproduction, edited by Arthus Bertrand, London, 1837. In: Camacho, Fabio. *Aspectos de Lima.* Lima: Editorial Incazteca de F. Camacho, Empresa Publicitaria Expresión, 1929, p. 3.

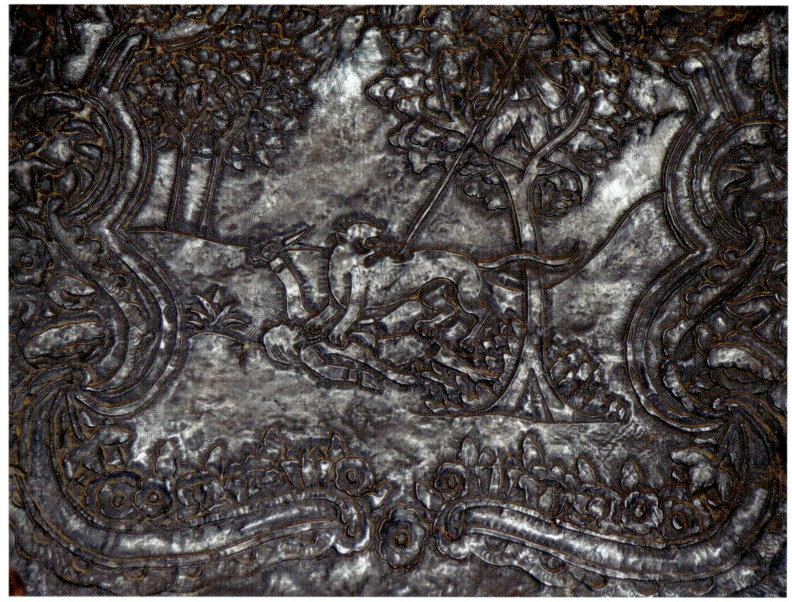

It is noteworthy that some seats, such as Renaissance *fraileros* or friar's chairs, showed a renewed style in the use of *cabriole* legs and outward-curving arms; details which made them definitely anachronistic. Two *fraileros* are worth mentioning, whose backrests were made from embossed cordovan. The first is decorated with thick foliage framing a hunting scene with a character dressed in the 18TH-century European fashion. The second portrays a street fight between three male characters also dressed in European fashions of the time. Both compositions are contained within central designs with intertwined curves, *rocaille* and asymmetric plant motifs.

**FRIAR'S CHAIR**
[LEFT] Backrest detail.
Banco Interbank - Casa del Mariscal Orbegoso, Trujillo.
18TH century.
Height: 111 cm. Width: 58 cm.
Depth: 54 cm.

**FRIAR'S CHAIR**
[RIGHT] Backrest detail.
Banco Interbank - Casa del Mariscal Orbegoso, Trujillo.
18TH century.
Height: 109 cm. Width: 60 cm.
Depth: 57 cm.

## BARE CARVED WOOD

Rococo pieces for both secular and ecclesiastical use were made in the Viceroyalty of Peru. Both uses reveal the dominant presence of an 18TH-century style which took France and England as points of reference.

Four-poster beds were found in main bedrooms of great mansions. One such bed, made by unknown artisans, is exhibited in the master bedroom of Casa de Aliaga, in the city of Lima.[4]

The structure consists of a footboard and a headboard of different heights and a canopy with curtains which is attached to the wall. The fashion of the time

4 Tord, Luis Enrique and Gjurinovic, Pedro. *El Palacio de Torre Tagle y las Casonas de Lima.* Lima: Asociación de Funcionarios del Servicio Diplomático del Perú, 2010, p. 161.
Arrarte, Eduardo R. *et al. Casa Solariega de Aliaga.* Lima: Stimulus, 2004, p. 51.

**FOUR-POSTER BED**

[TOP]

Casa de Aliaga, Lima.

18TH century.

Width: 140 cm. Length: 220 cm.

Backrest height: 190 cm.

**ARMCHAIR**

[BOTTOM, LEFT AND RIGHT] Front view and coat of arms detail on reverse.

Prado Heudebert family collection, Lima.

18TH century.

required a red silk damask bedspread matching the canopy curtains. In this case, those elements have obviously been renewed.

The solid mahogany of the piece was decorated with a profuse and interesting carving recreating an asymmetrically arranged *rocaille*, of evident European inspiration, and the structure is supported by *cabriole* legs, as dictated by the style. The piece has a clear lacquer finish and is in very good condition.

This desk armchair from the Prado Heudebert family collection is a classic example of a piece designed for a man. It was made in the mid-18TH-century Rococo style with equally evident French and English influences.

The armchair, upholstered in leather and featuring carved and polished wood mouldings, reveals typical Rococo features in its outward-curving arms and *cabriole* legs ending in goat feet —following the main trend of Old World countries— which are connected by an H-shaped crosspiece and decorated with elements appropriate to the style. Those elements are also seen in the gentle fiddle-back movement on the side stiles of the Louis XV-inspired backrest and in the cresting carved with plant motifs.

This anonymously-made piece has a wooden supporting structure and its

seat and backrest front have been reupholstered with studded leather. The original leather on the back of the seat shows a polychrome and gilded coat of arms revealing the original owners' lineage.

This armchair is in very good condition.

There is a throne or armchair, which may have been for either ecclesiastical or secular use, in the Salón Arzobispal of the Museo del Palacio Arzobispal, in the city of Lima. It is a striking Rococo piece with undeniable English influence, which reached the Spanish-American coasts in the 18TH-century. It clearly reveals the refined and capable, yet anonymous, hands of its makers in the city of Lima.

The special feature of this piece lies in its morphology: a seat with stunning backrest, fretted crest rails and sides, a central upholstered splat and outward-curving arms. It rests on *cabriole* legs which end in pad feet and are strengthened by an H-shaped crosspiece.

The solid mahogany supporting structure was carved and fretted with decorative motifs, such as *rocaille* and leaves, on both the crest rail and the skirt. The wood was covered with clear lacquer, which enhances its natural shine. Also, new fabrics cover the seat and part of the backrest.

The piece is in excellent condition.

**ARMCHAIR**
[LEFT] Museo del Palacio Arzobispal de Lima.
18TH century.
Height: 163 cm. Width: 76 cm.
Depth: 60 cm.

**ARMCHAIR**
[RIGHT] Compañía de Jesús.
Comunidad de San Pedro, Lima.
18TH century.

In the sacristy of the Iglesia de la Compañía de Jesús - Comunidad de San Pedro, in the city of Lima, there are two locally produced armchairs which were likely made in the second half of the 18TH-century.

Their key feature lies in their structure, which has an obvious Queen Anne English influence. That is why there are carved and fretted splats in the centre of their backrests, which are held by curved stiles and crowned by a carved *rocaille.* The chairs have outward-curving arms and *cabriole* legs strengthened by turned H-shaped crosspieces.

All the previously mentioned elements characterise a typical utilitarian seat, for secular or, eventually, ecclesiastical use. These armchairs were built from solid wood which was subsequently dyed in a dark colour; the seats were upholstered in red velvet. The armchairs are in good condition.

In the Salón de los Azulejos, at Casa de Aliaga, Lima, there is a splendid four-bodied bench made during the mid-18TH-century in the Rococo style. It is a seat for secular use, of a type which was usually placed in the drawing rooms of the most important houses in the Viceroyalty. These seats were occasionally made in pairs and placed against walls facing each other. They may be conceived as key features of interior design for the time, and high society ladies settled themselves on those pieces during receptions and wakes.

BENCH
Casa de Aliaga, Lima.
18TH century.
Height: 116 cm. Width: 192 cm.
Depth: 56 cm.

The consecutive backrests of this piece feature a series of fretted splats crowned by gold-leafed carvings, as well as curved arms and *cabriole* legs ending in club feet; all these elements evoke the Queen Anne style. Turned crosspieces connect legs and strengthen the structure. The key decorative element, typical of the time, is the *rocaille* repeated several times on the backrest and placed there with great attention to detail by unknown artisans.

The piece was made from solid Nicaraguan cedar wood and decorated by the application of direct carving, fretting, turning and partial gilding techniques. This bench is in very good

condition, although some backrest pieces may have been replaced. There are some patina traces.

In Don Juan Luis de Aliaga's collection, located in the city of Lima, there is a two-bodied bench for secular use with the mid-18TH-century characteristics of the Rococo style and an obvious English influence.

The piece is characterised by a backrest with straight stiles, where two splats indirectly remind us of a Ming-dynasty (China, 1368-1644) seat. The piece has *rocaille* as a main ornamental element, and curved arms and *cabriole* legs resting on club feet and demonstrating, once again, the characteristic subtle undulations of the Queen Anne style.

**BENCH**
Don Juan Luis de Aliaga's collection, Lima.
18th century.

There is a flat wooden seat, suitable for the placing of a cushion, and a slightly undulating skirt. A turned crosspiece makes the piece stronger.

This bench was made from solid wood and partially gilded by skilful anonymous artisans.

The piece is in very good condition.

## LARGE CENTRE TABLES, AN ORNAMENT IN THEMSELVES

Centre tables are a type of secular furniture which would be centrally placed in drawing rooms of great mansions. They are detached pieces, as all four sides, exquisitely decorated, are visible.

These tables rest on four *cabriole* legs at the corners, which are occasionally connected by crosspieces in the shape of a Saint Andrew's cross. However, one of the salient features of this style —demonstrating its development and improvement— is that builders usually managed without crossbars: a building challenge which made the pieces remarkably graceful. They usually have multifoil, undulating and projecting tops resting on wide skirts which may contain one or more drawers.

In the city of Trujillo, a magnificent centre table decorates the hall of the grand home of Don Alfredo Pinillos, the owner of a great furniture collection from the colonial period.

The piece was built in the 18TH-century (c. 1770-1780), in a dazzling and pure Rococo style with obvious French influence. It is a regular-sized item of furniture for secular use; useful for the placing of ornaments.

The most appealing features are the great carved and fretted aprons decorating all four sides of the skirt. It has a large multifoil top with curved angles resting on four *cabriole* legs which end in pad feet.

**CENTRE TABLE**
[OPPOSITE PAGE, TOP]
Don Alfredo Pinillos' collection, Trujillo.
18TH century.
Height: 84 cm. Width: 149 cm.
Depth: 95 cm.

**CENTRE TABLE**
[OPPOSITE PAGE, BOTTOM]
Don Alfredo Pinillos' collection, Trujillo.
18TH century.
Height: 81 cm. Width: 158 cm.
Depth: 97 cm.

**CENTRE TABLE**
[BOTTOM] Apron detail and full view.
Fundación Banco Continental BBVA - Casa de la Emancipación, Trujillo.
18TH century.
Height: 93.3 cm. Width: 221 cm.
Depth: 166 cm.

The piece was made by anonymous Trujillo craftsmen who had a marked inclination toward this style. For the ornamentation they chose phytomorphic motifs, curves and counter-curves, as well as the essential and omnipresent *rocaille*.

This table was made from solid Figueroa cedar; the carving and fretting techniques were applied without adding superfluous details, which were unnecessary considering the beauty of the piece.

The piece is in very good condition.

Right across from the one previously mentioned, there is another strictly ornamental centre table for secular use, which is also part of Don Alfredo Pinillos' collection.

The piece was made in Trujillo, in the purest Rococo style, by unknown artisans who were influenced, at the time (c. 1780), by aesthetic trends arriving from France.

It is a large item of detached furniture, whose four sides are visible. There is an ample carved and fretted apron on the waist supporting a large projecting top. It rests on four *cabriole* legs ending in pad feet.

The decorative elements include the omnipresent *rocaille* and sinuous curves and counter-curves, all asymmetrically distributed, even on the pronounced knees. The piece was made from solid Figueroa cedar, a material which enabled its makers to easily display their carving and fretting skills, producing a decoration which, as with the rest of the piece, remained bare with nothing but the natural shine of the wood. This table is in very good condition.

The centre table in the hall of Banco Continental BBVA - Casa de la Emancipación, in the city of Trujillo, was acquired by said institution from the Lima art

market. It has Rococo features with a distinct French influence. The table is a secular piece, of those which used to be centrally placed in drawing rooms of important houses throughout the Viceroyalty of Peru.

There is a flat multifoil top and four strong legs connected by a Saint Andrew's cross. In the skirt, there is a drawer covering the entire front and ornamented by movable fittings.

The table is profusely decorated with a repeated *rocaille*, leaves, cornucopia on the centre of both aprons, a blank cartouche, acanthus leaves and other ornaments. This piece was anonymously made from solid walnut decorated with the direct carving technique, covered by a layer of lacquer which provides an intense shine and adorned with engraved bronze handles on the front.

The piece is in very good condition.

The centre table in the Salón de los Azulejos, in the Casa de Aliaga, Lima, is a secular piece whose creators are unknown. It has European Rococo features.

The main characteristics are a multifoil projecting lid, a profusely carved skirt and four strong *cabriole* legs resting on spheres.

It is worth mentioning the abundant *rocaille* flanking the double-headed eagle in the centre of the skirt, which reappears on the sides of the piece, as well as the coat of arms of the Aliaga family, which is escorted by griffins. Symmetrical acanthus leaves and scales surround and complete the ornamentation.

CENTRE TABLE
Casa de Aliaga, Lima.
Height: 86 cm. Width: 160 cm. Length: 240 cm.

**GUERIDON**
Full view and apron detail.
Doña Mariana Berckemeyer Prado's collection, Lima.
18TH century.
Height: 65 cm. Width: 84 cm.
Depth: 65 cm.

A layer of clear lacquer reveals the direct carving underneath, which was applied to solid mahogany with order and moderation.

The piece is in very good condition.

The gueridon from the Prado Heudebert collection is currently in the city of Lima and its owner is Doña Mariana Berckemeyer Prado. Of unknown makers, it was produced in Lima in the mid-18TH-century with the characteristic sobriety and sophistication of the Rococo style and an obvious English influence.

It is a regular-sized piece intended for secular use, comprising a flat multifoil top, a drawer in the skirt and four carved *cabriole* legs for support.

Asymmetrically arranged leaves and flowers were selected for decoration, as well as the *rocaille*, which defines the style.

Made from dark waxed mahogany, the piece was adorned with carving and fretting techniques.

This piece is in good condition.

The centre table in Casa del Moral, in the city of Arequipa, is a typical piece decorated in a rustic Rococo style.

The top has several curves; there is a moulded drawer in the skirt and four curved legs with carvings on the knees, which are connected by straight cross-

pieces. An apron adorned with a rustic and remarkable carving stands out on the front and matches the side decoration.

**CENTRE TABLE**
La Casa del Moral - Banco de Crédito del Perú, Arequipa.
18TH century.
Height: 86 cm. Width: 122 cm.
Depth: 86 cm.

Made from dyed solid wood and decorated with *rocaille*, this table also has a scallop in the centre and curves on both sides. This piece is in good condition, even though some elements have been replaced.

A centre table[5] generously donated by the Prado family to the Museo de Arte de Lima was made by Lima artisans during the second half of the 18TH-century in Rococo style with a distinct French influence.

It is a utilitarian piece for secular use. Four cabriole legs support an undulating quadrangular top and there are large wood aprons carved on each face; these are adorned with asymmetrically distributed *rocaille*, plant elements, *rinceaux* and scrolls. The ornaments were created by fretting and direct carving onto a solid wood structure, which was subsequently covered with a clear lacquer finish.

This table, as almost every piece made in the "City of Kings" at the time, was built by anonymous craftsmen and preserved in good condition. It is complete and has not been restored.

5 Recorded in the archives of Asociación Museo de Arte de Lima under file N° V. 2.3 N° 00010. Catalogued by José Centurión Padilla on September 7, 1987.

At the Casa de Aliaga, in the historic centre of Lima, there is an English-inspired Rococo dresser with three moulded drawers, made by anonymous artisans probably in the last quarter of the 18TH-century.

This utilitarian container has an undulating front with drawers arranged in descending order, generous aprons on its three sides and *cabriole* legs, following the style of the time.

The dresser was made from solid mahogany —a kind of wood native to the

DRESSER
Detail of the side and full view.
Casa de Aliaga, Lima.
18TH century.
Height: 110 cm. Width: 137 cm.
Depth: 60 cm.

Americas— and decorated using fretting and direct carving. It is hand polished with the application of several layers of lacquer on all its faces and has metal fittings. The piece is in good condition, even though one *tirette* is missing.

## IMPRESSIVE AND EMBLEMATIC BUREAU BOOKCASES

Bureau bookcase and *secrétaire* are the names given to this splendid container built in the mid-18TH-century following the stylistic standards of the time. The piece belongs to Don Juan Luis de Aliaga's collection, located in the city of Lima. It is worth mentioning the English influence on the morphology of this magnificent utilitarian piece.

The bureau has two bodies: the upper one is crowned by a broken pediment and has glass doors which reveal three shelves for storing books. The lower body has an oblique folding lid —functioning as a desk— and five drawers carved in bas-relief on an undulating front, which ends in a profusely carved apron resting on four legs: the front of which are bevelled.

The piece is decorated following Chippendale-inspired Rococo canons. As is usual in this style, the cresting has a striking triangular broken pediment, profusely decorated with asymmetrical *rocaille* and plant details, and a bunch of feathers at the centre. On the apron, there is a carving of a Spanish-American mythological face surrounded by flowers and leaves on both sides; a detail which shows once again the syncretism present in these kinds of creations inspired by Spanish-American ancestry.

The piece was made from an attractive blonde solid wood, which was carved and fretted. Its ornamental details were partially gold-leafed producing a highly contrasting effect. The fittings were made from engraved bronze.

It is in superb condition.

In the Sala Sánchez Carrón of the Banco Central de Reserva del Perú —Casa Urquiaga[6]— in the city of Trujillo, a magnificent bureau bookcase is on display. It is a strictly utilitarian piece said to have been used by Simón Bolívar during his stay in the city. It was made in the 18TH-century in Rococo style with a clear English influence by unknown artisans of the Trujillo school.

The piece is a typical, large, two-bodied container. The upper body has two front glass doors topped by a very striking carved and fretted pediment. The lower has a curved front *arbalète*, a folding lid and three drawers with fretted

**BUREAU BOOKCASE**
[OPPOSITE PAGE] Detail of cresting and anthropomorphic figure, and full view.
Museo del Banco Central de Reserva del Perú - Trujillo Branch, Casa Urquiaga.
18TH century.
Height: 300 cm. Width: 115 cm.
Depth: 60 cm.

**BUREAU BOOKCASE**
[BOTTOM]
Don Juan Luis de Aliaga's collection, Lima.
18TH century.

[6] Currently owned by Banco Central de Reserva del Perú - Trujillo Branch.

bronze fittings. It ends in an undulating apron and rests on *cabriole* legs. The decorative motifs add luxury and elegance to the piece, revealing the high social and economic level of its original owner. They include a pair of lions facing each other and holding a central urn, *rocaille*, anthropomorphic columns, child corbels and faces of native characters, baskets on undulating side panels, as well as leaves and flowers.

This bureau was made from carved and polished Figueroa cedar. Its carvings were highlighted with gold leaf and polychrome on certain corners of the piece. Fittings were made from bronze. The piece is in very good condition but the original hinges have been replaced.

## THE INEVITABLE WARDROBES

In the city of Lima, as part of the Prado Heudebert family collection, there is a stunning wardrobe for secular use, a magnificent Cajamarca piece in Rococo style with a marked mid-18TH-century French provincial influence.

It is a useful container for storing household equipment or personal belongings, with gently curved front and sides and two front doors. Each door has a pair of carved wood panels framed by a frieze, as well as carved stiles on both sides.

This wardrobe is adorned with a multifoil upper frieze and topped by unique asymmetrical crestings on the three visible sides of the piece. It rests on four legs, the front of which are in the shape of lions' paws.

Unknown craftsmen applied their unparalleled carving and fretting skills to the solid blonde mahogany, repeatedly and asymmetrically distributing *rocaille*,

**WARDROBE**
[BOTH PAGES] Cresting detail and full view.
Origin: Cajamarca.
Prado Heudebert family collection, Lima.
18TH century.
Height: 270 cm. Width: 180 cm.
Depth: 68 cm.

curves and fruits of the land. The piece is hand polished with the application of several layers of clear lacquer. It is in very good condition.

Another magnificent wardrobe, donated by the Prado family, is exhibited in the Museo de Arte de Lima.[7] It is a typical example of Lima school furniture, inspired by the European Rococo of the last third of the 18TH-century.

**WARDROBE**
[BOTTOM, LEFT]
Museo de Arte de Lima collection.
Donated by the Prado family.
18TH century.
Height: 320 cm. Width: 134 cm.
Depth: 64 cm.

7 Recorded in the museum's Archive under file N° V-2.3 - 00122.

**WARDROBE**
[OPPOSITE PAGE AND THIS PAGE] Full view and coat of arms and cresting details.
Museo del Palacio Arzobispal de Lima.
18TH century.
Height: 290 cm. Width: 130 cm.
Depth: 67 cm.

The front of this large container has a pair of doors decorated with undulating panels containing profuse asymmetric ornamentation consisting of *rocaille* and leaves, reminiscent of French wardrobes in this style. Both sides have matching decoration. A comb on the upper frieze has a fretted *treillage* with a central *rocaille*, decoration demonstrating English influence from the Chippendale period. It ends in an undulating apron with a scallop in the centre and *cabriole* legs.

The piece was made from solid local wood —probably mahogany— and ornamented by applying carving and fretting techniques.

The piece is in good condition. Although it has been restored, some pieces of wood are missing and some fittings have been replaced.

In Sala Santiago Apóstol of Museo del Palacio Arzobispal, in Lima, there is a magnificent wardrobe for secular use, which was anonymously made in Lima during the 18TH-century following French-inspired Rococo canons.

It is a large container with two front doors crowned by an impressive fretted comb. The piece rests on four sturdy *cabriole* legs which end in claws and leaves.

On the front and sides there are carved panels with highly curved mouldings. The piece is richly ornamented with urns, *rocaille*, leaves and coats of arms flanked by columns, in an exceptionally symmetrical arrangement of elements.

This wardrobe was made from local carved and fretted woods. It is in very good condition, having been restored and the fittings replaced.

In one of the halls of the Museo del Monasterio de las Nazarenas, which belongs to the Discalced Carmelites Order of the city of Lima, there is a splendid

**WARDROBE**
Apron detail and full view.
Museo del Monasterio de las Nazarenas, Lima.
18TH century.
Height: 325 cm. Width: 147 cm.
Depth: 69 cm.

wardrobe for household use that was a key component of domestic equipment. It was made in French Rococo style during the second half of the 18TH-century by unknown craftsmen.

The piece is a container with two front doors and carved side panels. It is crowned by a striking carved cresting, which was fretted in the shape of subtle lace and matches the apron. The piece rests on four *cabriole* legs.

Decorative motifs on both comb and apron include *rocaille* and roses with stems and leaves in French-inspired Rococo style, whereas the fittings are neo-classical; a common feature in a piece which was widely used or renewed in response to the changing demands of fashion.

It was made from solid blonde mahogany and Nicaraguan cedar and has iron fittings. The piece is in very good condition.

WARDROBE
Banco Interbank - Casa del Mariscal Orbegoso, Trujillo.
18TH century.
Height: 283.5 cm. Width: 153 cm.
Depth: 78 cm.

The wardrobe in the main hall of Banco Interbank - Casa del Mariscal Orbegoso, in the coastal city of Trujillo, is an interesting piece for household use made in that city by unknown artisans. Its Rococo style highlights once again the mid-18TH-century French inspiration on both its lines and decoration.

This container features two front doors which are topped by an impressive carved and fretted cresting and supported by an undulating base. It has shelves inside and two utilitarian drawers in the skirt.

The front is decorated with four undulating panels where flower and leaf motifs are neatly distributed at the corners. In the centre of the upper panels, as well as on the comb, there are several coats of arms of the original owner.

The piece was built from a type of wood locally referred to as Figueroa cedar, which was carved and fretted. It has iron hinges. Despite some cracks and missing elements, the piece is in good condition.

In the Sala Víctor Andrés Belaúnde of the Palacio de Torre Tagle, a grand and historic house built in 1760 —currently the Peruvian Foreign Ministry— there is another large wardrobe made by local builders from solid mahogany, which was carved, fretted and polished in European Rococo style.

It is a utilitarian piece for secular use which has a pair of front doors decorated with multi-curved panels and topped by a fretted cresting in the shape of a triangular pediment. It ends in an undulating apron and stands on four *cabriole* legs. The piece is in excellent condition.

In the magnificent collection of Don Juan Luis de Aliaga —part of one of the oldest and most traditional houses of Lima— there is a splendid wardrobe made during the last quarter of the 18TH-century. It is a true exponent of Lima production of the time.

Both the wardrobe and the dresser, which replaced the traditional chest or *petaca* so widely used in previous centuries, were useful for storing linen or other valued personal belongings during long periods of sedentary life.

This particular piece is a flat utilitarian container with large front doors divided into panels and a remarkable cresting placed on a traditional "cardinal's hat" which aims to create an aesthetic discourse.

It also has an interesting apron with many curves, ending in *cabriole* legs. All these elements reveal, once again, the Bourbon influence on a piece which is similar to French provincial pieces.

The cresting is profusely decorated using carving and fretting techniques, and features *rocaille*, sharp curves and floral motifs. The light-coloured solid wood of

the four front panels was carved to form undulating mouldings. The piece is in very good condition.

### ANCIENT CHINESE INFLUENCES: BARE WOOD OR WOOD COVERED IN PASTEL-COLOURED PATINA

This continuous three-bodied bench is exhibited in the Salón de los Azulejos in the Casa de Aliaga, city of Lima. The piece has English influences in its structure and Venetian style in its decoration; evoking, once again, the spirit of Ming furniture.

The bench has the typical Queen Anne backrest, with a succession of fretted splats of eloquent harmony and simplicity. The seat with outward-curving arms rests on a skirt with profuse curves and four *cabriole* legs ending in "claw and ball" feet.

The structure, made from solid carved and fretted cedar wood, was treated with patina in a light-green shade on both bodies; partial gold-leaf highlights the ornamental details, including the usual *rocaille* and rosettes within diamonds.

The piece is in very good condition.

In the Sala de Labores of the Museo del Monasterio de Santa Catalina de Sena, a Congregation of the Dominican Order in the city of Cusco, we find an

**WARDROBE**
[OPPOSITE PAGE, TOP]
Palacio de Torre Tagle, Peruvian Ministry of Foreign Affairs, Lima.
18TH century.
Height: 288 cm. Width: 134 cm.
Depth: 73.5 cm.

**WARDROBE**
[OPPOSITE PAGE, BOTTOM LEFT] Full view and cresting detail.
Don Juan Luis de Aliaga's collection, Lima.
18TH century.

**BENCH**
Casa de Aliaga, Lima.
18TH century.
Height: 125 cm. Width: 210 cm.
Depth: 70 cm.

**BENCH**
[BOTTOM]
Museo del Monasterio de Santa Catalina de Sena, Cusco.
18TH century.
Height: 104 cm. Width: 206 cm.
Depth: 48.5 cm.

**PARLOUR CHAIR**
[OPPOSITE PAGE, LEFT]
Museo del Monasterio de Santa Catalina de Sena, Cusco.
18TH century.
Height: 94 cm. Width: 53 cm.
Depth: 40 cm.

**CHAIRS**
[OPPOSITE PAGE, RIGHT]
La Mansión del Fundador, Arequipa.
18TH century.
Height: 130 cm. Width: 56 cm.
Depth: 48 cm.

individual bench which is comparable to other previously described pieces. It was made by unknown artisans, probably in Cusco, in the last quarter of the 18TH-century. The Rococo style has an evidently English influence from the Chippendale period.

This bench for ecclesiastical or secular household use has a fretted backrest with successive and alternately decorated splats. The flat skirt features interesting and elegant carvings and gildings. It stands on *cabriole* legs connected by a triple crosspiece and has outward-curving arms.

The decorative motifs consist of the ubiquitous *rocaille*, canes and ribbons. All these elements were carved and fretted onto solid wood and highlighted with a gold leaf finish. Light brown patina demonstrates the artisans' efforts to link this piece to others of Venetian origin.

The piece is in delicate condition, there are some cracks and the patina has deteriorated.

In the same Sala de Labores of the Museo del Monasterio de Santa Catalina de Sena, in Cusco, there is an interesting parlour chair dating from the mid-18TH-century. It is a small chair whose backrest is considerably taller than the seat. These types of pieces were generally used by 18TH-century society ladies in a wide meeting room known as a *estrado*. This chair is a piece of secular furniture which may have belonged to a novice.

The piece has an obvious Rococo style and a marked English influence demonstrated by the central carved and fretted splat, as well as a Venetian influence, which can be seen in the use of pastel-blue patina and gildings. The seat, covered with traces of embroidered fabric, rests on *cabriole* legs connected by a triple crosspiece.

The chair, made from solid wood, probably of local origin, is decorated with a highly symbolic heart carved on the upper centre of the splat, along with *rocaille*, canes and rosettes, distributed among curves and *rinceaux*. It is in delicate condition. Given its great quality, the piece deserves to be restored.

This pair of Queen Anne chairs belongs to the private collection of La Mansión del Fundador, located in the city of Arequipa. The set was made during the mid-18TH-century in Rococo style.

These chairs for secular use consist of carved and fretted backrests with splats in the centre —a detail demonstrating, once again, the adoption and consolidation of English styles for colonial seats— a seat for placing a cushion and *cabriole* front legs resting on plugs and connected by a crosspiece ending in a suggestive carving.

The chairs are ornamented with *rocaille*, scallops, curves and counter-curves and gilded mouldings around the perimeter of each segment, contrasting with a suggestive light-blue background.

They are in good condition, but the patina needs to be restored.

In the Palacio del Arzobispado del Cusco, there is a sedan chair or litter: a portable seat for secular use which was built in the 18TH-century following Rococo guidelines. It was donated to the institution by its former owner, Doña Elvira González. This chair is a seat for one person which would be carried by four men. It is akin to those usually found in European palaces, which were designed for ladies not to step in the mud.

PORTABLE SEAT, SEDAN CHAIR OR LITTER
Museo del Palacio del Arzobispado del Cusco.
Donated by Doña Elvira González.
18TH century.
Height: 197 cm. Width: 126 cm.
Depth: 75 cm.

The piece is a container with an internal seat, a small side door, and windows at the front and on both sides. It is crowned by a dome-shaped canopy and rests on bases ending in carved and gilded felines. There are metal brackets on both sides to hold the poles used for carrying the litter.

Made from local wood which was partially carved and curved, the litter has a pastel background fully decorated with compositions painted on the front, back and both sides, such as *rocaille*, shells and curves, which were framed by mouldings gilded in the Rococo style. The themes are based on urban landscapes, seascapes and columns, created with the expressive language which was characteristic of the Cusco school. The first owner's coat of arms is placed on the back.

The piece is in very good condition.

In a bedroom of Don Alfredo Pinillos' ancestral home, located in the city of Trujillo, there is a bed made in the mid-18TH-century by anonymous, probably local, artisans. The Rococo style of the headboard decoration has a clear French influence in its stylistic ideas and its finish resembles Venetian furniture of the time.

The flat headboard is flanked by columns, covered with greenish patina and polychrome ornamentation, which gives the piece the gentle and refined appearance so characteristic of the Rococo style.

**BED**
Backrest detail.
Don Alfredo Pinillos' collection, Trujillo.
18TH century.
Height: 141 cm. Width: 131 cm.
Depth: 7.3 cm.

The surface has gilded reliefs in the form of *rocaille*, leaves, flowers and scrolls, surrounded by an undulating moulding made from solid wood.

The piece is in very good condition.

### FOR DISPLAYING RELIGIOUS IMAGES, ORNAMENTS OR FAMILY MEMORABILIA

The glass image display case in the Museo del Monasterio de las Nazarenas of the Discalced Carmelites Order, in Lima, is a container for ecclesiastical or secular use intended for the display of particularly venerated religious images. Different images would be displayed following the religious calendar. The frequent use of this type of furniture demonstrates the domestic devotion of both cloistered nuns and viceregal society ladies. In some cases, kneelers were placed in front of the pieces.

The piece was built and decorated in the Rococo style in vogue during the 18TH-century and reveals French and Venetian influences. This piece is divided

**IMAGE GLASS DISPLAY**

[BOTH PAGES] Apron, carvings and cresting details, and full view.
Museo del Monasterio de las Nazarenas, Lima.
18TH century.

into two bodies; the upper is an image container, while the lower is for support. The main structural characteristics of this display case are a front door with moulded glass and see-through glass panes on the sides. It is crowned by a semi-dome, ending in pinnacles and surrounded by a triple cresting which gives special significance to the piece. It rests on an *ad hoc* support table with four *cabriole* legs connected by carved crosspieces.

On a hazel patina background, painted flowers and leaves cover the entire surface; just like the pieces of Rococo Venetian furniture which were decorated with *lacca povera*. The rest of the decoration consists of *rocaille*, scallops and asymmetrical carved and gilded curves. On the four corners, there are corbels in the shape of children with cane headdresses.

This display case was made from solid carved and fretted wood, covered with patina and pastel polychrome; it has a gilded moulding and a dark fillet providing contrast. The piece is in very good condition, even though it has not been restored. Covering furniture with patinas in a light palette became a trend in the mid-18TH century, especially in peripheral production centres, such as Venice, Spain, Portugal, and in the New World, which adopted this finishing technique that gave the pieces the features appropriate to their time in order to replace lacquers from the East, as they were so expensive and, sometimes, unaffordable.

In one of the halls of the Palacio Goyeneche, in the city of Lima,[8] there is a strictly ornamental, glass, corner display-case for secular use. This type of display-case, placed in the corners of drawing rooms in the most important houses, was used to present ornaments and family memorabilia, fans or hard rocks. This piece was made by anonymous Lima craftsmen in French-inspired Rococo style, probably in the third quarter of the 18TH-century.

It is a triangular container topped by an undulating and partially moulded and fretted cresting. Glass front doors reveal its contents. The piece is supported by a pair of *cabriole* front legs and a quadrangular rear leg.

The outer sides are covered in bright-red patina and gilded mouldings. The interior, divided by shelves, is decorated with a succession of gallant scenes filled with 18TH-century characters wearing elegant Bourbon garments. These scenes make up a sequence, where the story is strung together by establishing a relationship between the French aristocracy of the time and Oriental characters.

The case was made from carved and fretted solid local wood; gold leaf, patina and polychrome on light backgrounds were used for decoration.

The piece is in very good condition.

**CORNER GLASS DISPLAY**
Detail of gallant and Chinese-style scenes on the background, and full view.
Banco de Crédito del Perú - BCP, Casa Goyeneche, Lima.
18TH century.
Height: 254 cm. Width: 130 cm.
Depth: 96 cm.
Courtesy of BCP.

## ECCLESIASTICAL FURNITURE MADE FROM BARE CARVED WOOD

With a renewed aesthetic vision after the earthquake which devastated the city of Lima in 1746, ecclesiastical furniture also followed Rococo structural and decorative patterns in remarkable pieces of furniture. These pieces accompanied the architectural changes resulting from the reconstruction of most places of worship, monasteries and convents.

In turn, these stylistic changes spread to the province of La Libertad; thus, some exceptional examples of liturgical furniture can be found in certain Trujillo churches.

Sacristy furniture, pulpits, cathedrae, choir stalls, sacristy tables, thrones, domestic chapels, mirrors, pedestals and image cradles (for enthroning religious images), biers or catafalques are examples of religious pieces decorated in Rococo style that would also feature the stylistic changes that took place in Europe.

These pieces were made and decorated with the usual materials and tech-

[8] Former Goyeneche family collection - Banco Central de Reserva del Perú. Casa Goyeneche was inaugurated in 1771 by its first owners, the Cavero y Vásquez de Acuña family, and inherited in 1894 by the descendants of the Goyeneche y Gamio family. Heritage archives of Banco de Crédito del Perú.

niques: direct carving, fretting, lacquering, polychrome and gilding applied to mahogany, cocobolo and Figueroa or Nicaraguan cedar.

It is worth mentioning the individuality and magnificence of a sacristy chest of drawers in the sacristy of the Basílica y Convento de Nuestra Señora de la Merced, city of Lima. It was produced by anonymous builders and carpenters from Lima, who had a Rococo influence and revealed the marked English inspiration in vogue from the mid-18TH-century until 1773.[9]

9 Bernales Ballesteros, Jorge. "Evolución estilística de Lima: del mudéjar al neoclásico". In: Ortiz de Zevallos, Augusto. *Lima a los 450 años.* Lima: Centro de Investigación, Universidad del Pacífico, 1986, pages 126-127.
Camacho, Fabio. Op. cit., p. 34.
Bonet Correa, Antonio. *Monasterios Iberoamericanos.* [n.p.]: Ediciones El Viso, 2001, p. 206.

**SACRISTY PIECE**
Side detail.
Basílica y Convento de Nuestra Señora de la Merced, Lima.
18TH century (before 1773).
Chest of drawers height: 122 cm.
Depth: 124 cm.

**SACRISTY PIECE**
[LEFT AND BOTTOM] Central niche with image on central alcove and *églomisé* glass panel. In detail. Basílica y Convento de Nuestra Señora de la Merced, Lima. 18TH century (before 1773). Chest of drawers height: 122 cm. Depth: 124 cm.

**CATHEDRA**
[OPPOSITE PAGE] *Rocaille* detail and full view. Museo del Palacio Arzobispal de Lima. 18TH century. Height: 500 cm. Width: 230 cm. Depth: 70 cm.

The most attractive feature is the original glass panels painted on the reverse and placed on the upper body, using a decorative technique which was widespread in China during the Kangxi period (1662-1722). This technique is called *églomisé* and was widely used in France, England and Italy during the 18TH-century. The panels recount scenes from the Bible —both the Old and New Testaments— populated with characters, some of them wearing 18TH-century attire. These compositions are framed by Venetian-style, acid-etched, glass panels.

This ecclesiastical utilitarian piece, in the shape of a large U, would be placed against sacristy walls. It is divided into two bodies; the upper is decorated with

illustrated panels alternating with mirrors. There is a central alcove where the image the Virgin of Mercy is enthroned. On the lower body, a chest of drawers with *bombé* fronts and three large drawers alternates with doors for storing clothes and liturgical utensils. This chest also has a curved and richly carved apron, which completes the piece.

Decorative elements include: *rocaille*, distributed to form various shapes; leaf motifs in which symmetry is an additional attribute; a remarkable cresting topping each panel; and corbels on alternate bays. The central alcove is topped by a broken pediment and flanked by columns. The composition is completed with children faces, bishop tassels and indigenous faces on the legs.

The chest was made from mahogany, which was carved, fretted, curved and finished with clear lacquer; bat-shaped bronze fittings were installed on each drawer and the entire piece was decorated with painted glass and mirror fragments.

The piece is in delicate condition.

A majestic cathedra dominates Salón del trono of Museo del Palacio Arzobispal, in Lima. It is a classic piece of ecclesiastical furniture intended for the prior of a religious order to preside over a Chapter.[10] The piece was designed and constructed in Lima during the 18TH-century using a Mannerist structure and French-inspired Rococo decoration.

The piece is divided into two bodies. The upper takes the form of a cresting in the shape of a "cardinal's hat", functioning as a round arch, on top of the backrest. On the lower, where the armchair is located, there is a high backrest with decorative elements contained within a round arch placed under a pediment. The side bays unify both bodies.

The profuse decoration includes a Sacred Heart on the top, canes, a blank cartouche, asymmetrical *rocaille* in the background covering almost the entire surface, flowers, rosettes and large corbels placed on both sides. All these elements were applied to carved Nicaragua cedar wood; hand polished with the application of several layers of lacquer.

10 Piece was included in Museo del Palacio Arzobispal de Lima collection during the 20TH century (c. 1970). Information provided by Monsignor Ricardo Wiesse Thorndike and Monsignor Raúl Chau, assistant to the Archbishop of Lima.

This piece is in very good condition, since it has been restored.

In the Museo de los Descalzos - Convento de los Franciscanos Descalzos, Rímac, city of Lima, there is a cathedra with a tribune for ecclesiastical use. It has a unique morphology, which may have been specifically commissioned in order to serve two functions: a throne presiding over the Chapter and a small pulpit. The combination being designed to fit a reduced space: *...a small pulpit from under which a semicircular seat for the local prior emerges; since theological studies were presented [at the institution], so courses and discussions may have taken place there.*[11] The cathedra was made by unknown craftsmen during the second half of the 18$^{TH}$-century in Rococo style with a marked English influence, as was usually the case in Lima during that period.

The piece has a small pentagonal tribune, with an additional cathedra attached to the front. It has outward-curving arms and *cabriole* front legs.

Each body has overlapping multifoil panels divided by flat columns; these panels were decorated with simple motifs such as corbels and stylised leaves.

The piece was made from partially carved mahogany and finished with clear lacquer.

It is in good condition.

CATHEDRA WITH A TRIBUNE
Museo de los Descalzos - Convento de los Franciscanos Descalzos, Rímac, Lima.
18$^{TH}$ century.
Total height: 160 cm.
Tribune height: 106 cm.
Width: 97 cm.
Depth: 108.5 cm.

In the Salón de los Diezmos, Museo Catedralicio de la Basílica Menor de Trujillo,[12] there is a bench which was originally placed in the lower choir of the cathedral. It was produced in Trujillo in the Rococo style, of unquestionable European influences, that was in vogue during the second half of the 18$^{TH}$-century, when it was adopted and frequently used by the Church as a means of artistic expression.

This bench is supported by two planks set on both ends, with carvings depicting the duality of the viceregal world. There is a feline or indigenous face on one side and an angel sticking out its tongue on the other, which may symbolise the Spanish rule.[13] Both planks rest on sturdy bases, connected by a crosspiece placed almost at floor level for reinforcement.

---

[11] Bernales Ballesteros, Jorge. *Lima, la ciudad y sus monumentos.* Seville: Escuela de Estudios Hispano-Americanos de Sevilla, 1972, p. 212.

[12] It currently belongs to the Trujillo - La Libertad Metropolitan archbishopric.

[13] Information retrieved from the museum by the author.

**CHOIR STALL**
"Plank" leg and anthropomorphic figure details.
Museo Catedralicio, Basílica Menor de Trujillo.
18TH century.
Height: 79 cm. Width: 181 cm.
Depth: 52 cm.

In addition to the abovementioned anthropomorphic carvings, *rocaille* and plant motifs surround and complete the decoration.

The piece was made from Amazonian mahogany and hand polished with the application of several layers of lacquer. A padded and studded leather cushion is placed on the seat, which has been restored.

The piece is in good condition.

The domestic chapel in a private Lima collection[14] is a piece for secular use. It was made in Rococo style in 1771, according to the inscription on the cartouche placed on the cresting.

Under its magnificent cresting, on the outer face, there are two front doors with a carved panel on each. Inside, there are many niches containing a crucifix and other religious images. Under the central niche, and with an irregular front, there is a display case consisting of three glass sides, which houses a Nativity

[14] It used to belong to the family of its current owner.

**DOMESTIC CHAPEL**
Cartouche detail and full view.
Private collection, Lima.
18<sup>TH</sup> century (c. 1771).
Height: 188 cm. Width: 111 cm.
Depth: 36 cm.

scene. It is also decorated with round arches separated by turned anthropomorphic columns. The lower body has a pair of small drawers and *tirettes*, in the English style, where the candlesticks illuminating the images would be placed.

The markedly asymmetrical decorative motifs include *rocaille*, children faces and leaves. Anonymous Lima artisans built this piece from solid Nicaraguan cedar, which was carved and pierced, and decorated with gold-leaf details. The piece is in very good condition.

The sacristy table in the centre of the sacristy anteroom at the Basílica Catedral de Lima is a large detached piece which was used to hold liturgical implements before and after ceremonies. Made during the second half of the 18TH-century in the Rococo style, it demonstrates the expressive freedom of the period.

Following the dictates of this style, its makers resorted to asymmetry to

**SACRISTY TABLE**
Full view and apron detail.
Basílica Catedral de Lima.
18TH century.
Height: 90 cm. Width: 210 cm.
Depth: 135 cm.

distribute *rocaille*, leaves, flowers and *rinceaux*. It has a multifoil top resting on a skirt, which has large carved and fretted aprons, and stands on eight sturdy and profusely decorated *cabriole* legs.

The table was made from solid Nicaraguan cedar and covered with a thin layer of clear lacquer, which gives it a moderate shine.

The piece is in excellent condition.

The centre table in the sacristy of Compañía de Jesús - Comunidad de San Pedro, in Lima, is a utilitarian piece intended for the placing of liturgical implements before and after ceremonies. It was designed and built with features similar to those of Queen Anne furniture, which were dominant in England during the first quarter of the 18TH-century.[15]

This piece stands out for its sobriety. It has a large rectangular projecting top resting on a broad skirt.

Supported by four cabriole legs, the coffee table has a unique and undulating crosspiece in the shape of a Saint Andrew's cross, which is connected at the centre by the carved image of a hound.

---

[15] Camacho, Fabio. Op. cit., p. 32.

**SACRISTY TABLE**
[OPPOSITE PAGE] Detail of a hound on Saint Andrew's cross and full view. Compañía de Jesús, Comunidad de San Pedro, Lima
18TH century.

**PEDESTAL**
[RIGHT] Museo de Arte Religioso of the Basílica Catedral de Lima.
18TH century.
Height: 58 cm. Width: 87.5 cm.
Depth: 46 cm.

**MIRROR**
Full view and cresting detail.
Basílica de Santo Domingo, Convento del Santísimo Rosario de Lima.
18TH century.
Height: 230 cm. Width: 150 cm.

The table, made from solid mahogany, is covered only with a clear lacquer finish. The piece is in very good condition.

In one of the Salas Brazzini in the Museo de Arte Religioso of the Basílica Catedral de Lima, there is a base or pedestal: an ornamental piece designed for enthroning a religious image. It has soft curves, typical of the Rococo style in vogue during the 18TH-century, and rests on five small legs.

This item was made from carved solid walnut wood, which was later covered with clear lacquer. The piece is in very good condition.

This mirror —part of a set of four— is to be found in the sacristy of the Basílica de Santo Domingo, Convento del Santísimo Rosario, in Lima. It was made in the 18TH-century through the remarkable efforts of anonymous artisans, who revealed their inclination towards the European Rococo spirit.

This is a decorative arts piece which had the purpose of propagating light; it could also have been an ornamental piece for ecclesiastical or secular use.

There is a vertical mirror with a profuse and asymmetrical decoration on its cresting, which is repeated on the rest of the piece. The structure was made from solid mahogany, adorned with exceptional carvings and fretwork, and was hand polished with the application of several layers of lacquer in order to highlight the decoration and preserve the piece. The piece is in very good condition.

In the sacristy of the Basílica y Convento de Nuestra Señora de la Merced, in Lima, there is a magnificent built-in wardrobe held by a frame, with two front doors. This Rococo piece dates from 1776; information revealed on its upper pediment. Because of its function, it is a piece of ecclesiastical furniture, although it

WARDROBE
Cresting, in detail.
Basílica y Convento de Nuestra Señora de la Merced, Lima.
18TH century (c. 1776).
Height: 300 cm. Width: 153 cm.

might also be a secular piece. The French influence can be seen in the plethora of ornaments placed on the comb, including *rocaille*, curves and asymmetrical elements. The solid wood doors are divided into four carved panels creating an effect of moving lines. The piece was decorated with carvings combined with exquisite fretwork on the mahogany, and was hand polished with the application of several layers of lacquer. This wardrobe is in good condition, even though its lock does not match the style or the period.

## CARVED WOOD ECCLESIASTICAL FURNITURE WITH COLOUR AND GOLD LEAF FINISHINGS

In the nave of the Parroquia San Antonio de Padua - Iglesia San Agustín de los P.P. Franciscanos, in the city of Trujillo, there is a magnificent pulpit sounding board[16]

[16] González, Elena (ed). *Trazos del pasado: El período colonial en La Libertad.* Lima: Asociación Marsa, 2008, p. 55.

for liturgical use. It was built in Trujillo in the purest French Rococo style during the 18TH-century. The rest of the pulpit was later replaced, since it was destroyed in an earthquake and only the upper body remained intact.

A magnificent carved, fretted and gilded comb stands on a huge scallop called "fan-shaped shell". Other ornaments include asymmetrically arranged *rocaille*, floral motifs, leaves, curves and counter-curves. On the sides, cherubs and guardian angels flank the image of San Francisco Solano which crowns the piece.

The sounding board was made from solid wood by unknown craftsmen who fully covered and enhanced the piece with gold leaf and partially decorated it with polychrome. The piece is in excellent condition.

In the presbytery, behind the high altar, of the Iglesia de San Pedro Mártir - Catedral de Juli[17] there are three liturgical thrones made during the second half of the 18TH-century in Rococo style with an English influence.

These seats are hierarchically organised according to their size and their magnificent backrests, whose fretted central splats are decorated with Chippendale

---

[17] The pieces currently belong to the Prelature of Juli, Museo Religioso de San Pedro, Department of Puno, Province of Chucuito. Data from the Departamento de Registro y Catalogación del Instituto Nacional de Cultura, Puno.

**PULPIT**
[OPPOSITE PAGE] Sounding board detail.
Parroquia San Antonio de Padua - Iglesia San Agustín PP. Franciscanos, Trujillo.
18TH century.

**CEREMONIAL THRONE**
[BOTTOM] Cresting, in detail.
Iglesia de San Pedro Mártir - Catedral de Juli, Department of Puno.
18TH century.
Height: 156 cm. Width: 68 cm.
Depth: 56 cm.

interlaced ribbons. They also have outward-curving arms and *cabriole* legs ending in pad feet. The seats are flat wood, suitable for the placing of cushions.

The central throne has a striking cresting which sets it apart from the rest. Dominant decorative motifs include shells, a central cartouche ornamented with a pineapple and some leaves, as well as curves and *rinceaux* on each side.

Made from carved and fretted solid wood by anonymous artisans, the thrones were covered in a variety of vibrantly coloured polychrome subsequently highlighted with gold-leafed mouldings.

The piece is in good condition, although some elements added to the backrests do not match the style.

The Monasterio de las Nazarenas, of the Discalced Carmelites Order, in Lima, is ... *one of the most complete Rococo monuments in Lima; erected in 1766-1771 [...]. This building shows the eagerness for innovation in traditional Baroque floorplans, with changes that were also introduced by Spanish architects, who were influenced by French trends.*[18] The pedestal in the museum of this monastery, designed for enthroning a religious image, consists of a single piece of reduced height.

Made in Venetian-inspired Rococo style, it has multifoil shapes on its three visible sides and a pastel polychrome finish.

This proves the existence of Rococo furniture production in peripheral locations, such as Venice, Spain, Portugal and the New World, which drew inspiration from French and English aesthetic trends during most of the 18TH-century.

Unknown builders made this piece by carving a wood base, and covered the background in hazel patina. Other elements worth mentioning are dark mouldings and gold leaf. Evenly distributed asymmetrical curves and floral motifs were selected as decorative elements. Finally, gilded *rocaille* and scallops complete the ornamentation. The piece is in very good condition, since it was duly restored.

The Sala de Labores at the Real Monasterio de Clarisas de Santa María de Gracia, in the city of Trujillo, exhibits an image cradle. It is a small Spanish-inspired piece, intended for ecclesiastical use, which was made during the 18TH-century in Rococo style with a European influence.

The piece was designed to display the image of a reclining Infant Jesus for worship. The headboard and footboard are of different heights and feature turned columns ending in pinnacles of various shapes; both are decorated with feathers and an oriental landscape painted in bright colours. The piece rests on four *cabriole* legs.

---

[18] Bernales Ballesteros, Jorge. *Lima, la ciudad y sus monumentos.* Op. cit., p. 339.

PEDESTAL
Museo del Monasterio de las Nazarenas, Lima.
18TH century.
Height: 59 cm. Width: 58 cm.
Depth: 37 cm.

This cradle was made by unknown craftsmen from a type of wood which was most probably local. The piece was carved, turned and covered in polychrome; a gold leaf finish highlights its carvings. The piece is in very good condition.

In the Sala De Profundis of the Monasterio de Santa Catalina, in Arequipa, there is a catafalque or bier whose function was to hold the lifeless corpse of a congregation member during a twenty-four hour wake and then transport it to its final place of rest. Square shaped, with a Chippendale (c. 1750) perimeter balustrade, it also has pinnacles on the corners and two poles for transportation.

The image of St. Catherine of Siena, with angels on both sides, is reproduced on the headboard, which was carved in low relief, fretted and painted.

This item was made from wood and has a patina and polychrome finish. It is a piece of conventual ecclesiastical furniture. The piece is in good condition, although the paint has deteriorated.

IMAGE CRADLE
Real Monasterio de Clarisas de Santa María de Gracia, Trujillo.
18TH century.

**CATAFALQUE OR BIER**
Headboard detail and full view.
Monasterio de Santa Catalina, Arequipa.
18TH century.
Height: 132 cm. Width: 70 cm.
Length: 330 cm.

# XI

## NEOCLASSICAL FURNITURE

## CARVED, GILDED, POLISHED, AND POLYCHROMED WOOD WITH MARQUETRY OR INLAY

Liturgical and household, ecclesiastical and secular use

LIMA, CUSCO, AREQUIPA AND TRUJILLO

# XI

## APPRECIATION AND REINTERPRETATION OF ART FROM ANTIQUITY

The discoveries at Herculaneum in 1738 and Pompeii in 1748 led to a Classical World revival. European artists drew on Greco-Roman aesthetics and neoclassicism emerged as an art movement.

These illustrious Old World trends turned against Baroque and Rococo aesthetics, becoming an inspiration to art theorists and a driving force during the last quarter of the $18^{TH}$-century.

The neoclassical style was based on canons which were initially developed in architecture, imposing once again an inclination towards distinct, simple and geometrical lines. Neoclassicism was characterised by the survival of columns with Doric, Ionic or Corinthian capitals, barrel vaults, niches and round arches to house sculptures, among other ornamental details.

During the reign of Louis XVI (1754-1793), France embraced the new style, continuing this aesthetic trend —after the French Revolution— with the Consulate, Directory and Empire styles. Meanwhile in England, with a sick George III (1738-1820), the work of architect Robert Adam and his fervent followers in North America became renowned.

At the same time in Spain, during the reign of Ferdinand VI (1746-1759), an enthusiastic sponsor of the research and study of antiquity, the Real Academia de San Fernando was founded in 1752 with that goal in mind; remaining open until 1840. The monarch ordered the translation into Spanish of the *Vitruvius' Treatise* and studies by the great Renaissance masters, to impart theoretical teachings to artists and students of the time.

**FLOOR LECTERN**
[OPENING] Lectern detail.
Museo de Arte Religioso of Convento San Francisco y Catacumbas, Lima.
Late $18^{TH}$ or early $19^{TH}$ century.
Height: 151 cm. Width: 70 cm.
Depth: 26 cm.

**ALTAR**
[OPPOSITE PAGE] Panel detail.
Monasterio de Santa Catalina, Arequipa.
Late $18^{TH}$ century.
Height: 98 cm. Width: 238 cm.
Depth: 65 cm.

*This leads to a better understanding of the figure of Charles III as a promoter of archaeology and as a central character in the history of archaeology; a fact which is rarely acknowledged.*

*Educated by his mother, Elizabeth Farnese, in the appreciation of antiquity, he is responsible for such a crucial event as the discovery of and the first excavations at Pompeii, Herculaneum and Stabiae, [...] because [...] he sponsored and promoted the entire enterprise as a royal patron...*[1]

The scientific interest of cultural institutions of the time was enriched by the influence of the Enlightenment rationalism, which later spread to the American colonies.

In 1777 the Spanish Crown delegated to the Church the supervision of architecture and additional applied arts which would be developed throughout the Spanish Empire. *New communities adopted neoclassicism as the official liturgical ornament for the creation of their architectural work and the growth of sculptural spaces.*[2]

Prelates were in charge of controlling artists, placing a special emphasis on the design of altarpieces for their sees. These had to represent and reflect a classical and defined style; in addition, the use of wood in architecture was expressly forbidden, in order to promote the use of masonry and stucco decoration.

Those measures aimed to do away with art practices which were considered morally unsuitable, since, according to the thinking of the time, the Rococo style "contributed to the creation of backward peoples".

The illustrious Lima of the last quarter of the 18TH-century continued with a process of beautification, which had begun during the viceroyalty of Don Manuel Amat y Junyent Planella Aymerich y Santa Pau (1761-1776), featuring works of a visibly French style, but placing emphasis on artistic changes occurring in Europe. *...decorative forms acquired extraordinary originality and became finer and more*

---

1 Almagro-Gorbea, Martín. "De Pompeya a Palenque: la arqueología ilustrada y la Corona de España". *Reales Sitios*, year XLVII, vol. Nº 183, first quarter of 2010, pages 42-63.

2 Pignoli, Giorgio, Rosenberg, Lucio and Altmann, Kenneth. *Diccionario de Estética*. Buenos Aires: Quadrata, 2003, p. 109.

**COUNTER-PULPIT**
[OPPOSITE PAGE, TOP] Cresting detail.
Iglesia y Convento de San Francisco de Lima, Basílica Menor, Lima.
Attributed to Prb. Arch. Matías Maestro or artisans from his workshop.
Late 18TH century.
Height: 240 cm. Width: 120 cm.
Depth: 50 cm.

**LECTERN**
[OPPOSITE PAGE, BOTTOM] Detail of panel with monogram.
Museo de los Descalzos - Convento de los Franciscanos Descalzos, Rímac, Lima.
Early 19TH century.
Height: 208 cm. Width: 122 cm.
Depth: 122 cm.

**ARMCHAIR**
[TOP] Leg detail.
Museo de Arte Religioso of Convento San Francisco y Catacumbas, Lima.
Late 18TH or early 19TH century.
Height: 131 cm. Width: 77 cm.
Depth: 64 cm.

*typical of Lima; there was a pompous and graceful transition from Rococo to Louis XVI's neoclassicism ...*[3]

Despite the general promulgation of ideas throughout the whole Viceroyalty, considerable distances made it difficult for new artistic trends to arrive, thus these fashions were often limited to the more illustrious urban settings. Martha Barriga Tello claims that... *in Peru the Andean region developed an artistic production which was independent to that of the coastal areas, and particularly of Lima production; it was formally closer to Upper Peru, in present-day Bolivia."*[4]

The educated population who easily adapted to changes related to classical forms lived mainly in the most important cities. With reference to the reinterpretation of classical art, Ramón Gutiérrez states: ... *neoclassicism was limited to urban elites and some enlightened religious people, who tried to impose an official art that imitated classical models. This universal and abstract modernity turned its back on reality and created a fictitious world which was distant from Spanish-American landscapes as well as indigenous and Creole customs.*[5]

In turn, Jorge Bernales Ballesteros believes that: ... *despite the catastrophic neoclassical fashion, which could hardly impose rules on essentially spontaneous and lavish peoples, it is not surprising that this passing fashion did not reflect the artistic sensitivities of the people of Lima the way the golden Baroque of the 17TH- and 18TH-centuries had. [...] Undoubtedly, the Baroque tradition would not perpetuate indefinitely; the cycle had to be closed; but the linear fashion of severe and fixed canons failed to impose itself on the Peruvian taste and died out after becoming a novelty for a short season, and after having destroyed quite a few altarpieces and even churches from the past splendour of Lima.*[6]

The changes that were taking place, which became aesthetic links, were seeds for the dominant neoclassical furniture of the time in the coastal regions of the Viceroyalty of Peru. This furniture would later give rise to the Republican style - in vogue throughout most of the 19TH-century —after the Declaration of Independence of Peru, as part of a universal phenomenon.

---

3 Velarde, Héctor. *Arquitectura peruana.* Mexico: Fondo de Cultura Económica, 1946, p. 86.

4 Barriga Tello, Martha. *Influencia de la Ilustración borbónica en el arte limeño: siglo XVIII.* Lima: Fondo Editorial de la Universidad Nacional Mayor de San Marcos, 2004, p. 87.

5 Gutiérrez, Ramón. "Artes utilitarias en el Virreinato de Perú". In: Gutiérrez, Ramón (coord). *Pintura, escultura y artes útiles en Iberoamérica, 1500-1825.* Colección Manuales Arte Cátedra. Madrid: Arte Cátedra, 1995, pages 345-346.

6 Bernales Ballesteros, Jorge. "La moda neoclásica". In: *Lima, la ciudad y sus monumentos.* Seville: Escuela de Estudios Hispano-Americanos de Sevilla, 1972, pages 343-344.

## MATÍAS MAESTRO, ARCHITECT OF THE TURN TO NEOCLASSICISM

In 1791, Charles IV of Spain (1748-1819) ratified his predecessor's measures and, in Lima, Archbishop Juan Domingo González de la Reguera (1720-1805) commissioned the Basque priest and architect, Matías Maestro, to remodel the Archbishopric see. Maestro was born in 1766 in Vitoria, the capital of Álava, in the Basque Provinces of Spain, and died in Peru in 1835. He was an architect and artist with an academic background who earned his reputation from his vast culture and versatility. He settled in Lima before 1790, where he took holy orders in 1793.

To replace beautiful and unique Baroque and Rococo works of art, he designed and implemented new fronts for altars, altarpieces and other liturgical elements in neoclassical style. Among his works, it is worth mentioning the altars of Compañía de Jesús - Comunidad de San Pedro, Iglesia y Convento de San Francisco, and the Catedral, all in the city of Lima. The latter was re-inaugurated in 1805. After the

**COUNTER-PULPIT**
Cresting detail.
Basílica Catedral de Lima.
Late 18$^{TH}$ century.
Height: 280 cm.

mid-18TH-century earthquake, the altar had to be restored using neoclassical ornamentation, following this new artistic impetus. Maestro also erected the Casa de Ejercicios de Santa Rosa and the Colegio de Medicina de San Fernando and designed the layout for the Cementerio General of the city of Lima.

Friar José Llera, praising the decisions made by the Basque architect Matías Maestro, reflected on the matter thus: *In order art has attempted / To ease Tuscan rudeness, / Enhance the admired Ionic, / In Doric and Corinthian gentleness; / From this compound the result being, / with more charms, grace, strength, / proportion and sculpture of its ways, / Altarpiece is Maestro, archetype of all.* [7]

Changes inspired by the Greco-Latin world pervaded other artistic expressions, such as churches and secular buildings, made or modified as appropriate, making a strong impact on the society of the time. Their influence was partly due to the saturation provoked by the outdated Rococo style and its high cost.

*Nevertheless, and although he was not entirely to blame because in his time the Baroque was being scorned, his work was rather destructive and harmful to the art of these countries.* [8] During this stage of religious art modernisation, the Creole priest José Manuel Bermúdez (1742-1830) wrote … *a translation, unpublished to date, of the classic work by Friar Juan Interián de Ayala,* Pictor Christianus Eruditus *—based on the Latin edition printed in Madrid in 1730— summarising the precepts of the doctrinal orthodoxy on religious art in order to prevent "mistakes often made when painting and sculpting the Holy Images"* [9], concepts which reinforce the idea of renewal of art in general by returning to the sources.

## NEW AND FINAL ARTISTIC LANGUAGES IN THE TWILIGHT OF THE VICEROYALTY

### CARVED FURNITURE FOR ECCLESIASTICAL USE, WITH OR WITHOUT GOLD LEAF

By the end of the colonial period —late 18TH- and early 19TH- centuries— due to the above political and religious decisions and the resulting classical influences on art, the characteristics of ecclesiastical furniture production resembled those

---

7 Mujica Pinilla, Ramón. "Arte e identidad: las raíces culturales del barroco peruano". In: Mujica Pinilla, Ramón *et al. El Barroco Peruano.* Vol. 1. Colección Arte y Tesoros del Perú. Lima: Banco de Crédito del Perú, 2002, p. 22.

8 Vargas Ugarte, S.J., Rubén. *Ensayo de un diccionario de artífices coloniales de la América Meridional,* [n.p.]: Talleres Gráficos A. Baiocco, 1947, p. 322.

9 Wuffarden, Luis Eduardo. "Imágenes en defensa del dogma: El grabado religioso, entre la Contrarreforma y la Ilustración." In: Michaud, Cécile and Torres Della Pina, José (eds). *De Amberes al Cusco. El grabado europeo como fuente del arte virreinal.* Lima: Centro Cultural Pontificia Universidad Católica del Perú, 2009, p. 33.

of furniture for secular and household use. Strictly ecclesiastical furniture includes pulpits, counter-pulpits, thrones, benches, lecterns and table top lecterns. Secular and household furniture includes seats, beds, centre tables, wardrobes and corner cupboards.

As a result of the aesthetic change which was taking place in the West, and in tune with the shapes of furniture produced in this style, new furniture acquired a great classical serenity. Salient features were the predominance of right angles on an essentially linear silhouette.

Master carvers, artisans and builders applied direct carving and fretting techniques, as well as totally or partially gilded light patina finishes; and they resorted to polychrome or a clear lacquer finish to cover local woods. There were also some pieces of furniture whose ornamentation included marquetry technique in partial combination with carvings on bare wood.

These methods facilitated the addition of flutings, tracery, columns with capitals of various orders, garlands, bows, draperies, Greco-Roman mythological

**BED**
[TOP] Side detail.
Don Alfredo Pinillos' collection, Trujillo.
Last quarter of the 18TH century.
Height: 204 cm. Width: 182.5 cm.

**CHAIR**
[TOP LEFT] Skirt frieze detail.
Ministry of Culture/Museo Nacional de Arqueología, Antropología e Historia del Perú, Lima.
c. 1800.

**PULPIT**
[BOTTOM LEFT AND OPPOSITE PAGE]
Pendant, pineapple and tribune details.
Basílica Catedral de Lima.
Late 18TH century.
Total height: 636 cm.

figures and other motifs which followed those changes. On the neoclassical furniture produced in these parts of the world, local motifs are no longer present. This not only means that, over time, these forms were refined, becoming purer and more distinct, but also that this aesthetic experience became universal; fading and blurring the rich artistic heritage which once inspired ancient indigenous beliefs and culture. Thus, the syncretism prevailing during most of the Baroque disappears, and this also takes place, to a lesser extent, in the Rococo period.

The viewing of neoclassical furniture is useful as an iconographic argument. This type of furniture should be appreciated, since not only does it demonstrate aesthetic changes, but it also testifies to the historical reasons which gave rise to renewed taste and sensibility in the lifestyles of the late 18TH- and early 19TH- centuries.

## CARVED AND GILDED ECCLESIASTICAL AND LITURGICAL FURNITURE

The pulpit of the Basílica Catedral de Lima is on the right hand side of the nave; it is neoclassical in style and has all the characteristics of a piece of furniture for ecclesiastical use in liturgical ceremonies.[10]

It was made in the late 18TH-century, when the Cathedral was restored after

[10] Basílica Catedral de Lima archives. Survey conducted on 12/10/84 by the Instituto Nacional de Cultura.

the 1746 earthquake, and remodelled in the purest neoclassical style.[11] The anonymous craftsmen who made the piece gave it a profuse ornamentation.

Attached to the wall, the pulpit has a hexagonal tribune with a slight inward curve on its base and access stairs on the side. Carved images of St. Peter and St. Paul flank both sides of the backrest, decorated with cherubs in the centre and placed between fluted columns with Corinthian capitals. The soundboard is crowned by the image of St. John the Evangelist.

The piece also has neoclassical motifs: garlands, pineapples, Greek friezes, acanthus leaves and mantlings, all of them carved with marked volume and enhanced with a suitable amount of gold leaf, thus achieving a subdued effect.

The piece is entirely built from carved solid cedar. Its panels are covered with stucco and a faux marble finish in greenish pastels with black, yellow and gray veins. The piece has been recently restored and is in excellent condition.

The ecclesiastical piece of furniture inspiring the homily delivered by the officiating priest to the faithful is a counter-pulpit. This piece is located on the left hand side of the nave of the Basílica Catedral de Lima, in front of the pulpit. It was also built in the late 18TH-century after the 1746 earthquake.

It is a hanging shrine supporting an image for worship. This piece has three concave sides divided by columns. On the centre panel there is a crucified Christ made from carved ivory, flanked by angels. The cresting is topped by an image of the Paschal Lamb surrounded by symbolic rays of light.

The structure was decorated in the same style as the pulpit: fluted columns with Corinthian capitals on the corners, cherubs, garlands, mantlings, draperies, rosettes and, as required by the style, a base of acanthus leaves ending in pineapples.

Like the pulpit, this piece was made from local wood and covered with light patinas and ornamental details highlighted with gold leaf.

The piece is in excellent condition.

In the nave of the Iglesia y Convento de San Francisco, Basílica Menor, city of Lima, there is a pulpit made in neoclassical style during the last decades of the 18TH-century (c. 1790). Its authorship is attributed to presbyter and architect Matías Maestro or to carvers from his workshop, who skilfully left a Greco-Latin mark on Lima production of the time.

This is a liturgical piece from which the officiating priest, located on the

**PULPIT**
[LEFT] Basílica Catedral de Lima.
Late 18TH century.
Total height: 636 cm.

**COUNTER-PULPIT**
[RIGHT] Basílica Catedral de Lima.
Late 18TH century.
Height: 280 cm.

[11] Lohmann Villena, Guillermo, *et al. La Basílica Catedral de Lima.* Colección Arte y Tesoros del Perú. Lima: Banco de Crédito del Perú, 2004, pages 74-75.

tribune, delivered his sermon during the mass. It consists of a polygonal tribune, a soundboard crowned by the image of the patron saint and a perimeter apron. The backrest has a half-relief image of the Immaculate Conception flanked by plain columns topped with Ionic capitals; there are also access stairs.

Other selected, strictly neoclassical, decorative elements include concave panels housing half-relief carvings of saints crowned by garlands, and various

**PULPIT**
[LEFT]
Iglesia y Convento de San Francisco de Lima, Basílica Menor, Lima.
Attributed to Prb. Arch. Matías Maestro or artisans from his workshop.
Late 18TH century.

**COUNTER-PULPIT**
[OPPOSITE PAGE]
Iglesia y Convento de San Francisco de Lima, Basílica Menor, Lima.
Attributed to Prb. Arch. Matías Maestro or artisans from his workshop.
Late 18TH century.
Height: 240 cm. Width: 120 cm.
Depth: 50 cm.

classical friezes, flutings, bows, rosettes, pineapples, cartouches and tassels. To this remarkable piece, artisans applied the carving and half-relief carving techniques on cedar wood and, to create a suitable volumetric effect, they used partially distributed gold leaf. The piece is in very good condition.

In the same nave of the Iglesia y Convento de San Francisco, Basílica Menor, city of Lima, attached to a sturdy column, there is a counter-pulpit which matches the abovementioned pulpit. Also attributed to the presbyter Matías Maestro or his artisans, it was made in neoclassical style during the late 18TH-century (c. 1790).

The piece is a functional liturgical decoration, useful for inspiring the officiating priest's sermon during the mass. To that end, it has a crucified Christ image on the central panel, crowned by a "cardinal's hat", which is flanked by plain columns topped with Ionic capitals on both sides and an apron.

The elements which complete the decoration are an oval laurel wreath surrounding the Franciscan emblem of crossed arms on the top, and flutings, classic friezes, garlands, draperies, ribbons, rosettes, pineapples and tassels.

The piece was made from solid cedar wood enriched with gold leaf and patinas to highlight its volume.

It is in very good condition.

On the patio of the Museo de los Descalzos-Convento de los Franciscanos Descalzos, Rímac, in the city of Lima, there is a lectern or rotating stand made in neoclassical style by unknown artisans, which dates from the early 19TH-century.[12]

It is a piece for liturgical use which would invariably have been located in the centre of the church choir to support large scores and choir books.

It is a tall, two-bodied piece: the upper body is a

[12] Recorded under file N° 0000062935.

stand in the shape of a truncated pyramid, with four oblique sides, which rotates around a central shaft; the lower is an octagonal container with an access door.

The stand bears the JHS monogram. One of the base sides reads: *Justo Dei Judicio / sine Verbo moritur / qui in divino officio / negligenter loquitur* and below it, there is a print with the image of the Virgin and the Infant Jesus.

Built from barely carved solid wood, the piece has ovals made in relief on each side of the base, divided by pilasters, with alternating ornaments. The piece is complete and in need of restoration.

**LECTERN**
Museo de los Descalzos - Convento de los Franciscanos Descalzos, Rímac, Lima.
Early 19TH century.
Height: 208 cm. Width: 122 cm.
Depth: 122 cm.

The hearse in the nave of the Iglesia de la Sagrada Familia, Basílica Catedral del Cusco, is a liturgical piece made following neoclassical canons. It was used for Tenebrae of Good Friday, a solemn moment when its candles would be put out one-by-one until there was total darkness.

It is a piece in neoclassical style made by unknown highlanders. Judging by its stylistic features, it was made at a time when Church authorities regulated the way in which the churches were decorated inspired by the classical world, in order to remove the instabilities inherent in the Rococo style.

The piece is a typical large candelabrum. Its structure consists of an upper triangular body and fifteen metal sockets —to hold candles— resting on dados. The triangle, placed on a diamond, is supported by a polygonal central shaft resting on a base. The decoration consists of classical friezes surrounding a central cartouche with the papal crown and coat of arms. The cartouche is placed within symmetrical carved and fretted curves. Corbels, acanthus leaves, flutings and pearls are some of the other ornamental motifs.

The piece is made from solid wood and covered with pastel patinas and gold leaf, which enhance the volume of details. It is in very good condition.

**HEARSE**
Iglesia de la Sagrada Familia - Basílica Catedral del Cusco.
Late 18TH or early 19TH century.

A floor lectern is on display in the library of the Museo de Arte Religioso of the Convento San Francisco y Catacumbas, in Lima. It is a support for liturgical or choir books useful to allow reading while standing. The lectern was made in the late 18TH-century.[13] This piece is a representative example which transmits serenity and simplicity: features of the neoclassical style that was in vogue at the time. There is an oblique stand on the top, supported by a shaft which rests on a tripod.

Made from carved wood and completely gilded with gold leaf, the lectern has symmetrically distributed ornamentation revealing a European influence. A large oval stands out containing a central rosette, topped by an interesting apron with carved fringes forming a mantling, both on the front and on the sides. The oval is crowned by a garland and has a pair of roses in the centre.

Despite the fact that there is a crack on the backrest and some gold leaf is missing, the piece is in good condition.

A pair of table top lecterns, exhibited in the library of the Museo de Arte Religioso of the Convento San Francisco y Catacumbas, in Lima, were made in

[13] Bonet Correa, Antonio. *Monasterios Iberoamericanos.* [n.p.]: Ediciones El Viso, 2001, p. 206.

**FLOOR LECTERN**
[LEFT]
Museo de Arte Religioso of Convento San Francisco y Catacumbas, Lima.
Late 18TH or early 19TH century.
Height: 151 cm. Width: 70 cm.
Depth: 26 cm.

**TABLE TOP LECTERN**
[RIGHT] Museo de Arte Religioso of Convento San Francisco y Catacumbas, Lima.
Late 18TH or early 19TH century.
Height: 50 cm. Width: 56 cm.
Depth: 45 cm.

**THRONE**
[OPPOSITE PAGE] Full view and cresting detail.
Museo de Arte Religioso of the Basílica Catedral de Lima.
Donated by Auxiliary Bishop Monsignor Alberto Brazzini Díaz Ufano.
Late 18TH century.
Height: 142 cm. Width: 80 cm.
Depth: 56 cm.

neoclassical style by unknown craftsmen during the late 18TH- or early 19TH-century. They are missal holders with foldable stands and short legs and can be placed on altars.

These lecterns have remarkably symmetrical decorations, which are characteristic of this style, such as a classical bow crowning the piece, as well as rosettes, tassels and fringes, and end in outstanding aprons.

Made from local wood, the carvings were highlighted with gold leaf and bright-red patinas. The lecterns are in good condition.

### UTILITARIAN SEATS IN RELIGIOUS SETTINGS

In the chapel of the Salas Brazzini, in the Museo de Arte Religioso of the Basílica Catedral de Lima, there is a throne —appropriate for the solemnity of ceremonies— which used to belong to the private collection of Auxiliary Bishop Monsignor Alberto Brazzini Díaz Ufano.

The throne has a high backrest with an important cresting emphasising the hierarchy of the person sitting upon it. The cresting is supported by a pair of oblique stiles; it has an apron with carved, fretted and gilded

**BENCH**
Full view and backrest detail.
Compañía de Jesús, Comunidad de San Pedro, Lima.
Late $18^{TH}$ or early $19^{TH}$ century.

leaves spilling towards both sides of the skirt. The piece has curved arms and rests on four straight legs strengthened by crosspieces.

It is a seat whose style is somewhere between Rococo and neoclassical, since its arms have less evolved aesthetics and are decorated with *rocaille*, two clear signs of this transition.

Ornamental motifs include flowers and leaves forming garlands which adorn a central urn, as well as leaves applied to *rocaille* on the skirt and front legs ending in cylinders. Both seat and backrest are upholstered in red velvet, which has been replaced. The structure of this throne was made from solid wood, probably local, which was carved, fretted, turned and patinated. Patinas are covered in gold dust and partially gilded. The piece is in very good condition.

ARMCHAIRS
Museo de Arte Religioso of Convento San Francisco y Catacumbas, Lima.
Late 18TH or early 19TH century.
Height: 131 cm. Width: 77 cm.
Depth: 64 cm.

There is a bench in the sacristy of the Iglesia de la Compañía de Jesús - Comunidad de San Pedro de Lima which belongs to the ecclesiastical utilitarian furniture group. It was made between approximately 1790 and 1810, and its salient feature is its classical serenity.

The bench seats several people and its multiple backrest has a series of ovals crowned by broken pediments. Each oval contains letters which, put together, read “Nuestra Señora de la O”, a statement of Jesuit devotion; ovals alternate with flat fluted columns. It also has curved arms maintaining the Rococo style and straight legs decorated with cylindrical dados.

The piece also has symmetrically distributed neoclassical decorations, such as flutings, gadroons, dentils, rosettes, leaves and flowers.

This bench was made from solid wood, and its volume was achieved by means of direct carving.

The piece is in good condition. It is worth mentioning that the wood was later blackened and the red velvet upholstery of the seat has been renewed.

A set of four neoclassical armchairs made in the early 19TH-century are on display in the library of the Museo de Arte Religioso of the Convento San Francisco y Catacumbas, in the city of Lima.

These are utilitarian pieces, since they are appropriate and necessary equipment for a place of study and research.

The backrests have stylised ovals moulded with garlands and with an oval sunflower in the centre. The arms end with inward scrolls; the straight front legs have bulbs with acanthus leaves, and the rear legs are sabre-shaped. Seats and backrests are upholstered in dark leather. Decorative elements were symmetrically arranged, following the dictates of the style, on the structure made from local wood. The pieces are in good condition.

## EXCEPTIONAL LITURGICAL PIECE FROM THE SOUTH ANDEAN REGION

In the novitiate chapel of the Monasterio de Santa Catalina, in Arequipa, there is an altar front with flat lines made by anonymous builders from the Arequipa school. It is a strictly liturgical piece which was built and decorated in neoclassical style during the late 18TH- or early 19TH-century, which might indicate that the new aesthetic language arriving from the metropolis at the time occasionally reached, as in this case, the South Andean region.

ALTAR FRONT
Monasterio de Santa Catalina, Arequipa.
Late 18TH century.
Height: 98 cm. Width: 238 cm.
Depth: 65 cm.

The front is decorated with panel painting technique using a vibrant palette on light backgrounds. Three interrelated images were selected for this purpose, which are separated by turned half-columns with gilded bases and capitals. The lid has no decoration. With rusticity and simple techniques, the images were painted on cartouches: Saint Dominic with attributes on the centre; the shield of the Order on the right; and a hound carrying a lit torch in its mouth (a Dominican symbol) on the left.[14] Cartouches are crowned by garlands, surrounded by plant elements and topped with three acanthus leaves. The supporting structure is made from wood, most likely willow, which is abundant in the Colca Canyon. The piece is in good condition, although some elements are missing.

## THE CLASSICAL WORLD REACHES DOMESTIC LIFE

In Peru, there are relatively few pieces of furniture for secular use which follow classical aesthetic patterns and reflect the changes that took place in Europe during the last third of the 18TH-century.

The new stylistic language from the Old World, based on classical antiquity, found it difficult to make the journey and was little understood in areas isolated from the major urban centres of the Viceroyalty. This is why it is safe to say that furniture maintained the spontaneity of the Baroque and Rococo styles, without falling into a decorative concept which was certainly new, although strange in its idiosyncrasy. The limited neoclassical furniture repertoire for household use found in the coastal region includes chairs and armchairs, consoles and centre tables, and corner cupboards.

**CHAIR**
Ministry of Culture/Museo Nacional de Arqueología, Antropología e Historia del Perú, Lima.
c. 1800.

Among the examples of seats with ovals and planimetric elements, it is worth describing a pair of chairs made in an unquestionable neoclassical style during the late 18TH-century, which are on display in the Casa Quinta de los Libertadores, owned by the Museo Nacional de Arqueología, Antropología e Historia del Perú, in Lima. This *Casa Huerta, a late-18TH-century place for rest and recreation, commissioned by Viceroy Joaquín de la Pezuela (1816-1821),* [...] *was the headquarters of libertadores Don José de San Martín (1821-1822) and Don Simón Bolívar (1823-1826) during the process of Independence.*[15]

The backrests have not been upholstered. They have carved and inlaid

14 Ferguson, George. *Signos y símbolos en el arte cristiano.* Buenos Aires: Emecé, 1956, p. 166.
15 Ministry of Culture of Peru. *Agenda cultural* [online]. June 2012 [retrieved on: June 3, 2012]. <http://www.mcultura.gob.pe/agenda_cultural_museos_mc-junio_2012.pdf>

**ARMCHAIR**
Full view, monogram and fretted backrest details.
Prado Heudebert family collection, Lima.
Early 19TH century.

central splats forming an oval and pagoda-shaped crestings. Those ornaments have subtle Chippendale lines, evoking the English Rococo, and rest on large oblique stiles; the projections form volutes. Faithful to the style, the skirt perimeter is decorated with Greek friezes inlaid with woods of contrasting colours. The straight legs, ending in fluted cylinders, are connected by carved H-shaped crosspieces. These chairs were anonymously built from local wood and finished with a clear lacquer layer. They are currently being restored.

In the Lima collection of the Prado Heudebert family, there is a set of neoclassical armchairs evoking those French seats from the late 18TH- and early 19TH-century: the troubled Consular period. Their structure responded to changes taking place in Europe at the beginning of the 19TH-century due to the Industrial Revolution; these changes reached Peru later, after its independence.

A worth mentioning morphological feature of the armchairs is their backward-curving backrests —one of the details demonstrating those changes— which are decorated with fretted ribbons and spheres, an inlaid monogram and pendants on both sides. Remarkable straight arms emerge from the backrest crestings. The legs are connected by carved H-shaped crosspieces; front legs are straight and adorned by the characteristic bulb-shaped cylinders. A Greek frieze on the skirt deserves special mention; it was also made with marquetry using different shades of wood and is useful for accurately dating the piece. The solid blond mahogany structure was covered with clear lacquer, enhancing its natural shine. The seats have been reupholstered. These armchairs are in very good condition.

The bed headboard, part of the regular household equipment in an important house, belongs to Don Alfredo Pinillos's collection, located in the city of Trujillo. Originally owned by the Martínez Pinillos family, it was made in neoclassical style by anonymous artisans in the late 18TH-century.

**BED**
Headboard detail.
Don Alfredo Pinillos' collection, Trujillo.
Last quarter of the 18TH century.
Height: 204 cm. Width: 182.5 cm.

**BED**

Full view and backrest detail.
Don Alfredo Pinillos' collection, Trujillo.
Early 19TH century.
Height: 212 cm. Width: 138 cm.
Total height: 220 cm.

This sumptuous piece has the traditional "cardinal's hat" shape and is flanked by fluted columns, which are topped by urns. It is decorated with a central oval containing a rosette, surrounded by a laurel wreath and crowned by a bow. A garland placed on *rocaille* and symmetrically distributed flowers adorn its cresting. All these elements have little volume. The piece was made from solid wood, which was carved and partially fretted. The supporting structure is covered with patinas, polychrome in certain areas and with gold leaf highlighting ornamental details. The headboard is in good condition, although the patina is deteriorated.

The Regency bed, inspired by English tastes —a final neoclassical expression occurring in the first quarter of the 19TH-century— also belongs to Don Alfredo Pinillos's collection, located in the city of Trujillo. This piece consists of a headboard, a footboard and four straight columns at angles which continue as legs.

The selected decorative motifs, suitable for this artistic language, comprise a peacock's tail, stars, interlaced leaves, and curves towards the ends. All these elements were placed on the most visible areas using a technique known as "bitter": wood inlaid with bronze. The bed is built from solid mahogany and held by four columns carved with stylised motifs and decorated with pineapples on top. The piece is in good condition.

The gueridon in the infirmary of the Real Monasterio de Clarisas de Santa María de Gracia, in the city of Trujillo, is an anonymously made neoclassical

**GUERIDON**
Real Monasterio de Clarisas
de Santa María de Gracia, Trujillo.
Late 18TH or early 19TH century.

piece with a distinct Italian influence; it dates from the late 18TH- or early 19TH-century. This is a detached support piece, whose four sides can be fully appreciated. The top has a pronounced rectangular broken projection and a drawer in the skirt with teardrop-shaped *tirettes.* It rests on four turned legs with cylinders serving as dados: an ornament related to Italian aesthetics.

The piece was built from Figueroa cedar; the marquetry work was made using different shades of local wood to form classical friezes on the top and drawer perimeter. These elements are its only decoration and its simple and refined style makes it a unique piece.

It is in very good condition and the drawer front has been restored.

The neoclassical gueridon for secular use which belongs to a private collection in the city of Arequipa has characteristics similar to those of the above pieces. It is a detached table —i.e. its four sides are visible— with a rectangular top and a drawer in the skirt. It stands on four filleted legs, demonstrating the Italian inspiration of the late 18TH- or early 19TH-century.

GUERIDON
Full view and drawer detail.
Private collection, Arequipa.
Late 18TH or early 19TH century.
Height: 75.5 cm. Width: 83 cm.
Depth: 47 cm.

**CENTRE TABLE**
Top and drawer details; full view.
Ministry of Culture / Museo Nacional de Arqueología, Antropología e Historia del Perú, Lima.
c. 1800.

There are a series of herringbone friezes and an oval at the centre of the top, along with sober neoclassical linear decorations and a predominance of right angles. The piece was probably made from willow, which was abundant in the Colca Canyon. It was decorated with marquetry using woods of different colours to emphasise contrasts and covered with clear lacquer. The drawer knob was made of bronze.

The piece is in excellent condition.

Two centre tables are on show at the Casa Quinta de los Libertadores, owned by the Museo Nacional de Arqueología, Antropología e Historia del Perú, in Lima. They are pieces for secular use, made in the early 19TH-century in neoclassical style, in which the Italian and English aesthetic influences persist.

Both pieces have rectangular tops with subtle curved angles, resting on four straight legs, inherent to the style. They show, however, slight structural and ornamental differences. The first piece has the top and the two drawers in the skirt framed by perimeter friezes; the second piece has the same perimeter moulding on the top and a single large drawer in the skirt, as well as wooden handles. One piece has straight legs ending in fluted cylinders, while the other has bulb-shaped legs.

These representative pieces are decorated with elements which provide them with great classical serenity and highlight the style: a central oval on the top, urns,

**CORNER CUPBOARD**
Basílica Catedral de Lima.
Late 18TH or early 19TH century.
Height: 233 cm. Width: 116 cm.
Depth: 84 cm.

ribbons, a flower bouquet and profuse geometric friezes surrounding them. The tables were made from solid local wood and inlaid with dyed or contrasting woods. Their entire surfaces are covered with clear lacquer.

The pieces are in extremely delicate condition and need to be restored.

The corner cupboard in one corner of the Sala del Tesoro of the Museo de la Basílica Catedral de Lima was made in neoclassical style by unknown craftsmen during the last quarter of the 18TH-century or early 19TH-century.[16]

The cupboard is a triangular utilitarian container with two of its sides placed against the wall. Having straight lines, it is subtly decorated with a triangular broken pediment framed by dentil carvings and a central oval representing a sunflower.

There is a pair of front doors divided into panels and adorned with inlaid perimeter friezes and ovals, which reappear on the upper and lower edges of the piece. There is a concealed lock in the centre and the front legs are bracket-shaped. All of the above results in a sober and refined piece which clearly demonstrates the equally strong influence of the Italian and English neoclassical styles.

This cupboard was made from solid local wood and other woods of various contrasting colours, then covered with clear lacquer. The hinges are made from iron. Despite some missing and replaced elements, the piece is in good condition.

In the Casa Quinta de los Libertadores, owned by the Museo Nacional de Arqueología, Antropología e Historia del Perú, in Lima, there are a pair of corner cupboards. They are containers for secular use with marked Italian and English neoclassical influences: styles which were in vogue during the last quarter of the 18TH-century.

The cupboards are both triangular and linear, with a predominance of straight angles. Both have two front doors, as well as shelves and drawers inside for everyday use; their front legs are bracket-shaped.

Even though they form a pair, the pieces display some differences: one of them has wood-moulded glass doors which reveal its contents, while the other has two-bodied doors; the upper body is made from glass and the lower, from

[16] Catedral de Lima archives. Survey conducted by the Instituto Nacional de Cultura on 12/10/84.

**CORNER CUPBOARD**
Frieze detail.
Ministry of Culture / Museo Nacional de Arqueología, Antropología e Historia del Perú, Lima.
c. 1800.

**RINCONERO**
Full view and detail of the inside.
Ministry of Culture - Museo Nacional de Arqueología, Antropología e Historia del Perú, Lima.
c. 1800.

wood. Ornaments were made with marquetry or inlay and direct carving techniques and finished with a layer of clear lacquer. These cupboards were made from local raw materials.

Decorative motifs, in the strictly neoclassical style of the time, include linear friezes and ovals, as well as dentils on the upper friezes.

Both pieces were simply and austerely built from local wood and other types of contrasting wood; their fittings are made from iron.

These pieces are in delicate condition and need to be restored.

In the old Trujillo manor of Don Alfredo Pinillos, as part of his collection, there is a large wardrobe with a sophisticated and elegant cresting. Anonymously made in the late 18TH-century, this ornament simulates a delicate filigree of great stylistic purity.

It is a wardrobe comb with classical motifs, such as a central urn at the top, neatly arranged leafs and flowers, interlaced elements and arches. All these ornaments were carved and fretted from bare solid Figueroa cedar.

The piece is in good condition.

**WARDROBE**
Cresting, in detail.
Don Alfredo Pinillos' collection, Trujillo.
Late 18TH century.
Cresting height: 88 cm. Width: 148 cm.

SINCHI ROCA INGA II
MAYTA CAPAC INGA IV
CAPAC YUPANGUI INGA V
TOPA YUPANGUI INGA XI
HUAYNA CAPA INGA XII
CARLOS II REY XIX
FELIPE V REY XX

MAMA HVACO
1ª COYA, o REYNA Madre y Muger de Manco Capac Inga, o Rey 1º del Perù

# APPENDIX

Triunfo Evangelico nueva
exaltacion de la fee gloria de la SS.ma Cruz

## POLITICAL ORGANISATION OF THE VICEROYALTY OF PERU

The Royal and Supreme Council of the Indies was founded in Spain during Charles V's rule, in 1524, with the aim of supervising and ensuring, with supreme authority, the interests of the Crown in the Spanish American colonies. *The Council's responsibilities were to recommend civil and ecclesiastical officers to the king, supervise documents for and about the Indies, draft laws for the Indies, oversee administration and justice, and even perform Treasury-related functions.*[1]

Viceroys were the King of Spain's representatives in the colonies, his *alter egos*. They held noble titles and were favoured with the monarch's utmost trust. They would be appointed the supreme authority over a viceroyalty by the monarch. These representatives were in charge of administering justice, managing the treasury and ensuring the evangelisation of the natives. They were also responsible for the fortification and maintenance of ports such as El Callao and their defence from attacks by privateers and pirates. The Viceroys were in command of the army as well, which consisted of their own guard and the captain generals.

The term of office originally lasted three years but, due to the long and exhausting journeys and the time it took to become acquainted with the administrative and political situation in the Viceroyalty, the Indian Council extended it to five.

The Viceroy resided in a palace in Lima, the "City of Kings", capital city of the Viceroyalty, surrounded by luxury and riches, and protected by a guard of honour. He was in charge of a social organisation, the *oidores* of the *Real Audiencia*. These ▸

***SUCESIÓN DE LOS INCAS Y LOS REYES ESPAÑOLES DEL PERÚ***
[OPENING]
Basílica Catedral de Lima.
Anonymous from Cusco.
c. 1725.
185 x 250 cm.
Courtesy of Monsignor Raúl Chau.

***EL REQUERIMIENTO O ENCUENTRO DE FRANCISCO PIZARRO CON EL INCA ATAWALLPA EN CAJAMARCA***
[OPPOSITE PAGE]
Convento de Santo Domingo de Cusco.
Anonymous from Cusco.
Late 16TH century.
Oil painting on canvas.

[1] Aguilera, Concha (coord). *La España donde no se ponía el sol.* Colección Grandes Imperios y Civilizaciones. Madrid: SARPE, 1985, p. 98.

## GOVERNORS AND VICEROYS OF PERU

### 16th CENTURY

**FRANCISCO PIZARRO** (1478-1541), was the governor from 1534 to 1541.

**CRISTÓBAL VACA DE CASTRO** (1492-1562) was the governor from 1541 to 1544.

**BLASCO NÚÑEZ VELA** was the 1st Viceroy of Peru, from 1544 to 1546. He ruled briefly, as he was murdered by Francisco Pizarro.

**PEDRO DE LA GASCA** (1494-1565) presided over the *Real Audiencia* from 1546 to 1549.

**ANTONIO DE MENDOZA Y PACHECO** (?-1552) was the 2nd Viceroy of Peru from 1551 to 1552. He was appointed Viceroy of Peru after leaving his post as Viceroy of New Spain.

**MELCHOR BRAVO DE SARAVIA** and **ANDRÉS DE CIANCA** were *Oidores Decanos* (senior judges) of the *Real Audiencia* of Lima from 1552 to 1553.

**ANDRÉS HURTADO DE MENDOZA** (?-1561), 2nd Marquis of Cañete, was the 3rd Viceroy of Peru, from 1556 to 1560.

**DIEGO LÓPEZ DE ZÚÑIGA Y VELASCO**, Count of Nyeva (?-1564), was the 4th Viceroy of Peru from 1561 to 1564.

**JUAN DE SAAVEDRA** and Licentiates **PONCE DE LEÓN, SALAZAR DE VILLASANTE Y MATIENZO** were *Oidores Decanos* of the *Real Audiencia* of Lima for a few months: February to September, 1564.

Licentiate **LOPE GARCÍA DE CASTRO** was the governor, captain general and president of the *Real Audiencia* of Lima from 1564 to 1569.

**FRANCISCO DE TOLEDO** was the 5th Viceroy of Peru from 1569 to 1581. After forty years of administrative disarray, the Viceroyalty of Peru found in him an efficient ruler, who achieved order and established a political and administrative framework which would remain in force for years.

**MARTÍN ENRÍQUEZ DE ALMANSA** (?-1583) was the 6th Viceroy of Peru from 1581 to 1583.

**CRISTÓBAL RAMÍREZ DE CARTAGENA** was *Oidor Decano* of the *Real Audiencia* of Lima from 1583 to 1586.

**FERNANDO DE TORRES Y PORTUGAL**, Count of Villar-don-pardo, was the 7th Viceroy of Peru from 1586 to 1589.

**GARCÍA HURTADO DE MENDOZA**, 4th Marquis of Cañete, was the 8th Viceroy of Peru, from 1589 to 1596.

**LUIS DE VELASCO Y CASTILLA** (?-1617) was the 9th Viceroy of Peru from 1596 to 1604. When appointed to the Viceroyalty of Peru, he was the Viceroy of New Spain.

### 17th CENTURY

**GASPAR DE ZÚÑIGA Y ACEVEDO**, Count of Monterrey (?-1606), was the 10th Viceroy of Peru from 1604 to 1606.

**JUAN DE MENDOZA Y LUNA**, Marquis of Montesclaros, was the 11th Viceroy of Peru from 1607 to 1615. He founded the Consulate Court of Lima and the Arequipa, Huamanga and La Paz bishoprics in 1609. Among other construction works, he built the *Alameda de los Descalzos* in 1611.

**FRANCISCO DE BORJA Y ARAGÓN**, Prince of Esquilache (?-1658), was the 12th Viceroy of Peru from 1615 to 1621.

**DIEGO FERNÁNDEZ DE CÓRDOBA**, Marquis of Guadalcásar, was the 13th Viceroy of Peru from 1621 to 1629, after being the Viceroy of New Spain.

**LUIS JERÓNIMO FERNÁNDEZ DE CABRERA, BOBADILLA, CERDA Y MENDOZA**, 4th Count of Chinchón (?-1641), was the 14th Viceroy of Peru from 1629 to 1639.

**PEDRO DE TOLEDO Y LEYVA**, Marquis of Mancera (?-1654), was the 15th Viceroy of Peru from 1639 to 1648.

**GARCÍA SARMIENTO DE SOTOMAYOR**, Count of Salvatierra (?-1659), was the 16th Viceroy of Peru from 1648 to 1655.

**LUIS ENRIQUE DE GUZMÁN**, Count of Alba de Liste, was the 17th Viceroy of Peru from 1655 to 1661, after handing over the Viceroyalty of New Spain to his successor.

**DIEGO DE BENAVIDES Y DE LA CUEVA**, Count of Santisteban, was the 18th Viceroy of Peru from 1661 to 1666.

**PEDRO ANTONIO FERNÁNDEZ DE CASTRO**, Count of Lemos, was the 19th Viceroy of Peru from 1667 until his death, in 1672. He stood out for his profound religiousness and exquisite taste. Order, severity and rigour characterised his period in office.

**BALTASAR DE LA CUEVA Y ENRÍQUEZ, ARIAS DE SAAVEDRA PARDO TAVERA Y ULLOA**, Count of Castellar (1626-?), was the 20th Viceroy of Peru from 1674 to 1678.

**MELCHOR DE LIÑÁN Y CISNEROS**, Archbishop of Lima (1629-1708), was the 21st Viceroy of Peru from 1678 to 1681. He remained the head of the Archdiocese until his death.

**MELCHOR DE NAVARRA Y ROCAFUL**, Duke of la Palata in the kingdom of Naples, was the 22nd Viceroy of Peru from 1681 to 1689. He undertook the arduous task of building the walls of the city of Lima; the work was finished in 1685.

**MELCHOR PORTOCARRERO LASSO DE LA VEGA**, 3rd Count of la Monclova (?-1705), was the 23rd Viceroy of Peru from 1689 to 1705, after ruling the Viceroyalty of New Spain.

## KINGS OF SPAIN DURING THE PERUVIAN COLONIAL PERIOD (1534-1824)

### HOUSE OF HABSBURG

**CHARLES V** (1500-1558) ruled Spain under the name of Charles I from 1516 to 1556, when he abdicated in favour of his son Philip II. He was also the Holy Roman Emperor from 1520 to 1558.

**PHILIP II** (1527-1598) reigned from 1556 to 1598.

**PHILIP III** (1578-1621) ruled from 1598 to 1621.

**PHILIP IV** (1605-1665) reigned from 1621 to 1665. He handed over the rule of Spain to his favourite, Count-Duke of Olivares (1587-1645), who was king from 1621 to 1643.

**CHARLES II** (1661-1700) his mother, Mariana of Austria, was the regent of the kingdom from 1665 to 1675, when Charles came of age. As he was a sick man and died without descendants, he was the last monarch of the House of Habsburg.

### THE HOUSE OF BOURBON

**PHILIP V** House of Bourbon, Duke of Anjou (1683-1746) was the grandson of Louis XIV of France and ruled Spain from 1700 to 1746.

**LOUIS I** (1707-1724) reigned briefly in 1724; he died young and his father, Philip V, resumed his reign until his death in 1746.

## $18^{TH}$ CENTURY

**FERDINAND VI** (1713-1759) ruled from 1746 to 1759.

**CHARLES III** (1716-1788) was Duke of Parma and King of Naples and Sicily; he ruled Spain from 1759 to 1788. In 1778 he passed the Decree of Free Trade in the colonies.

**CHARLES IV** (1748-1819) ruled from 1788 to 1808.

**MIGUEL NÚÑEZ DE SANABRIA**, *Oidor Decano* of the *Real Audiencia* of Lima, and *Oidores* Nicolás de Paredes y Armendáriz, Pablo Vásquez de Velasco, Gonzalo Ramírez de Baquedano, Pedro Gregorio de la Canal and Lucas Francisco de Bilbao la Vieja took over government from 1705 to 1707, when the new Viceroy arrived.

**MANUEL DE OMS Y SANTA PAU**, Marquis of Castell-dos-rius, was the $24^{TH}$ Viceroy of Peru from 1707 to 1710. His fondness for things French, partly due to the accession of the Bourbons to the throne of Spain, was one of his personal characteristics.

**DIEGO LADRÓN DE GUEVARA**, Bishop of Quito, was the $25^{TH}$ Viceroy of Peru from 1710 to 1716, following the death of his predecessor.

**CARMINE NICOLAO CARACCIOLO**, Prince of Santo Buono, was the $26^{TH}$ Viceroy of Peru from 1716 to 1720. In 1718 the King decided to create the Viceroyalty of New Granada, for which purpose he separated the province of Tierra Firme from the Viceroyalty of Peru.

**FRAY DIEGO MORCILLO RUBIO DE AUÑÓN**, Archbishop of Charcas (1642-1730), was the $27^{TH}$ Viceroy of Peru from 1720 to 1722.

**JOSÉ DE ARMENDÁRIZ**, Marquis of Castelfuerte, was the $28^{TH}$ Viceroy and Captain General of Peru from 1724 to 1736.

**JOSÉ ANTONIO DE MENDOZA**, Marquis of Villagarcía, was the $29^{TH}$ Viceroy of Peru from 1736 to 1745.

**JOSÉ ANTONIO MANSO DE VELASCO**, Count of Superunda, was the $30^{TH}$ Viceroy of Peru from 1745 to 1761. He took office in dramatic circumstances, after the earthquake which destroyed most of Lima and El Callao in 1746. He devoted all his efforts to rebuilding them, which is why he is considered their second founder.

**MANUEL AMAT Y JUNYENT PLANELLA AYMERICH Y SANTA PAU**, of Catalan origin, was the $31^{ST}$ Viceroy of Peru from 1761 to 1776. During his administration, in 1767, the Society of Jesus was expelled from the entire kingdom and the Spanish crown expropriated their substantial assets. In 1776 the residents of Lima were instructed to keep the front of their homes illuminated and work began on paving the city.

**MANUEL DE GUIRIOR**, Lieutenant general of the Spanish Army, was the $32^{TH}$ Viceroy of Peru from 1776 to 1780. During his administration part of the territory became the Viceroyalty of Río de la Plata, founded in 1776.

**AGUSTÍN DE JÁUREGUI Y ALDECOA** was the $33^{RD}$ Viceroy of Peru from 1780 to 1784.

**TEODORO DE CROIX**, Knight of Croix (1730-?), was the $34^{TH}$ Viceroy of Peru from 1784 to 1790.

***FREY* DON FRANCISCO GIL DE TABOADA, LEMOS Y VILLAMARÍN**, was the $35^{TH}$ Viceroy of Peru from 1790 to 1796. During his term in office, Puno province, which had once been part of the Viceroyalty of Río de la Plata, was reinstated into the territory in 1796.

**AMBROSIO O'HIGGINS**, Marquis of Osorio (1720/25-?), was the $36^{TH}$ Viceroy of Peru from 1796 to 1801, after being Captain General of the Kingdom of Chile and President of the *Real Audiencia* of Santiago.

## $19^{TH}$ CENTURY

**FERDINAND VII** (1784-1833) was the King of Spain between March and May 1808, and from December 1813 until his death, except for a brief period in 1823 when he was replaced by the Regency Council.

**GABRIEL AVILÉS Y DEL FIERRO**, Marquis of Avilés (?-1810), was the $37^{TH}$ Viceroy of Peru from 1801 to 1806.

**JOSÉ FERNANDO DE ABASCAL Y SOUSA**, was the $38^{TH}$ Viceroy of Peru from 1806 to 1816. He founded the Colegio de Medicina de San Fernando and the Drawing and Painting Academy.

**JOAQUÍN DE LA PEZUELA Y SÁNCHEZ, MUÑOZ DE VELASCO** (1761-1830), was the $39^{TH}$ Viceroy of Peru from 1816 to 1821.

**JOSÉ DE LA SERNA E HINOJOSA** (1770-1832), was the $40^{TH}$ Viceroy of Peru from 1821 to 1824. He was wounded and taken prisoner during the battle of Ayacucho. Being the last Spanish official holding the title of viceroy, he was coldly received by the king upon his return to Spain.[2]

---

2 Porras Barrenechea, Raúl, and Vargas Ugarte S.J., Rubén *et al. Historia general de los peruanos.* Lima: Peisa, 1988, pages 605-691.

*oidores* were members of the superior courts of justice. In turn, the *corregidores* had privileges granted by the king, and had to prove their lineage, so very few would be eligible for this post. From the 18TH-century they were in charge of *intendencias*.

At the end of his term, the Viceroy was required to deliver to his successor a *relación*, an official document which gave account of the most significant features of his administration. The *encomienda* was an institution granting the *encomendero* almost unlimited power over the indigenous population. Sometimes all kinds of abuses were committed. An individual was granted vast lands to implement this institution, and the population in his charge was made to work relentlessly, sometimes to an extent akin to slave labour. This was an unwarranted situation, as the *encomendero* was supposed to defend the people under his charge, help them progress and teach them catechism; duties that were rarely met.

In the 17TH-century, the Spanish authorities turned to the native ruling class, the Inca nobility known as *orejera* composed of *orejones* or *curacas* (*Quechua* for "chief"), since they deemed it appropriate to get them to interact with the local population in order to achieve an effective and rapid control over the region; this lasted until the mid-18TH-century.

It is worth clarifying that each community or *ayllu* was led by a *curaca*, who reported directly to the Spanish *corregidor.* He guaranteed order and collected taxes; this privilege was inherent in his rank prior to the Spanish conquest. Thus, he helped those exerting the central power, since he understood the ancestral customs and practices of his *ayllu*; over time, this contributed to the preservation of traditions.

*The Inca image in Peru was tied to the construction of colonial power from the very beginning […] the image of the Inca is a complex and productive hybrid simultaneously evoking European and Andean meanings.*[3] Accordingly, in the early 17TH-century, the Colegio del Príncipe was founded in Lima and the Colegio de San Francisco de Borja in Cusco, where the descendants of the Inca nobility enjoyed the rare privilege of being instructed in disciplines such as mathematics, Spanish, poetry, music and religion, which allowed them to integrate into the colonial society. In 1697 the Spanish Crown gave access to religious and military orders to the descendants of the ancient Inca royalty who had proven their purity of blood.

Throughout the 18TH-century, the Inca nobility continued its search for identity before the eyes of the royal authority and the society of the time. To that end,

---

[3] Macchi, Fernanda. *Incas ilustrados. Reconstrucciones imperiales en la segunda mitad del siglo XVIII.* Madrid: Vervuert - Iberoamericana, 2009, p. 228.

they commissioned portraits in which they wore their most luxurious garments, displaying the sun embroidered with gold threads on their chests, a symbol of their former power and wealth. With the same ostentation, they participated in public festivities and celebrations, for instance parading on horseback through the Plaza de Armas in Lima, during the celebration of the marriage of King Philip V's children; described in *Jvbilos de Lima* by Pedro de Peralta Barnuevo,[4] a distinguished writer and historian of the time.

## HISTORICAL PERIODS OF ANCIENT PERU

Oral transmission was vital in these cultures, since they were preliterate civilisations. All the testimonies and information available are based on stories and legends collected and written down during the colonial period. That is why there is little reliable information about these pre-Hispanic civilisations, other than what has been discovered from archaeological remains which have been found and researched.

*The distinguished historian Garcilaso de la Vega —the "Inca Garcilaso"— was responsible for the remarkable task of reconstructing this period in his* Comentarios Reales, *a work in which he describes the glorious development of the empire and its tragic end. This author, the most authentic and authoritative to report the immediate past of his country, was born in the city of Cuzco in 1539. His father was of Spanish origin and his mother, an Inca descendant of the royal dynasty. He left his country at the age of twenty one to settle permanently in Spain, where he wrote the above-mentioned work.*[5]

| PERIODS | DATES | CULTURES |
|---|---|---|
| VI PRE-CERAMIC PERIOD | 2700-1800 BC | |
| INITIAL PERIOD | 1800-1200 BC | |
| EARLY HORIZON PERIOD | 1200-200 BC | CHAVÍN |
| EARLY HORIZON PERIOD | 700 BC– 200 AD | PARACAS |
| EARLY INTERMEDIATE PERIOD | 200 AD - 550 AD | MOCHICA AND NAZCA |
| MIDDLE HORIZON PERIOD | 550-1000 AD | TIAHUANACO AND HUARI |
| LATE INTERMEDIATE PERIOD | 1000-1476 AD | CHIMÚ |
| LATE HORIZON PERIOD | 1438 - 1532 AD | INCA |

## PRE-HISPANIC CULTURES IN THE REGION

Until about 1200 BC, almost nothing is known of the first peoples to inhabit vast regions of the Peruvian territory, enclosed by mountains and the sea and characterised by a variety of climates and environmental conditions. There were settled

4 Macchi, Fernanda. Op. cit., pages 226-230.

5 Kirchhoff, Herbert. *Perú ayer y hoy. Past and present.* Buenos Aires: Guillermo Kraft, 1951, p. VIII.

tribes distributed over the jungle, the coast and the highlands whose livelihood was dependant on hunting, fishing, raising llamas and emerging farming activity.

CHAVÍN CULTURE (1200-200 BC): one of the most ancient civilisations preceding the Inca Empire, located in the central zone of the Andes at Chavín de Huantar, between the Marañón and Santa rivers, where their archaeological remains have been found. Chavín art was based on the extensive and efficient dissemination of their religious beliefs, rather than their military conquests. Their temples exhibited sculptures of terrestrial and aquatic animals, such as jaguars in anthropomorphic postures, fanged snakes, alligators, eagles and hawks, and anthropomorphic figures, occasionally in combination. The "god of the cane or walking stick," always upright and front facing, was a recurring (male or female) image in the various cultures until the arrival of the Spanish conquerors; it had a walking stick or corn cane in each hand, possibly representing the creator god.

PARACAS CULTURE (700 BC - 200 AD): This culture thrived on the Paracas Peninsula in present-day Pisco Province. During a certain period of time, it was contemporary with the Chavín culture settled in the north of Peru. According to archaeological excavations carried out between 1920 and 1925 in Paracas, Cavernas and Necrópolis, these peoples were expert weavers of camelid wool and cotton, and skilled in the production of flat needle embroideries with a vibrant palette. They were also identified by their burials, where mummies were wrapped like bales with funerary shrouds of extraordinary manufacture and accompanied, according to their rank, by their belongings. They are thought to have performed skull trepanations for medicinal as well as ritual purposes. The geographic and climatic conditions of the desert favoured the preservation of these archaeological sites.

MOCHICA CULTURE (200 BC - 550 AD): one of the dominant civilisations during the first six centuries of our era on the northern coast. Mochicas settled in the valley of Lambayeque, extending to Huarmey, present-day province of La Libertad. They occupied a 600-sq km area from Piura to Áncash where, in semi-desert valleys, they built magnificent irrigation canals, roads and large fortifications for defence, which were striking, monumental works. The Mochicas stood out for the high quality of their gold and silver artefacts, their mastery of various metal alloys and their sculptures, sacred images and utensils produced using the lost-wax casting technique. They were also producers of fabric and remarkable potters, leaving behind fine painted ceramic works. The discovery of graves revealed that high dignitaries were buried with their rich belongings, thus leaving a legacy of impressive and magnificent pieces, proof of such splendour.

**NAZCA CULTURE** (200 BC - 550 AD): the dominant civilisation on the southern coast of Peru, in a region covering the valleys of Chincha, Pisco, Ica, Nasca and Acari.[6] They were characterised by their inexplicable and famous network of lines; a distinctive, eloquent and colourful ceramic production; figurative or abstract feather art; and magnificent fabrics of a rich and vibrant palette, revealing the influence of the Paracas culture. These elements represent local phytomorphic and zoomorphic figures, as well as beheaded human beings.

**TIAHUANACO CULTURE** (550-1000 AD): this pre-Inca culture dominated the Collao Plateau, on the Altiplano by the southern shore of Lake Titicaca, present-day Bolivia. Agriculture and cattle-raising were the basis of their livelihood.

Tiahuanaco was a major religious centre of pilgrimage, attracting people from other Andean regions, and becoming a place of worship, where important temples and monumental monolithic sculptures were erected. This culture depicted winged figures, feline profiles and the ancestral "god of the cane or walking stick" always facing to the front. The latter was of paramount importance, since it was likely a representation of Viracocha: the god creator in later Highland cultures. Displayed on fabrics, ceramics and lithographs are a complex iconography through the representation of mythological characters and religious scenes, where the repeated use of elements is evident.

**HUARI CULTURE** (550-1000 AD): an Andean civilisation which flourished in the Highlands, to the east of present-day Ayacucho, expanded north to Lambayeque and Cajamarca, and south to Arequipa; its borders reached jungle areas to the north of Cusco. It peoples were focused on military activities, devoting much of their energies to conquest in order to expand their territory. The Huari or Wari Empire, however, excelled at their architectural works, and colourful and refined fabrics made from cotton or camelid wool, and used to make their characteristic four-cornered caps. Also worth mentioning are their ceramic and metal production and stone carving works.

**CHIMÚ** or **CHIMOR CULTURE** (1000-1476 AD): an empire which emerged after the decline of the Huari Empire. Based in the northern coastal area of Peru, in the Moche Valley, its capital was Chan Chan, on the Pacific coast. Their rulers were believed to be of divine descent. They dominated the region until 1476, when they were defeated by the Incas. These peoples were experts in shaping the finest metals and experimenting with the resources thus obtained. They were masters of the

---

[6] Mujica, Marisa *et al. Perú. 10.000 años de pintura. Desde la época rupestre hasta nuestros días.* Lima: Universidad de San Martín de Porres-Fondo Editorial, 2008, p. 78.

casting, welding, lost-wax casting, filigree, and gold and silver plating techniques. Also, they applied to painted fabrics their delicate aesthetic sense, including repeated images of sea birds, two-headed snakes and aquatic fauna in general. Their architectural works were based on the use of adobe and brick.

INCA CULTURE (1438-1532 AD): this was the last pre-Hispanic period in Peru. It began when notably warlike Inca ethnic groups settled to the north of Lake Titicaca managed to conquer an area of about one hundred thousand square kilometres. Their territory stretched from present-day southern Colombia and Ecuador to central Chile, with Cusco as its capital city. From there, successive Incas extended their power through successful military campaigns, establishing the *Tahuantinsuyo* or "Land of the Four Parts or Regions", which became the largest empire in pre-Hispanic America. However, their glory was short lived: it lasted barely one hundred years.

The Inca Empire was based on a pyramid structure: privileged classes made up the aristocracy and provided the state with political, military and religious leaders; it had both political and organisational significance. Under the Inca rule, Peru benefited from the foundation of major urban centres, pavement of roads and construction of suspension bridges, which provided the area with an efficient communication network and elaborate irrigation systems. The economy was based on extensive agriculture, llama and alpaca raising, and fishing.

While the official language was Quechua, the peoples of conquered regions continued to speak their own languages. Diversity characterised the Inca world, and their cultural background and religious beliefs reveal the positive influence of cultures with deep artistic traditions which preceded them, such as the Chimú, who were subjugated by the Incas. Inca architecture consisted of temples, public buildings and fortifications which were made of adobe or *quincha* in coastal areas and of stone on the Altiplano. In turn, they had striking skills in metalworking, since they made beautifully crafted ornaments and utilitarian objects in bronze, copper, gold, and silver.

The Inca cosmogony was centred on Lake Titicaca. They held the sun, the moon and the stars, as well as the ancestors of men, in a prominent position. These came from the lake when everything was dark, and Viracocha emerged, the creator who gave birth to the world. The Incas worshipped their ancestors and death, because they were convinced of their influence on the world of the living; this was the central axis of their beliefs. In this way, they adapted rituals which were practiced by previous civilisations. Feather art had special significance throughout the entirety of ancient Peru, as shown by archaeological discoveries including magnificent pieces over 3,000 years old. That artistic language reached the Incas; it was believed that feathers had great symbolic value. Cloaks and headdresses —with which the nobility were dressed for funeral rites and other ceremonies— were decorated with multicoloured feathers from parrots and other difficult-to-hunt birds, such as the *corequenque.*

The recurrent iconography with repeated symbolism, characteristic of earlier cultures, such as fantastic feline-human figures, the above "divinity of the cane or walking stick", or hawk-headed warriors, is one of the examples which survived during the Inca Empire, and [...] *provides significant arguments to the assumption that mythological Inca traditions were the result of a long process of innovation, which borrowed and adapted myths that are projected across Andean societies.*[7]

## INCA DYNASTIES

*The reigns previous to Viracocha Inca come from Cabello's chronicle (Lib. 3-1951). Data prior to 1532 must be considered mere approximations.*[8]

The Cusco *Curacazgo* (kingdom) included 13 consecutive sovereigns who ruled for over 300 years. The most authoritative chroniclers were: Gómez Suárez de Figueroa, called "Inca Garcilaso de la Vega", Betanzos, Cieza de León, and Montesinos. Garcilaso's chronicles are considered to be the most reliable.[9]

| *HURIN CUSCO* (LOW CUSCO) DYNASTY WHOSE TERRITORY DID NOT EXTEND BEYOND LOCAL BOUNDARIES | *HANAN CUSCO* (HIGH CUSCO) DINASTY *TAHUANTINSUYO* OR INCA EMPIRE | |
|---|---|---|
| | INCA ROCA | |
| | YAHUAR HUACAC | |
| | INCA VIRACOCHA | (? -1438) |
| INCA MANCO CAPAC | INCA PACHACUTEC | (1438-1471) |
| SINCHI ROCA | TUPAC INCA YUPANQUI | (1471-1493) |
| LLOQUE YUPANQUI | INCA HUAYNA CAPAC | (1493-1525) |
| MAYTA CAPAC | HUAFCAR INCA | (1525-1532) |
| CAPAC YUPANQUI | ATAHUALLPA[10] | (1532-1533) |

Manco Inca II (1533-1544), son of Huayna Capac, was invested Inca by Francisco Pizarro, following his triumphal entry to Cusco in 1533. His three children, two legitimate and one illegitimate, Sayri Tupac (1544-1558), Titu Cusi Yupanqui (1558-1570) and Tupac Amaru I (1570-1572), moved to Vilcabamba, invested as Incas with theoretical power.

---

7 Urton, Gary. *Mitos Incas.* Madrid: Akal Ediciones, 2003, p. 24.

8 Conrad, Geoffrey W. and Demarest, Arthur A. *Religión e imperio. Dinámica del expansionismo azteca e inca.* Madrid: Alianza Editorial, 1988, p. 126.

9 Espasa-Calpe. *Diccionario enciclopédico abreviado.* Vol. IV. Madrid: Espasa-Calpe, 1974, pages 979-984.

10 Vega, Garcilaso de la (El Inca). *Primera parte de los Commentarios Reales, que tratan del origen de los Yncas, Reyes que fveron del Perv, de sv idolatría, leyes y gouierno en paz y en guerra: de sus vidas y conquistas, y de todo lo que fue aquel Imperio y su República, antes que los Españoles passaran a el.* Lisbon: Pedro Crasbeeck, 1609.

ATILIO DELL'ORO MAINI

GLOSSARY
BIBLIOGRAPHY

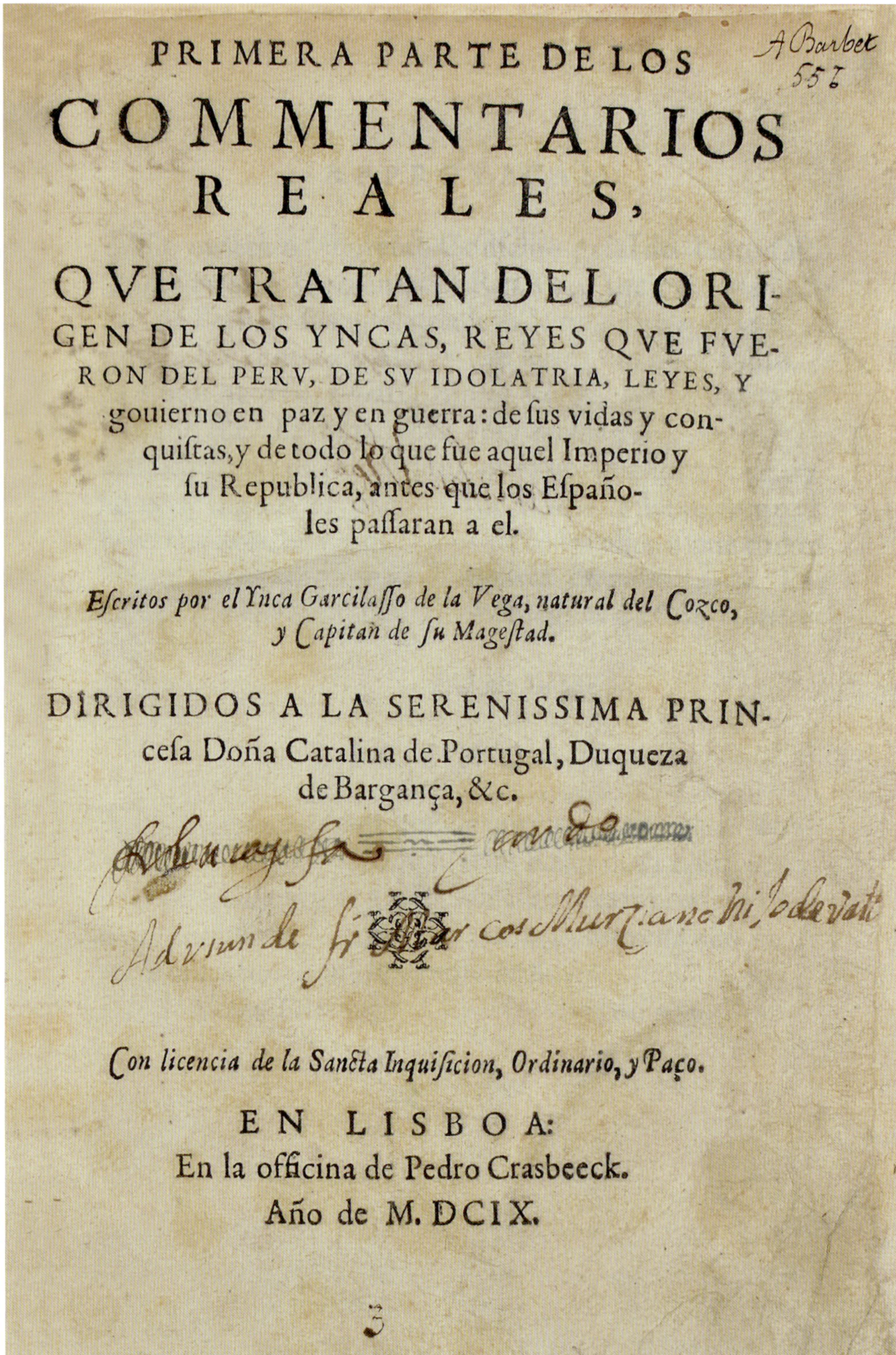

PRIMERA PARTE DE LOS
COMMENTARIOS
REALES,
QVE TRATAN DEL ORIGEN DE LOS YNCAS, REYES QVE FVERON DEL PERV, DE SV IDOLATRIA, LEYES, Y gouierno en paz y en guerra: de ſus vidas y conquiſtas, y de todo lo que fue aquel Imperio y ſu Republica, antes que los Eſpañoles paſſaran a el.

*Eſcritos por el Ynca Garcilaſſo de la Vega, natural del Cozco, y Capitan de ſu Mageſtad.*

DIRIGIDOS A LA SERENISSIMA PRINceſa Doña Catalina de Portugal, Duqueza de Bargança, &c.

*Con licencia de la Sancta Inquiſicion, Ordinario, y Paço.*

EN LISBOA:
En la officina de Pedro Crasbeeck.
Año de M.DCIX.

**COVER OF *PRIMERA PARTE DE LOS COMMENTARIOS REALES, QVE TRATAN DEL ORIGEN DE LOS YNCAS, REYES QVE FVERON DEL PERV…***
Author: Garcilaso de la Vega (El Inca).
Lisbon: Pedro Crasbeeck, 1609.
Courtesy of María Marta Larguía de Arias.

**SET OF ANTIQUE BOOKS**
[OPENING]

## GLOSSARY

### A

**Acanthus:** a Classical ornamental device based on the prickly, indented leaves of the acanthus plant, used especially on the capitals of Corinthian columns.

**Alcove:** central niche-shaped space for the placing of images or sculptures. There could be several in a piece, one on top of the other.

**Alder:** *(alnus acuminata)* whitish or yellowish softwood tree, native to the Cusco region. It was used by both the Incas and the Spanish conquerors.

**Allegory:** symbolic representation of an abstract quality or idea.

**Altarpiece façade:** outer church façade whose decoration is similar to the altar inside the church.

**Ambo:** liturgical piece of furniture similar to a pulpit; built in pairs, they would be placed on either side of the high altar and used for reading the Epistle and Gospel during Mass. An ambo is made up of a rostrum with a lectern and an access stairway, if necessary due to its height.

**Anthropomorphic:** human representation.

**Apron:** decorative fragment emerging from the skirt, both on the front and sides of the piece, connecting the upper parts of the legs.

**Arabesque:** intricate abstract, linear surface decoration of Arab origin with curves and flowing lines.

***Arbalète:*** [French] type of furniture front particularly found on dressers; resembles a crossbow seen from above.

**Archiepiscopal throne:** important chair used by ecclesiastical dignitaries.

**Armrest:** segment on the sides of seats for resting arms or elbows.

**Ashlar:** fine-grained, easily-carved white stone widely used on architectural fronts in the Arequipa region.

**Assembler:** skilled carpenter who builds altars and other major woodworks. Such skills were passed down from fathers to sons, which resulted in assembler dynasties.

***Aymara:*** Amerindian people living in the Lake Titicaca Basin. Also the name of the indigenous language spoken by those people.

### B

**Backrest:** segment located in the upper body of a piece for resting one's back.

**Baluster:** each of the small posts or pillars which make up a balustrade. Generally circular in cross-section and with a curving outline, whether turned or not.

***Bamboccio:*** [Italian] face carved on solid wood which was used as a drawer knob.

***Bargueño:*** [Spanish] square and flat cabinet in the traditional Spanish style, with Islamic roots. It has a front lid and drawers of various sizes and shapes, usually including secret drawers and outstanding bronze, iron, or silver fittings. It was both useful and a symbol of the owner's prestige. Designed to be used by men to keep valuables and documents.

**Base:** flat section piece which rests on the floor and supports the leg of the piece of furniture.

**Bay:** vertical, central and/or side division of spaces in a piece of furniture using columns or pilasters. The central bay may be symmetrically arranged with respect to side bays.

**Beads:** ornament comprising round shapes strung together in a linear fashion resembling a rosary, used on furniture legs and arms, especially in Baroque pieces.

**Bearded man:** representation of a mythical bearded face; frontal or in profile.

**Bedstead:** bed structure comprising a frame and legs.

**Bench:** a piece of furniture which can seat several people at the same time. They were usually placed in pairs facing each other. Found in hallways or entrances of houses, convents and monasteries.

**Bevelled:** cut or shaped into a bevel, where the angle which one surface or line makes with another is not perpendicular.

**Body:** horizontal division of furniture decoration, either continuous or discontinuous.

***Boiserie:*** [French] decorative panels made of various woods; used for covering walls.

***Bombé:*** [French] in dressers, a convex shape on two or more axes.

**Bone:** material used for the same decorative purpose as ivory; it stands out for being more yellow.

**Bracket feet:** flat leg used in English pieces, typical of 18TH century furniture.

**Builder:** artisan or mason who laboured in workshops and on architectural works.

**Bun feet:** name given in Europe to a leg shaped like a flattened onion, which may be decorated or fragmented, and serves as support in baroque furniture.

**Bureau cabinet:** a piece of furniture consisting of two bodies, one on top of the other. The upper body has two front doors for storing books. The lower is a desk with an oblique lid covering a container with several large drawers.

## C

***Cabriole:*** [French] referring to furniture legs, a curved shape emerging from the skirt with a pronounced knee, which can end in various types of feet. Its origins can be traced back to Ming furniture in China.

**Candelabra:** holder for two or more candles.

**Candlestick:** single-candle holder.

**Canopy:** draped fabric supported by a frame, partially or fully covering beds, cradles or thrones.

**Capital:** the separate ornamentation which crowns a column pilaster or pillar.

**Cardinal's hat:** type of furniture cresting, curved in the centre and straight on both sides.

***Cartapesta*** [Italian] or ***papier–mâché*** [French]**:** material made by mixing paper with water and flour; upon drying, it acquires a certain strength.

***Cartonnier:*** [French] segment which can be placed on a desk or table; has shelves and drawers for storing documents.

**Cartouche:** ornamental panel, often a stylised shield, which is decorative in itself but can also carry an inscription, monogram or crest.

**Carver:** master carver and sculptor adept at carving wood for altarpieces or furniture.

**Caryatid:** straight column representing a female figure.

***Cassapanca:*** [Italian] a piece of furniture which seats several people, similar to a bench. The piece has a backrest and may have armrests on both sides. The seat forms a chest with a lid for storing personal belongings.

**Catafalque:** open and portable funeral bed where cloistered nuns were placed for their wake in the *De Profundis* room, before being taken to their final place of rest.

**Cathedra:** piece of furniture consisting of two bodies, the upper being the backrest, and the lower, the armchair. It was used by the prior of a religious order when presiding over a Chapter meeting.

**Cavity:** in furniture, a hole made in a solid body for ornamental purposes.

**Cedar:** a species of tree native to the Amazon basin, frequently found in Ecuador, Nicaragua, Colombia, Venezuela, Guyana and Peru. The precious wood is used for making furniture. The so-called "cedro de altura" *(cedrela lilloi)* has high-quality wood; the Cigar-box cedar *(cedrela odorata)* is taller and larger; both were used in the production of furniture and altars.

**Central design:** in an object, a space which contains ornaments and is surrounded by a frame.
**Central niche:** the central and tallest space in multi-bodied pieces.
**Centre table** or ***gueridon:*** [French] small portable table which can be used in any room.
**Chapterhouse:** room in a monastery or convent where everyday Chapter meetings take place.
**Chest of drawers:** container consisting of multiple drawers.
**Chest:** rectangular wooden container, with a flat or roof-shaped lid, featuring one or more front locks and having handles for transport; decorated using various techniques, depending on its origin.
**Child corbel:** ornamental motif representing the face, torso or entire body of a child with native features; an element which appears to support the weight of another.
**Chinese junks:** small boats used by Chinese traders to transport goods from one port to another.
***Chinoiserie:*** [French] Chinese decoration.
**Choir stalls:** religious piece of furniture where choristers gather and sit or stand in order to sing together. They can be rood screened or low choir stalls depending on their location within the church.
**Claw and ball:** leg termination in the shape of a bird's claw holding a sphere.
***Coa:*** [Taíno] wooden tool ancestrally used in South America to till the land and sow the grain.
**Coat of arms:** blazon symbolising the nobility of a family or place.
***Cocobolo*** **or** ***granadillo:*** [Spanish] *(Dalbergia retusa)* tropical tree native to Central America. Its orange or reddish brown wood is very hard, heavy and oily.
**Coffered ceiling:** name given to the internal covering of the roof of a building, either secular or religious, which is decorated with polygonal or volumetric mouldings according to the Renaissance style.
**Comb:** in furniture, a large decoration carved and fretted on top of the piece.
**Confessional:** liturgical piece of furniture used for administering the sacrament of confession.
**Convent:** building in the centre of a settlement where a religious congregation lived and carried out its evangelical work.
***Coquera:*** [Spanish] small container with an upper lid for storing coca leaves.
**Corbel:** related to furniture, an ornamental element which supports the weight of another.
**Cordovan:** thick and tanned goatskin used for covering *petacas*, making suitcases or upholstering friar's chairs. It was embossed and occasionally polychromed or gilded.
**Corner bead:** reinforcement in the corners of a container.
**Cornice:** rectilinear ornament located at the top of a container.
**Cornucopia:** ornament representing a horn overflowing with the fruits of the land; it symbolises abundance.
**Counterpulpit:** liturgical piece of furniture hanging from a wall or column in the nave of a church opposite the pulpit, where a religious image was enthroned to inspire the officiating priest while he delivered his sermon.
**Coya:** princess, wife of the Inca.
**Cresting:** ornament on the top of a piece of furniture.
**Crossbar:** decorated wood segment connecting the front legs of seats.
**Crosspiece:** elongated segment connecting the legs of a piece.
***Cuadra:*** [Spanish] area of the house for receiving visitors

## D

***De Profundis*** **room:** room in a monastery or convent, adjacent to the refectory, for praying and holding wakes for the mortal remains of congregation members.
**Detached** (may refer to furniture or columns): an ornament separate from the main or central structure. The piece does not lean against another surface, so the observer can move around and have an unobstructed view of every side.
**Detached column:** decorative column which is neither attached to the structure nor acting as support.
**Diamond point:** decorative geometric carving in low relief.
**Direct carving:** technique for carving on solid wood.
**Dome:** in furniture, semicircular body topping or crowning a piece.
**Double-headed eagle:** imperial symbol consisting of a frontal representation of an eagle with two heads and spread wings.

## E

**East India Company:** shipping company which traded and transported goods from the East.
**Ebonised:** darkened wood, simulating ebony.
**Ebony:** tree native to South India, Sri Lanka *(Diospyros ebenum)* and Western Africa *(Diospyros dendro)*. Species which provides very dense dark wood (it sinks in water) with a very tight grain; it has a notable shine when polished and is greatly valued as ornamental wood.
**Egg:** volumetric oval decoration forming classical guards.
***Eglomise:*** [French] glass painted on the reverse.
**Elder:** *(Sambucus)* tree native to temperate and subtropical regions in both hemispheres. It stands out for the hardness and durability of its wood, which was used in cabinetmaking and the production of rural tools.
**Emblem:** symbolic object which represents something else; occasionally used for decorating furniture.
**Embossing:** leather working technique, involving the use of a hot iron to create a volumetric effect on surfaces.
***Encomendero:*** [Spanish] during the colonial period, a person who had the authority to organise Indians and make them work in the transportation and trade of goods.
**Engraving:** technique for working metal or stone with a chisel.
**Enthrone:** to place an image in a relevant location for worship.
**Escritoire:** small portable piece designed for writing.
***Estipite:*** [Spanish] flat foot with four sides shaped like an inverted pyramid.
***Estofado:*** [Spanish] technique consisting of carving, with the appropriate tools, the gold surface covering wood or leather, in order to extract the underlying colour from it or decorate it with polychromes.
***Estofador:*** [Spanish] craftsman specialised in applying the *estofado* technique to flat surfaces, such as leather or wood.

## F

**Fan-shaped shell:** open scallop resembling a fan.
**Fillet:** fine moulding of contrasting colours embedded in wood.
**Fitting:** external element completing the decoration of a piece.
**Floating column:** decorative column which does not rest on the floor, and therefore does not support the structure.
**Floor lectern:** a liturgical or choir book holder, useful for reading while standing. It consists of an oblique board resting on a tall shaft.
**Fluted** or **grooved column:** column with classical decoration achieved by carving grooves along its structure.
**Footboard:** lower segment of a bed, attached to the frame.
**Footstool** or **footrest:** small piece of furniture for resting one's feet while seated.
***Frailero:*** [Spanish] Spanish Renaissance style of armchair with a rectangular, leather-covered seat and a leather or velvet back; generally having a broad front stretcher, which is often carved. Sometimes hinged to allow folding and easy transportation.
**Frame:** a rigid construction attached to a soft material in order to stretch it.
**Fretwork:** technique of drilling or carving a material in order to decorate it with cavities.
**Friar's chair:** synonym for frailero.
**Frieze:** rectilinear segment on which the top ornament rests.
**Frontal projection:** broken front, whose centre emerges from the plane, protruding with respect to the side bays of a piece, or vice versa.

## G

**Gadroon:** ornamentation consisting of volumetric grooves forming a frieze.

**Garland:** ornament consisting of intertwined flowers or fruits.

**Geometrician:** person responsible for taking the geometric measurements of lines and surfaces; together with an architect, they would apply such measures to a plan or layout.

**Gilding:** technique for applying thin gold leaves to a surface using agate stone.

**Gold leaf:** extremely thin layer of gold used for decorating wood or other surfaces.

**Green man:** representation of a mythical face with leaves coming out of its mouth or representing its whiskers or forehead; it is a symbol of life and fertility which has existed since the dawn of time.

**Grotesque:** classic ornament derived from those found on Pompeian walls; they inspired Renaissance, Classical and Neoclassical decoration, where ornamental elements were intertwined and symmetrically distributed.

***Guadamecí*** or ***guadamecil:*** [Spanish] name given in Andalusia to sheepskin which, being malleable, soft and thin, could be decorated with elaborate polychromed and gilded *estofado* designs. Used for covering walls of chapels and fronts of domestic altars, as well as on floors and cushions in ladies' parlours.

**Guild:** an association of people with similar trades, who swore to abide by strict rules, for protection and the achievement of beneficial common goals. A practice carried out from the 15TH century in Spain by craftsmen who were trained in various skills, such as carpenters and cabinetmakers.

## H

**Half-relief carving:** carving with a certain volumetric sculptural effect.

**Half round:** semicircular, longitudinally cut framing.

**Hallway:** in a house, a corridor from the entrance to the first patio.

**Handle** or ***tirette:*** [French] element made of metal, wood or other materials, of various shapes and sizes, for opening and closing doors and drawers.

**Harquebusier archangel:** angelic figure representing the Virgin's armed guardian. Dressed in rich European military garments, it was very important in the Americas. The main archangels are Michael, Raphael, Gabriel and Uriel. Represented in Flemish prints, they arrived in Lima during the first half of the 17TH century. Their images spread in the South Andean iconography from Cusco to Arequipa, from Lake Titicaca to Trujillo, and southward, to the north of Argentina.

**Headboard:** upper segment of a bed, attached to its frame.

**Hearse:** large candelabra resting on a tall base, with a triangular upper body which holds fifteen candles. Used for Tenebrae on Good Friday, when its candles were extinguished one-by-one.

**Heresiarch:** a heretic or a person who commits a heresy.

**Heterogeneous bays:** in a piece of furniture, front body divisions of various heights for decorative purposes.

**Heterogeneous bodies:** (see **body**) having different sizes or decoration.

***Hierbera:*** [Spanish] small container with an upper lid for storing yerba mate.

**Hinge:** fitting comprising two metal plates with a common shaft. These plates are fastened to the two structures to be joined, allowing them to move without coming loose.

**Homogeneous bays:** in a piece of furniture, front body divisions whose sides have comparable heights.

**Homogeneous bodies:** (see **body**) having similar sizes or decoration.

***Horror vacui:*** fear of emptiness; in art it encourages artists to cover every space.

**Huaca:** in the Inca culture, sacred room or object for worshipping gods and honouring deceased ancestors.

**Huamanga Stone:** local type of alabaster made up of a conglomerate of volcanic material. Due to its ductility, it can be easily carved, as well as polychromed and gilded. Being translucent, it was often used instead of glass in church windows and skylights, both in the coastal region and on the Peruvian Altiplano.

**Huamanga:** ancient city of San Juan de la Frontera de Huamanga, present-day Ayacucho, located in the central Peruvian Andes and renowned for its alabaster quarries.

## I

**Iconography:** descriptive representation in a work of art from which historical or symbolic information can be obtained.
**Image cradle:** small cradle for placing sacred images for worship.
**Indigenous:** relating to the native population.
**Inlay:** contrasting wood or other materials inserted in wood following a predefined layout.
***Intarsia:*** [Italian] see **inlay**.
***Inti:*** sun god worshiped by the Incas, from whom their monarchs were descended.
**Ivory palm:** *(Phytelephas seemannii, Phytelephas macrocarpa)* palm tree growing in tropical and humid areas of South America. Vegetable ivory is obtained from its seeds.
**Ivory:** material extracted from elephant tusks, used for partially or completely inlaying luxury furniture or making art objects. During the period we are dealing with, it came from India.

## K

***Kantuta:*** or K'antu flower *(Cantua buxifolia)*, a flower which grows at high altitudes in the South Andean region (2,500/3,200 m above sea level). It was dedicated to the sun god by the Incas.
**Kneeler:** piece of furniture for praying on one's knees.
**Knob:** handle for easily opening drawers or doors.

## L

**Lacquer:** clear solution comprising a resin extracted from a conifer *(Rhus vernicifera)* and volatile thinners, such as alcohol. Wood surfaces were covered with it to make them shine and preserve them from external agents such as insects and damp. To achieve the desired colour the solution was mixed with natural pigments, such as cochineal, from which vermilion was obtained.
**Lamp:** element of various sizes and shapes used for illumination.
**Large candle holder:** a torch holder consisting of a central shaft and a supporting leg; useful for special celebrations, such as the Easter Sunday Mass.
**Lattice:** metal strips or crossed wood used for isolating purposes, while allowing the passage of air.
***Lattimo:*** [Italian] Venetian treatment of opaque white glass, either forming the whole body of the object or used as decoration in stripes, festoons or threads.
**Leaves:** decoration representing moving foliage.
**Lectern:** oversized piece for religious use located in the centre of the choir. Useful for supporting choir books which had to be read from a distance. It is a two-bodied piece: the upper body is a stand with several oblique sides; the lower is an octagonal container with a door.
**Leitmotiv:** feature repeatedly written or represented in art, becoming the focus of attention.

## M

**Maguey:** *(Agave americana)* plant with large fleshy leaves which stem directly from the root. Its fibres are useful for producing fabrics and weaving ropes with which the Incas made everything from sandals to bridges.
**Mahogany:** *(Swietenia spp / Swietenia macrophylia)* tree which grows in vast areas of Central America, as well as Peru and Bolivia. The most widely used variety, due to its unbeatable quality, is from Santo Domingo. Its incorruptible wood, highly resistant to damp and insects, is a deep, bright red. The wood is highly valued in furniture production.
**Marquetry:** a technique for completely inlaying a surface following a predefined layout; to this end, various shades of wood or other materials were used, produced contrasting effects.
***Martelé:*** [French] decorative treatment given to metal by hammering its surface.

**Mascaron:** ornament shaped like a human face.

**Master assembler:** carpenter who, leading a workshop and other builders, designed and assembled altars.

**Master cabinetmaker:** degree awarded to the master carpenter specialising in designing and building high quality furniture.

**Mermaid:** universal mythological figure represented, in the *mestizo* or Andean Baroque art world, on furniture fronts or architectural façades, with feathered or flowered headdresses, and a *charango* or guitar in her arms.

***Meuble d'apparat:*** [French] a strictly ornamental piece of furniture, with no utilitarian function.

**Misericorde:** small seat placed on the back of choir stalls, which allowed choristers to take some of the weight off their feet.

**Monastery:** building outside the cities where a religious congregation lived and carried out their evangelical work. Their sustenance was based on farming and animal husbandry.

**Monogram:** seal-shaped abbreviation symbolising a sacred or famous emblem.

**Monstrance:** liturgical object placed on altars during the blessing. Usually made of metal and richly decorated, it consists of a shaft holding a central glass container displaying a consecrated host and surrounded by a highly symbolic halo of rays.

**Mother-of-pearl inlay:** Oriental technique deriving from the *Namban* lacquer technique, whose decorative effect is produced by inlaying mother-of-pearl, tortoiseshell and occasionally, mahogany plates, in adequate and balanced proportions, on a wooden base.

**Mother-of-pearl:** also called nacre; fine scale-shaped plate extracted from the shell of certain multi-coloured bivalves. Used for decorating inlaid furniture.

**Moulding:** frame of decorative composition, either with or without volume.

***Mountain Caracara:*** very difficult to hunt bird, with white and black feathers**.** These feathers were used for making coats and other garments worn by the Inca nobility during important ceremonies. These birds had a high symbolic value since, according the Incas, they flew in pairs, an allusion to the original couple.

**Mudejar:** Spanish-Muslim artistic style which had a powerful influence on Christian art.

**Multifoil arch:** circular arch made with a series of curves on the inner edge.

## N

**Nacre:** see **mother-of-pearl.**

***Namban* lacquer:** Japanese technique based on the use of lacquers and mother-of-pearl; its name comes from *Namban*, a Japanese term for "Southern barbarians", i.e. foreigners. It was used to decorate pieces of furniture for export, whose morphology had European —chiefly Spanish— style and repertoire.

**Native:** referring to the native population with deep roots in their land.

**Nativity scene or Nativity chest:** container with front and top lids and side handles. When the chest was opened, characters were seen representing sequential scenes of Biblical History. Images were made from moulded paste and other materials. The purpose of the piece was to teach catechism to indigenous peoples.

## O

**Oblong:** rectangular shape arranged so that the longer sides are horizontal.

***Obraje:*** [Spanish] workshop where artisans of the same trade gathered to work.

**Order:** Catholic religious congregation authorised by the Pope, which brings together individuals who take vows, honour a patron saint and follow established rules.

## P

**Pad feet:** name given, in certain South American regions, to the end of *cabriole* legs.

**Paired columns:** columns arranged in pairs, an ornament replicated on both sides of the centre.

**Panel:** in architecture or furniture, a segment within a frame.

**Parlour:** exclusive room for women, derived from the *harem*, placed on a platform covered with fabrics and decorated with ad hoc furniture.

***Pastiglia:*** [Italian] technique for artistically moulding a wet plaster surface in low relief and subsequently gilding it when the surface dries.

**Pasto varnish:** lacquer of Spanish American origin which is extracted from the resin of a shrub called mopa-mopa *(Elaeagia pastoensis)*. According to some historians, during pre-Columbian times, the native population of the Pastos territory, in the Viceroyalty of New Granada (present-day Colombia), applied it in layers to wood or pottery pieces.

**Patina:** colour treatment, useful for covering wood or any other surface.

**Pearling:** a classical decoration forming a frieze, which gives the appearance of being made of pearls.

**Pedestal:** medium sized portable structure which rests on the floor; it can be used for placing lamps or other objects.

**Pediment:** triangular cresting, similar to an architectural pediment, which is also used in furniture.

**Pendant:** turned or carved decoration hanging from the bottom of a piece.

***Petaca:*** [Spanish] regular size chest, with a top lid, built with local wood and covered with leather. It has a metal lock and side handles for easy transportation.

**Phytomorphic:** related to a plant ornament.

***Piedra del lago:*** [Spanish] type of alabaster found in the Collao basin, by Lake Titicaca.

**Pilaster:** half column attached to the front of a piece for ornamental purposes.

**Pinnacle:** turned or carved ornament placed on top of a piece of furniture.

**Plain column:** basic straight column, with no decoration.

**Planiform decoration:** flat ornaments, with no relief.

**Plateresque:** Spanish art style characterised by the abundant decoration used by the silversmiths of the time.

**Pole:** long wood or metal segment for carrying a throne, litter or sedan chair on people's shoulders.

**Polychromed:** piece of furniture decorated with polychromy.

**Polychromy:** technique for applying a rich colour palette to a given material.

**Portable** or **positive organ:** small wind instrument operated with bellows insufflating air; it is played via a keyboard.

**Portable platform:** piece of furniture used for supporting and carrying sacred images during liturgical processions.

**Print:** series of figures or landscapes made using a printing press.

**Projecting lid:** an oversized lid with respect to the body on which it rests.

**Pulpit:** elevated piece consisting of a rostrum, a sounding board, stairs and an access door. Used by officiating priests to deliver their sermon during Mass; thus, a piece for liturgical use.

**Putto:** decorative figure in the shape of a plump child, typical of the Baroque style.

**Pyrography:** technique for using a hot metal tip to partially or completely decorate various materials.

## Q

**Quarter:** to divide into distinct sections.

***Quechua*:** indigenous language spoken by the Quechua people on the Altiplano.

**Quicksilver** or **mercury:** liquid metal used for purifying silver and making mirrors. In the Viceroyalty of Peru, this mineral was obtained in Huancavelica.

***Quincha:*** [Quechua] indigenous technique for building walls and roofs, widely used in seismic zones. It involved fastening canes together using leather thongs, and covering them with mortar or adobe.

## R

**Religious image sculptor:** artist or craftsman who carves religious images.

**Ribbons:** related to furniture, decoration made of ribbons.

*Rocaille:* [French] characteristic Rococo ornament; a concave representation of an eroded shell on a plane.

**Rood screen gate:** quartered fence dividing the area in the upper part of the nave from the rest of the church.

**Roof-shaped lid:** semicircular container lid resembling a roof tile.

**Rosette:** ornament in the shape of a stylised flower made up of acanthus leaves.

**Rostrum:** elevated piece of furniture attached to a wall, located on high, latticed balconies so people could attend ceremonies without being seen. Central body of the pulpit where officiating priests would stand when delivering their sermons.

**Rotating base** or **terminal:** metallic device located in the centre of a piece allowing it to rotate.

**Round arch:** a semicircular arch, from Roman art, later used in the Romanesque, Renaissance, Classicist and Neoclassical styles.

## S

**Sacramentary stand** or **holder:** preconciliary piece of furniture on which Scripture passages and psalms were placed to be read. Consisting of one or more regular-sized moulded frames, it rested on legs and was placed on the altar.

**Sacristy chest of drawers:** large container with drawers from top to bottom and doors on the upper body; usually located in church sacristies. It is used for storing the liturgical utensils and the garments worn by priests during Mass.

**Sacristy:** area adjacent to the church, where officiating priests changed into their liturgical garments before religious ceremonies. Equipped with large functional containers, it was useful for storing liturgical garments and utensils.

**Saturated:** referring to an excess of ornaments or colour.

**Scale:** in furniture, scale-shaped decoration made using various techniques.

**Scallop:** convex shell-shaped ornament.

**Sedan chair:** type of seat for transporting high dignitaries and ladies of the society on short journeys; carried on the shoulders of two or more people.

**Semi column:** half column attached to a structure and decorated only on its visible side.

**Semi-dome:** flat dome or low half-sphere used in architecture and furniture. It is supported by pinnacles or columns, and crowns visible areas in furniture.

**Semi-oval pediment:** Renaissance top decoration in the shape of a half oval, placed on architectural façades or furniture fronts.

**Sequential scenes:** descriptive and fragmented ornamentation whose scenes are interrelated representing a single story.

**Sewing box:** small container designed to hold sewing materials and implements for women who sewed; usually having one or more drawers fitted with partitions.

**Sgraffito:** [Italian] technique for decorating wood or other materials by making burin incisions imitating engravings, which are enhanced using vegetable dyes.

**Shaft:** structure which supports a body and extends from the centre of the piece to the floor.

**Shelf table or *dressoir:*** [French] sideboard supported by four legs. There is another body on top of its lid. Chapter I of this book refers to those placed by the altar in religious ceremonies to support liturgical utensils.

**Shrine:** small architectural construction which imitates Greek temples.

**Silver:** Precious metal of extraordinary purity, quality and malleability. Useful for making tableware and luxury furniture fittings.

**Skirt:** in furniture, part of the piece supporting a table's top and a chair's seat, or dividing the upper and middle bodies of wardrobes with drawers.

**Small candlestick:** holder for a single candle, with a side handle for carrying; used for individual lighting.

**Socket:** rectilinear bottom segment resting on the floor which supports a piece of furniture. Sometimes used instead of legs.

**Socket:** the metal part of an altar lamp which holds the candle.

**Sofa table:** table with straight lines, supported by legs at its ends, which features a large drawer in its skirt. Its main characteristic is a rectangular top with folding sections or drop leaves on each side to allow resizing.

**Solomonic:** in architecture and furniture, the helical format of a column shaft, with a marked volume, characteristic of the Baroque style.

**Sounding board:** canopy on the top of a pulpit.

**Spanish-Arab:** idiosyncrasy with Spanish and Arab features.

**Splat:** carved or fretted vertical segment placed in the centre of a backrest, an element of English origin and Chinese influence.

**Stall:** high or low seat in church choirs, with a backrest, a misericorde on the back, and armrests.

**Stereotomy:** art of cutting and carving stone for architectural works developed by Peruvian natives, who were skilful and meticulous in this art.

**Stile:** vertical wood segment in the structure of a piece which is assembled into crossbeams for strength.

**Structure:** in furniture, it is the wooden skeleton supporting the ornamentation.

**Stud:** metal nail (made of silver, bronze or iron) with a large head. Used in furniture for attaching fabrics or leather to a frame.

**Suitcase:** a medium-sized quadrangular container made of cowhide —with no wooden frame— and simply decorated with embroidered leather thongs. Useful for transporting clothes, tapestry, linen, silverware, crockery and books.

**Supporting structure:** wood, canvas or metal frame which is the base for an art work. In furniture, it is usually a wooden structure.

**Syncretism:** the merger of two or more cultures or forms of belief.

## T

**Tabernacle:** small sacred vessel with a front door and a key used for storing the ciborium containing consecrated hosts.

**Table top lectern:** holder for missals or other books. It takes the form of an oblique board supported by short legs so it can be placed on an altar or table.

**Temporary** or **portable altar:** small piece of furniture, used for celebrating the Holy Mass or other religious rituals. It could be transported to any location.

**Torch:** large candle.

**Tortoiseshell:** raw material extracted from the shell of a turtle and used to inlay a wood supporting surface and give it a very beautiful appearance. From the shell, eight of the thirteen panels were selected; each being two or three millimetres thick. These were softened by a moist heat and then pressed flat as they cooled, thus becoming suitable for use. This material comes from the hawksbill sea turtle *(Eretmochelys imbricata)*, abundant in the Marañón basin, a tributary of the Amazon River in Peru; the Charapa turtle *(Podocnemis expansa)*, one of the largest turtles in South America, whose shell can grow up to seventy centimetres; or the Brazilian giant tortoise *(Geochelone denticulata)*, whose shell can measure up to eighty-two centimetres.

***Treillage:*** [French] rhomboidal ornament widely used as background in Rococo decorative compositions; it recreates the fences of Chinese buildings.

**Triangular pediment:** classical top decoration in the shape of a triangle, placed on architectural façades or furniture fronts.

***Trompe l'œil:*** [French] technique for simulating reality by means of perspective. Used to expand spaces and give a convincing illusion of reality.

## V

***Veduta:*** [Italian] a topographically accurate landscape painting, as opposed to a fanciful one.
**Viringo:** Peruvian hairless dog.
**Volute:** Baroque ornament which appears to support a body.

## W

**Walnut:** *(Juglans neotropica)* in Peru, this tree grows at high altitude (1,000/3,000 m above sea level). Its wood is excellent for building pieces of furniture and musical instruments.
**Wardrobe:** regular-sized container with front doors; useful for storing clothes or personal belongings. It may have drawers in its skirt or above the legs.
**Weeping willow:** *(Salix humboldtiana)* tree growing on river banks, found throughout the Americas, although it was planted by the Incas in the Colca canyon, near Arequipa.
**West India Company:** shipping company which traded and transported goods from the Americas to Europe and vice versa.
**Wick:** the piece of thread in a candle, which burns when lit.
**Wood turner:** artisan who uses a lathe to shape wood.
**Writing desk:** small-sized desk.

## Z

**Zoomorphic:** animal-shaped ornament.

## BIBLIOGRAPHY


**Aguilera, Carmen *et al.*** *El mueble mexicano: Historia, evolución e influencias.* Mexico: Fomento Cultural Banamex, 1985.

**Aguilera, Concha (coord).** *La España donde no se ponía el sol.* Colección Grandes Imperios y Civilizaciones. Madrid: SARPE, 1985.

**Aguiló Alonso, María Paz.** *El Mueble en España: siglos XVI y XVII.* Madrid: Antiqvaria, 1993.

**Aguiló Alonso, María Paz.** *Orden y decoro. Felipe II y el amueblamiento del Monasterio de El Escorial.* Madrid: Coleccionarte, 2001.

**Aguiló, María Paz.** *El mueble clásico español.* Colección Cuadernos Arte Cátedra. Madrid: Cátedra, 1987.

**Aguiló, María Paz.** "Aproximaciones al estudio del mueble novohispano en España". Barcelona: Ayuntamiento de Barcelona, 2008.

**Alfonso Mola, Marina *et al.*** *El Galeón de Manila.* Madrid: Ministerio de Educación, Cultura y Deporte, Aldeasa, 2000.

**Alfonso Mola, Marina and Martínez Shaw, Carlos (eds).** *Oriente en Palacio: Tesoros asiáticos en las colecciones reales españolas.* Madrid: Patrimonio Nacional-Ediciones El Viso, 2003.

**Almagro-Gorbea, Martín.** "De Pompeya a Palenque: la arqueología ilustrada y la corona de España". *Reales Sitios,* year XLVII, vol. Nº 183, first quarter of 2010, pages 42-63.

**Arrarte, Eduardo R. *et al.*** *Casa Solariega de Aliaga.* Lima: Stimulus, 2004.

*Artes de México. La pintura de castas.* Mexico: Artes de México y del Mundo, Nº 8, summer of 1990.

*Asia en las Colecciones Reales del Museo Nacional de Artes Decorativas.* Santillana de Mar: Fundación Santillana, 2000.

**Bailey, Gauvin Alexander.** *Art of Colonial Latin America.* New York: Phaidon, 2005.

**Bákula Budge, Cecilia *et al.*** *Mestizo. Del renacimiento al barroco andino.* Lima: Impulso Empresa de Servicios, 2008.

**Barriga Tello, Martha.** *Influencia de la Ilustración borbónica en el arte limeño: siglo XVIII.* Lima: Fondo Editorial Universidad Nacional Mayor de San Marcos, 2004.

**Barros Arana, Diego.** *Compendio elemental de Historia de América.* Buenos Aires: Cabaut y Cía.-Librería del Colegio, 1915.

**Becker, Udo.** *Enciclopedia de los símbolos.* Barcelona: Swing-extra, 2008.

**Bennassar, Bartolomé and Vincent, Bernard.** *España. Los siglos de Oro.* Barcelona: Crítica, 2000.

**Bérchez, Joaquín (dir).** *Los Siglos de Oro en los Virreinatos de América 1550-1700.* Madrid: Museo de América-Ediciones El Viso, 2000.

**Bernales Ballesteros, Jorge.** *Lima, la ciudad y sus monumentos.* Sevilla: Consejo Superior de Investigaciones Científicas, Escuela de Estudios Hispano-Americanos de Sevilla, 1972.

*Boletín de Lima.* Lima: El Pino, 1998, vol. XX, Nº 114.

**Bonet Correa, Antonio.** *Monasterios Iberoamericanos.* [n.p.]: Ediciones El Viso, 2001.

**Bourne, Jonathan *et al.*** *Lacquer. An International History and Collector's Guide.* Marlborough: The Crowood Press - Phoebe Phillips Editions, 1984.

**Bruce-Mitford, Miranda.** *El libro ilustrado de signos y símbolos. Miles de signos y símbolos de todo el mundo.* Buenos Aires: El Ateneo, 1997.

**Bueno, Cosme.** *Geografía del Perú Virreinal (siglo XVIII).* Published by Daniel Valcarcel. Lima: [n.n.], 1951.

**Burckhardt, T.** *El mudéjar americano: del Islam al Nuevo Mundo.* Granada: El legado Andalusí, 1995.

**Camacho, Fabio.** *Aspectos de Lima.* Lima: Editorial Incazteca de F. Camacho, Empresa Publicitaria Expresión, 1929.

**Campos Vera, Norma (ed).** *Barroco y fuentes de la diversidad cultural: Memoria del II Encuentro Internacional sobre Barroco.* La Paz: Vice Ministry of Culture, Unión Latina and UNESCO, 2004.

**Campos Vera, Norma (ed).** *Manierismo y transición al barroco: Memoria del III Encuentro Internacional sobre Barroco.* La Paz: Unión Latina - Centro de Estudios Indianos, 2005.

**Carty, Charles L.** *Arequipa, ciudad inolvidable.* Arequipa: [n.n.], 2008.

**Cassinelli Del Sante, Gino.** *Árboles y arbustos del Valle Sagrado.* Lima: [n.n.], 2006.

**Checa Cremades, F., García Felguera, M. S. and Moran Turina, M.** *Guía para el estudio de la Historia del Arte.* Cuadernos Arte Cátedra. Madrid: Cátedra, 1987.

**Cieza de León, Pedro de.** *La Chronica del Perv, nvevamente escrita por Pedro de Cieza de León, vezino de Seuilla.* Anveres: Martin Nuncio, 1554.

**Cirlot, Juan Eduardo.** *Diccionario de símbolos.* Colombia. Grupo Editor Quinto Centenario, 1995.

*Conjunto Monumental "San Francisco de Asís".* Lima: [n.n.], [n.d.].

**Conrad, Geoffrey W. and Demarest, Arthur A.** *Religión e imperio. Dinámica del expansionismo azteca e inca.* Madrid: Alianza Editorial, 1988.

*Convento de Santo Domingo. Qorikancha.* Cusco: Asociación Cultural Laudare, 2011.

**Cotterell, Arthur (ed).** *Enciclopedia de mitología universal.* Barcelona: Parragon Books, 2008.

**Duarte, Carlos F.** *Grandes maestros carpinteros del período hispánico venezolano.* Caracas: Cantv, 2004.

**Eguiguren Molina, José and Eguiguren Molina, Javier (eds).** *El Mate en América.* Buenos Aires: Eguiguren y Vega, 2004.

**Espasa-Calpe.** *Diccionario enciclopédico abreviado.* Vol. IV. Madrid: Espasa-Calpe, 1974.

**Feduchi, Luis.** *El Mueble Español.* Barcelona: Ediciones Polígrafa, 1969.

**Feduchi, Luis.** *Historia del Mueble.* Barcelona: Blume, 1986.

**Ferguson, George.** *Signos y símbolos en el arte cristiano.* Buenos Aires: Emecé, 1956.

**Fisher, Herbert A. L.** *Historia de Europa.* Vol. II. Buenos Aires: Sudamericana, 1958.

**Fontana, David.** *The secret language of symbols. A visual key to symbols and their meanings.* San Francisco: Chronicle Books, 1994.

**Fuentes, Manuel Atanasio.** *Lima: apuntes históricos, descriptivos, estadísticos y de costumbres.* Paris: F. Didot, 1867.

**Fukumoto, Mary.** "Migración japonesa al Perú". *Boletín de Lima.* 1998, year 20, vol. XX, Nº 114.

**Fundación Pedro y Angélica de Osma Gildemeister.** *Museo Pedro de Osma.* Lima: [n.n.], 2004.

**Gesualdo, Vicente (ed).** *Enciclopedia del Arte en América.* Buenos Aires: Bibliográfica OMEBA, 1968.

**González, Elena (ed).** *Trazos del pasado: El período colonial en La Libertad.* Lima: Asociación Marsa, 2008.

**Goss, John (ed).** *Gran Atlas de Johannes Blaeu. El Mundo del Siglo Diecisiete.* Madrid: Libsa, 1991.

**Gruber, Alain (ed).** *The History of Decorative Arts. The Renaissance and Mannerism in Europe.* New York: Abbeville Press, 1994.

**Grupp, Franz and Mercado de Grupp, Zully.** *El Monasterio de Santa Teresa de Arequipa.* (Unpublished.)

**Gutiérrez, Ramón (coord).** *Barroco iberoamericano. De los Andes a las Pampas.* Barcelona: Lunwerg, 1997.

**Gutiérrez, Ramón (coord).** *Pintura, escultura y artes útiles en Iberoamérica, 1500-1825.* Colección Manuales Arte Cátedra. Madrid: Cátedra, 1995.

**Gutiérrez Haces, Juana (coord).** *Pintura de los Reinos. Identidades compartidas. Territorios del mundo hispánico, siglos XVI-XVIII.* Vol. II. Mexico: Fomento Cultural Banamex, 2008.

**Juan, Jorge and Ulloa, Antonio de.** *Relación Historica del viage a la America Meridional hecho de orden de S. Mag. para medir algunos grados de Meridiano Terrestre, y venir por ellos en conocimiento de la verdadera Figura, y Magnitud de la Tierra, con otras varias Observaciones Astronómicas y Phisicas.* Vols. I and III. Madrid: Antonio Marin, 1748.

**Kagan, Richard L.** *Imágenes urbanas del mundo hispánico 1493-1780.* [n.p.]: Ediciones El Viso, 1998.

**Kawamura Kawamura, Yayoi.** "Obras de laca del arte *namban* de los Monasterios de la Encarnación y de las Trinitarias de Madrid". *Reales Sitios,* year XXXVIII, Nº 147, pages 2-12.

**Kelemen, Pál.** *Baroque and Rococo in Latin America.* New York: Dover Publications, 1967.

**Kirchhoff, Herbert.** *Perú ayer y hoy.* Buenos Aires: Guillermo Kraft, 1951.

*La Biblia de Estudio. Dios habla hoy con Deuterocanónicos.* Brazil: Sociedades Bíblicas Unidas, 2004.

"La Virgen de las siete espadas". Historiarte.net [on line] [last accessed: February 29, 2012, 4:30 pm] <http://www.historiarte.net/iconografia/sieteespadas.html>. Source: Réau, Louis. *Iconografía del arte cristiano.*

**Lofstrom M., William.** *Espacios Virreinales: El arte mobiliario y decorativo en la ciudad de La Plata.* Sucre: [n.n.], 2009.

**Lohmann Villena, Guillermo *et al.*** *Historia marítima del Perú: siglos XVII y XVIII.* Vol. IV. Lima: Instituto de Estudios Histórico-Marítimos del Perú, 1975.

**Lohmann Villena, Guillermo *et al.*** *La Basílica Catedral de Lima.* Colección Arte y Tesoros del Perú. Lima: Banco de Crédito del Perú, 2004.

**Macchi, Fernanda.** *Incas ilustrados. Reconstrucciones imperiales en la segunda mitad del siglo XVIII.* Madrid: Vervuert - Iberoamericana, 2009.

**Majluf, Natalia and Wuffarden, Luis Eduardo.** *La piedra de Huamanga. Lo sagrado y lo profano.* Catalogue from the "La piedra de Huamanga. Lo sagrado y lo profano" exhibition. Lima: Museo de Arte de Lima, 1998.

**Martínez Shaw, Carlos and Alfonso Mola, Marina (eds).** *La ruta española a China.* Madrid: Ediciones El Viso, 2007.

**Menegazzo, Rossella.** *Japón.* Colección Los Diccionarios de las Civilizaciones. Barcelona: Random House Mondadori, 2008.

**Mesa Figueroa, José de *et al.*** *El retorno de los ángeles.* [n.p.]: Unión Latina, [n.d.].

**Meyer, F. S.** *Manual de ornamentación.* Mexico: G. Gili, 1999.

**Michaud, Cécile and Torres Della Pina, José (eds).** *De Amberes al Cusco. El grabado europeo como fuente del arte virreinal.* Lima: Centro Cultural Pontificia Universidad Católica del Perú, 2009.

**Ministerio de Cultura del Perú.** *Agenda cultural* [on line] June 2012 [last accessed: June 3, 2012] <http://www.mcultura.gob.pe/agenda_cultural_museos_mc-junio_2012.pdf>

**Morel, Héctor V. and Dalí Moral, José.** *Diccionario mitológico americano.* Buenos Aires: Distar Libros, 1978.

**Mujica, Marisa *et al.*** *Perú. 10.000 años de pintura. Desde la época rupestre hasta nuestros días.* Lima: Universidad de San Martín de Porres-Fondo Editorial, 2008.

**Mujica Pinilla, Ramón *et al.*** *El Barroco Peruano.* Vol. I. Colección Arte y Tesoros del Perú. Lima: Banco de Crédito del Perú, 2002.

**Mujica Pinilla, Ramón *et al.*** *El Barroco Peruano.* Vol. II. Colección Arte y Tesoros del Perú. Lima: Banco de Crédito del Perú, 2003.

**Mujica Pinilla, Ramón.** "La devoción al Niño Jesús". In: *Orígenes y devociones virreinales de la imaginería popular.* Lima: Universidad Ricardo Palma; Instituto Cultural Peruano Norteamericano-ICPNA, 2008.

**Mujica Pinilla, Ramón *et al.*** *Visión y símbolos. Del Virreinato criollo a la República Peruana.* Colección Arte y Tesoros del Perú. Lima: Banco de Crédito del Perú, 2006.

**Museo Nacional de Arte.** *El mueble virreinal. El bargueño.* Catalogue from the "El mueble virreinal, el bargueño" exhibition organized by the Museo Nacional de Arte, October 1997. La Paz: Museo Nacional de Arte, 1997.

**Oliphant, Margaret.** *Atlas de las Grandes Culturas.* Madrid: Debate, 1992.

**Oricaín, Pablo José.** *Compendio breve de discursos varios sobre el Obispado del Cuzco.* Lima: Ministerio de Relaciones Exteriores del Perú, 2004.

**Ortiz de Zevallos M., Augusto.** *Lima a los 450 años.* Lima: Centro de Investigaciones de la Universidad del Pacífico, 1986.

**Outram, Dorinda.** *Panorama de la Ilustración.* Barcelona: Blume, 2008.

**Paz, Octavio.** "El Uso y la Contemplación". In: Alcolea Gil, Santiago *et al. Historia General del Arte: Artes decorativas I.* Madrid: Ediciones del Prado, 1994.

**Peck, Amelia *et al.*** *Period Rooms in the Metropolitan Musem of Art.* New York: Metropolitan Museum of Art, 1996.

**Pérez-Valiente de Moctezuma, Antonio.** *Muebles coloniales: La colección de Don Gustavo M. Barreto.* Buenos Aires: [n.n.], 1931.

**Pignoli, Giorgio, Rosenberg, Lucio and Altmann, Kenneth.** *Diccionario de Estética.* Buenos Aires: Quadrata, 2003.

**Porras Barrenechea, Raúl and Vargas Ugarte, S. J., Rubén.** *Historia del Perú desde los orígenes hasta el presente. El Perú virreinal.* Lima: Sociedad Académica de Estudios Americanos, [n.d.].

**Porras Barrenechea, Raúl, Vargas Ugarte, S. J., Rubén *et al.*** *Historia general de los peruanos. Vol. 2: El Perú Virreinal.* Lima: Peisa, 1988.

**Prado Heudebert, Javier.** *Lima: Arquitectura y Escultura Religiosa Virreynal.* Lima: Talleres Gráficos P.L. Villanueva, 1996.

**Pulgar Vidal, Javier.** *Geografía del Perú. Las ocho regiones naturales. La regionalización transversal. La sabiduría ecológica tradicional.* Lima: Peisa, 1996.

**Ravines, Rogger.** "Migración y colonización en el Perú: Preámbulo necesario". *Boletín de Lima.* Lima: El Pino, 1998, vol. XX, Nº 114.
*Recorridos. Guía de las colecciones del siglo XVII del MNAD.* Madrid: Secretaría General Técnica, 2007.
**Riccardi-Cubitt, Monique.** *The Art of Cabinet.* London: Thames and Hudson, 1992.
**Rishel, Joseph J. and Stratton-Pruitt, Suzanne (eds).** *Revelaciones: Las artes en América Latina 1492-1820.* Mexico: Fondo de Cultura Económica, 2007.
**Rivero L., Víctor T.** *Cuzco Incaico y Colonial.* Madrid: Ediciones Serrano, 1966.
**Rivero Lake, Rodrigo.** *El Arte Namban en el México Virreinal.* Madrid: Estilo México Editores -Turner, 2005.
**Rodríguez Bernis, Sofía.** *Diccionario de mobiliario.* Madrid: Secretaría General Técnica, 2006.
**Rostworowski de Diez Canseco, María.** *Estructuras andinas del poder. Ideología religiosa y política.* Lima: Instituto de Estudios Peruanos, 1983.
**Royston Pike, Edgar.** *Diccionario de Religiones.* Mexico: Fondo de Cultura Económica, 1960.
**Saldívar Antúnez de Mayolo, Liliana.** *Magic and Enthrallment. The Cathedral of Cusco and the Temples of La Sagrada Familia and El Triunfo.* Cusco: Arzobispado del Cusco, 2007.
**Sancho, José Luis.** *Real Monasterio de San Lorenzo de El Escorial.* Madrid: Reales Sitios de España, 2002.
**San Cristóbal, R. P., Antonio.** *Arquitectura Virreinal de Lima en la primera mitad del Siglo XVII.* Lima: Fondo Editorial INI-FAOA, 2003.
**Schenone, Héctor, Ribera, Adolfo Luis and Curt Lange, Francisco.** *Historia General del Arte en Argentina.* Vol. II. Buenos Aires: Academia Nacional de Bellas Artes, 1983.
**Schenone, Héctor.** *Santa María: iconografía del arte colonial.* Pontificia Universidad Católica Argentina "Santa María de los Buenos Aires". Buenos Aires: Educa, 2008.
**Snodin, Michael and Llewellyn, Nigen.** *Baroque 1620-1800. Style in the Age of Magnificence.* London: V&A Publishing, 2009.
**Stratton-Pruitt, Suzanne and Castro, Mark A. (eds).** *Journeys to New Worlds. Spanish and Portuguese Colonial Art in the Roberta and Richard Huber Collection.* Philadelphia Museum of Art, 2013.
**Tabar de Anitua, Fernando.** *Lujo asiático. Artes de Extremo Oriente y chinerías en el Museo Cerralbo.* Catalogue from the "Lujo Asiático. Artes de Extremo Oriente y chinerías en el Museo Cerralbo" exhibition held in Madrid in 2004. Madrid: Secretaría General Técnica, 2004.
**Taullard, A.** *El mueble colonial sudamericano.* Buenos Aires: Peuser, 1947.
**Teijeira Pablos, María Dolores.** *Las sillerías de coro en la escultura tardogótica española. El grupo leonés.* León: Ediciones Universidad de León, 1999.
**Toman, Rolf (ed).** *El Barroco. Arquitectura. Escultura. Pintura.* Barcelona: Ullmann & Könemann, 2007.
**Tord, Luis Enrique.** *Arequipa artística y monumental.* Lima: Banco del Sur del Perú, 1987.
**Tord, Luis Enrique and Gjurinovic Canevaro, Pedro.** *El Palacio de Torre Tagle y las casonas de Lima.* Lima: Asociación de Funcionarios del Servicio Diplomático del Perú, 2010.
**Toro Montalvo, César.** *Grandes Obras Maestras. Resúmenes. Literatura Hispanoamericana.* Vol. 3. Lima: Editorial San Marcos, 1998.
**Trusted, Marjorie.** *The Arts of Spain. Iberia and Latin America 1450-1700.* London: V&A Publications, 2007.
**Urton, Gary.** *Mitos Incas.* Madrid: Akal Ediciones, 2003.
**Vargas Ugarte S. J., Rubén.** *Ensayo de un diccionario de artífices coloniales de la América Meridional.* [n.p.]: Talleres Gráficos A. Baiocco, 1947.
**Vega, Garcilaso de la (El Inca).** *Primera parte de los Commentarios Reales, qve tratan del origen de los Yncas, Reyes qve fveron del Perv, de sv idolatría, leyes y gouierno en paz y en guerra: de sus vidas y conquistas, y de todo lo que fue aquel Imperio y su República, antes que los Españoles passaran a el.* Lisbon: Pedro Crasbeeck, 1609.
**Velarde, Héctor.** *Arquitectura Peruana.* Colección Tierra Firme. Mexico: Fondo de Cultura Económica, 1946.
**Villacorta Ostolaza, Luis Felipe.** *Faces of Ancient Peru. Rostros del Perú Antiguo.* [n.p.]: AFP Integra, 2008.
**Viñuales, Graciela María.** *El Espacio Urbano en el Cusco Colonial: uso y organización de las estructuras simbólicas.* Lima: Epígrafe Editores - Cedodal, 2004.
**Vogt, Richard C.** *Tortugas amazónicas.* Lima: Gráfica Biblos, 2008.
**Wust, Walter H.** *Guía de identificación de especies de la flora y la fauna del Perú.* Lima: Peisa, 2003.

PRINTED IN NOVEMBER 2013 IN MADRID, SPAIN.

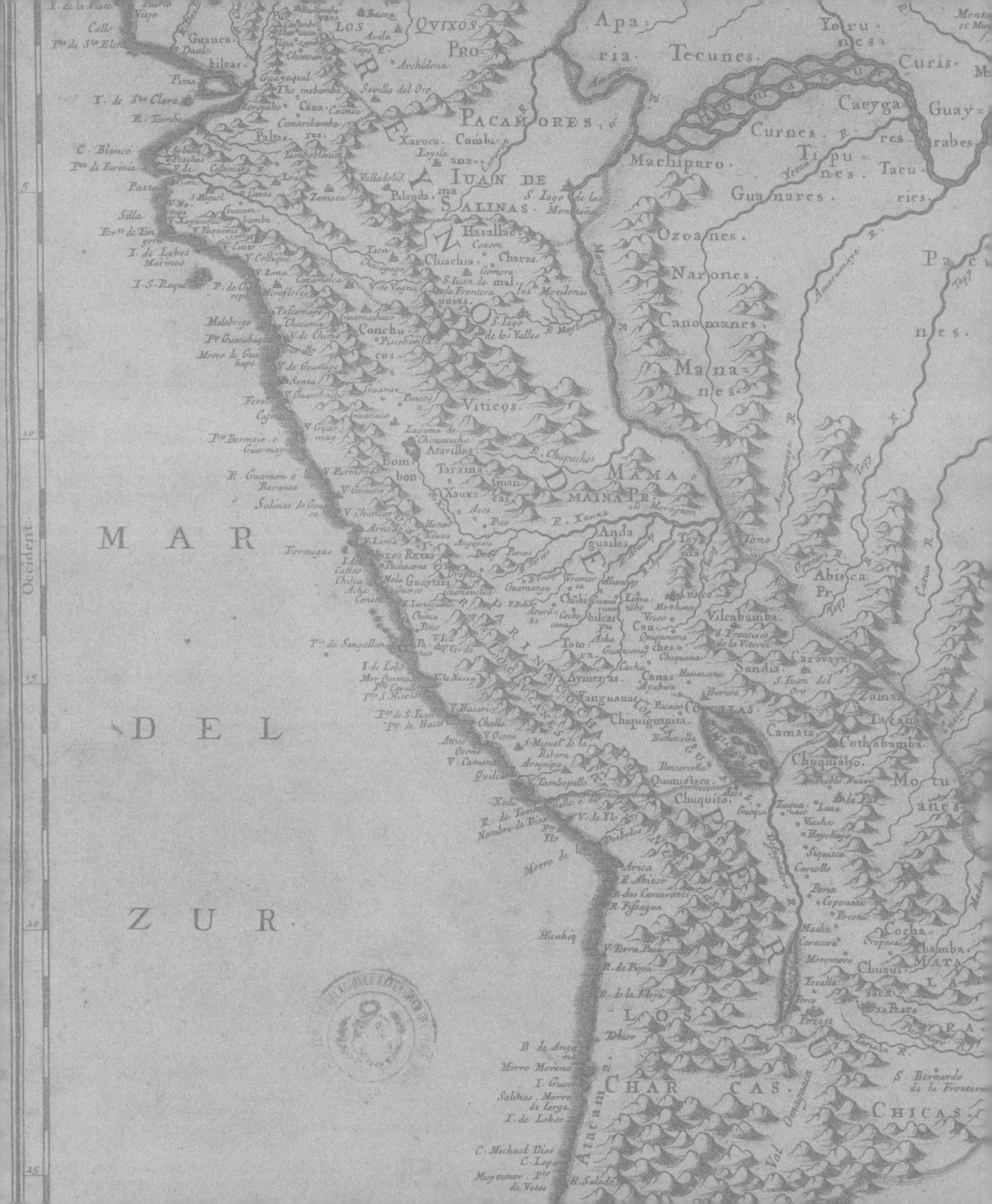

MAR
DEL
ZUR
Occident
LOS QUIXOS
PACAMORES, ó
IUAN DE SALINAS
Machiparo
Guanares
Ozoanes
Narones
Canomanes
Mananes
Tecunes
Curnes
Caeyga
Curis
Tipunes
Tacunes
ries
Viticos
Bombon
Atavillos
Tarama
Xauxa
MAMA
MAINA PR.
Anda guaylas
Guamanga
Vilcabamba
Abisca Pr.
Cusco
Caravaya
Sandia
S. Iuan del Oro
Zamas
Tacana
Cothabamba
Chuquiabo
Motuanes
Chuquito
Aymeras
Yanguanas
Chiquiguanita
Collas
Arequipa
Arica
R. Pissagua
Potosi
Cochabamba
CHARCAS
CHICAS
S. Bernardo de la Frontera
LOS
Atacama
R. Salado
Guayaquil
Puna
Y. de Sta Clara
R. Tumbes
C. Blanco
Pta de Parinia
Paita
Silla
I. de Lobos Marinos
I. S. Roque
Malabrigo
Pto Guanchaquo
Morro de Guañape
Santa
Ferol
Casma
Pto Bermejo o Guarmay
R. Guaman o la Baranca
Salinas de Guaura
Formigas
LOS REYES
Callao
Pachacama
Chilca
Mala
Guaytara
Guanavellica
Chinca
Pisco
Pta de Sangallan
I. de Lobo
Pto S. Nicolas
Pto de S. Iuan
Chala
Ocona
Camana
Quilca
V. Tambopalle
V. de Flo
Morro de
Micahiq
R. de Pisua
R. de la Ploya
B. de Angu
Morro Moreno
I. Guon
Salinas, Morro de Lorge
I. de Lobos
C. Michael Dios
C. Lope
Muytamor, Pto de Vetos
Loyola
Valladolid
Zamora
Palanda
Xaroca
Cumbinama
Archidona
Sevilla del Oro
Avila
Baeza
Chaxas
Hasallao
Cluachia
Conchucos
Piscobamba
Guanuco
Laguna de Chincacocha
R. Chupaches
R. Xauxa
Chuquisaca
Tarija
la Plata
la Paz
Oruro
Ciquisaca
Paria
Misqui
Chuquisaca
Omaguaca
Vol